ABOUT THE SMILING STUDENT ON

Dalia was a student in Renay Sadis's third grade class at P.S. 87 on the Upper West Side of Manhattan, a classroom in which issues of social justice take center stage in reading, writing, and conversations. During the summer of 2020, as the pandemic kept students sheltered inside their apartments, Dalia shared a letter with Renay—a letter she wrote at home, on her own. Renay graciously and proudly shared the letter with me, and my heart skipped a beat. Dalia had gone above and beyond, using writing as you or I might— to make a difference in the world. Isn't that a powerful goal for all teachers of writing?

In the fall, New York City schools reopened in a hybrid model, part remote and part in small in-school cohorts. Renay arranged for Dalia, now a fourth grader, to visit her empty classroom. Dalia removed her mask for the few seconds it took for Renay to snap this photograph in her well-ventilated classroom. Dalia is holding a copy of her precious letter. It is no wonder that she is smiling with such joy and pride. Hopefully, the forty-sixth president of the United States read this letter with joy and pride as well.

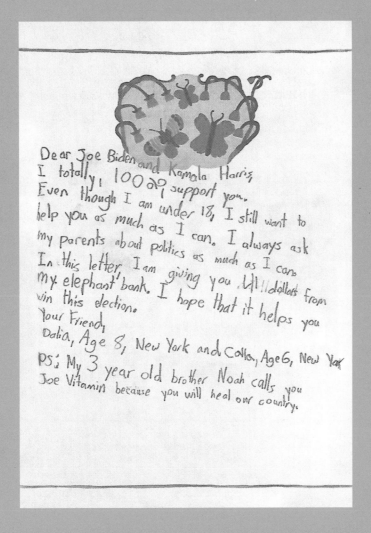

Dear Joe Biden and Kamala Harris,
I totally, 100% support you.
Even though I am under 18, I still want to
help you as much as I can. I always ask
my parents about politics as much as I can.
In this letter I am giving you 41 dollars from
my elephant bank. I hope that it helps you
win this election.
Your Friend,
Dalia, Age 8, New York and Calla, Age 6, New York
PS: My 3 year old brother Noah calls you
Joe Vitamin because you will heal our country.

"This book extends joyful, engaging invitations to children across grade levels to develop expertise, read and research meaningfully, and write for authentic, rewarding purposes. For teachers who want to capture the spirit and heart of the writing workshop, Shelley Harwayne's ideas provide motivation and inspiration to innovate, along with practical support, detailed approaches, student and teacher examples, and sets of rich book lists that point the way for young writers."

—Anne Atwell Merkel, classroom teacher and co-author of *The Reading Zone*, Second Edition

"In the same way a beautiful photograph can do, Shelley Harwayne's writing takes us back to our roots: as teachers of writing, as creative thinkers, and as educators who marvel at what our students can do. As we've come to expect from Shelley, her writing is filled with personal anecdotes, concrete examples, and ideas she herself has developed and executed with young writers. Always the researcher, Shelley is honest in her delivery of information and in sharing both the successes and challenges of being a teacher of writing."

—Joanne Hindley, Principal

"Shelley Harwayne roots us in writing workshop, generous to those pioneers among whom she worked. Above and beyond these origins, she unveils an abundance of ingenious lessons, each one culturally inclusive, each one infused with opportunities for empathy and joy. Almost without our noticing, the grace of the text transforms us, awakening us to the wonders of the world, more curious and able to discover lessons and qualities of successful writing."

—Andrea Lowenkopf, Education Consultant

"*Above and Beyond the Writing Workshop* is a must-read for anyone who feels they have lost the heart of writing workshop in their classroom. Shelley's words harken back to the original spirit ignited years ago by Donald Graves and others to inspire and energize today's teachers. Each chapter provides readers with creative, powerful ideas to enliven their writing instruction. In a time when student writing sometimes feels formulaic and over-processed, Shelley reminds us of the importance of honoring experimentation, choice, and celebration within writing workshop."

—Jennifer Allen, Literacy Specialist

"Rooted in authenticity, *Above and Beyond the Writing Workshop* shares a constellation of writing strategies to engage kids and activate them as writers. In an era where prescriptive writing programs dominate the curriculum, Shelley Harwayne offers a refreshing alternative that urges us to teach kids to write like real writers in writing workshops that celebrate their curiosity, creativity, and individuality."

—Stephanie Harvey, co-author of *Strategies That Work*, Third Edition

"The writing challenges in *Above and Beyond the Writing Workshop* inspired my teachers to think differently about writing workshop. Their creativity and risk-taking helped my students to develop a passion for writing. This book is a must-read for all who want to breathe new life into their teaching of writing."

—Monica R. Berry, Principal

"*Above and Beyond the Writing Workshop* is a treasure trove of joyful and inspiring ideas. It is Shelley at her best, bringing craft to life while demonstrating incredible potential for lifting the level of writing. Enjoy the fresh lens she brings to topics. Reclaim the value of choice, voice, intention, and writing with authentic purpose that will engage an audience."

—Sharon Hill, Principal

"Shelley challenges us to remember who we are, where we came from, and whose shoulders we are standing on. She invites us to reclaim and revive the dignity, passion, and hope that is fostered when writing instruction is elevated to life. With a relentless sense of urgency, Shelley waves the banner, and I join in her crusade."

—Michael Oliver, Principal

ABOVE and BEYOND
the Writing Workshop

ABOVE and BEYOND
the Writing Workshop

SHELLEY HARWAYNE

Stenhouse
PUBLISHERS

Portsmouth, New Hampshire

Stenhouse Publishers
www.stenhouse.com

Library of Congress Cataloging-in-Publication Data
Names: Harwayne, Shelley, author.
Title: Above and beyond the writing workshop / Shelley Harwayne.
Description: Portsmouth, New Hampshire : Stenhouse Publishers, [2021] |
   Includes bibliographical references. |
Identifiers: LCCN 2021013086 (print) | LCCN 2021013087 (ebook) | ISBN
   9781625314307 (Paperback) | ISBN 9781625314314 (eBook)
Subjects: LCSH: English language—Writing—Study and teaching (Elementary)
   | English language—Composition and exercises–Study and teaching
   (Elementary)
Classification: LCC LB1576 .H279 2021 (print) | LCC LB1576 (ebook) | DDC
   372.62/3044—dc23
LC record available at https://lccn.loc.gov/2021013086
LC ebook record available at https://lccn.loc.gov/2021013087

Cover design, interior design, and typesetting by Cindy Butler

Printed in the United States of America

This book is printed on paper certified by third-party standards for sustainably managed forestry.

27 26 25 24 23 22 21   4371   9 8 7 6 5 4 3 2 1

. . . .

dedicated to the memory of my sister and brother-in-law,
Barbara and Michael Abraham

and in celebration of their children and grandchildren
Josh, Karen, Cooper, Millie, David, Lilach, Ellie, and Miki

and with endless love for Neil, Michael,
Alison, Ben, Zach, J.J., Andie, Will, and Sasha

. . . .

CONTENTS

ONLINE RESOURCES
ACCESS INFORMATION

Above and Beyond Resources include access to twenty-five carefully curated book lists for downloading and printing. These extensive bibliographies support each of the writing challenges. The publications are a mix of brand-new titles as well as older ones I discovered in classroom, school, and public libraries. Unfortunately, picture books go out of print way too quickly. Therefore, the reader may find that some of the titles listed in these booklists are difficult to purchase. The good news is that these vintage volumes can still be found on the shelves of school and public libraries, and secondhand copies can often be found in online searches. Then too, some of my most treasured finds have been made at flea markets, estate sales, public library fund raisers, and in the bedroom collections of young friends and family members. It was impossible for me to eliminate these "oldies but goodies," as students gain so much from carefully selected, well-crafted material, no matter the publication dates. The online booklists will be updated periodically. In addition to these online book lists, readers will find current titles at the end of each chapter under the heading, "A Few Titles to Enrich Your Teaching."

To access the Online Resources, please follow the directions below.

Access Information:

1. Go to https://www.stenhouse.com/content/above-and-beyond-the-writing-workshop

2. Fill out the form, click Submit.

3. When prompted, enter this passcode: Aboveandbeyond21

4. You will immediately receive an email that gives you the link to access the resources. This is the link you will use from here on, so please bookmark it for easy access.

5. You may need to enter the passcode each time you access this page.

You will now have access to:

PROLOGUE: WHY THIS BOOK

I have spent the last eighteen years of formal retirement from the New York City public schools, learning from my young grandchildren, volunteering in their schools, both urban and suburban, as well as consulting in classrooms across this country.

Above all, my main interest has remained the teaching of writing, and I must admit I have been saddened by what has become of this groundbreaking movement, a movement that reenergized teachers across our nation during the 1980s and 1990s. How thrilling it was to learn something new, something authentic, something that mattered. Now, amid all the homogenizing of classroom instruction, the process approach has become sanitized, sequenced, and scripted. We've lost our sense of adventure, playfulness, and experimentation, and as Tom Newkirk (2009) so eloquently reminds us in *Holding On to Good Ideas in a Time of Bad Ones*, "When we stop experimenting, we stop living as teachers."

In short, many writing teachers have lost their right to try new things in their writing workshops. Under increasing pressure to cover more and more curriculum mandates, in shorter and shorter blocks of time, many teachers have been forced to download packaged units of study and squeeze them into brief blocks of time. Shortened blocks of time often result in the elimination of such workshop essentials as daily writing time, one-on-one conferring, and opportunities for young writers to critically reread, experiment with possibilities, and solve problems in their drafts. Instead, students and their teachers are being rushed to crank out the next mandated grade-level requirement. Just as processed foods are not considered healthy, so, too, processed teaching materials should not be on our instructional menus. This standardization and bastardization of the workshop approach to teaching writing has disappointed me, and I am not alone.

Jane Fletcher Geniesse, wrote a biography of Freya Spark, a British adventurer, explorer, and writer who lived to be one hundred years old. It was titled *Passionate Nomad* (2001). In it, the author presents Spark's belief that "there can be no happiness if the things we believe in are different from the things we do." Although not particularly intended for a teacher audience, her words ring true for those of us who call schools our second home. Many teachers across the country find themselves in situations in which much of what they are asked to do does not mesh with what they believe in, with what they hold to be true about teaching and learning. These are the educators who have been asked to focus on isolated skill-and-drill materials, assign seemingly endless test-prep paragraphs instead of real books, and eliminate field trips and the arts in lieu of getting back to basics. It's no wonder that these teachers are not happy.

Back in the good old days of teaching writing, when Don Graves and his colleagues first offered teachers a meaningful and exhilarating way to teach children how to write with enthusiasm and expertise, our workshops were filled with such essentials as genuine curiosity, playful exploration, individual choice, big blocks of time, quality conversations, and powerful literature. As such, teachers felt empowered, professionally alive, and incredibly invested in their teaching. Today, it is extremely difficult to feel those groundbreaking moments when we are being asked to follow scripted lessons, in a prescribed order, for predetermined blocks of time.

This book is my response to all that scripting, sequencing, and homogenizing of the teaching of writing. It is a call to reengage with the trailblazer spirit of bygone years. It is my hope to honor the professors, researchers, writers, and classroom teachers, who in decades past paved the way for us to create writing workshops in our classrooms. We honor our roots when we make the teaching of writing a top priority in our classrooms. We honor our roots when we refuse to let our writing time become stale, never settling for the same old same old. We experiment, take risks, and follow students' leads. We give students time, choice, and response to their work in progress. We put content before form, revision before editing, all the while balancing process and product.

Recently, my husband and I traveled to New Orleans to tour Tulane University with our granddaughter Andie. While there, I was moved by a sign I spotted on a passing bus. It read, "Every child deserves two things. Above and beyond." It is my sincere hope that this book offers teachers the inspiration and information to go above and beyond in their writing workshops. This would be the greatest tribute to the educators who introduced us to the writing process approach.

My goal, therefore, in the chapters that follow is to ignite in readers the spirit of imagining, inventing, and innovating, while appreciating that teachers do have to meet district mandates and requirements. We can satisfy the powers that be and at the same time reignite that professionally alive spirit. We can create joyful writing workshops, ones filled with what Eleanor Duckworth (2006) in her classic book described as "the having of wonderful ideas." Duckworth stresses the importance of "finding problems that really interest the learner," providing learners with "the body of information (content knowledge)" that will enable learners to solve those problems, and creating settings in which "it is safe to take risks." Duckworth's insight about the importance of having wonderful ideas applies especially well to teachers of writing.

Another goal, which is always at the forefront of my mind, is to raise global citizens, children who respect, honor, and appreciate diversity. Not too long ago, the acclaimed Israeli writer Amos Oz passed away. When I read about his life, I was impressed to discover The Order of the Teaspoon, a Swedish organization whose motto is "Together for diversity and tolerance." The inspiration for this organization was Amos Oz's (2010) work *How to Cure a Fanatic*. In it, Oz poses three ways to respond to a calamity, for example, a fire. He suggests that one can either run away, write an angry letter of protest, or bring a bucket of water and throw it on the fire. Oz goes on to suggest that if you don't have a bucket, bring a glass of water, and if not a glass, bring a teaspoon. In other words, we can all do our part in the face of a calamity. Intolerance for others, for people who are different, is a calamity in today's world. Teachers who ask students to treat one another with kindness, who read aloud carefully selected literature, who invite students to write about their beliefs and their experiences, and who encourage caring conversations in response to the written word are fighting intolerance. As Oz so eloquently points out, "And yes, I know a teaspoon is little and the fire is huge but there are millions of us and each of us has a teaspoon." So too, every teacher has a piece of writing that will spark conversation about treating one another with humanity, integrity, and respect, no matter our religion, our skin color, our language, or our sexual orientation. I hope that teachers will find in this volume, as well as in the online resources, additional titles that push back against the calamity of intolerance.

It took me a long time to complete this book as I struggled with a seeming contradiction in my thinking. If I was opposed to packaged units of study, how could I write a book brimming with descriptions of yet more writing challenges? Certainly, calling them "challenges" doesn't eliminate the possibility that they will simply serve as substitute units of study. (Isn't that just like Kraft calling their salad dressing "salad frosting" to entice children to eat salad?) It was a relief to finally realize that the teaching ideas that follow are different in several ways. Most basically, they are not scripted, sequenced, or assigned set blocks of time to accomplish. They are not carved in stone, not filled with "thou shalts," and to the best of my knowledge have never become mandated units of study. Some were tried only once by a classroom teacher and never again. Other teachers have returned to a challenge two or three times, tweaking their plans as they proceeded. Some were used merely as a kernel idea and reshaped to meet the needs of different students and different teachers. Many inspired teachers to experiment with their own original ideas, and I must admit, that outcome was the most satisfying.

Throughout this book, I note the importance of the teachers' own reading and writing. Throughout these challenges, the teachers' own literacy serves as a cornerstone to the work at hand. All the ideas in this book can be traced to my own reading—of newspapers, of children's literature, of adult novels and nonfiction. Similarly, throughout the book, the teachers' own writing serves a critical role. Teachers are consistently asked to serve as mentors, writing alongside their students, not merely to do cursory or superficial "pretend" writing but completing the challenge and celebrating alongside their students. Perhaps the most important component attached to all the challenges in this book is the feel of being an original thinker. There is a quality in the air of a classroom, one that is hard to name or define, when students and their teachers are trying something brand new. Perhaps it is an openness to possibility, a genuine feeling of not having all the answers, a premium placed on the ability to think on one's feet, to do as the late Don Murray suggested and expect the unexpected.

Additionally, I have described on pages 4–6 the essential elements that I have come to value, depend upon, and use as a filter when designing teaching and learning opportunities.

Note that when describing classroom practice, I occasionally switch from my first-person account to the more inclusive *we*. The reasons for this are varied. Planning for instruction was usually a collaborative effort. I frequently cotaught with classroom teachers becoming full participants in all aspects of the workshop. In addition, since I usually visited only once a week, classroom teachers carried on quite enthusiastically and successfully in our time apart. Depending on the school, as well as on the availability of substitute coverage, classroom teachers welcomed visiting colleagues into their classrooms when I conducted a demonstration lesson. Observing teachers were also invited to participate in many aspects of the writing workshop. Hence, the use of the pronoun *we*.

Background on Writing Challenges

As has been said before, all the writing challenges that follow have the same goal in mind: to remind teachers to keep the groundbreaking spirit alive in our classrooms. Nothing would please me more than to inspire teachers to experiment in their writing workshops, trying things they have never tried before, even if they never try them again. It is my sincere desire that the writing challenges that follow are never turned into mandated units of study. Instead, I offer them as inspiration for teachers to design their own. I hope the ideas contained motivate educators to take back their writing workshops, to find time for professional collaborations, to try out new ideas in the company of colleagues, and, if possible, to find ways to share their discoveries with wider audiences through publications and presentations.

My goal is to remind students just how fascinating this world is. I recently came across a small volume of sketches and brief writings entitled *The Illustrated Compendium of Amazing Animal Facts*, written and illustrated by Maja Safstrom (2016). With every page, I got that feeling of "I never realized that; isn't that unbelievable?" ("Crocodiles can survive without food for three years." "Owls have three eyelids"—one is for blinking, another for sleeping, and a third for cleansing their eyes. "Sharks' moms lose their appetite before they give birth, so they won't be tempted to eat their own babies!") I hope this same sense of awe will fill our writing workshops—the thrill of learning something new and then sharing that with others. Most of the challenges in this collection are, therefore, in the nonfiction arena, as elementary-age students seem to take extra delight in figuring out how things in the world work and then teaching others what they have learned.

Time and again, when I reflect on the most successful writing workshops I know, I discover that certain qualities cut across all these classrooms. These qualities make it possible for teachers and students alike to do their best work. Here are short descriptions of four essential big-ticket items:

- **Students' best work stems from their ability to get up from their desks.** This permission is rooted in their teachers' acknowledgment that students don't simply belong to a class; they belong to an entire school and to the community in which their school is located. Throughout all the challenges that follow, no matter the grade, we encouraged students to see the world as their classroom—searching, researching, interviewing, observing, documenting, visiting, sketching, photographing, and the like. We must pay attention to the outside world. Students can't do their best work sitting at their desks. No, they must be out and about.

- **Camaraderie in the writing workshop serves writers well.** I don't mean students being asked to collaborate on writing projects. Instead, I am talking about the thrilling, energetic hum in a classroom when children know one another's areas of interest and make serendipitous discoveries that are shared. Teachers make sure that everyone in the class and in the school is aware of the topics being studied. You never know who has access to important information, connections to experts, or admission to just the right museum, shop, or library. When classrooms are marked with camaraderie, children learn to pitch in, support one another, and feel free to pore over texts and screens together in the joyous search for needed information.

- **Students need to expect their work to be original and of high quality.** I often suggest to teachers that the tricky part about asking young children to write nonfiction is that students usually don't have anything new to say about their topics. As much as many of them would like to, they can't pack a duffle, go on safari, and report firsthand information about the eating habits of rhinos in Africa. In other words, they can't gather information that no one has already discovered. Instead, we need to show them that their work can be high quality and memorable if they design original or borrow clever and accessible formats to contain their thoughts, or focus in on unusual aspects of their topic, or craft their thoughts in fresh and surprising ways.

- **A teacher audience of one is never enough.** When a writing assignment demands interaction with the reader, an adult or a peer, it is more likely that students will work hard to make it their best. Better yet, if the completed work is turned into a gift for a friend, becomes a family heirloom, or takes up permanent residence in the school or classroom library, students work hard to make the work their best. The message is clear: we need to give students real-world reasons to work hard. Students need to see that their words can make a reader smile, sigh, nod, laugh, or even tear up. They need to see that their words can change their readers' behavior or attitude, or make someone rethink an issue or solve a new problem.

In addition to the four big qualities described, an additional dozen elements follow, which guide the work I do. Rarely, does any challenge meet all twelve criteria, but I do work toward their inclusion. I also encourage teachers to think about these elements when they design their own writing challenges. (See "Elements to Think About as You Design Writing Challenges" on page 286.)

1. **Choice:** Students have options as to topic, design, language, and so on.

2. **Appeal to children:** The challenges tap into children's interests, attitudes, and strengths. I laughed out loud when I read a short article in *Real Simple* magazine ("If Language Phrase Books Reflected Actual Travel Experiences..."). Shannon Reed (2019), the author, created a language phrase book for parents traveling with children, and she was spot on. The phrase she chose in Finnish translates to, "Chicken nuggets. All the chicken nuggets. Only chicken nuggets. Every chicken nugget. Chicken nuggets." The author understands what appeals to children.

3. **High-quality literature to inspire and support:** When teachers come across an appropriate and intriguing piece of writing, they wonder if their students can do likewise. They ask themselves, "What can my students learn from this?"

4. Teachers take on the challenge themselves: Teachers become full participants in the writing workshop, using their own writing as models. Teachers share their research techniques, problem-solving moments, revision strategies, and so on.

5. Span grade levels: Challenges can be offered across several elementary grade levels, not limited to just one. Student interest seems more important than an arbitrarily assigned grade level.

6. Accessible formats: Challenges belong to the Little League of writing, not Yankee Stadium. Formats and requirements are age appropriate.

7. Expectation of high-quality finished work: Teachers present information on writing techniques alongside other demands of the writing challenge, recognizing that the simpler the container, the higher the quality of writing that can be asked for.

8. Short duration: Challenges can be completed in short amounts of time, thereby sustaining children's interest and attention.

9. Opportunities to experiment with more than one piece within each challenge: The short nature of each challenge allows students to "have a go" more than once and to therefore tap into what they learned from their first attempt as they craft their second.

10. Scaffold with templates if necessary: Teachers can provide differentiation of instruction for students that need extra support.

11. Ease of publication: Simple formats and short time frames allow for frequent publications.

12. Presence of joy for students and teachers: Challenges bring energy to the writing workshop, offering delight, not drudgery.

Structure of Writing Challenges

All the challenges in this book contain a similar structure. The components follow:

COMPONENTS OF EACH CHALLENGE

- **Student Exemplar:** A student writing sample provides an image of where the challenge is headed.

- **Exploring the Roots of the Writing Challenge:** An explanation is provided of what inspired the creation of the challenge.

- **Engaging Students in the Challenge:** Suggestions are given for launching the challenge.

- **Continuing to Support Students' Efforts:** Several ways to support students' work follow.

- **Sharing Your Own Writing:** The teacher accepts the writing challenge.

- **Gathering Information:** Students conduct research as needed.

- **Lifting the Quality of Student Writing:** Craft suggestions are provided, along with presentation of tools in the writer's toolbox.

- **Student Writing Samples:** Additional examples of student work are shown.

- **Carving Out Time for Celebration:** Suggestions for sharing completed work are given.

- **Books Noted:** Published material mentioned in the chapter are listed. (Additional bibliographies appear online.)

- **A Few Titles to Enrich Your Teaching:** Current publications that support student writing are listed. (Additional bibliographies of these also appear online.)

BOOKS NOTED

Duckworth, Eleanor. 2006. *"The Having of Wonderful Ideas" and Other Essays on Teaching and Learning.* New York: Teachers College Press.

Geniesse, Jane Fletcher. 2001. *Passionate Nomad: The Life of Freya Stark.* New York: Modern Library.

Murray, Don. 1989. *Expecting the Unexpected: Teaching Myself—and Others—to Read and Write.* Portsmouth, New Hampshire: Heinemann.

Newkirk, Tom. 2009. *Holding On to Good Ideas in a Time of Bad Ones.* Portsmouth, NH: Heinemann.

Oz, Amos. 2010. *How to Cure a Fanatic.* Princeton, NJ: Princeton University Press.

Reed, Shannon. January 2019. "If Language Phrase Books Reflected Actual Travel Experiences . . ." *Real Simple*, 112.

Safstrom, Maja. 2016. *The Illustrated Compendium of Amazing Animal Facts.* Berkeley, CA: Ten Speed Press.

PART ONE

GETTING UP
FROM YOUR DESK

The writing challenges presented in the pages that follow require young writers to gather information and ideas in active and interactive ways. All involve tapping the resources of the school and the community, as well as members of the students' own families. All require students to learn the art of interviewing, a skill that will serve them well throughout their lives.

When students are asked to write a traditional school report, instant answers seem to abound. Siri and Alexa often become their research partners, especially if their assignments are particularly straightforward. There is no longer a need for browsing and searching, for seeking out experts in the field, for viewing of documentaries, or for trips to the public library. I suppose the way to undo that press-of-a-button, instant-gratification form of information-gathering is to eliminate the straightforward assignment.

For elementary students, this means bidding farewell to the state report, the country report, the everything-you-ever-wanted-to-know-about report. After all, state capitals, population counts, natural resources, famous cities, and so on are just a click away. Those assignments too easily become mere stenography. Students can easily lift someone else's information and, if they are a bit ambitious, jazz it up with a clever lead, a solid ending, and careful editing of their finished work. I've come to believe that it is hard to craft writing filled with voice if you have nothing new to say. Bland assignments often result in voiceless pieces of writing. And unfortunately, teachers must read them and, in most settings, grade them.

The question facing teachers becomes, "How do we give students opportunities to write about things that perhaps no one else has thought to write about and to write about them in fresh, surprising ways?"

Way back in 1988, I attended an orientation for parents of incoming members of the freshmen class at Harvard University and recall one professor describing a writing assignment that he gave to all his new students. He asked, "What beliefs about the world did the 1865 alumni have in mind when they selected the architect's design for the iconic Memorial Hall on campus?" He lamented that most of his freshmen students think they can rush to the library (no Internet resources back then) and simply look up the answer. His was *not* a straightforward assignment. It needed thinking through. It needed culling, puzzling over possibilities, walking a mile in someone else's shoes, and making things add up. In other words, his assignment was more thought-provoking, more rigorous, and no doubt more interesting for the writer and the reader. We aimed at the elementary level to do likewise, to design an appropriate challenge that would require students to think more, work harder, and craft an enticing and memorable work of nonfiction.

Chapter 1: Across-the-Globe Writing (Grades 3–5)

Chapter 2: Quirky Questions and Biographical Sketches (Grades 3–5)

Chapter 3: Playing Favorites (Grades 1–2)

Chapter 4: Learning from One Writer (Grades 1–2)

CHAPTER 1
Across-the-Globe Writing

(Grades 3-5)

"SAVE ROOM FOR DESSERTS!"
BY RUBY AND AUDREY

Is it dessert time yet? Do you have a sweet tooth? Do you feel your mouth watering and the dessert calling your name? Are you craving a vanilla cupcake, pie, or an ice-cream cone? After you read this article, we bet you may love something different. Many people around the world enjoy different kinds of desserts. If people all over the world love them, then maybe you will too. Enjoy!

Bang, Boom, Bingsu!
Are you ever really hot? Do you need an icy treat? If you want an icy, cold, and yummy treat, you should try Bingsu from Korea. Bingsu is shaved milk ice sorbet with decorations like sweetened condensed milk, sweet rice cakes, or jellies and fruit. Bingsu melts in your mouth. Guess what? You don't need teeth to eat Bingsu. Are you anxious to try this? Order up!

Beaver Tail Maniac
Do you like beavers? Well, if you do then you should try . . . a beaver tail! (Not a real beaver tail!) Canadian people love this tasty treat that is deep fried with brown sugar and butter. Beaver tail gets its name because it is flat, smooth, and it looks like a beaver's tail. BUT it does not taste like a beaver's tail. You can add nuts, Nutella, chocolate candies, and more! Yummy, YUM, YUM!

(continues)

"SAVE ROOM FOR DESSERTS!"
BY RUBY AND AUDREY
(continued)

At Your Command—Syrniki!
Russians love this classic dessert called *syrniki*. Syrniki is like a pancake which is a fresh dairy product with cheese. It has a texture like sour cream. Syrniki is fried and served with either jam, apple sauce, sour cream, or honey.

Doce de Leite
Do you really want a chewy, sticky, and creamy dessert? You are not supposed to make this in your apartment or a house because it might explode to the roof. There is a lot of condensed milk in it. You boil it until it turns to dark caramel. Try this yummy caramel treat called *Doce de Leite* that comes from Brazil. Delicious!

Soursop, the Juicy Madness
In Trinidad, a popular fruit is soursop. It is cooling, delicious, and yummy! Soursop is a fruit that can be made into different desserts like ice cream. On the outside of soursop, it is spiky like a zombie egg. The inside of soursop is soft, sweet, and juicy. Just open it fast! It is really, really, really juicy, and if you open it slowly, the juice will explode on your outfit! And trust me, you do not want that to happen!

Kononkrok—Soft, Creamy Love!
Are you ever in the mood for creamy coconut pancakes? Well, if you are, try this Thai coconut milk pancakes called *kokonkrok*. (It's not really a pancake, but has similar texture.) On the bottom of this treat is rice flour mixed with palm sugar. The palm sugar comes from the coconut of the palm tree. The top has coconut milk. It tastes like a rice cake crossed with a banana.

Was your mouth watering? Did your favorite dessert change after reading this article? Dessert time is big in many other countries.

Exploring the Roots of the Writing Challenge

In New York, the state requirement in social studies for grade three includes a study of communities around the world. One requirement is for students to learn how communities are culturally similar as well as different. In New York City, China became a popular country to study, probably because of our large Chinese population as well as the ease of school field trips to our famous and fabulous Chinatown neighborhood. The traditional school report usually includes such predictable subtopics as holidays, government, food, and language. Information about these topics is usually readily available for students online and in nonfiction picture books. Some subjects, especially the topic of food, can be much more interesting, as class trips often include a lunch in Chinatown. The problem perhaps is that for the most part, the students all say the same thing about Chinese holidays, government, language, climate, religion, geography, and culture. Imagine having to read twenty-five similar paragraphs about the government of China or the language spoken there. It is very hard for children to write these with energy, voice, and surprise when they are all taking notes on the same articles, chapters, and teacher-prepared handouts.

Rather than ask students to report on all these subtopics, we decided to try something new, something more joyful, and something that would enable students to write about things that perhaps no one had ever written, and certainly had never written about in just the same way. We decided that rather than students selecting just one country, they would probe topics of real interest that cut across many countries. (Think Christiane Amanpour's *Sex and Love Around the World* documentaries on CNN.)

Engaging Students in the Challenge

I began by sharing pages from the cookbook *In Her Kitchen: Stories and Recipes from Grandmas Around the World* by Gabriele Galimberti (2014a). The book brims with incredible photographs of grandmothers in their kitchens, the world over, assembling the ingredients for their signature dishes. After a discussion of what it means to have a signature dish and the students telling stories about the signature dishes of folks in their own families, we studied the photos in the book, guessing the home countries of the featured cooks.

The quiet hallway provides the perfect workplace for students to share their writing.

My aim was to make sure that the third graders found the world to be a fascinating place. How could I miss? They oohed and aahed when they saw a grandmother from Malawi preparing caterpillars in tomato sauce, a Honduran grandma sharing her recipe for iguana with rice and beans, and a Canadian grandmother explaining that the bison in her recipe was caught and butchered by her own son. Of course, we made sure that no negative comments would be tolerated—no "Yucky!"; no "Gross!"; no "How could they?" I explained to students that the author traveled the world, researching grandmothers and their cooking. Third graders were most interested to learn that Gabriele did the same with children and their toys (*Toy Stories: Photos of Children from Around the World and Their Favorite Things*) (2014b).

(I must confess, a friend introduced me to Gabriele, and he included me in his grandmother cookbook. I was very proud to represent New York. His documentary/photography book, *My Couch Is Your Couch: Exploring How People Live Around the World* (2015) is fascinating but appropriate only for an adult audience.)

I could have also made sure that our students took delight in learning about people around the globe, by sharing a stack of carefully selected children's picture books. For example, *Pancakes to Parathas: Breakfast Around the World* by Alice B. McGinty (2019) makes a perfect model for children about to research topics that cross the globe. Not only does the author provide poetic as well as prose information about traditional breakfasts in different countries, she also locates these countries on a map, and Tomoko Suzuki beautifully illustrates each country and its popular breakfast food. The short prose passages provide a perfect image of where students might be headed with their own writing. In the following days, teachers also read aloud such picture books as:

Back to School: A Global Journey by Maya Ajmera and John D. Ivanko (2019)

Kids Cooking: Students Prepare and Eat Food from Around the World by George Ancona (2018)

Throw Your Tooth on the Roof by Selby Beeler (2001) (losing a tooth traditions)

Mazes Around the World by Mary D. Lankford (2008)

My Librarian Is a Camel: How Books Are Brought to Children Around the World by Margreit Ruurs (2005)

Birthdays Around the World by Margreit Ruurs (2017)

It is also possible to come across newspaper articles that can engage students in topics that cut across many countries. In recent months, I have come across articles about ice-cream flavors, first day of school rituals, family vacations, children's museums, popular candy, basketball players, New Year's Eve celebrations, and wedding traditions around the world. (See bibliography in online Book List 1.) Then too, simply browsing the Internet with such key words as "Top ten, surprising, unusual, or weird . . . around the world" will result in some intriguing articles to share with children. Student favorites included snacks that kids around the world leave for Santa at Christmas time, unusual winter sports, and ways that people the world over greet one another.

An alternate method of launching this writing challenge would be to gather and share real-world artifacts. Travel-loving teachers often collect interesting items from the countries they visit during their school breaks. When I came across "15 Unexpected Good Luck Charms from Countries Around the World," an Internet publication written by Jacob Shamsian and Diana Yukari (2017) for *Business Insider*, I realized I had several of the items mentioned in my own home. I brought in a wooden red Dala horse from Sweden, a hamsa keychain from Israel, and a Native American dream catcher. After sharing these good-luck charms with children, they often talk about the kinds of souvenirs their families collect when they travel. Some may lead to topics for research. For example, if your family collects musician figurines, you might be interested in the study of unusual musical instruments around the world. Or if your family collects salt and pepper shakers, you might want to explore popular spices around the world. Or if your mom buys scarves whenever she travels, you might be interested in learning about women's head coverings in different cultures.

When children seemed filled with enthusiasm about what they were learning, we asked what other topics piqued their curiosity. Some responses were rather predictable, including snacks, sports, and school life around the world. Others were less so, including how people fished, what playgrounds looked like, and how kids celebrated their birthdays around the world. Even if students selected the same across-the-globe topic as those in the published works we had shared, we trusted that their finished pieces would be original as we knew the students would get information by interviewing people in our community who came from places that differed from those in the books shared.

Then too, we provided support for children who could not readily decide on an interesting topic.

DISCOVERING ACROSS-THE-GLOBE RESEARCH TOPICS

- Imagine you are writing a pen pal letter to a new friend in a foreign country. What questions would you probably ask? Could any of these be turned into across-the-globe studies (school lunches, homework policies, pets, favorite board games, chores at home, and so on)?

- Think about the main character in the book you are currently reading. Does the character have a pastime that intrigues you, a household chore that surprises you, or an important life event that is about to occur? Would you want to find out how children in other places respond in similar situations?

- Do you have a friend that comes from another country? Is there something about your friend's life in that country that you would like to know more about? Is there something your friend already told you about life in that other country that surprised you, and you now wonder how such an issue would be handled in other countries?

- Do you have any family stories about relatives that grew up in other places? Are there topics connected to those?

- Allow children to browse related reference materials including the picture books and articles listed at the end of this chapter as well as in online Book Lists 1 and 2. Encourage chatting, sharing, and swapping of resources. Classrooms come alive when children are supporting one another, not competing with one another. (See section on camaraderie on page 58.)

- Continue clipping and sharing related newspaper and magazine articles. Encourage students and their families to browse publications and share the discoveries that might lead to a research topic.

Continuing to Support Students' Efforts
Sharing Your Own Writing

Whenever I think about a new writing assignment, I think back to the wise words of Donald Graves. When he visited classrooms at the Manhattan New School, he was delighted when he witnessed teachers taking care of their own writing. He would frequently ask, "If it is not for us, why should it be for them?" Teachers can become the most meaningful mentors for their students because if students admire us, they will want to be like us. If we are enthusiastic, serious, and hardworking when it comes to our own writing, so might our students be. When we write in the genre that our students have been asked to write, we learn about the appropriateness of the challenge, the availability or lack of resources, and any valuable writing techniques. So, the first way to support students' efforts is to attempt the writing challenge yourself.

I chose hats as my topic, thinking about the classic hats that are well known in different countries. I found it helpful to then imagine my finished work as a picture book, and I came up with the title, *Hats Off to You!* After the introductory remarks on the first page, I envisioned turning pages for each country with a photo or drawing of each hat and a short passage describing the hat and its use. The last page, of course, would have some concluding remarks about hats across the globe. My opening passages follow:

> There was a time in the United States, when people wore hats whenever they left home. Men wore fedoras in the cold weather and switched to straw ones called boaters when the weather warmed. News boys, in the early 20th century became famous for wearing Gatsby hats and men wore top hats on formal occasions. Abraham Lincoln is associated with a version of the top hat called a stovepipe hat. Women loved pillbox hats with veils or felt hats with feathers attached. For the Easter parade, women created wild and outrageous hats that attracted everyone's attention. Westerners wore cowboy or cowgirl hats. And of course, babies wore bonnets.
>
> Today, fewer people wear hats whenever they leave home, except when the weather is extremely cold or extremely hot. Hats help us keep warm and head coverings protect us from the rays of a very hot sun. Then too, lots of people wear baseball caps that announce their favorite teams or political positions and lately it has become popular for women and girls to wear pink knit hats to stand up for women's rights.
>
> Living in New York City, we meet lots of people from other countries. Some are tourists and others are immigrants. If you see people wearing the kinds of hats described in the pages that follow, you might be able to guess the country they come from or ones they have visited.

On the pages that followed, I described the Turkish fez, the French beret, the English bowler, the Russian ushanka, and the Mexican sombrero, making sure to include why that hat design is so important to the country it represents. For example, I explained that the fez began in a Moorish school and came to represent intelligence. In England, the bowler represented two very different occupations, the butler or valet, a servant to the rich, or in the big city it was worn by rich lawyers, stockbrokers, and bankers. The beret is still considered the national hat of France and is often worn by artists and movie directors.

On the last page of my picture book, I wrote:

> Do you think we have a hat that symbolizes our country, the United States of America? If so, what hat would that be and why would it be a good choice? If you don't think there is one all-American hat, can you explain why we might not have one hat to represent us? Hats off to you!

Gathering Information

In the author's note to *Throw Your Tooth on the Roof,* Selby Beeler (2001) offers great advice for students. The author suggests, "I quickly discovered that the best way to learn what people do with their baby teeth is simply to ask them … I talked to people on the street, in stores, in taxicabs and airplanes and buses. I visited the embassies of many nations in Washington, D.C. and wrote letters and e-mail to people at universities, cultural centers and UNICEF offices all over the world." In other words, the in-person or in-print interview became a really important tool for this researcher/writer. Similarly, Margreit Ruurs, the author of *Birthdays Around the World*, (2017) begins her back-of-the-book note to parents and teachers with the statement, "The information shared in this book is based on interviews with real people from the different countries that are featured." She goes onto to advise children to interview people from different countries or cultures. And so, the interview became our students' main way to gather information.

A few years ago, my grandson Zach was fortunate enough to be selected as a kid reporter for *Sport Illustrated Kids*. As part of his training for this yearlong commitment, he was given several very helpful interview tips. These included preparing questions beforehand, recording the interview, making eye contact, and asking follow-up questions.

The importance of asking pertinent follow-up questions cannot be stressed enough. It is so important that I prepared the following handout for students who tend to rush through their prepared questions, not really paying attention to the answers they were given, not recognizing the importance of seeking clarification, and not appreciating the potential of getting their subjects to say more. I borrowed the follow-up format from *Sports Illustrated Kids*, substituting sports questions with questions from several around-the-globe topics.

ASKING FOLLOW-UP QUESTIONS WHEN YOU INTERVIEW

Ask follow-up questions to get more specific or more surprising information or to draw out interesting anecdotes or stories. The following follow-up questions may come in handy.

- Can you say more about that?
- I am not sure I understand what you meant. Can you explain that idea?
- Can you tell any stories that illustrate your point?
- Can you be more specific?

Responses to follow-up questions like these might lead to the kind of raw material that will add richness to your writing. See examples below:

Question: What kind of snacks do kids in your country prefer?

Answer: Sweet ones.

This answer is too general.

Follow-up question: Can you tell me the names of some sweet treats that I probably wouldn't be able to find in the United States?

Question: What kinds of breaks do you get at school in your country?

Answer: We get recess twice a day, and we call our snack break high tea.

(continues)

ASKING FOLLOW-UP QUESTIONS
WHEN YOU INTERVIEW *(continued)*

This answer has great potential and you might want to seek even more information.

First follow-up question: What kinds of activities are popular with students during recess, and how long does recess last?

Second follow-up question: What kinds of things do students eat and drink during high tea?

After studying the art of interviewing, we practiced by tapping into the expertise and diversity of several staff members. Student interviewers focused on their across-the-globe areas of interest. Anne Kay, a Korean American teacher, taught us about Kungi fishing in which women, known as *haenyeo*, deep-sea scuba dive for abalone without fancy tools. The fisherwomen are native to the island of Jeju, and they collect shellfish in the Korean Strait. They catch marine snails by scraping them off rocks with tiny sticks that look like hoes. Children were also fascinated to learn that there are animal cafés in Korea where you can pet cats, dogs, or even reptiles. Students were also surprised to hear that young people are expected to bow to their elders, that soccer is a very popular sport, and that Korean cakes are often decorated with whipped cream, not frosting.

In addition, students were given time to browse the nonfiction shelves of the school library. They looked at picture books about different countries, scanning tables of contents and indexes to see if their topics were included. They were also given time to use Chromebooks, browsing appropriate sites on the Internet. (See page 101 for a listing on Internet sites.) Teachers, aides, student teachers, and family members also helped students gather additional and appropriate information.

Lifting the Quality of Student Writing

As students began to gather information, we carved out time to study how authors put this information together into a meaningful whole. We read and reread picture books and short articles. One article that proved particularly helpful for grade three students was titled, "Snack Time Favorites from Around the World," written by Dan Kois (n.d.) and published in *The New York Times*. The article begins with an intriguing lead followed by short descriptions of snack food from four different countries including *mamón chino* from Costa Rica, *paua* from New Zealand, *stroopwafel* from the Netherlands, and deep-fried crickets from Thailand. The author also includes France, but quite humorously lists "nothing" as the preferred snack, explaining that French parents do not usually approve of eating between meals.

Upon reading and rereading the article, we named the tools the author lifted from his writer's toolbox to create such an effective piece, one that in its brevity and simplicity of format proved to be a helpful model for eight-year-olds. The tools noted included:

- Direct address that creates a conversational tone

- Questions to encourage the reader to interact with the information

- Similes that help readers understand the new fruit by comparing it to familiar things ("*Mamón chino* looks like an alien egg but tastes like a Sour Patch Kid crossed with a grape.")

- Precise verbs that give more exact information (*grab, pry, fry*)

- Sensory details that help the reader feel like they are taking part in the event or scene, putting the reader's senses to work

- Power of three that makes the writing more rhythmic and memorable ("They're crunchy, salty and good.")

- Specific and accurate information that teaches the reader about the subject and proves the writer is an authority on the subject ("Pry the mollusk from an undersea rock …")

- Humorous lines throughout that enrich the conversational, casual tone and help create a satisfying ending

• enhancing w drawings or maps

In addition to these writer's tools, we called students' attention to the author's use of paragraphing to separate description of each snack, bold print and uppercase letters to name the snack, and parentheses to reveal the name of the countries. These techniques can all be borrowed if students plan to write short articles about their topics.

Teachers followed up by sharing several other texts including those listed at the end of this chapter and those included in the bibliography in online Book List 1. After reading aloud and inviting response to the important ideas and information in these books, teachers helped students tease out what each author had effectively done. Wade Bradford, in *Around the World in a Bathtub: Bathing All Over the Globe* (2017), demonstrates that sensory details can make the opening page of a book more appealing. He writes, "Somewhere right now, water is filling up a bathtub, steam is fogging up a mirror, washcloths and rubber duckies are waiting …" Giles Laroche in *If You Lived Here: Houses of the World* (2011) proves that he is an authority on his subject because he weaves in specific bits of accurate information. In describing a house in a Ndebele village in South Africa, he writes, "If you lived here, your brightly decorated home would be easy to find. With a brush or your fingertips, you and your mother and sisters would have painted the outside walls of your house in bold geometric patterns and shapes that look like flowers, leaves, and birds. Each house façade in your village is decorated by its family, and each has its own recognizable expression—just like a person's face."

Student Writing Samples

The following pieces of writing were both written by third graders in Laura Liebman and Andrea Garvey's class at P.S. 87.

"AMAZING WAYS TO GO FISHING" BY MAX AND MILES

If you like waking up at 2:00 am, you would be a good fisherman. Also, if you are patient, you would be a good fisherman. It takes practice to catch lots of fish. Some kinds of fishing don't even require using a hook. There are many different ways to go fishing around the world.

(continues)

"AMAZING WAYS TO GO FISHING" BY MAX AND MILES
(continued)

Dive!
Grab a wet suit, a mask, and a sharp tool to dive under water. Haenyeo or sea women of Korea, catch mollusks, abalone, octopus, conch and other creatures for a living. They practice holding their breath and they swim a lot. They dive underwater and hold their breath about a minute searching for sea creatures and bringing them back up.

Cold
In Canada, when it is cold, go to a frozen lake. Fishermen use a machine that goes through ice and makes a hole. When the ice is really strong sometimes, they drive cars on the ice. They set fishing rods with bait in the holes. They sometimes sleep overnight and see if they catch anything in the morning. Popular fish you could catch are pike, bass, walleye and whitefish.

"TRANSPORTATION AROUND THE WORLD" BY JACOB AND PHILIPP

How do you get around town? Do you use a car, a train, a bus? In other countries, transportation is very different than transportation here. You will be amazed by how people get around all over the world.

Chicken Bus
What bus do chickens ride? A chicken bus is in Guatemala and Panama. It gets its nickname by chickens boarding and traveling to market. They get on board for no money. Lucky chickens!

Skidoo and Skiing
What if it is a snowy day in chilly Canada? Grab a skidoo. A skidoo has 2 skis in front and a caterpillar tread at the back. If you don't take a skidoo to work, some people in Canada ice skate along the river to get to work.

See Appendix 1 for more examples of students' writing.

Carving Out Time for Celebration

Students learned a great deal by listening to one another present their findings as well as reading one another's finished work in a published anthology that was copied and distributed to each student. Students learned about a wide range of topics that cut across many, many countries. These included such surprising and child-centered topics as popular breakfast foods, summertime activities, birthday traditions, new baby celebrations, and first day of school rituals. Student publications were enhanced by drawings and maps.

BOOKS NOTED

Ajmera, Maya and John D. Ivanko. 2019. *Back to School: A Global Journey.* Watertown, MA: Charlesbridge.

Ancona, George. 2018. *Kids Cooking: Students Prepare and Eat Food From Around the World.* Somerville MA: Candlewick.

Beeler, Selby. 2001. *Throw Your Tooth on the Roof.* Boston, MA: Houghton Mifflin Books for Children/ Houghton Mifflin Harcourt.

Bradford, Wade. 2017. *Around the World in a Bathtub: Bathing All over the Globe.* Watertown, MA: Charlesbridge.

Galimberti, Gabriele. 2014a. *In Her Kitchen: Stories and Recipes from Grandmas Around the World.* New York: Clarkson Potter.

_____. Galimberti, Gabriele. 2014b. *Toy Stories: Photos of Children from Around the World and Their Favorite Things.* New York: Abrams Image.

_____. Galimberti, Gabriele. 2015. *My Couch Is Your Couch: Exploring How People Live Around the World.* New York: Potter Style/ Penguin Random House.

Kois, Dan. n.d. "Snack Time Favorites from Around the World." *The New York Times.*

Lankford, Mary D. 2008. *Mazes Around the World.* New York: Collins/HarperCollins.

Laroche, Giles. 2011. *If You Lived Here: Houses of the World.* Boston: MA: Houghton Mifflin Books for Children/Houghton Mifflin Harcourt.

McGinty, Alice B. 2019. *Pancakes to Parathas: Breakfast Around the World.* New York: Little Bee Books/ Simon & Schuster.

Ruurs, Margreit. 2005. *My Librarian Is a Camel: How Books Are Brought to Children Around the World.* Honesdale, PA: Boyds Mills.

_____.Ruurs, Margreit. 2017. *Birthdays Around the World.* Toronto, Canada: Kids Can Press.

Shamsian, Jacob, and Diana Yukari. 2017. "15 Unexpected Good Luck Charms from Countries Around the World." *Business Insider*, March 16.

A FEW TITLES TO ENRICH YOUR TEACHING

Cohen, Medeia. 2018. *Hats of Faith.* San Francisco, CA: Chronicle.

DePalma, Kate. 2019. *Let's Celebrate: Special Days Around the World.* Cambridge, MA: Barefoot Books.

de Regil, Tania. 2019. *A New Home.* Somerville, MA: Candlewick Press.

Diaz, Natalia, and Melissa Owens. 2015. *A Ticket Around the World.* Toronto: Owlkids.

DK. 2016. *Children Just Like Me: A New Celebration of Children Around the World.* New York: DK

Hughes, Susan. 2017. *Up: How Families Around the World Carry Their Little Ones.* Toronto: OwlKids Books.

Kostecki-Shaw, Jenny Sue. 2011. *Same, Same but Different.* New York: Henry Holt and Co.

Lamothe, Matt. 2017. *This Is How We Do It: One Day in the Lives of Seven Kids from Around the World.* San Francisco: Chronicle Books.

Ogburn, Jacqueline K. 2012. *Little Treasures: Endearments from Around the World.* Boston: MA: HMH Books for Young Readers.

Paul, Baptiste, and Miranda Paul. 2018. *Adventures to School: Real-Life Journeys of Students from Around the Globe*. New York: little bee books.

Tavangar, Homa Sabet. 2019. *Global Kids: 50+ Games, Crafts, Recipes & More from Around the World*. Cambridge, MA: Barefoot Books.

Tahe, Rose Ann, and Nancy Bo Flood. 2018. *First Laugh—Welcome Baby!* Watertown, MA: Charlesbridge.

Walker, Sylvia. 2012. *Happy New Year Around the World*. New York: Dover.

Walrond, Beth. 2019. *A Taste of the World: What People Eat and How They Celebrate Around the Globe*. Berlin: Little Gestalten.

TEACHER REFERENCE MATERIAL:

Strauss, Marianne Julia. (editor). 2020. *Do You Read Me?: Bookstores Around the World*. Berlin, Germany: Gestalten.

See bibliography in online Book Lists 1 and 2.

CHAPTER 2
Quirky Questions and Biographical Sketches

(Grades 3-5)

Alexander, a third grader in Renay Sadis's class at P.S. 87, asked the question, "Do you have your face on money?" He then chose to write biographical sketches on Susan B. Anthony and George Washington. See Figures 2.1 and 2.2.

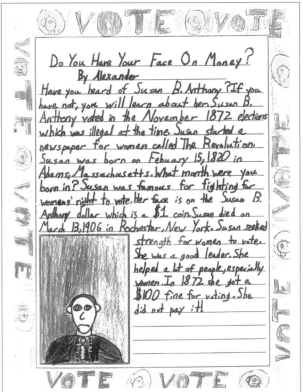

Figure 2.1

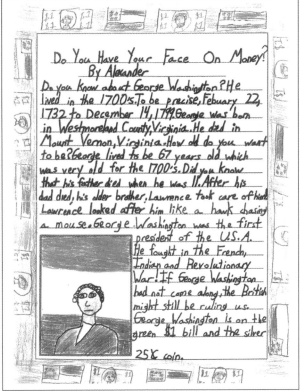

Figure 2.2

Exploring the Roots of the Writing Challenge

Years ago, I used to play an entertaining parlor game, back when our contact information wasn't contained on an electronic device. There was a time, much to my grandchildren's surprise, when most of us filled in the names, addresses, and phone numbers of family and friends in an alphabetized, paper phone book. (Back then, we didn't have email addresses or cellphone numbers to sit alongside our land lines numbers.) I remember the deep belly laughs when friends and I played "Guess who is coming to dinner!" The game was rather simple. We would take turns flipping to a random page in our phone books and read the list of names on a page, imagining what a dinner party would be like if all the folks on any one page, whose last names began with the same letter, were invited to the same get-together. What would my uncle, my gynecologist, my next-door neighbor, and a children's author talk about? How would they get along? I must admit, it was great fun to imagine bringing such a surprising mix of people together.

Recently, my husband and I were invited to another surprising gathering, this time for real. Calling it a vertical cocktail party, a friendly couple decided to bring together all the families that lived in the same line of apartments in our Manhattan apartment building. We lived at the same address and each had the same apartment layout, but we came from very different backgrounds and had very different family situations, careers, and interests. And our apartments looked oh so different. It was an entertaining and eye-opening get-together.

I thought about the power of bringing a surprising group of people together when I first read Eileen Spinelli's picture books *Do You Have a Hat?* (2004) and then *Do You Have a Cat?* (2010) and *Do You Have a Dog?* (2011). In this lyrical, informative, and delightful series of picture books, the author brings together a wide range of people who seemingly share little in common except for answering in the affirmative to the question asked in the title of the book. Abraham Lincoln, Carmen Miranda, Daniel Boone, Amelia Earhart, and Charlie Chaplin, to name but a few, would all say yes if asked if they had a hat. In fact, their hats became iconic, memorable, and closely associated with their celebrated lives.

Spinelli's book made me ask one of my favorite teaching of writing questions: Could our students do that? Instead of their usual biography-writing units, could our students think of an interesting question that would bring together a wide range of interesting and diverse people (much the way my imagined dinner party would). Then, could students research the people chosen and write about them? Spinelli's books are filled with short, poetic tributes to each of her famous hat wearers (and dog or cat owners), but we weren't interested in asking children to craft rhyming tributes. Instead, creating short biographical sketches seemed more in line with their grade-level curriculum goals.

Engaging Students in the Challenge

We introduced the idea of creating biographical sketches anchored to an interesting question by sharing Eileen Spinelli's books. It was joyful to read the title and ask students, "Who do you think the author may have included in this book? Do you know any famous people who are known for their hats?" Abraham Lincoln was the first one called out. Barack Obama was suggested for dog ownership, and students were disappointed that he was not included. They so wanted to read about Bo, his Portuguese water dog. The cat question stumped the children as well as the teachers gathered.

A third grader proudly displays a postcard he received from Harry Belafonte, one of the people he researched who have birthdays in March.

We then asked the children to do what Eileen Spinelli had done. We asked, "If you were to write a book like those of Eileen Spinelli, what question would you ask that would lead you to learn about a few interesting, famous, and diverse people?" Some of their interesting questions follow:

Do you have a birthday in January? (Any month would do.)

Do you have your face on a postage stamp?

Do you have a visual impairment?

Do you have a bridge, tunnel, concert hall, stadium, or office building named after you?

Do you have eyeglasses?

Do you have well-known initials?

Do you have a famous hairdo?

Do you have a uniform?

Do you have a twin?

Do you have an alliterative name?

Do you have a famous nickname?

Do you have a wheelchair?

Do you have a Canadian passport?

Of course, we had to help children eliminate questions that would not lead to appropriate or diverse people. For example, if students asked, "Did you win a Grammy?" they would bring together only people connected to the music industry. If they asked, "Do you have a swimming pool?" the list of names would probably be impossible to research, but more importantly this trait would not be as distinctive as would be needed to create an interesting book. If students asked, "Do you have a mustache?" their candidates would be male dominated.

To make the groupings more original and surprising, we also suggested that their questions needed to pull together people who had different occupations or accomplishments. When children eventually brought in their list of possible subjects, we also directed them toward those that represented diversity in gender, ethnicity, and age. When a fifth-grade teacher learned of third graders taking part in the Do You Have . . . ? challenge, her students rethought their own biographical essay assignments. Instead of writing a biography of just one person, they were asked to think of interesting ways to cluster several people. In Melissa Martinez's fifth-grade class, a student grouped Neil Armstrong, Lance Armstrong, and Louis Armstrong and wondered if their surnames were connected to their strength of character or physical strength. I would add Lil Hardin Armstrong, the wife of Louis Armstrong and a key figure in the history of jazz, to that list. Wouldn't they make for an interesting dinner party?

Continuing to Support Students' Efforts

After students chose an interesting question, we had two important instructional goals. First, students had to create a list of potential subjects, those who could answer yes to the organizing question they posed. For example, if students chose "Do you have your face on a postage stamp?" they could easily search the Internet for a list of potential subjects, talking to their family members about which would be interesting to study. Students could then share their list of postage stamp luminaries with their teacher. For example, such folks as Albert Einstein, Louisa May Alcott, Joe DiMaggio, Arthur Ashe, Susan B. Anthony, Johnny Appleseed, Maya Angelou, and George Washington Carver would be appropriate for third graders to research and then create biographical sketches. Teachers and students can decide on how many would make for a satisfying finished product. Students who chose the same organizing question but different people to research could combine their writings, creating a collaborative publication.

Our second goal was to decide what information would go into a biographical sketch, pointing out that it was not a fully developed biography like those in the Who Was . . . ? series with several chapters, dozens of pages, and timelines included. Nor was a biographical sketch as skimpy as the summary statements printed on the endpapers of Eileen Spinelli's Do You Have . . . ? books, which, for example, only states, "Abraham Lincoln was the sixteenth president of the United States." Surely, third-grade classmates would want to know more about Abraham Lincoln.

I read with interest Robert Caro's (2019) latest book titled, *Working: Researching, Interviewing, Writing*. In it, the biographer presents the importance of taking time to get to know your subject deeply when writing a biography. In a review of Caro's book in *The New York Times*, Sir Harold Evans (2019) notes, "He can't stop asking questions. He suspects that behind every answer there is another question. Most good reporters I know have a full quiver of 'whys?' but Caro is insatiable." Having real curiosity about your subject is an important lesson for even our youngest biographers. We ask them, "What do you want to know about the people you are presenting?" I asked students, "Besides knowing that Lincoln was our sixteenth president, what other questions do you want answered?"

Students were quick to list the questions they wanted answered, suggesting the additional information that should be added if they were to write a biographical sketch of Lincoln. These included the dates and location of his birth and death, his major accomplishments, as well as some information about the stovepipe hat that he wore.

Sharing Your Own Writing

Next, as has become a regular part of our instructional plans, I modeled my own writing, using the Spinelli format to create an original Do You Have . . . ? picture book. Creating an exemplar was a particularly essential step in this challenge as we borrowed only Spinelli's idea of an interesting, organizing question. We did not use her written text as a model. Her pages were filled with clever five-line rhymes, but we decided to challenge the third graders to write short prose paragraphs.

I chose the organizing question "Do You Have Eyeglasses?" and asked students and the teachers gathered for the demonstration lesson, to guess who might be included in my biographical collection. They accurately guessed Ben Franklin, Elton John, and Harry Potter. I then turned the pages of my book to reveal Mahatma Gandhi, Steve Jobs, Billy Jean King, Whoopi Goldberg, Sarah Palin, and John Lennon. (Wouldn't this crowd make for an interesting dinner party?)

Gathering Information

I then shared the questions I had about John Lennon and the notes I had taken about him. The notes were based on reading biographical material, chatting with friends, as well as counting on my background information about the Beatles. I showed the notes to the students and discussed additional questions I might research and the information I might include. Students reminded me that the memorial to John Lennon, Strawberry Fields, was in walking distance of the school, and teachers reminded me that Lennon had a first wife before Yoko Ono and that he had two sons, as I had only included his son Julian.

Once students had their own list of names and selected a few to research, we suggested that students jot down the questions they had about each of their subjects. Afterward, we guided students toward appropriate resource materials, so they could gather information to create their biographical sketches. Students benefited from school and classroom libraries that had abundant biographies, including the series, anthologies, and picture books listed in online Book List 3. Teachers also helped students download articles from appropriate Internet sites. Students were encouraged to talk to family members, recording their ideas about the famous folks chosen for their biographical sketches.

Lifting the Quality of Student Writing

Most prose biographical sketches that are appropriate for eight- to ten-year-old readers are often bland and rather matter of fact, the kind found in Wikipedia entries. We were interested in students learning to write well as they created short biographies of their subjects. To present models, we knew we had to create them ourselves. We had to weave the notes we took into a biographical sketch. The following first draft was written collaboratively with students as we posted chart paper and asked students how to proceed. "Which information should come first? Next? Do we have enough information? How might we end this biographical sketch?" Taking suggestions from the students, we produced the following first draft:

John Lennon was a famous singer, songwriter and peace activist from England who helped create the Beatles. He was born on October 9th, 1940 in Liverpool, England. He grew up to be a famous singer, songwriter and peace activist. He is most famous for cofounding the Beatles with Paul McCartney. They were joined by Ringo Starr and George Harrison and were very, very popular in the 1960s and 1970s. Fans were so crazy about them and their music that the popularity was called "Beatlemania." Lennon also performed with his second wife Yoko Ono and both of his sons, Julian and Sean, became musical performers. Unfortunately, John Lennon was killed on December 8th, 1980, by a mentally ill man right in front of the Dakota, his apartment building on the Upper West Side of Manhattan. Fans were so saddened by their loss that they created a memorial in nearby Central Park. Visitors gather there, leaving bouquets of flowers and sometimes playing their guitars. Although we can no longer hear any new John Lennon songs, we do have many old ones to still enjoy.

We then led students through a series of minilessons demonstrating how to improve the quality of our draft. We began with leads, then reviewed our study of tools in the writer's toolbox, and finally moved onto satisfying endings.

We shared and discussed other options for a lead, recording them on a chart that appears below.

POSSIBLE TYPES OF LEADS FOR JOHN LENNON BIOGRAPHICAL SKETCH

1. A broad summary statement: "John Lennon was a famous singer, songwriter, and peace activist from England who helped create the Beatles."

2. A brief question: "Have you ever heard of John Lennon?"

3. Asking for a reader response: "Most people love the Beatles and can name their favorite member of that band. Mine is John Lennon. Who's yours?"

4. A fictional story: "We were driving to the zoo when my mom turned to me and asked, 'Do you like the Beatles?' 'No,' I answered, 'but I do like ladybugs.' 'Not those kinds of beetles,' she said, 'the Beatles who sing. I want to play some music as we drive.' 'Of course, I love the Beatles,' I added, 'especially John Lennon.'"

5. Begin at the end: "December 8, 1980 was a sad day for New Yorkers, British people and music lovers throughout the world. It was the day that John Lennon passed away."

6. Quote from subject: "'I profoundly regret that I was not an American and that I did not grow up in Greenwich Village.' It comes as no surprise that John Lennon, a member of the famous British band The Beatles, would love this artistic neighborhood of New York City. After all, he was a wonderful musician, and his American fans adored him."

On another day, we discussed how the tools in our writer's toolbox can be used to improve the quality of our writing. I created handouts, containing lines lifted from biographical picture books that had previously been read aloud. I asked students to read and talk about the quality of the writing. A sampling of possible lines follows below. (See list of biographical picture books in online Book List 3.)

WRITERS USE TOOLS FROM THEIR TOOLBOXES

Can you name the tools used in these excerpts from biographical picture books?

1. From *Helen Keller: The World in Her Heart* by Lesa Cline-Ransome (2008)

   It was March in Alabama, and the warm spring air slipped through the open windows and mingled with the scent of sugar and vanilla. Helen longed to go outside and run barefoot through the still damp grass or climb the tall oak tree out in front, but the promise of the first bite of her favorite cake kept her inside close to the stove.

2. From *Roberto Clemente: Pride of the Pittsburgh Pirates* by Jonah Winter (2005)

   On an island called Puerto Rico, where baseball players are as plentiful as tropical flowers in a rain forest, there was a boy who had very little but a fever to play and win baseball.

3. From *Abe Lincoln: The Boy Who Loved Books* by Kay Winters (2003)

   The Cumberland Trail ran close to their new cabin. Abe saw peddlers, pioneers, politicians, traders . . . pass by. As Abe grew, he talked to travelers—heard where they'd been, where they were going. He saw their world was wider than his own. His ideas stretched. His questions rose. His dreams were stirred.

4. From *Tito Puente: Mambo King* by Monica Brown (2013)

   The Mambo King plays and sways as people dance the mambo, the rumba, and the cha-cha! . . . Tito performed at parties, restaurants, and clubs . . . When the Tito Puente Orchestra played . . . the tambourines sounded like rain on metal roofs . . . The dancers twirled, the lights swirled, and the mambo went on and on . . .

5. From *I Dissent: Ruth Bader Ginsburg Makes Her Mark* by Debbie Levy (2016)

   Ruth read about Nancy Drew, girl detective. She discovered Amelia Earhart, daring aviator. She learned of Athena, goddess of Greek myths. Here were independent girls and women, taking charge. Ruth read her way into this world. Around her, the sweet scent of books blended with savory aromas from the Chinese restaurant downstairs. Delicious! A girl could be anything.

6. From *Bambino and Mr. Twain* by P.I. Maltbie (2012)

   Bambino attacked the sunbeam dancing on the wardrobe door. Sam opened the door. The sunbeam shone on a white suit. Bambino swatted at it.

7. From *When Paul Met Artie: The Story of Simon & Garfunkel* by G. Neri (2018)

   Paul has seen Artie around the neighborhood, wearing a red Phillies cap or shaking boxes of Good & Plenty in the candy store. But until he sees Artie standing nervously onstage at the fourth-grade talent show, Paul hasn't given him a thought . . . That is, until Artie opens his mouth and out pours the Voice: smooth, hypnotic, and sounding just like the unforgettable Nat King Cole himself . . . This kid Artie is like a human jukebox, his voice casting a spell over the entire school auditorium.

(continues)

WRITERS USE TOOLS FROM THEIR TOOLBOXES
(continued)

8. From *Electrical Wizard: How Nikola Tesla Lit Up the World* by Elizabeth Rusch (2013)

The night of Nikola Tesla's birth, lightning zapped, crackled, and flashed overhead. For years after, booming thunder drew the poor Serbian boy to the window of his family's small house. Nikola gazed, mystified, as electrical bolts ricocheted across the sky . . . One day, when he was twenty-six, Nikola went for a walk with a friend. The sun set in a fiery blaze. The buzzing thoughts inside Nikola's head sparked together like a lightning bolt.

9. From *Martina & Chrissie: The Greatest Rivalry in the History of Sports* by Phil Bildner (2017)

Martina, she was all emotion, all the time. Slapping her thighs and yelling at herself and bursting into tears. Sometimes she'd even cry on the court. Martina had this lefty serve that was wicked, wicked. And she loved to rush the net: serve and volley, serve and volley, serve and volley. Guys, Martina OWNED the net.

10. From *Rosa* by Nikki Giovanni (2005)

Rosa Parks was the best seamstress. The needle and thread flew through her hands like the gold spinning from Rumpelstiltskin's loom. . . . And the people walked. They walked in the rain. They walked in the hot sun. They walked early in the morning. They walked late at night. They walked at Christmas, and they walked at Easter. They walked on the Fourth of July; they walked on Labor Day. They walked on Thanksgiving, and then it was almost Christmas again. They still walked.

11. From *Colorful Dreamer: The Story of Henri Matisse* by Marjorie Blain Parker (2012)

Years ago, a dreamy boy gazed out his bedroom window. He lived in a dreary village in France. It was an industrial town—choked with factories, clanking looms, and smoking chimneys. There were no gardens to wander, no museums to visit, no paintings to admire.

12. From *Julia Morgan Built a Castle* by Celeste Davidson Mannis (2006)

Julia prepared plans, details and models for a large main house to crown the highest hill, and three smaller guesthouses to hug its side. She also designed lush gardens and walkways to connect the buildings and give the project the look and feel of a dreamy hilltop village.

13. From *Radiant Child: The Story of Young Artist Jean Michel Basquiat* by Javaka Steptoe (2016)

Somewhere in Brooklyn, between hearts that thump, double Dutch, and hopscotch and salty mouths that slurp sweet ice, a little boy dreams of being a famous ARTIST.

WRITERS USE TOOLS FROM THEIR TOOLBOXES
(continued)

14. From *Words Set Me Free: The Story of Young Frederick Douglass* by Lesa Cline-Ransome (2012)

> On a Saturday when we sailed down the Miles River with all I owned in the world, my first pair of scratchy breeches and a shift, I did not cry. I was ready to leave Talbot County, Maryland, behind. We arrived at Smith's wharf on Sunday morning. Old Tom never told me that Baltimore looked as if it floated on a sea of waves.

We discussed the lines above at length, reminding students the names of the writer's tools and what effect each had on the reader. Students need to remember that if they choose to use any of these tools, it will affect their readers. Notes from that discussion are summarized next. The numbers refer to the numbered list of books in the previous text box.

1. Sensory details make readers feel like they are taking part in the event or scene, putting the readers' senses to work ("It was March in Alabama, and the warm spring air slipped through the open windows and mingled with the scent of sugar and vanilla").

   Precise verbs give more exact information (*slipped, mingled*).

   Specific and accurate information teaches content to reader and prove that the writer is an authority on the subject ("March in Alabama").

2. A simile helps the reader understand a concept by making a comparison to something familiar ("... where baseball players are as plentiful as tropical flowers in a rain forest").

3. Alliteration adds a comforting, musical quality to the sound of the writing ("peddlers, pioneers, politicians..."; "world was wider...").

   Long list sentence adds variety to sentence lengths in the writing and demonstrates author's rich content knowledge about the subject ("Abe saw peddlers, pioneers, politicians, traders... pass by").

   The power of three makes the writing more rhythmic and more memorable ("His ideas stretched. His questions rose. His dreams were stirred").

   Specific and accurate information teaches content to reader and prove that the writer is an authority on the subject ("The Cumberland Trail").

(continues)

4. The power of three makes the writing more rhythmic and more memorable ("the mambo, the rumba, and the cha-cha!"; "The dancers twirled, the lights swirled, and the mambo went on and on").

    A simile helps the reader understand a concept by making a comparison to something familiar ("the tambourines sounded like rain on metal roofs").

    Precise verbs give more exact information (*sway, twirl, swirl*).

5. The power of three makes the writing more rhythmic and more memorable ("Ruth read about Nancy Drew, girl detective. She discovered Amelia Earhart, daring aviator. She learned of Athena, goddess of Greek myths").

    Sensory details make readers feel like they are taking part in the event or scene, putting the readers' senses to work ("Around her, the sweet scent of books blended with savory aromas from the Chinese restaurant downstairs").

    Sentences of varied lengths make the writing more interesting for the reader, eliminating the monotony of too many similar-length sentences ("Around her, the sweet scent of books blended with savory aromas from the Chinese restaurant downstairs. Delicious! A girl could be anything").

6. Personification adds a lyrical and poetic quality to the writing ("the sunbeam dancing on the wardrobe door").

    Sensory details make readers feel like they are taking part in the event or scene, putting the readers' senses to work ("The sunbeam shone on a white suit. Bambino swatted at it").

    Precise verbs give more exact information (*attacked, shone, swatted*).

7. Sensory details make readers feel like they are taking part in the event or scene, putting the readers' senses to work ("Paul has seen Artie around the neighborhood, wearing a red Phillies cap or shaking boxes of Good & Plenty in the candy store").

    The power of three makes the writing more rhythmic and memorable ("smooth, hypnotic, and sounding just like the unforgettable Nat King Cole himself").

8. The power of three makes the writing more rhythmic and more memorable ("lightning zapped, crackled, and flashed").

   Precise verbs give more exact information (*zapped, crackled, flashed, gazed, sparked*).

   A simile helps the reader understand a concept by making a comparison to something familiar ("The buzzing thoughts inside Nikola's head sparked together like a lightning bolt").

9. Sensory details make readers feel like they are taking part in the event or scene, putting the reader's senses to work ("Slapping her thighs and yelling at herself and bursting into tears").

   Repetition shows emphasis and importance to the reader ("Martina had this lefty serve that was wicked, wicked"; "serve and volley, serve and volley, serve and volley").

   The power of three makes the writing more rhythmic and more memorable ("serve and volley, serve and volley, serve and volley.")

10. A simile helps the reader understand a concept by making a comparison to something familiar ("The needle and thread flew through her hands like the gold spinning from Rumpelstiltskin's loom").

    Repetition shows emphasis and importance to the reader ("They walked . . . They walked . . . They walked . . . They walked . . .").

    Specific and accurate information teaches content to reader and prove that the writer is an authority on the subject ("Christmas"; "Easter"; "Fourth of July"; "Labor Day").

11. The power of three makes the writing more rhythmic and more memorable ("choked with factories, clanking looms, and smoking chimneys"; "There were no gardens to wander, no museums to visit, no paintings to admire").

    Precise verbs give more exact information (*gazed, choked, wander, admire*).

    Sensory details make readers feel like they are taking part in the event or scene, putting the readers' senses to work ("It was an industrial town— choked with factories, clanking looms, and smoking chimneys").

(continues)

12. The power of three makes the writing more rhythmic and more memorable ("Julia prepared plans, details and models").

   Precise verbs give more exact information (*crown, hug*).

   Sensory details make readers feel like they are taking part in the event or scene, putting the readers' senses to work ("She also designed lush gardens and walkways to connect the buildings and give the project the look and feel of a dreamy hilltop village").

13. An engaging lead sentence pulls the reader into the story.

   Sensory details make readers feel like they are taking part in the event or scene, putting the readers' senses to work (". . . between hearts that thump, double Dutch, and hopscotch and salty mouths that slurp sweet ice . . . ,").

   Onomatopoeia words such as "thump" and "slurp" make the writing more vivid.

14. When writing is filled with specific bits of accurate information, it proves to the reader that the author is an expert on the topic (Miles River, Talbot County, Maryland, Smith's wharf).

   Poetic language makes the writing memorable (". . . Baltimore looked as if it floated on a sea of waves.").

Several days later, we talked about creating satisfying endings. We shared and discussed options for endings. I prepared and distributed a handout for the subjects in my collection: "Do you wear eyeglasses?" Students realized that although the thread holding my subjects together was the wearing of eyeglasses, only half of the endings mentioned that.

EXPERIMENTING WITH ENDINGS FOR BIOGRAPHICAL SKETCHES

1. "Whoopie Goldberg usually wears round, rimless eyeglasses that sit on the tip of her nose. They look attractive, don't you agree?" (Ends with a comment on the trait that brought the subject together and a quick question for the reader.)

2. "When children dress up as Harry Potter for Halloween, they always wear a hooded Hogwarts student robe with the Gryffindor crest and carry his magic wand and a thick book on witchcraft and wizardry. And, of course, their costume would not be complete without a pair of round-rimmed eyeglasses." (Ends with strong imagery and an opinion offered by the writer that connects back to the theme of the collection—eyeglasses.)

3. "Look at a painting of Ben Franklin. You can tell from his hairdo and his style of clothing that he lived in an earlier historic time period, but you still might see today people wearing those same round eyeglasses." (Ends with a comment about the physical appearance of the subject, suggesting the reader take a look at the image of the person and note the trait that connects all the subjects in this collection.)

4. "People all over the world remember Gandhi on his birthday, October 2d, and it is sometimes called The International Day of Non-Violence. Imagine if people the world over celebrated your birthday!" (Ends with an interesting fact and a surprising thought.)

5. "These songs make John Lennon live on forever in our hearts and minds." (Ends with a tug at the reader's emotions.)

6. Lead: "Billie Jean King was a famous trophy-winning tennis player, but perhaps more importantly she was a fighter for women's rights for equality." Ending: "Today, women tennis players owe a debt of gratitude to Billie Jean King, tennis player supreme, and advocate for equality for women athletes." (Ends by circling back to beginning information.)

After studying engaging leads, the qualities of good writing, and satisfying endings, students helped me revise my draft on John Lennon. In addition to a more engaging lead, we added a simile, used the power of three, added more bits of specific and accurate information, and revised our endings so that it would tug at the reader's emotions.

Most people love the Beatles and have a favorite member of that band. Mine is John Lennon. Who is yours?

John Lennon was born on October 9, 1940 in Liverpool, England. He grew up to be a famous singer, songwriter, and peace activist. He is most famous for co-founding the Beatles with Paul McCartney. They were joined by Ringo Starr and George Harrison and were very, very popular in the 1960s and 1970s. Fans were so crazy about them and their music that the popularity was called "Beatlemania." The Beatles became as famous as the Queen of England or the President of the United States.

John Lennon also performed with his second wife, Yoko Ono, and both of his sons, Julian and Sean, became musical performers. Unfortunately, John Lennon was killed on December 8, 1980 by a man with a mental health illness right in front of the Dakota, his apartment building on the Upper West Side of Manhattan. Fans were so saddened by their loss that they created a memorial in nearby Central Park called Strawberry Fields. Visitors gather there, leaving bouquets of flowers, lighting candles and sometimes playing their guitars.

(continues)

> Although we can no longer hear any new John Lennon songs, we do have many old ones to still enjoy. These include "I Am the Walrus," "Give Peace a Chance," "Strawberry Fields Forever," "Imagine," and "Happy Christmas (War is Over)." These songs make John Lennon live on forever in our hearts and minds.

During regularly scheduled writing workshops, teachers conferred with students after teaching mini-lessons related to taking notes, turning notes into cohesive paragraphs, crafting engaging leads as well as satisfying endings, and applying the tools in their writer's toolboxes when appropriate.

During conferences, teachers often addressed such problematic situations as students borrowing words and phrases that were not their own, omission of essential pieces of information, and students' attempt at using reference material that was too difficult. (Teachers helped locate more appropriate materials.)

Student Writing Samples

Molly, a third grader in Renay's class at P. S. 87, gathered people whose face appeared on a postage stamp. Two of her samples appear in Figures 2.3 and 2.4.

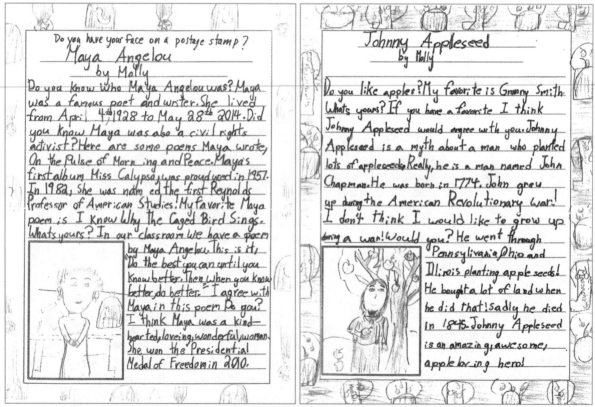

Figure 2.3   Figure 2.4

Zach, another of Renay's students, focused on folks who had a birthday in March including Harry Belafonte and Alexander Graham Bell. See his biographical sketches in Figures 2.5 and 2.6.

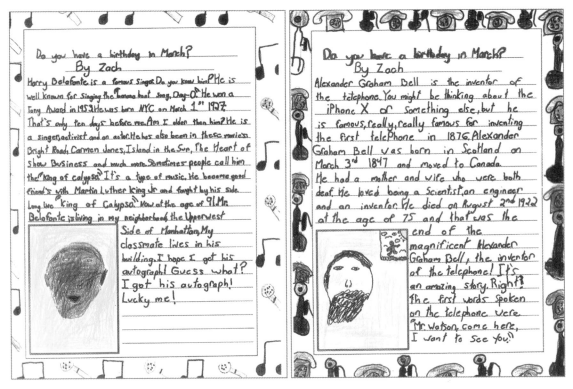

Figure 2.5   Figure 2.6

Carving Out Time for Celebration

In preparation for a publishing party, students downloaded photographs or made drawings of their subjects, and added these to enrich each revised and eventually edited biographical sketch. They separated each sketch with the repetition of their chosen question and affirmative answer, such as "Do you have eyeglasses? Billie Jean King had eyeglasses." If more than one student had the same question, they often combined their efforts, making their published work more substantial and announcing all contributing authors on the cover. Family members were invited in to celebrate the students' efforts.

In any one class, dozens of biographical sketches were produced, and students and adults became familiar with many new and noteworthy celebrities. Students delighted in introducing children and adults to such unfamiliar people as Vivien Thomas (surgical technician who stopped blue baby disease), Judith Heumann (disability rights advocate), Trischa Zorn Hudson (Paralympic swimmer), and Lee Duncan (trainer of the dog Rin Tin Tin).

BOOKS NOTED

The following were used for format:

Spinelli, Eileen. 2004. *Do You Have a Hat?* New York: Simon & Schuster Books for Young Readers.

———. 2010. *Do You Have a Cat?* Grand Rapids, MI: Eerdmans Books for Young Readers.

———. 2011. *Do You Have a Dog?* Grand Rapids, MI: Eerdmans Books for Young Readers.

The following books were used to teach craft techniques:

Bildner, Phil. 2017. *Martina & Chrissie: The Greatest Rivalry in the History of Sports.* Somerville, MA: Candlewick.

Brown, Monica. 2013. *Tito Puente: Mambo King.* New York: Rayo/HarperCollins.

Cline-Ransome, Lesa. 2008. *Helen Keller: The World in Her Heart.* New York: HarperCollins.

———. 2012. *Words Set Me Free: The Story of Young Frederick Douglass.* New York: Simon & Schuster.

Giovanni, Nikki. 2005. *Rosa.* New York: Henry Holt.

Levy, Debbie. 2016. *I Dissent: Ruth Bader Ginsburg Makes Her Mark.* New York: Simon & Schuster.

Maltbie, P.I. 2012. *Bambino and Mr. Twain.* Watertown, MA: Charlesbridge.

Mannis, Celeste Davidson. 2006. *Julia Morgan Built a Castle.* New York: Viking Juvenile.

Neri, G. 2018. *When Paul Met Artie: The Story of Simon & Garfunkel.* Somerville, MA: Candlewick.

Parker, Marjorie Blain. 2012. *Colorful Dreamer; The Story of Artist Henri Matisse.* New York: Dial Books for Young Readers/Penguin Group.

Rusch, Elizabeth. 2013. *Electrical Wizard: How Nikola Tesla Lit Up the World.* Somerville, MA: Candlewick.

Steptoe. Javaka. 2016. *Radiant Child: The Story of Young Artist Jean-Michel Basquiat.* New York: Little, Brown.

Winter, Jonah. 2005. *Roberto Clemente: Pride of the Pittsburgh Pirates*: New York: Atheneum/Simon & Schuster Children's Publishing Division.

Winters, Kay. 2003. *Abe Lincoln: The Boy Who Loved Books.* New York: Simon & Schuster Books for Young Readers.

TEACHER REFERENCE MATERIAL

Caro, Robert. 2019. *Working: Researching, Interviewing, Writing.* New York: Knopf.

Evans, Harold. 2019. "Biography as Obsession." *The New York Times*, Book Reviews, April 21.

A FEW TITLES TO ENRICH YOUR TEACHING

Chambers, Veronica. 2018. *Resist: 35 Profiles of Ordinary People Who Rose Up Against Tyranny and Injustice.* New York: HarperCollins.

Cline-Ransome, Lesa. 2020. *Not Playing by the Rules: 21 Athletes Who Changed Sports.* New York: Knopf.

Clinton, Chelsea. 2018. *She Persisted Around the World: 13 Women Who Changed History.* New York: Philomel.

Harrison, Vashti. 2019. *Little Legends. Exceptional Men in Black History.* New York: Little, Brown.

Hood, Susan. 2018. *Shaking Things Up: 14 Young Women Who Changed the World.* New York: HarperCollins.

Katz, Alan. 2019. *Awesome Achievers in Technology: Strange Facts About 12 Almost Famous History Makers.* Philadelphia, PA: Running Press Kids.

Kinew, Wab. 2018. *Go Show the World: A Celebration of Indigenous Heroes.* Toronto: Tundra Books.

King, Shani Mahiri. 2021. *Have I Ever Told You That Black Lives Matter?* Thomaston, ME: Tilbury House.

Lowe, Mifflin. 2020.*The True West: Real Stories About Black Cowboys, Women Sharpshooters, Native American Rodeo Stars, Pioneering Vaqueros and the Unsung Explorers, Builders and Heroes who Shaped the American West.* Charlotte, NC: Baker & Taylor.

Menéndez, Juliet, 2021. *Latinitas: Celebrating 40 Big Dreamers.* New York: Henry Holt.

Norwood, Arlisha. 2020. *Black Heroes: A Black History Book for Kids; 51 Inspiring People from Ancient Africa to Modern-Day U.S.A.* Berkeley, CA: Callisto Media

Peñas, Roberto. 2021. *Pedro's Yo-Yos: How a Filipino Immigrant Came to America and Changed the World of Toys.* New York: Lee & Low.

Pinkney, Andrea Davis. 2021. *Because of You, John Lewis.* New York: Scholastic.

Wallace, Sandra Neil and Rich Wallace. 2018. *First Generation: 36 Trailblazing Immigrants and Refugees Who Make America Great.* New York: Little, Brown.

Weatherford, Carole Boston. 2020. *R-E-S-P-E-C-T: Aretha Franklin, The Queen of Soul.* New York: Atheneum.

See additional bibliography of biographies for young readers in online Book List 3. These titles can be used for information on the subjects' lives as well as for close study of biographical writing.

CHAPTER 3
Playing Favorites
(Grades 1-2)

Lilah, a first grader in Corinne Daniels and Crystal Raymond's class, interviewed the district's assistant superintendent about her favorite animal:

> Dr. K's favorite animals are tigers. She likes them because they have beautiful patterns. Another reason she likes them is because they are interesting. A third reason she likes them is because they are smart.
>
> Dr. K wants to know if tigers will become extinct. Tigers that live in the wild are endangered because people are hunting them and moving into their habitats. Tigers need lots of space to hunt and live. There are about 3890 tigers left in the wild. Unfortunately, the prediction is that tigers in the wild may become extinct. This would make me depressed because these animals need to be treated better.

Exploring the Roots of the Writing Challenge

Children love the work of Eric Carle. They instantly recognize his brilliant and distinctive illustrations, be they caterpillars, ladybugs, spiders, chameleons, click beetles, seahorses, or crickets. Yes, they can spot an Eric Carle picture book, even before they have learned to read. Children and their parents love the simplicity and sensibility of his stories. Kids always want his books to be read aloud repeatedly, inevitably memorizing the words. It's no wonder that *Brown Bear, Brown Bear, What Do You See?* (2002) written by Bill Martin Jr. and boldly illustrated by Carle are often the most dog-eared titles on young children's bedroom shelves and in early childhood classrooms.

A recent series of picture books takes on a rather different feel as Carle taps the talents of a wide range of fellow children's book artists. In fact, these books boast Eric Carle and Friends as their creators. The titles ask such child-like questions as *What's Your Favorite Color?* (2014b), *What's Your Favorite Animal?* (2014a), and *What's Your Favorite Bug?* (2018). Turn the pages of these gloriously illustrated books and find the answers written and illustrated by over a dozen popular children's book artists. The royalties from the sale of these books are given to The Eric Carle Museum of Picture Book Art.

Read aloud any of these books to a classroom of young students and be prepared to have every hand raised in response. All the children have a favorite color and a favorite animal, and most can name a favorite bug. Students' enthusiasm for these books led to the early childhood writing challenge that follows.

Engaging Students in the Challenge

I began with *What's Your Favorite Animal?* knowing that at the elementary level all roads lead to animals. Children want to talk about the pets they currently have, the ones they used to have, and the ones they wish they had. They want to share which animals they spotted at the zoo, in their backyards, on vacation, and, for our city kids, even those on the subway tracks.

Classmates ask one another for feedback on their drafts.

After explaining how *What's Your Favorite Animal?* was created, I asked students which artists were familiar to them and if they were curious to find out which animal these artists had chosen. First graders squealed when I mentioned such literary luminaries as Lucy Cousins, Jon Klassen, Rosemary Wells, and Mo Willems, artists who not only illustrated but wrote many of the children's favorite picture books. They were thrilled to learn that Lucy Cousins adored leopards, Jon Klassan appreciated ducks, and Rosemary Wells preferred dogs. They were rather stunned to learn that Mo Willems selected the Amazonian Neotropical Lower River Tink-Tink, although most adults doubted that such a species existed. We talked about the meaning of collaboration and suggested that we could create our very own version of this research, right here at school. Students were quick to point out that we didn't have famous writers or illustrators in the school, but I suggested that we did have beloved staff members. "Aren't you curious to learn which animal is your kindergarten teacher's favorite? Your art teacher? Your physical education teacher?" Of course, they were, and our writing challenge took root.

Continuing to Support Students' Efforts
Gathering Information

We began by talking about the meaning of conducting an interview. Had they ever seen someone being interviewed? (Yes, on television was the most common answer. Young children knew that reporters interview important people to find out what they are doing or thinking or feeling.) We added that people who work for newspapers and magazines also do a lot of interviewing, as do authors who need to learn about a topic for a book they are writing. Teachers can also read aloud Micha Archer's (2019) picture book *Daniel's Good Day* in which the main character asks everyone he meets what makes for a good day or *Taking a Bath with the Dog and Other Things That Make Me Happy* by Scott Menchin (2007), in which the main character asks everyone she meets, "What makes you happy?" Then too, in Junot Diaz's beautiful picture book, *Islandborn* (2018), the main character asks people in her family and neighborhood what they like most about the Dominican Republic.

Asking students to choose a grown-up they would like to interview came next and turned out to be rather easy. Children readily chose their kindergarten teacher, a sibling's classroom teacher, a school specialist (music, art, physical education, librarian, computer, etc.), an administrator (principal, assistant principal), or other school personnel (nurse, security guard, or aide).

We then reread aloud Lucy Cousin's response in "What's Your Favorite Animal?" (Carle 2014a). We shared her choice of the leopard as her favorite animal and her explanation of why she loved leopards. Following that, we posed the question to first graders, "What questions would you ask to find out a person's favorite animal and why that person likes that animal?"

In addition, we anticipated that many adults, when asked about their favorite animal, would name their own pets. Not wanting to have children writing exclusively about cats and dogs, we added to the first question "that is not your pet?"

Their responses resulted in the interview sheet printed below:

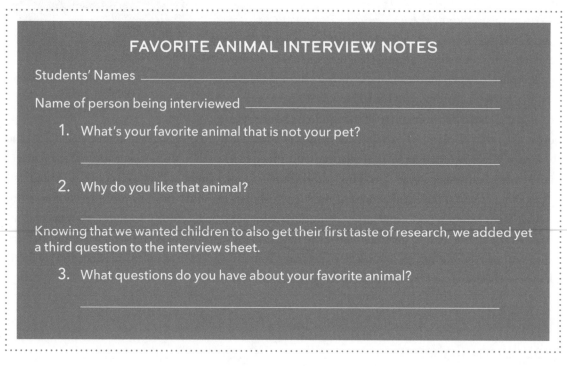

FAVORITE ANIMAL INTERVIEW NOTES

Students' Names _____

Name of person being interviewed _____

1. What's your favorite animal that is not your pet?

    _____

2. Why do you like that animal?

    _____

Knowing that we wanted children to also get their first taste of research, we added yet a third question to the interview sheet.

3. What questions do you have about your favorite animal?

    _____

Sharing Your Own Writing

Before asking students to conduct interviews with staff members, I shared how I used the interview sheet to find out about my husband's favorite animal. I told the children that I had to remind my husband not to answer "Cats," because we had cats as pets for many years. He finally decided on monkeys, and I turned his answers into the following paragraph. He told me why he likes monkeys, and I had to research to answer his question about them. Then, I put all the ideas together and wrote the following two paragraphs.

NEIL'S FAVORITE ANIMAL

Neil's favorite animals are monkeys. He chose these animals because he enjoys watching them at the zoo and even more when he saw them in the wild when he visited Costa Rica. He also loves monkeys because when his grandchildren were young, they loved listening to him read books about the monkey named Curious George and all those monkeys in *Caps for Sale*. Neil would like to know how many kinds of monkeys there are in the world today. He hopes that he gets a chance to see all those different monkeys when he travels around the globe.

I tried to answer Neil's question, and I discovered there are around 260 different kinds of monkeys. Some belong to a group called New World monkeys. They include marmosets, howler monkeys, and spider monkeys. The others belong to a group called Old World monkeys. These include baboons, mandrills, and macaques. Neil was surprised to hear that chimpanzees, gorillas, and orangutans are not part of these monkey groups. They belong to the ape family, not the monkey family. Are you surprised to hear that?

We pointed out to students how I answered the interview questions in the first paragraph. Readers found out Neil's favorite animal and why he likes them. In the second paragraph, I answered Neil's question about how many kinds of monkeys there are in the world.

After sharing my own writing, we asked a classroom teacher to volunteer for an interview to demonstrate how a good interview might proceed. With clipboard and interview sheet attached, two young children stood in front of the classroom, asking the three questions of the teacher, recording their answers as best they could.

Throughout the next week, children were sent in pairs at prearranged appointment times to interview the adults they had requested. The plan was for every child to write up his or her own interview, but children had partners as backup when they conducted an interview. This allowed students to help one another remember and record answers to the questions they asked.

A word of advice is in order. We realized that we should have given the adults chosen for interviews more background information on the challenge. They didn't realize that the first graders were going to attempt to answer their lingering questions. Some asked very complex questions that no six-year-old could research (Do monkeys show emotions? How come dolphins can see so well under water? What weather do elephants prefer?). We should have told the adults being interviewed to limit their questions to ones that first graders could successfully research. "Who are the zebras' predators?" would be more preferable to ask a six-year-old than, "Why do zebras have stripes?"

(See page 45 for suggestions for older students conducting interviews.)

For young students to answer their interviewee's research questions, we needed to fill the classroom shelves with easy-to-read animal books. (See online Book List 2 for a bibliography of some of the most useful books and series.) When questions were simple and appropriate, children were able to use the index or table of contents to locate the answers they needed. These included names of predators, eating habits, as well as parts of the world where this animal could be found.

Children who could not find answers to the questions posed often offered their own charming, best guesses. For example, when unable to find the answer to the question, "Can monkeys tell jokes?" a first grader wrote, "My best guess is no. Also, I think monkeys can be funny because they scratch their armpits." Another was asked, "How do pandas smell?" The student answered, "My best guess is that pandas smell bad because they live in the wild and they touch smelly things. And maybe they smell like bamboo." Another was asked, "What do tigers think about?" The student wrote, "Our guess is . . . 'What are these people doing here?'"

Students who were not interested in guessing often decided to share additional information about the animal that they found interesting. Most included what is often referred to as fun facts.

Lifting the Quality of Student Writing

In the days ahead, at the beginning of every writing workshop, we asked interview partners to share the results of their interviews. We worked collaboratively in the meeting area to turn those notes into meaningful passages. Our goals for these very young researchers were rather basic and included turning notes into full sentences, creating introductory or topic sentences, and moving from one piece of information to the next.

I led the children with a series of very basic and simple questions and recorded their ideas on chart paper. Ravens became the subject of our first modeled writing.

1. What is the first thing we should record? How do we introduce our readers to our topic?

2. Did they tell you why they like ravens? If they gave more than one reason, how would you include that?

3. What else would they like to know about ravens?

Our first chart read:

> Ms. F's favorite animal is the raven.
>
> She likes them because they are smart.
>
> She also likes ravens because they are black, and black is her favorite color.
>
> She wants to know if ravens have feelings.

Finding out if ravens have feelings is one of those questions that would prove to be too difficult for first graders. We talked about how to admit that you couldn't find the answer to interviewee's request, but you could teach your reader other interesting things about these favorite animals. We discussed how the word *but* helps you introduce a new idea as in the sentence below.

I couldn't find out if ravens have feelings, but I did learn other interesting things.

At a follow-up gathering, we talked about other ways to begin interview reports.

Instead of simply saying, "Ms. F's favorite animal is the raven," we brainstormed other possibilities including:

1. Would you like to know what Ms. F's favorite animal is?

2. We interviewed Ms. F to find out about her favorite animal.

3. Guess what? Ms. F's favorite animal is the raven.

These sentences were available to first graders as a reference when they worked on their own writing.

We talked about other ways to add on additional reasons. First graders learned that an alternative to using the word *also* was to use the words *one reason* or *another reason* . . .

Note that if our students had been older (second grade and higher), we would have taught them to ask more follow-up questions. For example, if someone says they like ravens because they are smart, the young interviewer might ask, "How do you know they are smart?"

Student Writing Samples

Ethan, a student in Corinne and Crystal's class, demonstrates in the interview report that follows that he has learned two different ways to add on additional information. First, he uses the words *one reason*, *another reason*, *a third reason* . . . Following that group of sentences, he adds on with the word *also*. He also learned to separate totally new information by beginning a new paragraph. After answering Ms. G's questions, he also chose to include extraneous information that he found interesting, beginning with the word *finally*. The clarity of Ethan's organization will serve him well as he continues to write throughout the grades.

Ethan's writing is memorable because he adds an element of surprise when he uses direct address, talking directly to the giraffes ("Giraffes, you better watch out for lions! You should also remember to kick your predators away, especially leopards and hyenas").

> Ms. G's favorite animals are giraffes. One of the reasons she likes them is because they have long necks. Another reason is they have beautiful patterns. A third reason is they have 18-inch tongues. Ms. G wants to know what giraffes eat. She also wants to know if they have predators.
>
> I was able to find the answers to Ms. G's questions. Giraffes like to eat hay and leaves. I also learned who their predators are. Giraffes, you better watch out for lions! You should also remember to kick your predators away, especially leopards and hyenas. Finally, I learned that giraffes live in the wild in Africa and they can be 18 feet tall.

In Lilah's interview included in the opening of this chapter, she presented her reasons clearly although, as noted earlier, if the interviewer had been an older student, we would have encouraged her to ask follow-up questions, weaving the additional information into her writing (such as "Why do you say tigers are interesting?" or "Can you say more about tigers being smart?"). Lilah's second paragraph is memorable because it is so filled with very specific bits of information. She also surprises the reader by including an opinion in the last sentence.

Carving Out Time for Celebration

The one- to two-page finished products made it easy to combine student work into a bound anthology to be copied and distributed to all students. Some teachers decorated each contribution with a photograph of the student and the person they interviewed. Others invited children to prepare watercolor illustrations of chosen animals. Some combined both a photograph and an illustration. I certainly appreciated being acknowledged in the dedication to one of these collections, which read, "A thousand grateful roars to Shelley for this fun animal interview project."

In addition to preparing bound books, perhaps my favorite method of celebration was a very public display of each child's work on an easy-to-read bulletin board. Passersby, young and old alike, couldn't resist finding out one another's choices for favorite animals.

BOOKS NOTED

For Inspiration and Format

Carle, Eric (and Friends). 2014a. *What's Your Favorite Animal?* New York: Henry Holt and Company.

_____. 2014b. *What's Your Favorite Color?* New York: Henry Holt and Company.

_____. 2018. *What's Your Favorite Bug?* New York: Henry Holt and Company.

Carle, Eric. 2002. *Brown, Bear, Brown Bear, What Do You See?* New York: Penguin.

Books with Main Characters Who Conduct Interviews

Archer, Micha. 2019. *Daniel's Good Day.* New York: Nancy Paulsen Books/Penguin Random House LLC.

Diaz, Junot. 2018. *Islandborn.* New York: Dial.

Menchin, Scott. 2007. *Taking a Bath with the Dog and Other Things That Make Me Happy.* Cambridge, MA: Candlewick Press.

Additional Picture Books Noted

Rey, H. A., and Margret Rey. 1973. *Curious George.* Boston, MA: Houghton, Mifflin, Harcourt.

Slobodinka, Esphyr. 1987. *Caps for Sale: A Tale of a Peddler, Some Monkeys and Their Monkey Business.* New York: HarperCollins.

A FEW TITLES TO ENRICH YOUR TEACHING

Barton, Bethany. 2015. *I'm Trying to Love Spiders.* New York: Viking.

_____. 2017. *Give Bees a Chance.* New York: Viking.

Buhrman-Deever, Susannah. 2020. *If You Take Away the Otter.* Somerville, MA: Candlewick.

Clarke, Ginjer. 2020. *The Fascinating Animal Book for Kids: 500 Wild Facts!* Berkeley, CA: Rockridge Press.

Davies, Nicola. 2015. *I Don't Like Snakes.* Somerville, MA: Candlewick Press.

Goebel, Jenny. 2020. *Adelita: A Sea Turtle's Journey.* Parkridge, IL: Albert Whitman & Co.

Jenkins, Martin. 2019. *Beware of the Crocodile.* Somerville, MA: Candlewick.

Jenkins, Steve. 2019. *The Frog Book.* Boston: HMH Books for Young Readers.

London, Jonathan. 2016. *Otters Like to Play*. Somerville, MA: Candlewick.

_____. 2015. *Hippos are Huge!* Somerville, MA: Candlewick.

Markle, Sandra. 2018. *What If You Had an Animal Tail?* New York: Scholastic Paperbacks.

Marotta, Millie. 2019. *A Wild Child's Guide to Endangered Animals*. San Francisco, CA: Chronicle Books.

Porter, Jane. 2020. *So You Want to Be An Owl*. Somerville, MA: Candlewick.

Saxby, Claire. 2017. *Koala*. Somerville, MA: Candlewick.

Suen, Anastsia. 2020. *Arctic Foxes*. Minneapolis, MN: Amicus Ink.

See the bibliography of animal resources in online Book Lists 2 and 4.

CHAPTER 4
Learning from One Writer
(Grades 1-2)

Maya, a second grader, interviewed her mom and created Professor Patty using Monica Wellington picture books as models. She includes many of the distinctive features of the author's picture books including a last page with a related, yet surprising topic and genre. See Figure 4.1.

Professor Patty
by: Maya Lily Litt-White

① Professor Patty teaches college students at a vivacious university. She strides onto the bright, beautiful, busy campus and sees students studying, playing, and chatting. Her students and other professors greet her with a wave and a smile. She finds her class room, Room 3073, and gazes at a full room of students ready to learn.

② Professor Patty begins discussing the topic of the day. She makes it interesting by explaining how the students can use it in their own lives. She uses tools like a computer, a whiteboard, and a large screen to conduct a long lesson. She is as exited and energetic as a bunny hopping through the forest.

③ Professor Patty breaks her students into groups to let them discuss a problem. She allows them 15 minutes to accomplish a task. After, each group proudly presents their ideas on how to solve the problem. Then the whole class chats about their ideas and reaches a conclusion. Professor Patty ends class and strolls to her office.

④ Professor Patty sits in her bright, warm, cozy office. She meets with students who need extra help understanding the lesson after class. She answers all of their questions and feels fantastic as a flamingo to help her students.

⑤ Next, Proffessor Patty works hard on a research project. She looks at all of her data, analyzes it, and writes about what she discovers. She hopes she can help the world understand her work and its meaning.

⑥ Professor Patty realizes she has an important committee meeting. She gathers together with other professors to discuss how to make the university a better place for their students. They are all given assignments to complete before they meet again next week.

⑦ Finally, Professor Patty packs up to go home. Her heart is as jumpy as a kangaroo because she taught so many lovely, valuable, helpful lessons today. She skips out with a big, bright, beautiful smile on her face knowing she makes her university and the world a happier place every day.

Now You be the Professor !!

① Pick a topic that interests you. Research the topic and create a presentation on what you find.

② Ask family and friends to be your students.

③ Perform your presentation and add activities to make it fun for your students. For example, ask them to solve a problem, play a game, or draw a picture that relates to your lesson.

④ Have fun with it! It is your class!

Figure 4.1

Exploring the Roots of the Writing Challenge

It's always thrilling to suggest an author that teachers might never have thought to study with their early childhood students. In the early grades, teachers frequently line their shelves with stacks of books by Eric Carle, Lucy Cousins, Donald Crews, Kevin Henkes, Angela Johnson, Ezra Jack Keats, and Rosemary Wells. I suggest they also become familiar with picture books written by Rita Gray, Martin Jenkins, Juana Medina,

Mary Murphy, Matt de la Peña, Kenard Park, Seth Fishman, Aram Kim, Monique Gray Smith, Richard Torrey, Sam Usher, Etta Kaner, and Monica Wellington. When choosing authors for our youngest writers to study closely, I search for authors whose beautifully written picture books are filled with memorable stories, important information, and insightful ideas. I also look for authors whose writing is very distinctive and whose tone and techniques cut across many of their titles. These are the kind of books that move young writers to say, "I know what that author is doing. I could do that! I want to try and do that." In other words, students have the urge to apprentice themselves to these published authors.

Monica Wellington's work proves to be a particularly powerful teaching tool in the early grades as many of her titles explore the lives of community workers, a social studies topic often discussed at these grade levels. Her books, including *Firefighter Frank* (2002), *Truck Driver Tom* (2007), and *Apple Farmer Annie* (2001) contain many distinctive features that young readers and writers can easily identify and emulate. Although I selected Monica Wellington for this study, there are many authors whose work is marked by distinctive features and can be emulated by first and second graders. (See bibliography in online Book List 5.)

Engaging Students in the Challenge

After reading aloud a stack of Monica Wellington books and sharing responses to them, I asked students what they noticed about all her picture books that present people with different jobs. It didn't take too long for young listeners to name some of the distinctive features in her books.

Students seemed especially interested in her style of illustrating, naming "bright colors, with some photographs mixed in with her drawings and pretty borders around big shapes filled with her words." They also pointed out that she adds something extra on the last few pages like recipes or how-to instructions. Young students paid attention to her catchy alliterative titles. In fact, they loved inventing their own. Monica Wellington's distinctive features are summarized here:

This first grader chose circle-shaped paper to craft his Monica Wellington–style book.

1. The works have alliterative titles. (The words in her titles often have the same beginning sounds.)

2. They use present tense. (Wellington follows the workers throughout their workday.)

3. Extra information is presented in a different genre on the last pages. (These include related recipes, tips, how-to instructions, labeled drawings, etc.)

4. Illustrations are mixed media combining photographs with drawings. (Children are given opportunity to clip magazine photographs and drawings.)

5. Decorative borders surround the words with words contained in circles, squares, ovals, or rectangles.

Continuing to Support Students' Efforts
Sharing Your Own Writing

I encourage teachers to begin by sharing their own Monica Wellington–style book. My simple book about Teacher Terri appears in Figure 4.2.

Figure 4.2

When I first show this book to students, I ask why they think I chose to write about the life of a teacher. They readily understand that I could write about a teacher's life because I have been a teacher. "You haven't had jobs yet, so how will you choose a job that you know a lot about?" Many students choose the occupation of a member of their family. If they don't, we talk about ways to research the chosen worker's life. Students come to understand that they can learn about jobs from other people, from books and videos, from field trips in the neighborhood.

Then we take a closer look at the Wellington-like book I prepared. We begin by simply looking at the cover of my homemade book. Students are quick to point out the alliterative title and the use of the photographed map and book covers in the cover illustration. I then share the easily understood dedication and the six pages that explore the typical day of a first-grade teacher. I comment that after studying the author's books, I decided to do what Monica Wellington does and begin with the start of the teacher's day and close with the end of her day. I point out that I used the power of three to create each page, a technique that first graders learn enthusiastically and easily. I also point out that I wrote the words in the present tense as if the worker is doing her job today, and I placed the words inside a rectangle on every page with the illustrations surrounding the shape.

Students are eager to see what kind of "surprise" writing I included on the last page, as Wellington never fails to delight. When I tell them that the last page contains a list titled "Teacher Terri's Favorite Books for First Graders," they are eager to predict which titles I included and cheer with recognition when I read them aloud.

Students are then encouraged to choose a worker and come up with an alliterative title. We asked the six-year-olds to think about jobs they know a lot about or jobs they would love to learn about. Children often chose the occupation of someone in their family. These included Architect Aaron, Druggist Dan, Librarian Louise, Mail Carrier Maria, and Zookeeper Zoe.

Gathering Information

We then talk about how they will get the information they need to help readers understand the life of that worker. We talk about using what they already know, reading related books, talking to family members, observing workers, and, if possible, interviewing those workers. We brainstorm questions they might ask the worker. These include:

How do you spend your day?

What do you do at work?

What tasks are the hardest?

Which tasks take the longest time to do?

Which tasks are the easiest to do?

Which tasks go quickly?

Who helps you at work?

It helps to invite a parent or two to come to class and sit for a public interview, demonstrating how to ask questions with follow-up questions and how to jot down important pieces of information. Whenever possible, teachers arrange to have classes go on field trips to see the work of the local librarian, the firefighter, the pharmacist, or the police officer. Children are encouraged to jot down notes as soon as they return to class and to share their observations and memories with the student who has chosen that occupation.

It is also helpful to have the class work on a book together. In Paola Jeon and Elisa Rios's first-grade class at P.S. 87, we began by creating a class book about Nurse Natalia. We chose a school nurse, as most first graders are familiar with their school nurse and the various tasks she performs.

Paola prepared several large sheets of paper, each one having a big circle right in the middle of the page. In each circle, she recorded the sentences that students created orally to describe a day in the life of a school nurse. Their collaborative text follows.

> ## NURSE NATALIA
>
> First thing in the morning, Nurse Natalia checks her thermometer, ice packs, and band-aids. (page 1)
>
> At 11 o'clock, a girl scrapes her knee on the metal in the playground. Nurse Natalia cleans the scrape, puts on a band-aid, and a friend takes the girl back to class. (page 2)
>
> At one o'clock, a boy with a headache goes to see Nurse Natalia. He has chills, feels warm, and feels tired. Nurse Natalia takes his temperature and calls his parents to take him home. (page 3)
>
> When the students all leave school, Nurse Natalia goes home tired but happy because she took care of tons of kids. (page 4)

Throughout the oral composing, we stressed the need to be specific, to be accurate, and to use the power of three if it made sense and sounded right. We also demonstrated that four pages would be enough, an amount we thought most first graders could produce. Second graders, like Maya, whose writing about Professor Patty appears in the opening of this chapter, were able to produce a lengthier and more sophisticated text, drafting and revising as she composed.

Lifting the Quality of Student Writing

Once students think they have enough information about their chosen jobs, they are offered a variety of preprepared blank books in which to record their ideas. These teacher-made books make it easy for students to use Wellington's design technique of a central shape containing the words, leaving space for illustrations surrounding the oval, circle, square, or rectangle. Each shape is filled with teacher-made lines to guide the formation of words. Students, of course, have their choice of papers.

Helpful minilessons for this challenge follow:

- We ask students to create an alliterative title. Some children might need help finding a name that matched the beginning sound of their chosen worker. Classmates are eager to offer suggestions.

- To begin, we brainstorm how to present the start of the workday, reminding students that they need not have their worker wake up, eat breakfast, or get dressed. Instead, they are encouraged to do as Monica Wellington does and begin by telling how the worker gets started at work. We talk about such phrases as "First thing at work," "At the start of her workday," "Early in the morning," "When Nurse Natalia gets to work."

- We remind students that writers write with information, the more specific the better. We make sure they understand the difference between general information and specific information. Sometimes we warm up their crafting minds by relying on point/counterpoint examples. We ask such questions as:

» Which is easier for you to picture in your mind's eye: "My new bathing suit is colorful," or "My new bathing suit is covered with blue dolphins, foamy waves, and orange sunsets"?

» Which is easier for you to picture in your mind's eye: "Today, my father packed my lunch," or "Today, my father packed a toasted bagel slathered with peanut butter and strawberry jam and a juicy clementine"?

» Which is easier for you to picture in your mind's eye: "My grandmother got a new dog," or "My grandmother got a tiny white teacup poodle"?

- We share the metaphor of being hungry when we read, hungry for information. I frequently ask young students to reread their work, asking themselves if their readers will be starving for information or feeling satisfied with the amount of information offered.

- We suggest writers check the sequence of their ideas. Which pages should go first, second, and so on?

- We suggest ways for writers to move from one part of their worker's day to the next. Such words and phrases as, *Then*, *After*, *A little while later*, *Following that* come in handy.

- We chat about the need to create an ending that sounds like an ending. We point out that Wellington's endings usually involve the close of the workday for the main character. My *Teacher Terri* book ends with the teacher going home feeling tired, proud, and lucky to work with young children.

- We ask students to choose a back-page surprise for their readers. How about a labeled map of the zoo for the zookeeper, a menu of flavors for the ice-cream vendor, a list of safety tips for the police officer, a picture dictionary of flowers for the florist, suggestions for having healthy teeth for the dentist, and recycling reminders for the sanitation worker?

- We discuss and model how to prepare illustrations in the style of Monica Wellington. We remind students that their illustrations should surround the words on each page. In addition to students preparing appropriate drawings, students are encouraged to clip appropriate magazine photos to create collage illustrations that resemble Wellington's technique. (If possible, collaborating with the art teacher to support students' efforts to learn from Monica Wellington would be a good idea.)

Learning from One Writer with Older Students

The third-grade teachers I know best often select Eileen Spinelli for close study in their writing workshops. Eight-year-olds love her picture books and her style of writing. Her books always lead to rich conversations about topics that matter to children. Later, teachers support students as they study Spinelli's writing tools. Students notice Spinelli's frequent use of refrains, particularly in *When No One Is Watching* (2013), *When*

You Are Happy (2006), *I Know It's Autumn* (2004), *Here Comes the Year* (2002), *In My New Yellow Shirt* (2001), and *Someday* (2007). Third graders enjoy listening to these books read aloud and then borrowing the refrain (structure/pattern) that will best convey their own ideas. (See Writing with Refrains on page 157.) Other popular writers with distinctive styles that can be studied by third graders include Byrd Baylor, Tom Brenner, Monica Brown, Jason Chin, Nicola Davies, Helen Frost, Sandra Markle, Tony Medina, Kadir Nelson, Pat Mora, Janet S. Wong, and Jacqueline Woodson. (See bibliography in online Book List 5 and see student writing inspired by Eileen Spinelli in Appendix 2.)

Student Writing Samples

Julia, a first grader in Corinne Daniels and Julie Giacomantonio's class at Dows Lane Elementary School, wrote *Train Driver Tracy*. In addition to creating an alliterative title, Julia wrote in the present tense as she described a day in the life of Tracy the train driver. Her illustrations were done in the Wellington style of borders, and the six-year-old even attempted mixed media in her illustrations. Her surprise additional writing on the final page presented instructions for drawing a train. See Figure 4.3.

Figure 4.3

The two Monica Wellington–style books in Figures 4.4 and 4.5 were written by young students in Paola Jeon and Elisa Rios's first-grade class at P.S. 87. Unfortunately, the students' work was interrupted when school was canceled during the coronavirus pandemic. They never had an opportunity to complete their days nor add that surprising last page. I wonder if Lila would have added instructions for handwashing to her *Doctor Delia* book, a topic on everyone's mind.

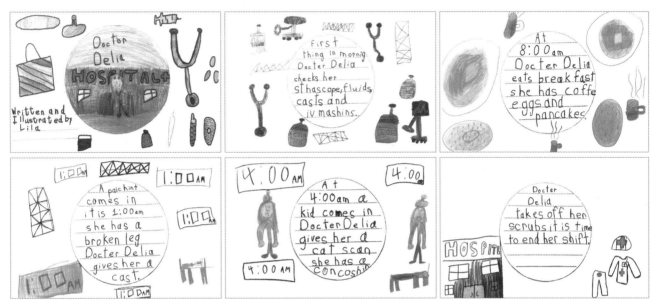

Figure 4.4

Figure 4.5

Carving Out Time for Celebration

Family members love attending these celebrations as they often see their own jobs take center stage. At the celebration, children can introduce and display Monica Wellington's books and explain how they went about learning from this author. Children from other first-grade classrooms can learn a great deal about jobs in the community by attending the celebration.

BOOKS NOTED

Spinelli, Eileen. 2001. *In My New Yellow Shirt.* New York: Henry Holt.

———. 2002. *Here Comes the Year.* New York: Henry Holt.

———. 2004. *I Know It's Autumn.* New York: HarperCollins.

———. 2006. *When You Are Happy.* New York: Simon & Schuster Books for Young Readers.

———. 2007. *Someday.* New York: Dial Books for Young Readers/Penguin Young Readers Group.

———. 2013. *When No One Is Watching.* Grand Rapids, MI: Eerdmans Books for Young Readers.

Wellington, Monica. 2001. *Apple Farmer Annie.* New York: Dutton Children's Books/Penguin Putnam Books for Young Readers.

———. 2002. *Firefighter Frank.* New York: Dutton Children's Books/Penguin Putnam Books for Young Readers.

———. 2007. *Truck Driver Tom.* New York: Dutton Children's Books/Penguin Putnam Books for Young Readers.

A FEW TITLES TO ENRICH YOUR TEACHING

Fishman, Seth. 2019. *Power Up.* New York: Greenwillow.

———. 2020. *A Hundred Billion Trillion Stars.* New York: Greenwillow.

———.2020. *The Ocean in Your Bathtub.* New York: Greenwillow.

Medina, Juana. 2016. *One Big Salad: A Delicious Counting Book.* New York: Viking Books for Young Readers.

———. 2017. *ABC Pasta: An Entertaining Alphabet.* New York: Viking Books for Young Readers.

———. 2018. *Sweet Shapes: A Forest of Tasty Shapes.* New York: Viking Books for Young Readers.

———. 2021. *I Will: A Book of Promises.* Boston: Versify.

Murphy, Mary. 2003. *The Alphabet Keeper.* New York: Knopf.

———. 2004. *I Kissed the Baby!* Somerville MA: Candlewick.

———. 2005. *I Like It When...* Boston, MA: Houghton Mifflin Harcourt.

———. 2020. *Only a Tree Knows It's a Tree.* Somerville, MA: Candlewick.

———. 2020. *What I Like Most.* Somerville, MA: Candlewick.

Park, Kenard. 2016. *Goodbye Summer, Hello Autumn.* New York: Henry Holt.

———. 2017. *Goodbye Autumn, Hello Winter.* New York: Henry Holt.

———. 2020. *Goodbye Winter, Hello Spring.* New York: Henry Holt.

See additional bibliography in online Book List 5.

PART TWO

CAMARADERIE
AMONG WRITERS

. . . .

The writing challenges presented in the pages that follow require young writers to support one another by sharing information discovered as they pore over classroom materials. These challenges demand that students have time to scan, browse, and otherwise flip pages searching for the answers to real questions, all the while aware of their classmates' concerns and areas of interest. There is a definite feel in these writing workshops that "We are all in this together and we can all help one another."

- Chapter 5: Simple Scaffolds, Grades 2–5
- Chapter 6: Curiosity at the Core, Grades 2–5
- Chapter 7: And the Award Goes to . . . , Grades 4–5
- Chapter 8: Could It Really Happen? Grades 3–5

CHAPTER 5
Simple Scaffolds

(Grades 2–5)

An informational alphabet book about the duck's life cycle created by Valentino, a student in Diane Berman's fourth-grade class at P.S. 87, can be seen in Figure 5.1.

D, d is for dabbling. It's also for a drake.

Dabbling is when a duck puts its rear in the air and puts its head underwater. Ducks do this to find food. A funny nickname for the dabbling duck is duck bot. Can you guess what a drake is?

Figure 5.1

Exploring the Roots of the Writing Challenge

Browse the nonfiction section of your local children's library and delight in such informative, yet simply designed books as question-and-answer books, books that boast a list of 100 things you should know about . . . , books that have repeated refrains such as "I didn't know that . . . ," and books that ask the reader to evaluate true-or-false statements.

Other simply designed nonfiction texts include those often found in a toddler's library, namely alphabet and counting books. When I choose to share these with students, I look for ones that have rich content information, hoping that even as an adult reader, I will learn something new. I know my teenage grandson Will, a serious musician and Metallica fan, was happy to receive *The ABC's of Metallica* (Abrams and Metallica 2019), an alphabet book in rhyme written by the band in collaboration with Howie Abrams. The authors explore the history of this classic band. So, too, alphabet books for young children can be filled with surprising content and fresh ways of looking at the world. Students might think that they belong in the kindergarten and are intended to merely teach the alphabet. Not true, of course. There are alphabet books on a wide range of topics, and they often include such extra sources of information as maps, glossaries, and author notes. Some are written in rhyming poetry, others in extended prose passages. Both might have content-rich sidebars. The same holds true for counting books. In Jerry Pallotta's (2017) *The Very Berry Counting Book*, I had to ask myself, "What are salmonberries? Have I ever seen or tasted them?" I knew that many young children would be surprised to learn about mulberries and elderberries. If children were to write a counting book, I ask myself, could they present information that would be new to their classmates? Could they add illustrations that could clarify and enrich that information?

Engaging Students in the Challenge

I am always amazed at how delighted students in grades 2–5 seem when you show them books from their earlier years. They are surprised to hear that they will have an opportunity to create their own alphabet or counting books. To keep the enthusiasm high, we fill the classroom with a large assortment of these simply designed books, ones that are rich in content and have more than a one-word label or short phrase on each page. I add nonfiction question-and-answer books and true-or-false books to the mix. (See bibliography in online Book List 6.) We borrow books from the school and public library and tap the resources of colleagues throughout the grades. We then set aside abundant browsing time. After students have looked over all the books gathered, we then ask them to share their discoveries with one another.

Some students prefer finding a very quiet place to write.

Students frequently comment that alphabet books require twenty-six different ideas and that some pages will be more difficult to prepare than others. The biggest challenge is reserved for the high-value letters on the Scrabble board—Q, X, and Z. It's worth spending time discussing how authors go about solving these problems. That discussion can begin with inviting students to pore over the stacks of content-rich alphabet books, searching for clever ways the authors has handled a difficult letter. Teachers can add any newspaper or magazine articles created with the alphabet structure. Students will probably discover that some authors solve the X problem by highlighting the X in the middle of the word like *Texas* or choosing words that end with an X. Others resort to the familiar phrase "X marks the spot" or use words that begin with the letters *ex*, as that certainly sounds like the name of X.

Students are likewise surprised that content-rich counting books are more complicated than they originally thought. They learn that these books require more than just increasing the number of items in an illustration. They realize they must choose content that matches the numbers in a significant way. For example, Jim Haskins and Kathleen Benson (2007), the authors of *Count Your Way Through Zimbabwe*, show that they are authorities on this country when they include four for the number of countries that border Zimbabwe and seven for the number of stripes on the flag of Zimbabwe. That's very different than simply drawing three mud and straw homes to illustrate number three.

Similarly, students realize that creating true-or-false statements about a topic offers its own challenge. They learn how clever they must be to come up with a false statement that might be considered true by their readers. When writing question-and-answer books, students' main concern is how to how to select a topic that is not too broad, how to place the questions in a sensible order, and how to ask the kind of question that cannot be answered with a simple yes or no or a one-word answer.

When all four formats have been reviewed, it is time to connect these formats to the classroom study at hand. Sometimes, teachers ask for topics connected to a social studies unit (like communities around the globe) or a science course of study (like birds in the neighborhood). In other rooms, students are invited to choose their own independent area of interest. In addition to alphabet and counting books, students are invited to choose the question-and-answer format or the true-or-false design.

Continuing to Support Students' Efforts
Sharing Your Own Writing

Becoming a full-fledged member of the writing workshop involves lots of decision making, and our instructional know-how improves when we can anticipate the process that lies ahead for our students. I decided to write about New York City because of my love for my hometown, and I decided to create a counting book. I let the students in on my decision, explaining that I eliminated a question-and-answer book because the questions that could be posed about New York City seemed infinite. I wasn't sure that I could narrow my focus. I eliminated creating an alphabet book because I had already seen several high-quality ones published about the Big Apple. I didn't attempt a true-or-false book as I struggled to think of telling an untruth about my city. A counting book seemed manageable and enticing, and the few that I have seen were intended for toddlers.

Planning on the usual 1–10 counting book, I claimed third graders as my audience and shared my planning and process with them. Some ideas came to mind instantly including: one Statue of Liberty, three bridges on the East River, five boroughs that make up our city. With each choice, I thought about whether the topic would be satisfying to write about. I also thought about the balance of the ten items. Would they refer to the whole city, not just Manhattan? Would they include man-made and natural items? Would they be of equal importance? Some of the remaining numbers required additional research. I spoke to family and friends, looked at guidebooks, and checked New York City tourist sites on the Internet. I also had to think about whether I would write an introduction and a conclusion, as some counting books contain. Following is the finished work I shared with students.

COUNTING ON NEW YORK CITY

It is very difficult to write a counting book about New York City, especially if you are only counting from 1 to 10. New York City is just too big a city, with too many people, too many passions and too many sights to see. Our skyscrapers have too many stories, our streets are filled with too many coffee shops, too many pharmacies and too many banks. No matter your interest, you can probably count to way over 10. How many museums do we have? How many Chinese restaurants? How many subway lines? I have had to rack my brain to find things that are limited to 10 and under. The following pages, made with love and labor, demonstrate how I have learned to count on my hometown, New York City.

One is for the Statue of Liberty. This gift from France has become a symbol of freedom and democracy. This huge copper statue that sits in the New York Harbor on Liberty Island was designed by the French sculptor Bartholdi. The statue is based on the Roman Goddess of Liberty and she holds a torch in her right hand and a tablet in her left. On the tablet is the date, July 4th, 1776 written in Roman numerals. This is the date of the signing of our Declaration of Independence from England. There are 354 steps to Lady Liberty's Crown, the top of the statue. Would you be willing to climb?

Two is for the tunnels that connect Manhattan to other boroughs. So many people who live in the outer boroughs travel to and from Manhattan, the most famous of all the five boroughs. They come for work, for shopping, for entertainment, for restaurants, for Broadway shows, and so much more. The Brooklyn Battery connects Manhattan to Brooklyn, and the Queens Midtown tunnel connects Manhattan to Queens. (There is also the Lincoln Tunnel, but that one brings folks to and from New Jersey to Manhattan).

Three is for the airports people use to travel to and from New York City. Imagine how many visitors from around the world come to New York City every day of the year. Add to that the number of residents of New York City that travel by airplane for work or pleasure. The airports all these people use are La Guardia and JFK in Queens and Newark Airport in New Jersey. It's no wonder these three airports are always busy!

Four is for the kinds of public mass transportation used by New Yorkers. Sure, some people ride bikes, some drive private cars and others walk to their destinations in New York City. But many, many folks choose to use mass transportation. They travel by subway (in all the boroughs except Staten Island, which has its own train system, not a subway), bus (in all five boroughs including express buses that travel directly into Manhattan), ferryboat (to all the boroughs from piers on the East River), as well as the famous Staten Island Ferry. You can also travel by tram (to and from Roosevelt Island).

See my entire counting book pages 1–10 in Appendix 3.

Gathering Information

Research is where the presence of camaraderie can really make a difference. Imagine classroom desks stacked high with nonfiction texts connected to New York City—guidebooks, picture books, magazine articles, and other assorted nonfiction books. Then imagine the teacher's request: "Please browse the books on your table-tops searching for topics that can be used for the NYC 1–10 counting book I am putting together. Let's get together in the meeting area in half an hour to share your discoveries. You can help me make great choices." Imagine the fun students would have learning to do such stress-free browsing, chatting, jotting, and sharing.

Now imagine they are asked to do the same for their own research in progress. All the topics that students are working have been posted publicly in the classroom, and children are surrounded with materials that connect to the broad theme being studied—animals, countries around the world, birds, museums, modes of transportation, and so on. Children browse the texts searching for the information they need, but also aware of the information needed by others. Luke is creating a counting book on train travel. Ethan has chosen an alphabet book on airplanes, and Grace is planning a question-and-answer book about water transportation. Whenever children come across something interesting related to a friend's topic, they are encouraged to share with the researcher in need. What an energetic hum would fill the classroom! How supported all young researchers would feel.

Lifting the Quality of Student Writing

Students throughout the grades benefit from reading and rereading well-written texts. They learn to appreciate the sound of literary language, and they come to value saving and savoring excerpts that move them. Even with the most basic and straightforward formats, teachers and children can note tools from the writer's toolbox, the techniques the writers use to turn okay writing into memorable writing.

A few excerpts follow from alphabet, counting, true-or-false, and question-and-answer picture books. They could effectively be shared during minilessons to encourage students to write well, to attempt to move their audiences even in these seemingly straightforward formats.

In *Amelia to Zora: Twenty-Six Women Who Changed the World*, Cynthia Chin-Lee (2005) uses the power of three to describe the art of architect Maya Lin. She writes, "She made crafts with any material she could find—paper, string, and even scraps of silver." She uses this tool again in describing the accomplishments of Wilma Pearl Mankiller, a chief of the Cherokee nation. She writes, "In her two terms as chief, Wilma strengthened the financial foundation of the nation, supporting medical clinics, daycare centers, and environmental cleanup." Students also notice her use of alliteration in the phrase "financial foundation."

In the question-and-answer books by Joan Holub, the author frequently uses similes to help her readers understand her meaning. For example, in *Why Do Rabbits Hop*? (2003), she compares the weight of a baby rabbit to "ten quarters" and the size of an adult guinea pig to the size and shape of an "adult's sneaker." In *Why Do Snakes Hiss?* (2004), the author suggests that a Komodo dragon can grow to be as heavy as "six second-grade children." Holub's work is also filled with strong, precise verbs often clustered in threes as in *Why Do Rabbits Hop*? She explains how guinea pigs communicate with the words: "They grunt, squeak or whistle when they want food or attention." In *Why Do Snakes Hiss?* she explains the dangers that reptiles face by suggesting, "Some reptiles are in danger because forests, ponds and other habitats are being destroyed, polluted or changed." The use of the power of three make these sentences very memorable, and the precise verbs prove that the author knows her subjects well.

Similarly, Sandra and William Markle (1998) in their book *Gone Forever! An Alphabet of Extinct Animals* also rely on comparisons to help the reader appreciate their meaning. In presenting the Elephant Bird for the letter *E*, they describe the bird as being "much taller than the tallest basketball player," noting that the empty shell from an Elephant Bird "could hold two gallons of milk!"

So, too, Frané Lessac (2017) in *A Is for Australian Animals* introduces the Tasmanian devil for the letter *T*. She explains, "The Tasmanian devil is the size of a small dog, but its jaws are almost as powerful as a leopard's." The clear and concise comparisons help the reader really appreciate the power of this Australian animal. She continues by using a simile as well as rich sensory details when she notes, "Like a skunk, the Tasmanian devil can squirt a smelly liquid from under its tail when it is threatened." She continues to prove she is an authority on Australian animals by including specific sensory information in a long-list sentence. She writes, "In a Tasmanian devil's poop, a wildlife biologist discovered: the head of a tiger snake, an owl's foot, a sock, aluminum foil, half a pencil, and the knee of a pair of jeans." Alphabet books can certainly be filled with startling surprises!

Jerry Pallotta, a very popular and prolific alphabet and counting book author, also depends on specific writing techniques to make his rich content come alive. In *The Underwater Alphabet Book* (1991), he chose the man-of-war to represent the letter *M*. He helps the reader appreciate the look of this type of jellyfish by including such comparisons as, "The top of its body is shaped like a sail on a sailboat" and letting the readers know that its tentacles "can grow as long as a telephone pole."

Brian Stokes Mitchell, the Broadway star, wrote an introduction to Harriet Ziefert's *Lights on Broadway: A Theatrical Tour from A to Z* (2009). Throughout, he enriches his personal commitment to the Great White Way by relying on the power of three. In part he writes, "There were no lights on the trusses, no scenery, and no players in the pit, only a thousand vacant seats facing the blank stage." He goes on to say, "I had reached that moment when all those years of training, practice, and dedication—trying, falling, and trying again—would be put to the ultimate test." He concludes, "So welcome to my house, my home, my Broadway!" Ziefert continues to use this same writer's tool when she provides examples for each letter of the alphabet. "C" stands for costume designer and the author writes, ". . . the person who imagines, designs, and creates the costumes and is responsible for the total look of the show's characters. The designer has to research the setting, time, and place of a play to determine which colors, fabrics, and accessories will authentically and believably transform an actor into a character."

Juana Medina relies on alliteration to add charm, humor, and a musical quality to her surprising circus alphabet book, *ABC Pasta: An Entertaining Alphabet* (2017). It's hard to resist reading aloud such memorable phrases as "rigatoni ringmasters, spaghetti spectators, and tortellini trapeze trio."

Quality writing appears in carefully selected counting books as well. In Jim Haskins and Kathleen Benson's (2007) *Count Your Way Through Zimbabwe*, one is for Victoria Falls, and the authors use a simile to describe the falls. They note, "The mist looks like smoke rising to the sky." In Sandra Markle's *How Many Baby Pandas?* (2009) the author reveals that a newborn baby giant panda is "the size of a hot dog!" In Katie Cotton's beautiful picture book *Counting Lions* (2015) she demonstrates how precise verbs, alliteration, and repetition add a satisfying, musical quality to her information-laden passage. On the page for number three, she writes, "Three giraffes with their heads in the sky pluck leaves from trees and chew, up and down, side to side, for up to twenty hours a day. They are peaceful patterned giants wandering from place to place, sleepless surveyors of the grasslands. Three wanderers. Three giraffes."

Yuyi Morales also offers crafting lessons for young writers in *Just a Minute: A Trickster Tale and Counting Tale* (2016). In addition to illustrating the meaning of a trickster tale, she also shows how the repetition of key phrases helps readers feel at home in the story and enables them to make predictions. With the turn of every page, listeners expect to hear the clever procrastinating grandma say, "Just a Minute Señor Calavero.

I will go with you right way." The author also demonstrates the power of precise and varied verbs. The skeleton-visitor showed his displeasure and impatience with waiting. He "sighed," "rolled his eyes," "frowned," "tapped his fingers," "threw up his hands," "shook his head in disbelief," finally shouting, "Enough!"

Students attempting to write true-or-false books would do well to apprentice themselves to Patricia Lauber, a most accomplished nonfiction writer. In her book *The True-or-False Book of Dogs* (2003), she frequently relies on the power of three to make her sentences meaningful and memorable. She describes the services of a Roman dog called a molossus with the statement, "It was used to guard property, pull carts, and attack enemy troops." She later suggests that "the Chinese were breeding dogs for hunting, guarding, and eating."

The more students hear well-written texts read aloud, the more they feel comfortable talking about how authors craft texts, the more they are encouraged to try out new techniques, the more likely students will internalize these tools and use them effectively when aiming to share information and move their audiences. The simplicity of the format of these challenges enables students to focus on lifting the quality of the writing. We can expect them to work hard and produce memorable work.

Student Writing Samples

In Laura Fine Leibman and Andrea Garvey's third-grade class at P.S. 87, all class members contributed to an anthology entitled *ABC China*. They handled the rare letters well, presenting *Qin Shihunag Di* for the letter *Q* (the first emperor of China), *Xi'an* for the letter *X* (the home of the Terra Cotta warriors), and *zodiac* for the letter *Z*, explaining the twelve animals in the Chinese zodiac. See Betty and Georgia's contribution for the letter *F* in Figure 5.2.

Ann Marie Reardon, teaching third grade at Dows Lane Elementary School, invited her students to choose from a wide range of formats when asked to study a foreign country. Iris created a Swiss alphabet book. She carefully researched information about Switzerland, and her classmates learned a great deal. For the letter *J*, they learned about Jeune Genevois, a holiday celebrated in Geneva in which lots of plum pies are eaten. For the letter *K*, students read about Koniz, an ancient town dating back to the 1100s. And for the letter *L*, Iris chose the word *languages* as Switzerland boasts four official languages—German, Italian, French, and Romansh, a language that students had never heard of.

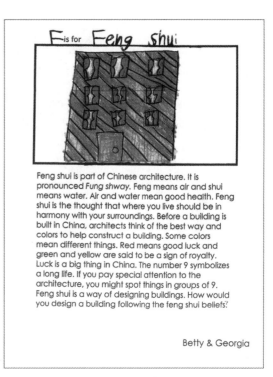

F is for Feng shui

Feng shui is part of Chinese architecture. It is pronounced *Fung shway*. Feng means air and shui means water. Air and water mean good health. Feng shui is the thought that where you live should be in harmony with your surroundings. Before a building is built in China, architects think of the best way and colors to help construct a building. Some colors mean different things. Red means good luck and green and yellow are said to be a sign of royalty. Luck is a big thing in China. The number 9 symbolizes a long life. If you pay special attention to the architecture, you might spot things in groups of 9. Feng shui is a way of designing buildings. How would you design a building following the feng shui beliefs?

Betty & Georgia

Figure 5.2

Ian, a third grader in Ann Marie's class, prepared the *True or False Book of Ireland* that appears next.

TRUE OR FALSE:

The Irish flag is blue, white and orange.

False!

The Irish flag is green, white and orange. The green stands for the native people of Ireland. The orange stands for the British supporters of William of Orange in Northern Ireland in the 17th century. The white stands for the peace of Ireland.

TRUE OR FALSE:

Polar bears were originally from Ireland.

True!

DNA tests on modern polar bears have shown that they were originally from Ireland. Their DNA matches the Irish Brown Bear suggesting that the bears left Ireland. During the last Ice Age, while other bears stayed back in Ireland, the bears that left Ireland became polar bears.

TRUE OR FALSE:

The national drink of Ireland is Guinness.

False!

Although Guinness is probably the most recognizable, the national drink is actually whiskey. The Irish have been making whiskey since 1000 A.D. so they made it a national drink.

TRUE OR FALSE:

If you go to the Blarney Stone, you lay on your belly and kiss it.

False!

You lay on your back and kiss it. Then it gives you the gift of the gab which is good luck!

TRUE OR FALSE:

St. Patrick was Irish, and parties are held every year on March 17th to celebrate him.

False!

St. Patrick got captured by pirates at the age of 16 and brought to Ireland where he was enslaved. He was born somewhere in Britain in the late 4th century.

TRUE OR FALSE:

Carrots are the most popular vegetable in Ireland.

False!

Potatoes are probably the most popular vegetable in Ireland. People say that Sir Walter Raleigh, the English explorer who lived from 1552-1618, was the first to bring the potato to Ireland. He discovered it on his travels to South America.

TRUE OR FALSE:

The Titanic was built in Ireland.

True!

The Titanic was built at Harland and Wolff shipyards in Belfast, Northern Ireland, between 1919 and 1912. At that time, Belfast was still a part of Ireland, but now it is not.

TRUE OR FALSE:

Leprechauns are Irish myths that have delighted children for years.

True!

The legend of the leprechauns dates to medieval times. They are considered in the fairy tale class, but in Ireland they are part of Irish folklore.

TRUE OR FALSE:

Ireland got its nickname, the "Emerald Isle", because there were once a lot of emeralds in Ireland.

False!

It got its nickname, the" Emerald Isle," from how green Ireland is. Actually, Ireland does not have that many emeralds in it.

And Elena, another of Ann Marie's third-graders, prepared a counting book.

COUNT TO TEN IN AUSTRALIA

There is only 1 Sydney Opera House.

Koalas eat 2 pounds of eucalyptus a day.

Australians celebrate 3 days of Easter.

There are 4 months of winter in Australia, June through September.

There are 5 famous cities in Australia: Melbourne, Sydney, Perth, Canberra and Alice Springs.

Australia has 6 states: Western Australia, New South Wales, South Australia, Queensland, Tasmania, and Victoria.

There are 7 continents and Australia is the smallest one and is the only continent that is also a country.

There are 8 famous foods including pavlova, shrimp on the barbie, roast lamb, meat pie, Vegemite, barbecued sausage, lamington, and Anzac biscuits. (tim tam, fairy bread)

There are 9 public holidays in Australia including New Year's Day, Australia Day, Good Friday, Easter Saturday, Easter Sunday, Easter Monday, Anzac Day, Christmas Day, and Boxing Day.

There are 10 deserts in Australia including Great Victoria, Great Sandy, Tanami, Simpson, Gibson, Little Sandy, Strzzeleki, Sturt, Tiran, and Perdika.

Carving Out Time for Celebration

Completed work often took the form of a picture book, as most children studied this genre for inspiration and information. Of course, the content could be presented as an article and gathered into a class anthology. Magazine articles are frequently presented in a question-and-answer format. Then too, the alphabet can be found as a structure for brief writing in magazines. Counting books are more likely presented in the picture book genre but can certainly be turned into short magazine articles. No matter the format, these completed works become worthy of celebration. Perhaps adding them to the class library in the nonfiction section would be the highest compliment.

BOOKS NOTED

Abrams, Howie, and Metallica. 2019. *The ABCs of Metallica.* Brentwood, TN: Permuted.

Chin-Lee, Cynthia. 2005. *Amelia to Zora: Twenty-Six Women Who Changed the World.* Watertown, MA: Charlesbridge.

Cotton, Katie. 2015. *Counting Lions: Portraits from the Wild.* Somervile, MA: Candlewick.

Haskins, Jim, and Kathleen Benson. 2007. *Count Your Way Through Zimbabwe.* Minneapolis, MN: Millbrook.

Holub, Joan. 2003. *Why Do Rabbits Hop? And Other Questions About Rabbits, Guinea Pigs, Hamsters and Gerbils*. New York: Penguin Young Readers.

———. 2004. *Why Do Snakes Hiss? And Other Questions About Snakes, Lizards and Turtles*. New York: Penguin Young Readers.

Lauber, Patricia. 2003. *The True-or-False Book of Dogs*. New York: HarperCollins.

Lessac, Frané. 2017. *A Is for Australian Animals*. Somerville, MA: Candlewick.

Markle, Sandra, and William Markle. 1998. *Gone Forever! An Alphabet of Extinct Animals*. New York: Atheneum Books for Young Readers/Simon & Schuster Children's Publishing.

Markle, Sandra. 2009. *How Many Baby Pandas?* New York: Walker.

Medina, Juana. 2017. *ABC Pasta: An Entertaining Alphabet*. New York: Viking.

Morales, Yuyi. 2016. *Just a Minute: A Trickster Tale and Counting Tale*. San Francisco: Chronicle Books.

Pallotta, Jerry. 1991. *Underwater Alphabet Book*. Watertown, MA: Charlesbridge.

———. 2017. *The Very Berry Counting Book*. Watertown, MA: Charlesbridge.

Ziefert, Harriet, and Brian Stokes Mitchell. 2009. *Lights on Broadway: A Theatrical Tour from A to Z*. Maplewood, NJ: Blue Apple Books.

A FEW MORE TITLES TO ENRICH YOUR TEACHING

Alphabet Books

Allman, John Robert. 2020. *B Is for Ballet: A Dance Alphabet*. New York: Doubleday.

Chen, Eva. 2019. *A Is for Awesome: 23 Iconic Women Who Changed the World*. New York: Feiwel & Friends.

Cortez, Rio. 2020. *The ABCs of Black History*. New York: Workman Publishing.

Fadipe, Sade. 2019. *A Visit to Grandad: An African ABC*. Abuja, Nigeria: Cassava Republic Press.

LaBarge, Melanie. 2020. *Women Artists A to Z*. New York: Dial Books for Young Readers.

Latham, Irene, and Charles Waters. 2020. *Dictionary for a Better World: Poems, Quotes, and Anecdotes from A to Z*. Minneapolis, MN: Carolrhoda Books.

Littlejohn, James. 2019. *G Is for Golazo: The Ultimate Soccer Alphabet*. Chicago: Triumph Books.

Rose, Tiffany. 2019. *M Is for Melanin: A Celebration of the Black Child*. New York: little bee books.

Thompson, Craig. 2015. *ABC's of Black Inventors: A Children's Guide*. Silver Spring, MD: Beckham Publishers.

Ziefert, Harriet, and Brian Stokes Mitchell. 2009. *Lights on Broadway: A Theatrical Tour from A to Z*. Maplewood, NJ: Blue Apple Books.

Counting Books

Chen, Eva. 2020. *3 2 1 Awesome: 20 Fearless Women Who Dared to Be Different*. New York: Feiwel & Friends.

Kurman, Hollis 2020. *Counting Kindness: Ten Ways to Welcome Refugee Children*. Watertown, MA: Charlesbridge.

Medina, Juana. 2016. *1 Big Salad: A Delicious Counting Book*. New York: Viking.

Nagara, Innocento. 2015. *Counting on Community*. New York: Triangle Square.

Thong, Roseanne. 2014. *One Is a Drummer: A Book of Numbers*. North Mankato, MN: Amicus.

See additional resources in online Book List 6.

CHAPTER 6
Curiosity at the Core
(Grades 2-5)

Sasha sent a series of questions in a letter to Josh Abraham, a television story producer. See Figure 6.1.

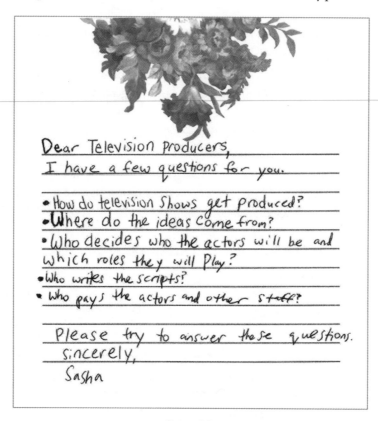

Dear Television producers,
I have a few questions for you.

- How do television shows get produced?
- Where do the ideas come from?
- Who decides who the actors will be and which roles they will play?
- Who writes the scripts?
- Who pays the actors and other staff?

Please try to answer these questions.
sincerely,
Sasha

Figure 6.1

Josh kindly emailed the following response:

Hi Sasha,

These are some great questions, and I'm thrilled to be able to offer my expertise. Thanks for thinking of me.

Please let me know if you need me to clarify anything.

1. How do television shows get produced?

   Television shows are created by a production company—a group of producers and crew to handle each job: writers, directors, editors, camera and sound people, and so on.

   Producers will work with each department to come up with ideas for stories, audition actors for the cast, assemble the locations, props, and costumers, and film the episode. Then they spend several weeks editing the episode, adding music and sound effects, before it is sent to the network to broadcast.

2. Where do the ideas come from?
   Ideas come from everywhere! Writers and producers will always draw on their own lives for inspiration, as well as the stories they hear from family and friends. Anytime we encounter a funny or interesting situation, we think "that could be a useful plot one day."

   Also, we are always reading the news and magazines to learn about different people and cultures, interesting jobs, and other worlds that would be fun to explore on television.

3. Who decides who the actors will be and which roles they will play?
   A casting director oversees finding the right actors for each role. Casting directors read the script, then hold auditions with dozens of actors (sometimes hundreds) to see who might be a good fit for each character.

   Once the casting director has selected some potential actors, they will recommend a small group to the director and producers, who ultimately pick the actors they think best fit the role.

4. Who writes the scripts?
   Screenwriters have the job of turning the ideas into stories—writing down all the dialogue, describing the action, coming up with surprises, and so on.

   Many shows have a group of screenwriters in a "writers' room," to work on ideas together. After brainstorming, each writer will take one idea to work on a different episode. Then they'll each bring their scripts back to the room, so everyone can work together again to improve the scripts.

5. Who pays the actors and other staff?
   A TV network gives the producers a budget to spend, which is an estimate of how much everything will cost: the actors' and crews members' salaries, as well as equipment, props, wardrobe, music, special effects, and everything else.

Exploring the Roots of the Writing Challenge

Years ago, I wrote about my wish that schools were judged not by students' scores on standardized tests but by the curiosity students exhibit. Wouldn't that change all our decisions about curriculum, assessment, teaching practices, and even the look, sound, and feel of our classrooms?

Isidor Rabi (1993), a Nobel laureate in physics, credits his mother for paving the way for him to become a scientist. Every day after school, his mom would ask him, "Did you ask a good question today?" rather than the more usual question, "What did you learn today?" According to Rabi, asking good questions made him become a scientist. When my city grandsons were preschoolers and we walked the streets of Manhattan, I was always impressed when they asked good questions, especially ones that I couldn't answer, ones that would require a bit of research. These included, "How come some street signs are brown, not the usual green?" "How come people swing their arms back and forth when they walk?" "How come there are bars on the first-floor windows in so many apartment buildings?" These were intriguing and honest questions, the kind a grandmother hopes her grandchildren will continue to ask as they move through the grades.

In this challenge, we put curiosity on a pedestal, making it the driving force of students' reading, writing, and researching. This challenge is not simply framing nonfiction writing into the simple question-and-answer design mentioned previously. Instead, students' curiosity about the world serves as the centerpiece of all the work to follow. Students ask their honest, burning questions and search for real answers from resources within the school community and beyond. If we don't get in the way, children's curiosity will be our North Star, guiding us to rich and thrilling areas of study.

My inspiration for this writing challenge has its roots in a wonderful book entitled, *Father Knows Less or "Can I Cook My Sister?" One Dad's Quest to Answer His Son's Most Baffling Questions,* written by journalist Wendell Jamieson (2007). In this thoroughly engaging nonfiction book for adults, the author presents dozens of questions he gathered from his own son and from the children of friends and family members. He then wrote to experts in the field who might be willing to respond to the children's queries. The book is a compilation of the questions asked and the letters of response. An emergency room doctor answers the questions, "What would hurt more: getting run over by a car or getting stung by a jellyfish?" A maritime professor answers the question, "Why do ships have round windows?" Former Mayor Ed Koch answers the question, "Why is New York City called the Big Apple?" The book is jam-packed with true-to-the-spirit-of-childhood questions and fascinating answers explained by well-informed authorities. We expect that all our students will likewise have authentic questions and that we will be able to find experts in the field to answer those questions.

Engaging Students in the Challenge

Teachers began this challenge by filling their classrooms with books that honored curiosity including *What Do You Do with an Idea?* by Kobi Yamada (2013), *Ideas Are All Around* by Philip C. Stead (2016), and *The Wonder* by Faye Hanson (2014). Picture books in which the main character is filled with curiosity also come in handy. These include Cathy Camper's *Ten Ways to Hear Snow* (2020), James Berry's *A Story About Afiya* (2020), Decur's *When You Look Up* (2020), Juan Felipe Herrera's *Imagine*, Sophie Spencer and Margaret McNamara's *The Bug Girl: A True Story* (2020), and Sophie Blackall's *If You Come to Earth* (2020). Then too, we shared picture books that inspire children to share the questions on their minds. We reminded students that teachers don't think they are clever only when they answer questions but when they ask good questions as well. The following titles will prime the question-asking pump: Kari Anne Holt's *I Wonder* (2019), Janice Harrington's *Buzzing with Questions: The Inquisitive Mind of Charles Henry Turner* (2019), Kimberly Derting and Shelli Johannes's *Cece Loves Science* (2018), and *Just Because* by Mac Barnett (2019). This last title will inspire students to think about the questions they have asked and the validity of the answered they received. The questions asked by the children in this book are followed by imaginative and fantastical answers. If you wonder about what makes rain, would you be satisfied to learn that rain is "the tears of flying fish"? Barnett offers beautiful poetic answers to the questions in the book, and most students sense there are factual ones as well.

Students are curious about their world, inside and outside of school.

We then handed students new, slim composition notebooks as a place to record the honest questions that, no doubt, would pop into their minds throughout the days to come. Although we suggested that easy-to-answer questions like "What's for lunch in the cafeteria today?" or "Is recess indoors or outside today?" need not be recorded, we knew students would probably record all the questions that crossed the minds. Rather than announce too many restrictions, we let students have full control of their jottings, knowing that we would ask them to become critical readers of their questions in a few days.

The students came up with titles for their new treasure chest, labeling their notebooks, with a wide range of headings including "Questions on My Mind, "My Book of Questions," and "Curiosity Leads to Questions." We announced that at the end of the week, we would carve out time to share some of their questions and that their questions would lead to our next writing challenge. (Students were invited to keep their book of questions going long after this challenge was completed, as students' questions always lead to engaged reading, writing, and research.)

A few days later, we explained where their questions would lead. We shared excerpts from Wendell Jamieson's book to demonstrate the challenge. We explained that the author gathered real questions, offered by real children, and then turned to real experts to answer the students' questions: "Is a rainbow hot or cold?" was answered by a meteorologist; "How and why do our ears make earwax?" was responded to by an ear, nose, and throat doctor; "How did the pineapple get its name?" was explained by the operations director of the Dole Food Company; and "Why do they call it soccer? They don't play in socks." The answer to this question was offered by the president of the U.S. Soccer Federation. Another source of inspiration for this challenge was suggested to me by Diane Berman, a fourth-grade teacher at P.S. 87. She raved about *Brains On!*, a science podcast produced by American Public Media (https://www.brainson.org/pages/about). During the coronavirus pandemic, children were invited to send their questions about the illness to the *New York Times*'s podcast *The Daily*. To hear their questions and the answers offered by science writer Carl Zimmer, visit nytimes.com/the daily.

Continuing to Support Students' Efforts
Sharing Your Own Writing

Just as I do with all writing challenges, I immersed myself in the task. I showed the students my own list of questions. These included:

1. Why are orchids so hard to care for?

2. How do you prepare meatballs so they always come out with your desired softness? (Same question applies to matzo balls.)

3. What would it take to get rid of the electoral college system of voting?

4. Why do teeth change color as you age?

Then I shared with students how I followed through on the last question above, writing to my dentist for an explanation of why my teeth seem to be changing color as I age. I talked to the students about the benefits of asking questions of known experts in the field instead of relying on a quick response from an anonymous source on the Internet. A real benefit of writing to a specific person is the possibility of asking follow-up questions or seeking clarification. I also talked about the advantage of having the dentist's answer in writing so that I could reread it and refer to it if needed. If I had only asked the question of the dentist, during a visit, he may not have had the time for such a thoughtful answer, and I may not have recalled all that he explained.

Dr. William Harwayne, my brother-in-law and my dentist, wrote the following:

> Teeth darken with age for several interesting reasons. Most teeth have varying degrees of orange and gray that combine to appear whitish. To understand what happens in aging, it helps to know a little tooth anatomy. In general, teeth are made up of three layers, an outer translucent layer of enamel, a darker middle layer called dentin, and the inner most layer called the pulp or nerve. As we age, that outer layer of white translucent enamel gets worn away and starts to show more of the middle, darker dentin. Additionally, the inner most layer of the pulp starts to recede and be replaced by even more of the darker dentin, so the teeth become both darker and less translucent, which makes them appear even darker. Finally, a lifetime of habits and diet can contribute to older teeth appearing darker. If you eat blueberries every day, you may have darker teeth than someone who doesn't, and if you chew betel nuts (not a healthy idea), as some cultures do, you will definitely have darker teeth.

Sharing Interesting Queries

We asked students to reread all their questions, searching for and highlighting those burning questions whose answers would require the help of an expert. We also found it necessary to help some students turn their interesting yes-or-no questions into broader ones. For example, one student wrote, "Will there be any snow days this year?" We explained that a meatier question would be, "How do weather forecasters get the information that helps them predict the weather?" In other words, we were asking student to reword their questions to create ones that could be fully answered by an expert in the field.

We had fun listing the questions chosen by students and then brainstorming what kind of experts were best to answer those questions. A few questions follow:

How does an ATM keep money inside if people keep taking it out? Wouldn't it run out of money?

How does water form? Does it just appear like magic?

Why do humans yawn?

Why can't birds see glass? (Why do they crash into windows and glass doors?)

How come some people are allergic to cats or dogs?

How do post offices keep track of all those packages and letters going all over the world?

How come football and soccer are different sports in Europe?

How do trees provide us with oxygen?

Where do last names come from?

Why are our hair colors different?

How does the Internet get its information?

Who started pierced ears?

When New York City restaurants are rated A, B, C, who does the rating, and what are the raters looking for?

We were surprised that many students did not have the vocabulary for specialized workers. Students were just as surprised that there were specific job titles for the experts that could answer their questions. New terms for students included obstetrician, ornithologist, botanist, and linguist.

Gathering Information

Next came the hunt for experts to write to via email or snail mail. We suspected that many of the questions could be answered by the students' pediatricians, the school science teacher, or family members in related lines of work. We certainly encouraged students to tap these local experts. We also reached out to family members and school staff to identify additional experts who might answer the students' questions. Schools that keep an ongoing and up-to-date community-wide directory of experts are at an advantage.

A list of the questions with the kind of expertise we were looking for was distributed to staff members as well as to family members. A partial list follows:

Why do some plants come back every year and others don't? (a local florist)

How do you get to be a teacher? (a teacher's college professor)

Why do squirrels attack bird feeders? (a park ranger)

How come Coney Island doesn't seem like an island? (chamber of commerce in Brooklyn)

We asked the adults for suggestions and connections to experts in the field. "Do you know an expert who could and would answer our students' questions?" Then too, we found ourselves searching the Internet for organizations, companies, and foundations that were related to the students' queries. We jotted down the names and addresses of representatives listed. We knew that some of the students' questions could be answered quickly with the press of a button on their computer screens. Often those explanations are not intended for young readers, but we sensed that experts who were aware that they were addressing children would write accordingly. We also wanted students to have the experience of writing and mailing letters as well as, hopefully, the thrill of receiving responses, ones that could be shared with others.

The student interested in finding out why birds crash into glass windows sent an email to the director of conservation and science at the New York office of the National Audubon Society. The student interested in finding out how ATMs always seem to have enough money wrote to a professor of computer science at the State University of New York in Albany who had written an article online about ATMs. The student who wanted to know why fancy cars are so expensive wrote to an executive vice president of the Alliance of Automobile Manufacturers, an advocacy group for the auto industry that represents many different car companies including Porsche, Mercedes-Benz, and BMW. The student who wanted to find out how the post office keeps track of letters and packages wrote to the postmaster general of the U.S. Postal Service at her office in Washington, D.C.

Lifting the Quality of Student Writing

Once we had the name and either the snail mail address or email address of the experts, we carved out time for students to write their letters of request. We made sure their letters were revised for meaningful and understandable content and edited for mechanics, grammar, spelling, as well as handwriting, for those that were sent by snail mail. We talked about how to write the kind of letter that people would take the time to respond to. We discussed and listed the following ideas:

Make sure that you . . .

- let the expert know that you are a student and include your age and grade
- let the expert know that you attend a public school in New York City
- acknowledge that the expert is probably very busy doing important work
- explain why you are interested in the topic of your question
- are gracious and thank the expert
- check your spelling and grammar
- use your best handwriting if the letter is handwritten

- include the name of a specific person (Try not to write just to an organization.)
- include all the specifics of the mailing address (the name and title of expert, a specific suite or room number, street address and name of city and state, and the zip code)
- include a way for the expert to send a response (an email address or home or school address)
- include "in care of . . ." with your teacher's name if you are corresponding via snail mail with your school's address

We made copies of all students' letters and even the emails that were sent knowing we would eventually create a display of letters alongside their responses. Finally, we took a class walk to the local mailbox to send off the snail-mail requests. And then we waited.

> *Would the repairman who takes care of the school's fax machines answer the question "How does a fax machine work?"*
>
> *Would the owner of our local school bus company answer the question "Why are school buses yellow?"*
>
> *Would a worker at the reptile house at the Bronx Zoo answer the question "How do snakes care for their young? "*
>
> *Would a representative from the sanitation department take the time to respond to "Why does snow melt faster in Manhattan than in the suburbs?"*

We anticipated several possible problems: What would we do for children who never receive an answer? (We'd refer to the school science teacher or tap other local experts.) What would we do if the experts' answers were way over the head of our young students? (We'd read their responses and explain their meaning to students.) What would we do if the response really did not answer the students' questions? (We'd teach students to ask follow-up or clarifying questions.)

Student Writing Samples

Lily wanted to know why our eyes couldn't see two things at once (see Figure 6.2). See Figure 6.3 for optometrist Dr. Dara Martin's response to Lily's letter.

Figure 6.2

Dear Lily,

Thank you for your wonderful question.

I have to first tell you that I laughed to myself when I read your question. During my exam as an Optometrist, I have all my patients follow my pen so I can check how their eye muscles work together. I tell them "I want you to follow my pen with your eyes and not move your head." Very often they ask me, "with both of my eyes?" I have always thought this is so funny because when we look at something both of our eyes always move together in the same direction, and we can't really only move one eye. This is because the brain does not want to see 2 different things at the same time. This would make it very hard for the brain to understand what it is seeing and would make the person see double. This would be very uncomfortable and make it very difficult to walk around or read a paper.

When we look at something, there are cells (rods and cones) in the back of the eye that are fired up to see an object. Both eyes move together and it fires up the cells all around the same area in the back of the eye on something called the retina. If each eye is in a different spot, then different parts of the retina see the same image and it will make the person see 2 of the same thing. This is what you probably know as being "cross eyed." There are some people who are born with a weak muscle which makes one eye move slower or stay looking in or out while the other eye does something different. This is a lazy eye. You may have a friend or a brother or sister that you can see one eye doesn't look at you when the other eye is looking at you. Some kids have to wear glasses, wear a patch or do exercises to try to fix this to make the eye stronger.

But I do want to tell you that is it possible to move one eye left and one eye right at the same time, but to do this you have to force it to happen. Here is an example. Take a pen or pencil and hold if far away. Look at the tip of the pen/pencil and slowly move it closer to your nose. At some point, you will start to see 2 of them as one eye moves differently than the other. Then, the brain will do what it can to make it 1 again, usually by making one eye turn away.

I hope this answers your question. Thank you for asking this because a lot of people have the same question.

Your friendly Optometrist . . .
Dr. Dara Martin

Figure 6.3

Carving Out Time for Celebration

As responses began to trickle in, we took time to acknowledge, appreciate, and celebrate each one. Students shared at morning meetings, teaching all of us what they learned. We talked about how different our learning would have been if we merely looked up the answer on the Internet. Students learned to respect the knowledge and authority of experts in the field. They also came to understand the power of letter writing. When some students did not receive a response, we resent the letter to a member of the staff who had some expertise in the area or tried to locate another expert in the field. When all students had a response to share, we set aside a date for families to attend a class celebration. Students displayed copies of the letters they wrote and the letters they received. We then displayed these sets of letters side by side for the entire school community to enjoy.

BOOKS NOTED

Barnett, Mac. 2019. *Just Because.* Somerville, MA: Candlewick.

Berry, James. 2020. *A Story About Afiya.* Oxford, UK: Lantana.

Blackall, Sophie. 2020. *If You Come to Earth.* San Francisco, CA: Chronicle Books.

Camper, Cathy. 2020. *Ten Ways to Hear Snow*. New York: Kokila.

Decur. 2020. *When You Look Up*. Brooklyn, NY: Enchanted Lions.

Derting, Kimberly, and Shelli R. Johannes. 2018. *Cece Loves Science*. New York: Greenwillow Books.

Hanson, Faye. 2014. *The Wonder*. Somerville, MA: Templar Books/Candlewick.

Harrington, Janice N. 2019. *Buzzing with Questions: The Inquisitive Mind of Charles Henry Turner*. Boyds Mills, PA: Calkins Creek.

Herrera, Juan Felipe. 2018. *Imagine*. Somerville, MA: Candlewick.

Holt, Kari Anne. 2019. *I Wonder*. New York: Random House.

Spencer, Sophie, and Margaret McNamara. 2020. *The Bug Girl: A True Story*. New York: Schwartz & Wade.

Stead, Philip. 2016. *Ideas Are All Around*. New York: Roaring Brook.

Yamada, Kobi. 2013. *What Do You Do with an Idea?* Seattle, WA: Compendium Kids.

TEACHER REFERENCE MATERIAL

Barbaro, Michael. March 27, 2020. "A Kids Guide to Coronavirus." *The New York Times*. https://www.nytimes.com/2020/03/27/podcasts/the-daily/kids-coronavirus.html.

Jamieson, Wendell. 2007. *Father Knows Less or "Can I Cook My Sister?" One Dad's Quest to Answer His Son's Most Baffling Questions*. New York: G.P. Putnam's Sons.

Rabi, Isidor. 1993. "Great Minds Start with a Question." *Parents Magazine*. September.

A FEW TITLES TO ENRICH YOUR TEACHING

Bryan, Nathan. 2019. *Look Up!* New York: Puffin.

de la Peña, Matt. 2021. *Milo Imagines the World*. New York: G.P. Putnam's Sons.

Dillon, Diane. 2018. *I Can Be Anything: Don't Tell Me I Can't*. New York: Blue Sky Press.

Fleming, Candace. 2018. *The Amazing Collection of Joey Cornell*. New York: Schwartz & Wade Books.

Karlins, Mark. 2021. *Kyoshi's Walk*. New York: Lee & Low.

Marinov, Isabel. 2021. *The Boy Whose Head Was Filled with Stars: A Life of Edwin Hubble*. Brooklyn, NY: Enchanted Lion.

Martin, Marc. 2018. *Everything & Everywhere: A Fact-Filled Adventure for Curious Globe-Trotters*. San Francisco, Ca: Chronicle Books.

Merino, Gemma. 2016. *The Cow Who Climbed a Tree*. Park Ridge, IL: Albert Whitman & Co.

McClure, Nikki. 2020. *What Will These Hands Make?* New York: Harry N. Abrams.

Regwan, Sol. 2020. *Geraldine and the Most Spectacular Science Project*. Atglen, PA: Schiffer Kids.

Rex, Adam. 2019. *Why?* San Francisco: Chronicle Books.

Robertson, David A. 2017. *When We Were Alone*. Winnepeg, Canada: HighWater Press.

Sanders, Joshunda. 2019. *I Can Write the World*. Houston, TX: Six Foot Press.

Spencer, Sophie, and Margaret McNamara. 2020. *The Bug Girl: A True Story*. New York: Schwartz & Wade.

Tanco, Miguel. 2019. *Count on Me*. Toronto: Tundra Books.

Tsarfati, Einat. 2019. *The Neighbors*. New York: Harry N. Abrams.

See additional bibliography in online Book List 7.

CHAPTER 7
And the Award Goes to . . .

(Grades 4–5)

Tess, a fourth grader in Diane Berman's class at P.S. 87, decided to create State Awards:

"STATE AWARDS" BY TESS

The Best State to Collect Seashells Award goes to Florida because of the stunning and amazing seashells that wash up on the sandy beaches of Sanibel Island. There are over 250 types of shells that you can find on the 15 miles of beaches that Sanibel is known for. It also has the most beautiful sunsets and amazing dolphin watching.

The Best State To Be a Tourist Award goes to New York because New York has New York City which has the Empire State Building, the Chrysler Building, the Statue of Liberty, Central Park, and many other famous monuments that teach us a lot about history and are the stars of the city.

The Best State to Visit Museums Award goes to Pennsylvania because a lot of the important things from the Revolutionary War happened in Philadelphia, so they have a lot of really interesting museums about the war.

The Best State to Eat Seafood Award goes to Massachusetts because Cape Cod has a lot of beaches, so a lot of people catch a lot of fresh seafood like lobsters and fish and then sell it to restaurants. Since the seafood is fresh it tastes a lot better and that is what makes the Cape so special.

The Best State to Eat Cheese Award goes to Wisconsin because they make a lot of cheese there so you could have a very wide variety of them. Some of the cheeses that they have there are mozzarella, Cheddar, Gouda, American, feta, Muenster, Swiss, and Gorgonzola.

The Best State to Go to Beaches Award goes to South Carolina because the beaches there are big, white, and flat, and they go on for miles at a time. The most fun thing to do there is ride your bike down the beach, then stop for ice cream at the end.

Exploring the Roots of the Writing Challenge

I listened with interest to a news report about a book club in Iowa in which readers were committed to reading books written by the 2020 candidates for president. Andrea Phillips, the organizer of the book club, is a vice chair of the Democratic Party in the state, and as soon as she posted information about the proposed book club on Facebook, over 700 people nationwide became members. I also read a related article titled, "Every 2020 Democratic Candidate's Memoir Reviewed"(Bookmarks 2019), which began with rather humorous, imaginative awards for those books. The Best Title Award was given to Kamala Harris's (2019) *The Truths We Hold: An American Journey.* The Most Poetic Title Award was given to Michael Bennett (2019) for his book, *Land of Flickering Lights: Restoring America in the Age of Broken Politics.* The reviewer also chose winners for the Worst Title, The Most Misleading Title, and the Longest Title. This article heightened my interest in fictitious awards.

A year before, the *New York Times* published a short, intriguing article entitled *"The Bird Awards: 5 of the Most Fantastic Feathered Artists,"* written by Mara Grunbaum (2018). In it, the journalist invented five awards for birds, giving the Coolest Dancer Award to the Wahnes's parotia, a bird found in Papua New Guinea, The Best Decorator Award to the bowerbird, The Most Stirring Singer Award to the Cuban solitaire, The Most Extraordinary Actor Award to the superb lyrebird, and the Boldest Fashion Icon Award to the satyr tragopan, a type of pheasant from Himalaya. In addition to illustrations, the author offered short descriptive and convincing paragraphs to explain each of her choices. This is the kind of newspaper article that inspires me to ask, "Would our students enjoy doing a version of that? What would students learn from so doing? How would they choose the categories for their imaginative awards?"

Children usually love being in total command of a project, and this challenge allows them to do so. They were asked to select a beloved topic of interest, create imaginative awards to connect with that interest, decide on the winners of those awards, and explain their choices. David Brooks (2019), a journalist for the *New York Times*, reminded his readers that "a key job of a school is to give students new things to love—an exciting field of study, new friends." He goes on to suggest that "what teachers really teach is themselves—their contagious passion for the subjects and their students." In the following challenge, students and their teachers have an opportunity to think deeply about one of their passions and give one another new things to love. This challenge also demonstrates that many of our students' interests stem from pop culture, and those topic choices remind us that there must be a place for pop culture in our classrooms.

Engaging Students in the Challenge

We began by sharing the imaginative bird awards that appeared in the newspaper. I also shared a poem by Allan Wolf (2019) titled "Saturn—And the Winner for Best Wardrobe Is . . ." in which the poet explains why Saturn is the best-dressed planet. "What other awards might you create for the planets?" I asked. The picture book by Etta Kaner (2013), *And the Winner Is . . . Amazing Animal Athletes* was additionally helpful. The author gives awards to animals in such categories as sprinting, weightlifting, and the long jump.

Students search for information to support their award choices.

I often tell students about my grandson Ben who loves sushi restaurants, especially conveyor belt sushi. When he was in second grade, his teacher Nancy invited students to present their passions to the class in a project she called "Off the Beaten Track." Ben chose to teach his classmates about the different conveyor belt sushi restaurants that he and his family had eaten at in New York City and around the country. Years later, I asked Ben what kind of awards he would invent if he were to give out sushi restaurant awards. We talked about the Least Expensive Sushi Restaurant Award, the Tastiest Sushi Restaurant Award, the Most Popular Item on a Sushi Menu Award, the Hardest Sushi Restaurant to Get a Reservation at Award, and of course, the Best Conveyor Belt Sushi Restaurant Award.

Teachers do not need the bird article mentioned previously, the Saturn award poem, the animal picture book, or a grandson who loves sushi to initiate this challenge. In one classroom, I simply introduced the challenge by asking students if they ever watched award shows on television. Most had. They had seen award shows for television shows, movies, music, and Broadway theater. I then asked if they had ever heard about Nobel Prizes and Pulitzer Prizes. Some had. We talked about the scope of these prestigious awards and some of the categories connected to each award. Students recalled books on their classroom library shelves that had award-winning stickers including the Coretta Scott King Book Awards, the Ezra Jack Keats Awards, the Caldecott Medal, and the Pura Belpre Awards. I also told them that various organizations give out awards that most people know little about. These include the Comedy Wildlife Photography Awards, Animal Hero Awards, and Animal Star Awards, which honors extraordinary things that humans and animals do for one another. (Stories and photos of award winners can be viewed on the Internet.) Teachers can also share the contents of a well-thought out listing in an article entitled, "50 Youth Sports Awards Ideas" (Eng 2019). The topic is sure to be of interest to the student athletes in the class.

After a general conversation about unusual awards, I asked the big question: "What topic do you know and care about that, if it were possible, you would love to invent awards and select the winners?" It turned out that this question was a great way to satisfy some students' interests in pop culture, as their initial responses included video games, superheroes, singers, bands, television shows, pizza restaurants, and roller coasters.

Continuing to Support Students' Efforts
Sharing Your Own Writing

First, as has become customary, I accepted the challenge myself, selecting a topic that I was passionate about. I hoped to spread what David Brooks calls that "contagious passion." It will come as no surprise that I chose children's literature. I wanted the categories to be original, surprising, and perhaps even whimsical. Then too, to serve as a model, I needed to support my awards with interesting facts and thoughtful observations. (It should be noted, though, that teachers who choose not to share their own writing might just as easily collaborate with students in creating an exemplary text. This can be done for many of the challenges in this book, and one example is described in more detail in Creating Glossaries on page 224).

I shared the following with fourth graders:

SHELLEY'S CHILDREN'S LITERATURE AWARD

Most dog-eared book award

And the award goes to . . . *Knuffle Bunny: A Cautionary Tale* by Mo Willems (2004). More than 750,000 copies of this book have been sold. Willems' books have been translated into over 25 languages, including French, Chinese, and Spanish. Whenever I visit early childhood classrooms, I notice very well-worn copies of the book, with even our youngest not-yet-reading-students choosing this title, having memorized most of the words. They hug the book as tightly as they do their favorite teddy bears.

Most revered book from childhood award

And the award goes to . . . Margaret Wise Brown's 1947 publication *Goodnight Moon*. Grown-ups instantly recognize the bold artwork in *Goodnight Moon*. They quote lines from the book. They surround themselves and their own children with *Goodnight Moon* memorabilia including stuffed bunny toys wearing pajamas, melamine dish sets decorated with scenes from the book, soft pillow-like editions of the books, tote bags, baby onesies, and *Goodnight Moon* t-shirts for young and old alike.

Most prolific author awards

And the award goes to . . . Jonathan London. London has published over 200 poems and 120 picture books, including over 30 titles in his very popular Froggy series. He has also written several chapter books for middle grade readers. His work appears in many different genres—fiction, realistic fiction, poetry, nonfiction, and even autobiography.

Most often quoted at graduations award

And the award goes to . . . *Oh, the Places You'll Go!* by Dr. Seuss (1990). Simply search on You Tube and you can watch several people refer to the now famous Dr. Seuss picture book when they deliver graduation speeches. Excerpts are shared by valedictorians, guest speakers, and school administrators all the way from elementary school to university celebrations. Of course, not everyone thinks this book serves graduates well, especially high school and college graduates. Kyle Smith (2014) wrote an article for the *New York Post* newspaper entitled, "Why This Dr. Seuss Book Should Never Again Be a Graduation Gift." He complains that it is filled with "insipid declarations" that are "trite, shallow . . . and childish, "especially for older students." The author would much prefer that students were offered material that is more thought-provoking and insightful. He'd probably prefer the inspirational messages in Peter Reynold's *Be You!* (2020), Emily Martin's *The Wonderful Things You'll Be* (2015), or Nancy Tillman's *You're Here for a Reason* (2015).

Most often referred to on op-ed pages award

And the award goes to . . . Judith Viorst's (1972) *Alexander and the Terrible, Horrible, No Good, Very Bad Day*. I have a file folder filled with references to this oft-quoted Judith Viorst title. In fact, the book's title often becomes the title of the newspaper article. *The Chicago Tribune* published "Trump's Terrible, Horrible, No Good, Very Bad Day" in August of 2018. *Christian Headlines* (Stonestreet and Carlson 2019) published an article titled, "The Media's Terrible, Horrible, No-Good Very Bad Week: When News Becomes a Game of 'Gotcha.'" *Adweek* (Sutton 2018) published a variation that read "Facebook's Terrible, Horrible, No Good, Very Bad Year." Viorst's classic book was first published in 1972 and has remained popular decades later. It's no wonder that journalists in their 30s and 40s still refer to it so frequently when they want to describe a time when things go really wrong.

After reading and discussing my awards, students had a better idea of the task before them, including the need to come up with interesting categories for their awards. (I did have to stop and read *Oh, the Places You'll Go!* so they could understand the critic's attitude about the book for older graduates.) I reminded the students that readers love to be surprised, and coming up with original awards was a prime way to satisfy that desire. Teachers can often find additional imaginative awards, in newspapers and television, especially at the end of the calendar year. Critics and newscasters often look back on the best and the worst of the year and create awards in many interesting categories. For example, in the Arts section of *The New York Times*, columnist Jason Zinoman (2019) wrote "A Critic's 2019 Picks for the Best Comedy." He lists such surprising awards as Best Scene Stealer, Funniest Online Character Comic, and Best Talent Cluster. CNN, in a show titled *All the Best/All the Worst of 2019*, announced such surprising awards as The Worst Trend to Put Parents on Edge (vaping), the Worst Long Good-Bye (Brexit), and the Worst Helicopter Mom Award (actresses in the college admissions scandals). (Note, the contents of these awards are for adults only.)

Gathering Information

Before asking them to make final decisions about their topics, we filled the room with stacks of informational texts that ranked and rated items in broad categories. We gave students time to browse and share surprising discoveries. The books whet their appetites for choosing topics as well as thinking about possible awards. The hottest books in the room included volumes of the *Guinness Book of World Records*, the oversized picture book *Highest Mountain/Smallest Star* by Kate Baker and Page Tsou (2018), and the top-ten sports books published by *Sports Illustrated Kids* including *Full Count: Top Ten Lists in Everything Baseball, Face Off! Top Ten Lists in Everything Hockey, Slam Dunk! Top Ten Lists in Everything in Basketball*, and *1st and 10: Top Ten Lists in Everything Football*.

Eventually, students selected their favorite topics. These included:

architectural feats

dinosaurs

mountains

extinct animals

sea creatures

circus acts

heavy metal bands

pasta dishes

cartoons

local pizza restaurants

comic books

national parks in the USA

basketball players

Yankees

New York City tourist sites

pets

desserts

board games

video games

jungle animals

farm animals

roller coasters

After students chose their topics, the real fun began. We asked, "What awards can you imagine giving out?" Students were asked to list as many awards that they could think of and then select their top five. Note, several students selected categories for their awards that were rather difficult to explore and explain because their award topic was too broad. For example, a student chose Company Awards but did not limit them to a particular type of company, so choosing the most hardworking company, the slowest-working company, or the coolest company would be hard to give out. Another chose Shoe Brand Awards and hoped to give out awards that included the best quality, worst quality, most popular, cheapest, and most expensive, all rather hard to research if not limited, for example, to a kind of shoe like sneakers. Another student wanted to give Restaurant Awards but didn't include a specific locale, which would make the task more manageable.

Indira, a fourth grader, decided to give out Cake Awards. She came up with great categories for her awards and at first had difficulty choosing winners. To support her, we had a small group chat about her topic, and we did some browsing on the Internet. She announced the following awards:

The hardest cake to make award goes to lemon meringue pie.

The most decorated cake award goes to the Fabergé Egg Cake made for a British man's 60th birthday.

The yummiest cake award goes to Brooklyn Blackout Cake.

The healthiest cake award goes The Ultimate Red Velvet Cupcake (made by Amy's Healthy Baking).

The most expensive cake to make award goes to Prince William and Kate Middleton's wedding cake that cost $78,000.

The most popular cake award goes to cheesecake.

Most students were eager to assign their award winners but needed to be slowed down to research and include specific reasons for their choices. Although the seeds of their awards were personal opinions, student had to support their choices with convincing information. When students explained their choices, they were engaging in a very solid form of persuasive writing. They had to prove that their award winners were well deserved. In other words, Indira needed to explain what healthy ingredients were in that red velvet cupcake, what made that royal cake so expensive, and what the Fabergé egg cake looked like. Similarly, students who created awards for playgrounds, Broadway shows, and Halloween treats could not simply offer the names of their winners but needed to provide the rationale for their choices, putting meat on the bones.

(Be prepared to be surprised by students' ideas. Sonia, a fifth grader in Melissa's dual-language class at P.S. 87, created a rather tongue-in-cheek collection of Emoji Awards. These included such surprising awards as the Most Popular Emoji, the Most Optimistic Emoji, the Most Romantic Emoji, the Most Shy Emoji, and the Most Ready for a Party Emoji. Her work could easily be published in a comedy magazine. Her topic and categories, however, did not lend themselves to the kind of research and documentation I had imagined for this challenge.)

A few student topics and award categories follow.

Jungle Animal Awards

Most Ferocious Animal in the Jungle Award

Fastest Animal in Jungle Award

Most Endangered Animal in Jungle Award

Most Beautiful Animal in the Jungle

Best Camouflaged Animal in the Jungle Award

Farm Animal Awards

Cutest Farm Animal Award

Sloppiest Farm Animal Award

Most Social Farm Animal Award

Easiest to Care for Farm Animal Award

Most Written About Farm Animal Award

Roller Coaster Awards

Makes You Wish You Stayed Home Award

Makes You Throw Up Award

Makes You Willing to Get on a Long Line to Repeat the Ride Award

Makes Your Knuckles Hurt from Holding On So Tight Award

Makes Your Eyeglasses Fly Off Award

To flesh out their ideas, students benefit from research time in the school and public library, use of Chromebooks, and time to browse any relevant materials from home, including magazines, cookbooks, travel brochures, game instructions, and guidebooks.

Lifting the Quality of Student Writing

Once students gathered enough information, they wrote up their five winning choices with accompanying short passages to support those choices. During our minilessons held at the beginning of each workshop, we focused on coming up with appropriate and clever names for the awards, deciding whether illustrations were needed, but mostly about putting the tools in their writer's toolbox to good use. Teachers who had a copy of Mara Grunbaum's (2018) "The Bird Awards," the article that inspired this project, were able to lift lines and discuss with students if the tools that were at the journalist's disposal were the same as the ones they have studied. They noted:

1. alliteration in her subtitle, "Fantastic Feathered Artists" and in her closing line, "What's fashion without flair?"

2. sensory details in such lines as "males fan their black feathers into puffy tutus and waggle six long plumes on their head" and "he unfurls a brightly patterned red-and-blue neck flap and inflates two neon blue horns"

3. precise verbs such as *groove, wobble, rave, fan, waggle,* and *freeze*

4. a simile such as "has a strange, layered call that sounds like a singing 'Star Wars' droid"

5. the power of three in the line "gather dozens of colorful objects—red berries, blue bottle caps and shiny beetle wings"

6. information that is specific as in "Male lyrebirds can mimic almost anything, from the cackle of a kookaburra to the wail of a car alarm"

Students seem pleased when they can spot and name a professional writer's crafting techniques. It's proof positive that what they are studying in school has a place in the world outside of school. Teachers who haven't tracked down this article can use the exemplars they themselves created for this challenge. When students reread my children's literature awards, they noticed that I counted on:

> **Long list sentences:** *"Goodnight Moon memorabilia including stuffed bunny toys wearing pajamas, melamine dish sets decorated with scenes from the book, soft pillow-like editions of the books, tote bags, baby onesies, and Goodnight Moon t-shirts for young and old alike."*
>
> **The power of three:** *"Willems' books have been translated into over twenty-five languages, including French, Chinese, and Spanish."*
>
> **Specific and accurate bits of information:** *"London has published over 200 poems and 120 picture books, including over 30 titles in his very popular Froggy series."*
>
> **A simile:** *"They hug the book as tightly as they do their favorite teddy bears."*

Writing these short paragraphs can also serve another purpose. It is a gentle introduction to the art of persuasive writing. After all, the author is trying to convince the reader why these awards are justified. They are presenting evidence to explain their choices. Teachers might choose to teach some persuasive techniques that would enrich the students' work. These include exaggerations, comparisons, precise word choice, quotes from experts, and data that prove how distinct the winner is.

We also conferred individually with students and occasionally met with small groups of students who needed similar assistance. During the short share times at the end of our workshops, students proudly read aloud some of the awards they created during that workshop or discussed any writing problems they had solved.

Fifth graders in Melissa Martinez's class wrote the awards that follow.

Student Writing Samples

"THE DOG AWARDS" BY LAYLA

The Dog That Drools the Most:
A Saint Bernard. It is a huge dog and it also has a huge mouth for drooling. They also have deep and loose lips, so the drool comes right out.

The Dog with the Longest Hair:
A Golden Retriever. Their hair hangs down like a waterfall. Long strands dangle from most parts of their bodies.

The Dog with the Longest Body:
A Dachsund. These dogs are low to the ground with skinny long bodies. When they walk, it looks like they are waddling.

The Best Dog for Hunting:
A Bloodhound. Bloodhounds have great senses of smell and they can sniff out animals for hunters.

"THE DOG AWARDS" BY LAYLA *(continued)*

The Dog That Barks the Most:
A Shetland sheepdog. These dogs were meant for guiding sheep back into their pen, and they use a lot of barking to do it.

The Fiercest Dog:
A Rottweiler. They are often used as guard dogs, and they grow to be large and very strong dogs.

The Chubbiest Dog:
An English Bulldog. These big guys have wrinkly faces and round short bodies. The wrinkles get smushed together, and that makes it look clumped up and large.

The Most Shy Dog:
A Yorkshire Terrier. These dogs come in very small sizes, and it is hard for them to interact with other dogs. Also, they are much smaller than almost everything in their lives, which makes them scared and more careful.

Hope you liked Layla's Dog Awards!

"BOARD GAME AWARDS" BY VERONICA

The Best Board Game with Dice: Yahtzee. A lot of board games with dice are fun, but this five-die game is always a WINNER.

The Most Realistic Board Game: Life as you can tell is very, very realistic although the new version may not be. So what? Doesn't everybody love vintage board games?

The Most Logical Board Game: Mastermind is, as the slogan says, "the cunning game of logic" and that is definitely true. In this logical game, you must use logic to uncover a code made by your opponent using clues from little 1¼ centimeter pegs–logical.

The Most Surprisingly Technological Game (of the past): Stop Thief uses a minicomputer-like mechanism to help you "find the thief." It might not seem that high tech except that it's from 1979. Now this award should make sense.

The Board Game with the Most Rules: Sagrada. Sagrada has a 2-page, 8½ by 11 booklet with diagrams. It can get really confusing, just like the real Sagrada Familia in Spain actually is.

Carving Out Time for Celebration

This writing challenge is particularly well suited to an interactive publishing celebration. Imagine inviting another class to the party and distributing a list of all topics with the categories to be awarded. Visiting students would have an opportunity to fill in the blanks, jotting down their own preferences for award winners. What would you choose for the most ferocious animal in the jungle, the cutest farm animal, the healthiest dessert, and so on? Visitors will listen differently to the presenters once they have voiced their own opinions.

BOOKS NOTED

Titles of books chosen for my literature awards and resources used:

Brown, Margaret Wise. 1947. *Goodnight Moon*. New York: Harper Brothers.

London, Jonathan. 2006. *Froggy Rides a Bike*. New York: Viking/ Penguin Young Readers Group (and many more Froggy titles).

Martin, Emily Winfield. 2015. *The Wonderful Things You'll Be*. New York: Random House

Reynolds, Peter. 2020. *Be You!* New York: Orchard Books.

Seuss, Dr. 1990. *Oh, the Places You'll Go*. New York: Random House.

Tillman, Nancy. 2015. *You're Here for a Reason*. New York: Feiwel & Friends.

Viorst, Judith. 1972. *Alexander and the Terrible, Horrible, No Good, Very Bad Day*. New York: Atheneum Books for Young Readers.

Willems, Mo. 2004. *Knuffle Bunny: A Cautionary Tale*. New York: Hyperion Books.

PICTURE BOOKS

Baker, Kate, and Page Tsou. 2018.*Highest Mountain/ Smallest Star*. New York: Penguin Random House/ Big Picture Press.

Editors of Sports Illustrated Kids. 2011. *1st and Ten: Top Ten Lists in Everything Football*. New York: Time Home Entertainment.

_____. 2012. *Full Count: Top Ten Lists of Everything in Baseball*. New York: Time Home Entertainment.

_____. 2014. *Slam Dunk: Top Ten Lists of Everything in Basketball*. New York: Time, Inc. Books.

_____. 2015. *Face Off! Top Ten Lists of Everything in Hockey*. New York: Time, Inc. Books.

Kaner, Etta. 2013. *And the Winner Is . . . Amazing Animal Athletes*. Toronto, Canada: Kids Can Press.

POETRY

Wolf, Allan. 2019. "Saturn—and the Winner for Best Wardrobe Is . . ." *The Day the Universe Exploded My Head: Poems to Take You into Space and Back Again*. Somerville, MA: Candlewick.

TEACHER REFERENCE MATERIAL

Bookmarks. 2019. "Every 2020 Democratic Candidate's Memoir, Reviewed." June 26. https:// bookmarks.reviews/every-2020-democratic-presidential-candidates-memoir-reviewed/.

Brooks, David. January 18, 2019. "Students Learn from People They Love." *The New York Times*. Op ed, page A23.

Chicago Tribune. August 21, 2018. "Trump's Terrible, Horrible, No Good, Very Bad Day." https://www. chicagotribune.com./news/opinion/editorials/ct-edit-trump-manafort-cohen-scandal-20180821-story.html

CNN Special Report. *All the Best/All the Worst of 2019*. https://archive.org/details/ CNNW_20191230_020000_CNN_Special_Report.

Eng, Kyle. 2019. "50 Youth Sports Awards Ideas." https://www.signupgenius.com/sports/award/-ideas. cfm.

Grunbaum, Mara. 2018. "The Bird Awards: 5 of the Most Fantastic Feathered Artists." *New York Sunday Times,* April 29. The Animal Issue.

Smith, Kyle. May 10,2014. "Why This Dr. Seuss Book Should Never Again Be a Graduation Gift." *New York Post*. https://nypost.com/2014/05/10/why-this-dr-seuss-book-should-never-again-be-a-graduation-present/

Stonestreet, Jones, and David Carlson. 2019. "The Media's Terrible, Horrible, No-Good Very Bad Week: When News Becomes a Game of "Gotcha." *Christian Headlines.* January 23. https://www.christianheadlines.com./columnists/breakpoint/the media's-terrible-horrible-no-good-very-bad-week-when-news-becomes-a-game-of-gotcha

Sutton, Kelsey. 2018. "Facebook's Terrible, Horrible, No Good, Very Bad Year," *Adweek*. December 26. https://www.adweek.com/performance-marketing/facebooks-terrible-horrible-no-good-very-bad-year/.

Zinoman, Jason. 2019 "A Critic's 2019 Picks for the Best Comedy." Arts section. *The New York Times*. December 26.

ADULT MEMOIRS

Bennett, Michael. 2019. *Land of Flickering Lights: Restoring America in the Age of Broken Politics*. New York: Atlantic Monthly Press/Grove Atlantic.

Harris, Kamala. 2019. *The Truths We Hold*. New York: Penguin Press.

A FEW TITLES TO ENRICH YOUR TEACHING

Chin, Jason 2020. *Your Place in the Universe*. New York: Neal Porter Books.

Cusick, Dawn. 2016. *Animals that Make Me Say Ewww!* Watertown, MA: Charlesbridge.

———. 2016. *Animals That Make Me Say Look Out!* Watertown, MA: Charlesbridge.

Derrick, Stuart, and Charlotte Goddard. 2018. *World's Strangest Predators*. Oakland, CA: Lonely Planet Kids.

———. 2018. *World's Strangest Creepy- Crawlies*. Oakland, CA: Lonely Planet Kids.

———. *2018. World's Strangest Ocean Beasts*. Oakland, CA: Lonely Planet Kids.

Drimmer, Stephanie Warren. 2018. *Ultimate Secrets Revealed: A Closer Look at the Weirdest, Wildest Facts on Earth*. Washington, D.C.: National Geographic Kids.

Harris, Michelle, and Julie Beer. 2018. *National Geographic Extreme Records: The Tallest, Weirdest, Fastest, Coolest Stuff on Planet Earth*. Washington, D.C.: National Geographic Kids.

Hawkins, Emily. 2020. *Atlas of Record-Breaking Adventures: A Collection of the Biggest, Fastest, Longest, Toughest, Tallest and Most Deadly Things from Around the World*. London: Wide-Eyed Editions.

Jenkins, Steve. 2013. *The Animal Book: A Collection of the Fastest, Fiercest, Toughest, Cleverest, Shyest, and Most Surprising Animals on Earth*. Boston, MA: HMH Books for Young Readers.

Sanchez, Anita. 2018. *Itch!; Everything You Didn't Want to Know About What Makes You Itch*. Boston, MA: Houghton Mifflin Harcourt.

Sanchez, Anita. 2019. *Rotten! Vultures, Beetles, Slime and Nature's Other Decomposers*. Boston, MA: Houghton Mifflin Harcourt.

Sayre, April Pulley. 2016. *Slowest Book Ever*. Honesdale, PA: Boyds Mills Press.

See bibliography in online Book List 8 for additional resources.

CHAPTER 8
Could It Really Happen?

(Grades 3-5)

After reading *The Very Hungry Caterpillar* (Carle 1969), Lily, a student in Diane Berman's fourth-grade class, wondered if caterpillars would eat human food and if they would gain a lot of weight. She researched the answers to her questions and wrote the answer in Figure 8.1.

TITLE: THE VERY HUNGRY CATERPILLAR FACTS

BY: LILIANA

QUESTION 1: CAN CATERPILLARS EAT HUMAN FOOD?

The diet of the Very Hungry Caterpillar is an interesting one. Unless it's in a fictional book caterpillars are not known for snacking on processed food. Most species are vegan, sticking to plant-based food sources. Butterflies and moths lay their eggs where their offspring will have the beast chance of survival. This usually means on the leaf of their foodplant, providing a 'ready meal' when they hatch. But there are always exceptions to the rule. The peculiar eating habits of some caterpillars do sound like made-up stories. But it may surprise you that caterpillars eat flowers, honeycomb, grass, bark and twigs, animal waste, ants, moss and lichen, hair, and creepily, eachother! Carnivorous caterpillars are quite unusual but those who are will feast on other moth caterpillars if the opportunity arises. They eat leaves most of the time but will happily swap their salad for caterpillars, even of their own kind, if the bump into them

QUESTION 2: CAN CATERPILLARS GET FAT?

Caterpillars are tiny when they emerge from the egg and need to grow a lot during this life stage so that's why they're so greedy. They get too fat for their skin so need to shed it and grow a new one four or five times. So, they do get fat, just not in a bad way.

Figure 8.1

Exploring the Roots of the Writing Challenge

An intriguing headline in *The New York Times* caught my eye several years ago. It read, "Story Time, Debunked" (Horowitz and Shea 2012). In it, the journalists, Alexandra Horowitz and Ammon Shea, analyze a few very popular children's books, offering scientific evidence as to whether the events of the stories, all of which have animals as main characters, could have really taken place. For example, we learn that the brown bear in Bill Martin Jr's (1996) *Brown Bear, Brown Bear What Do You See?* is not really capable of seeing the very vivid colors referred to in the tale and that the animal species in Arnold Lobel's (2003) *Frog and Toad Are Friends* would not really coexist as easily as the author suggests. The authors also probed the issue of monkey curiosity inspired by H.A. Rey's (1973) *Curious George* and the ability of pigeons to navigate routes based on Mo Willems's *Don't Let the Pigeon Drive the Bus* (2003). The article pushed me to ask one of my favorite teacher questions, "Could our students do that?" Could our students investigate whether the animals in favorite picture books could engage in the activities contained in the story? As we began this challenge, we realized that the main characters need not be animals and the research need not be limited to animal questions. No matter the characters, the questions that resulted formed the foundation of this writing/research challenge.

Engaging Students in the Challenge

I began this challenge by summarizing the findings of the authors of "Story Time, Debunked" (Horowitz and Shea 2012). Students were able to figure out the meaning of the word *debunked* after I shared what the journalists reported. I then suggested to students that they would all have an opportunity to debunk other children's books. Recently, the *New Yorker* magazine published a cartoon by Pia Guerra and Ian Bothby (2019) that showed a teacher reading aloud to a group of young children and suggesting to them, "Let's save all our questions about the story's veracity until it's over." With a similar thought in mind, I read aloud *Caps for Sale: A Tale of a Peddlar, Some Monkeys and Their Monkey Business,* by Esphyr Slobodkina (1987), a book the third graders knew from their early childhood years in school. After a rich and joyful discussion of this familiar text, I then asked the children if they thought monkeys really do copy humans behavior. In other words, does the old saying "Monkey see, monkey do" ring true? I asked, "Wouldn't it be fun if we took time to research the answer to that question or others posed by other popular picture books?"

Students enjoy listening to one another's ideas, responses, and questions.

To get children totally on board, we filled the classroom with carefully selected books, ones that would most likely inspire readers to ask, "Could it really happen?" Students found out, Esphyr Slobodkina did base the ending of her story on a grain of truth, but not all writers do likewise. We reminded students that authors are free to use poetic license, exaggeration, and their imaginations when they craft fictional picture books. We were preparing students to discover that sometimes the events in a fictional picture book could never really happen in real life. Having said this, we felt obliged to remind students that even though the events might not be able to happen in real life, we still count these books as wonderful works of art. We didn't want our study to detract from their appreciation of literature.

We gathered the following picture books from our school and public library and also borrowed some from colleagues in the lower grades. Students selected a book to read and jotted down their "Could it really happen?" questions. If questions were written in a yes-or-no format, children were encouraged to explain fully. In other words, if a student wanted to answer the question "Do insects bite animals?" a simple yes or no would not give enough information. Instead, the student would be asked to explain fully. If the answer is yes, the student might list which insects bite which animals. The student might also share information about the animals' symptoms, what can be done to help animals that get bitten, and what can be done to prevent animals from getting bitten.

A few books that led to "Could It Really Happen?" questions about animals follow:

> *Norman: One Amazing Goldfish!* by Kelly Bennett (2020): Is it possible for a goldfish to perform? Why or why not?

> *Crocodiles Need Kisses Too* by Rebecca Colby (2020): Do animals show affection? If so, how?

> *How to Heal a Broken Wing* by Bob Graham (2008): Can you really heal a bird's broken wing?

> *Crow and Hawk* by Michael Rosen (1995): Have birds ever hatched eggs belonging to other birds?

> *Red & Lulu* by Matt Taveres (2017): Would a male and a female cardinal search for one another?

> *The Mouse That Snored* by Bernard Waber (2000): Do animals snore?

A few titles that led to "Could It Really Happen?" questions on a wide range of topics follow:

> *Luci Soars* by Lulu Delacre (2020): Is it possible for someone not to have a shadow? Why or why not?

> *The Boy Who Went to Mars* by Simon James (2017): When do scientists expect people to visit Mars?

> *George Shrinks* by William Joyce (1985): Do human beings really shrink?

> *Leo the Late Bloomer* by Robert Kraus (1999): When are children considered to be late bloomers?

> *The Carrot Seed* by Ruth Krauss (1945): How big can a carrot really grow?

> *What Will You Dream of Tonight?* by Frances Stickley (2019): Is it possible to choose, plan, or predict what you will dream about?

> *Pecan Pie Baby* by Jacqueline Woodson (2010): Do pregnant women really have food cravings? If so, why?

My Blue Is Happy by Jessica Young (2013): Do people associate emotions with colors? If so, what colors are connected to which feelings?

(See additional animal and nonanimal titles and questions at the end of this chapter and in bibliography in online Book List 9.)

Some children needed help in formulating a question, and in those cases, we read aloud their picture book to the whole class and students brainstormed possible research questions. We also reminded students that they would need to present a full explanation, not merely a yes-or-no answer to their questions.

Continuing to Support Students' Efforts
Sharing Your Own Writing

We returned to our *Caps for Sale* inquiry. I selected two age-appropriate answers to that question online. I read them aloud, asking students to jot down the parts they thought important. We then turned our notes into the following collaborative passage, which we hoped would serve as a model for future individual investigations.

After reading Esphyr Slobodkina's *Caps for Sale: A Tale of a Peddlar, Some Monkeys and Their Monkey Business*, we wondered if monkeys really do copy human behavior. We researched that topic and discovered that it makes perfect sense that the monkeys threw off their hats when the peddler threw off his. Monkeys do copy human behavior. Researchers found that when they made faces at baby monkeys, including ". . . sticking out their tongues, smacking their lips, and opening and closing their mouths," the monkeys did likewise. Researchers at the University of Nevada also proved that monkeys learn by copying adults when they taught American Sign Language to chimpanzees. There are social reasons for monkeys doing all that copying. Monkeys communicate by copying actions. They imitate one another in order to find food, use tools, and recognize relatives. (Wonderopolis, "Do Monkeys Really Do What They See?" Wonder of the Day # 1299). Gaia Vince (2006), a reporter for *New Scientist* wrote an article titled, "Proved: Monkey See, Monkey Do." She confirmed that monkeys "imitate with a purpose." She reported that newborn rhesus macaques imitate the facial expressions of their mothers for up to two months. This imitation helps develop a healthy relationship between the mother monkey and her infants. The next time you read, *Caps for Sale*, remember that this work of fiction definitely contains some nonfiction information.

Gathering Information

In the days ahead, students researched online using their Chromebooks. We discussed how to go about using approved search engines to find relevant information. I also found it helpful to demonstrate how students might need to alter their questions to find answers. For example, in Mitra Modarressi's (2007) book, *Stay Awake Sally*, the raccoon wants to go to sleep at night and go to school during the day. The student's research question was, "Would a nocturnal animal ever be awake during the day?" We discovered that it was easier to find information when we asked about the specific animal. Using Google, I typed in "Would you ever see a raccoon during the day?" There, we learned that it is a possibility. In fact, we learned that it is a myth that seeing a raccoon during the day means that the animal is sick or has rabies. And the article continued with many reasons why a nocturnal animal might be seen during daylight hours, including finding an available food source, too much competition for food at night, having been frightened away from their daytime sleeping location, or being a mother raccoon hunting for food for her babies. Our student could now write an interesting answer to the question "Would a nocturnal animal ever be awake during the day?" and he could infer that the information applies to other nocturnal animals.

We also discovered, perhaps surprisingly, that sometimes a question could be too specific, and a broader question might lead to some answers. This was true for the student researching the question "Are there crickets that do not make sounds?" after reading Eric Carle's (1990) *The Very Quiet Cricket*. When he typed the more general question "Why do crickets chirp?" into his search engine, he discovered the answer to his question woven into the explanation. The student taught us that not all species of crickets can chirp, and of those that can, only the males chirp. He went on to explain the purpose of chirping. This student's research taught his classmates that you must be willing to read abundant related material to find the answer you are seeking.

Throughout the research phase of this challenge, as well as throughout the others in this book, not only did teachers teach students to modify their questions, they also taught them to use key words, to rely on approved sites, and to pay attention to the reliability of their sources. Of course, they also provided students with practice in taking notes and turning those notes into meaningful passages.

Much of the hunt for answers required students to use the important thinking skill of inferring. The student who read Trinka Hakes Noble's (1992) *The Day Jimmy's Boa Ate the Wash* could not find any information about boas eating fabric, but she could infer from all the information about the dietary habits of boas that they were carnivores interested in devouring opossums, deer, squirrels, bats, tapirs, and caiman and would not be interested in eating laundry hanging on a line. Further reading taught her about how the snake's digestive muscles contract to push the food into the snake's stomach, and she inferred that a boa would be unable to push down a large bedsheet or pillowcase. During this research, the room came alive with active minds, serious intentions, and interesting conversations.

Lifting the Quality of Student Writing

Students drafted, revised, and edited their answers during writing workshop time. The teacher's role was to work the room, helping with research, conferring about content, and noting what minilessons should be taught to the whole class.

Minilessons that were especially needed included how to include sources, how to use direct quotations, and the importance of rereading as you drafted. Although students had watched as we accomplished all three of these goals in our *Caps for Sale* writing, they still needed the skills to be reinforced in subsequent minilessons. In addition, at the beginning of writing workshops, we worked on:

1. the importance of including information that was specific and accurate
2. the need to be fussy about word choice
3. the use of similes to convey difficult concepts
4. the value of varying sentence lengths

Student Writing Samples

Diane Berman's fourth graders eagerly read our stack of picture books and chose to research the answers to some very interesting questions.

After reading Mercer Mayer's (1987) *There's an Alligator Under My Bed*, fourth-grader Miri wondered if alligators could stay alive under a bed. She researched the topic, and her answer appears in Figure 8.2.

> Alligators can't live on land long because the land doesn't have the things alligators need to survive such as small and big fish, turtles, and water insects. Although alligators eat things on land like snails, worms, and mammals, they are more comfortable in the water.
>
> Alligators live in fresh water such as slow moving rivers. Sometimes they even live in swamps, marshes, and lakes. Alligators can tolerate salt water for short periods of time but they don't have salt glands.

Figure 8.2

Tyler and Lincoln read Jessica Young's (2013) *My Blue Is Happy* and investigated whether colors are connected to people's feelings. Their discoveries appear in Figure 8.3.

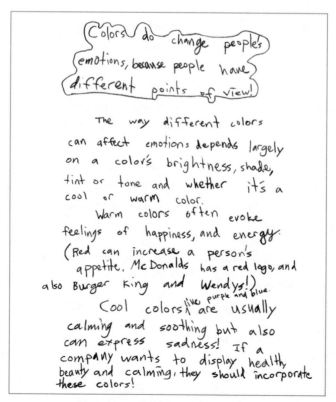

> Colors do change people's emotions, because people have different points of view!
>
> The way different colors can affect emotions depends largely on a color's brightness, shade, tint or tone and whether it's a cool or warm color.
>
> Warm colors often evoke feelings of happiness, and energy. (Red can increase a person's appetite. McDonalds has a red logo, and also Burger King and Wendys!)
>
> Cool colors like purple and blue are usually calming and soothing but also can express sadness! If a company wants to display health, beauty and calming, they should incorporate these colors!

Figure 8.3

Jacqueline Woodson's (2010) picture book *Pecan Pie Baby* inspired Natalia to ask, "Do pregnant women really get food cravings?" Her research answer appears in Figure 8.4.

> Do women really get cravings When they are pregant?
>
> Yes, women do get cravings when they are preganet. People really dont know why. The leading theories suggest that it has something to do with nutrients that you may be lacking. The cravings are your bodys way telling you it needs more nourishment.
>
> But what about those strange food combinations? The reason for this may have to do with hormones. When a woman is pregant, she starts to interpret smells and taste diffrently. While the idea of coco pufs and instant noodles may disgust a woman normally, it can suddenly taste amazing when she becomes pregant.

Figure 8.4

Two fourth graders, both named Charlie, read William Joyce's (1985) *George Shrinks* and wondered if people really do shrink. Their collaboration appears in Figure 8.5.

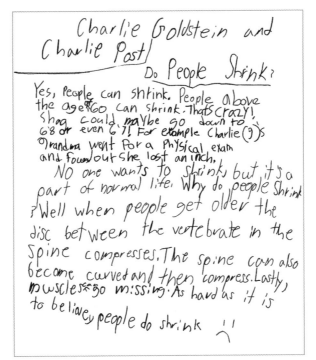

> Charlie Goldstein and Charlie Post
>
> Do People Shrink?
>
> Yes, People can shrink. People above the age of 60 can shrink. Thats crazy! Shaq could maybe go down to 6'8 or even 6'7! For example Charlie (9)s grandma went for a physical exam and found out she lost an inch.
>
> No one wants to shrink but its a part of normal life. Why do people Shrink? Well when people get older the disc between the vertebrate in the spine compresses. The spine can also became curved and then compress. Lastly, muscles go missing. As hard as it is to believe, people do shrink !!

Figure 8.5

Carving Out Time for Celebration

Celebrating a student's hard work could be stretched out over the course of a month with the classroom teacher or the student reading aloud the chosen title. Then the student could share the topic they chose to debunk as well as their findings. For example, a student or teacher could read aloud *The Boy Who Went to Mars* by Simon James (2017) and then pose the question "Do scientists really expect human beings to visit the planet Mars? If so, when? What would the challenges of such a journey be?" Even if the picture book seems intended for younger students, like *The Very Hungry Caterpillar* by Eric Carle (1969), older students usually love hearing familiar texts from their early childhood years and appreciate learning from their classmate's research.

BOOKS NOTED

Bennett, Kelly. 2020. *Norman: One Amazing Goldfish!* Somerville, MA: Candlewick.

Carle, Eric. 1969. *The Very Hungry Caterpillar.* New York: Philomel Books/Penguin Putnam Books for Young Readers.

———. 1990. *The Very Quiet Cricket.* New York: Philomel Books/PenguiPutnam Books for Young Readers.

Colby, Rebecca. 2020. *Crocodiles Need Kisses Too.* New York: Viking.

Delacre, Lulu. 2020. *Luci Soars.* New York: Philomel.

Graham, Bob. 2008. *How to Heal a Broken Wing.* Somerville, MA: Candlewick.

James, Simon. 2017. *The Boy Who Went to Mars.* Somerville, MA: Candlewick.

Joyce, William. 1985. *George Shrinks.* New York: Laura Geringer Books/ HarperCollins.

Kraus, Robert. 1999. *Leo the Late Bloomer.* New York: HarperCollins.

Krauss, Ruth. 1945. *The Carrot Seed.* New York: Harper & Row.

Lobel, Arnold. 2003. *Frog and Toad Are Friends.* New York: HarperCollins.

Martin Jr., Bill. 1996. *Brown Bear, Brown Bear What Do You See?* New York: Henry Holt.

Mayer, Mercer. 1987. *There's an Alligator Under My Bed.* New York: Dial Books for Young Readers/NAL Penguin.

Modarressi, Mitra. 2007. *Stay Awake Sally.* New York: Putnam Juvenile.

Noble, Trinka Hakes. 1992. *The Day Jimmy's Boa Ate the Wash.* New York: Puffin Books.

Rey, H.A. 1973. *Curious George.* Boston, MA: HMH Books for Young Readers.

Rosen, Michael. 1995. *Crow and Hawk.* San Diego: Harcourt Brace.

Slobodkina, Esphyr. 1987. *Caps for Sale: A Tale of a Peddlar, Some Monkeys and Their Monkey Business.* New York: HarperCollins.

Stickley, Frances. 2019. *What Will You Dream of Tonight?* Somerville, MA: Nosy Crow.

Taveres, Matt. 2017. *Red & Lulu.* Somerville, MA: Candlewick.

Waber, Bernard. 2000. *The Mouse That Snored.* Boston, MA: HMH Books for Young Readers.

Willems, Mo. 2003. *Don't Let the Pigeon Drive the Bus.* New York: Hyperion Books for Children/Disney Book Group.

Woodson, Jacqueline. 2010. *Pecan Pie Baby.* New York: G.P. Putnam's Sons/ Penguin Group.

Young, Jessica. 2013. *My Blue Is Happy.* Somerville, MA: Candlewick.

TEACHER REFERENCE MATERIALS

"Do Monkeys Really Do What They See?" wonderopolis.org. Wonder of the Day #1299. https://www. wonderopolis.org/wonder/do-monkeys-really-do-what-they-see/donate

Guerra, Pia, and Ian Bothby. 2019. *The New Yorker* cartoon. July 1.

Horowitz, Alexandra, and Ammon Shea. 2012. "Story Time, Debunked." *The New York Times*. January 1.

Vince, Gaia. 2006. "Proved: Monkey See, Monkey Do." https://newscientist.com/article/dn9916-proved-monkey-see-monkey-do/September 5.

INTERNET SEARCH ENGINES AND RESEARCH SITES FOR CHILDREN

www.kids.nationalgeographic.com

www.kiddle.co

www.wonderopolis.org

www.kidzsearch.com

www.ducksters.com

www.wonderlist.com

www.culturegrams.com/kids

www.natgeokids.com

www.switcheroozoo.com

www.arkive.org

www.zooborns.com

https://pbskids.org/

Students will need a wide range of books and articles to investigate their individual topics.

A FEW TITLES TO ENRICH YOUR TEACHING

Bentley, Tadgh. 2015. *Little Penguin Gets the Hiccups*. New York: Balzer + Bray. (Do animals get hiccups? If so, why and what would they do?)

Boelts, Maribeth. 2020. *Kaia and the Bees*. Somerville, MA: Candlewick. (Would a young child ever be allowed to work as a beekeeper? Why or why not?)

Choi, Susan. 2019. *Camp Tiger*. New York: G.P. Putnam's Sons. (Are wild animals ever domesticated?)

James, Simon. 2017. *Frog and Beaver*. Somerville, MA: Candlewick. (Would a beaver ever help other animals build homes? Why or why not?)

Johnson, Angela. 2004. *Violet's Music*. New York: Dial. (Can babies show a talent for music? Is musical ability inherited?)

Kang, Anna. 2016. *Can I Tell You a Secret?* New York: HarperCollins. (Would a frog ever be afraid of water? Why or why not?)

Lim, Hope. 2021. *I Am a Bird*. Somerville, MA: Candlewick. (Can people attract birds by making bird sounds?)

Nyeu, Tao. 2012. *Squid and Octopus: Friends for Always*. New York: Dial Books for Young Readers. (Would a squid and an octopus ever be alongside one another? Why or why not?)

Pignataro, Anna. 2018. *The Heart of a Whale*. New York: Philomel. (Do whales sing to attract a mate?)

Robbins, Jacqui. 2006. *The New Girl*. New York: Richard Jackson. (Are iguanas kept as pets?)

See also online Book List 9.

PART THREE

ORIGINAL AND HIGH QUALITY

· · · · · · · · · · · · · · · · · · · ·

The writing challenges presented in the pages that follow all remind students that their writing can be bold and memorable. Students learn that they can carve out fresh ways to look at their topics. They learn that they can craft lines that move their audience. They learn that they can design new and surprising formats to deliver their thoughts.

CHAPTER 9
Just for a Day
Writing

(Grades 2-5)

Dalia, the third grader who graces the cover of this book and a student in Renay Sadis's class at P.S. 87, imagined what it would be like to be an ornithologist studying birds in Central Park, just for one day. See Figure 9.1.

Name Dalia   Date___
A Day in the Life of an Ornithologist

Introduction: It's a bright summer day and the sun is beaming through your windows. You hitch up your overalls, eat your fill and leave. Your binoculars are gleaming in the brightness. You hurry to Central Park. After a nice stroll, you find what you're looking for. A Cuckoo in a Wren's nest!

The Cookoo is getting all the food because it is the biggest. It's mother Cookoo put it in a wren's nest because she could not care for her young. When it hatched the Cookoo tossed out all the other eggs. The poor mother and father wren couldn't have any more fledglings because the Cookoo always demanded food. You take the Cookoo under your arm. You will care for it in the lab. One mission done! After you drop the the Cookoo of at the Cornell Lab of Ornithology, you keep birdwatching. Now that it is summer, a ruby throated humming bird in drinking nectar. You know the hummingbird in tired because she is traveling from Canada to Mexico 600 days journey!

Tasty! While you eat your lunch, so does a kingfisher. He flies off his waiting post to catch some dragonflies. His iridescent blue feathers are gleaming behind him in the bright sunlight at noon. Click! Your camera does it's work as a Rock Dove flies by and grabs your tuna sandwich!

At 1:00, you see a pack of hungry vultures searching for their next bloody treat. They look upset because even their excellent eyesight cannot spot any dead animals. You walk away quickly. You DO NOT want to fall prey to the vultures.

Name Dalia   Date___
A Day in the Life of an Ornithologist

Then you go to the lake. A grey heron is silently creeping up on a poor little frog. You stare at them both as the frog goes inside the heron's long beak. You are not suprised. You know that grey herons are superb predator and that they creep silently before the big attack. What suprises you is something else you're seeing. You know Mandrin (MAN-DER-IN) Wood Ducks are only found in Asie. The Cornell Lab has to see that! When you walk away from the lake, your last glimse of a lake bird today is a beautiful male trumpet swan with lovely white feathers. You write down in your notebook." 2:30 "I just saw a trumpet swan. Swans have over 26,000 feathers. They are very beautiful birds."

Then, you close the notebook walk away.   You hear a pretty song. It is two male song thrushes in a singing competition. Their lovely voices enchant you to no end. Too bad you're not a female wood thrush. Dusk is almost over.

You see streetlights not too far away, and decide to end your day. As you walk out of the park, a flock of pigeons (otherwise known as Rock Doves) surround you. But when a child drops a piece of bread, they run to the sight Racing each other by and by.

Conclusion: Back at your house, you sit by the fire place and rest. Warmth, and heat surround your body and mind. As you close your eyes, the alarm clock rings. It's already morning and time for another birdwatching day!

Figure 9.1

Exploring the Roots of the Writing Challenge

In this challenge, young writers imagine one day in the life of a person connected to an area of their interest. I have seen teachers invite students to walk a mile in someone's else's shoes as part of a whole-class study; for example, when studying China, a teacher might suggest, "Imagine you wake up and you are a child living in China." On the other hand, teachers might invite students to do totally independent and individual studies without any overarching theme. Many authors use this slice-of-life format to share information about daily life in different time periods, in different cultures or to imagine a day in the life of a person with an interesting job. (See bibliography at the end of this chapter and in online Book List 10.) What adds a literary element to this challenge is a study of Joanne Ryder's Just for a Day books. The books in this series have very distinctive features that facilitate Ryder becoming an unwitting collaborator with young writers. If the Joanne Ryder books are hard to track down, Kelly Cunnane's beautifully crafted books *For You Are a Kenyan Child* (2006) and *Deep in the Sahara* (2013) would be just as effective. So, too, teachers who write their own "Just for a Day . . ." tales would serve as powerful mentors.

Ryder relies on this "day in the life of" structure, but her subjects are animals. The books in this imaginative series all begin with a child turning into an animal, and then the author describes a day in that animal's life. Ryder's books, however, have several unique elements that young writers can try on for size. Her features are easy to notice and to name. They are described next.

Engaging Students in the Challenge

We began this challenge in Renay's grade 3 classroom by reading aloud several of the books in this series and discussing the rich and intriguing contents. Later, we reread them to notice and name her distinctive and effective writing techniques. (Note, we did have to obtain several titles from the public library as this series is unfortunately out of print.) Working together, we discovered that Joanne Ryder's Just for a Day books contained several elements that cut across all the books. Our list follows:

Third grader receiving feedback on his draft.

1. Opening pages often begin with a description of that day's weather, as in "One chilly morning" or "One bright morning."

2. Books usually open with a child in bed who is about to magically become an animal.

3. Books are written in direct address as author is talking directly to the child turned animal. Pages are therefore filled with the words *you* and *your*.

4. Pages are packed with specific and accurate bits of information, teaching the reader a great deal about the highlighted animal.

5. Child-friendly similes abound. For example, in *Lizard in the Sun*, Joanne Ryder (1990) writes, "You are a lizard, small and thin, as light as a pencil, as light as a handful of popcorn."

6. The author uses lots of repetition to emphasize important ideas. For example, in *Lizard in the Sun*, the author repeats the phrase, "You are lean and green" several times throughout the book.

7. The author uses rich sensory details and onomatopoeia to make the readers feel like they have entered the setting and are going through the experiences described.

8. The books are filled with precise verbs, offering lots of information to the reader. For example, *Lizard in the Sun* boasts such strong action words as *wiggle*, *cling*, *dash*, and *bob*.

9. Events take place over just one day, frequently ending with the animal turning back into the child who is comfortable once again in his or her own bed. (Although most teachers frown on what is often called "bed-to-bed," stories, Joanne Ryder makes this structure work brilliantly to bring closure to her tales.)

Note that the Kelly Cunnane texts are similarly written in direct address, are rich in sensory details, contain repetition of important phrases, include effective similes, and have specific bits of information woven in. *For You Are a Kenyan Child* is studded with words and phrases in Swahili. *Deep in the Sahara* explores family customs in Mauritania.

After thoroughly exploring the Just for a Day series, we announced to the young students that they would have time to craft their own version of Just for a Day writing. Even though Ryder's books focused on animals, we were clear that students did *not* have to choose an animal to study. We also did not attempt to connect the writing to any content-area theme. The choice of topic was therefore wide open for students. We suggested that they think of topics they were interested in and what kind of work an expert in that field would do. In addition, we informed students that they would not have to morph into that worker when they awoke in the morning, but could just talk directly to that person, taking them through a typical day in their life.

Continuing to Support Students' Efforts
Sharing Your Own Writing

It was clear that students needed us to present an exemplar so they could picture where this challenge was heading. I suggested to the third graders in Renay's class that I thought their teacher could imagine being a car salesperson for a day, especially for Mini Coopers as she loves cars and owns one of those easy-to-park-in-Manhattan vehicles. Or, I continued, she could spend a day as a tour guide in Tel Aviv, Israel, because Renay had lived there for several years, working as a principal at an American international school. Then, too, she could pretend to be a member of the Grateful Dead, as she has long been a fan of that classic rock band. Next, I asked Renay to prove she was an expert on these topics by sharing some specific bits of information that she could weave into her narrative to teach us about her topics. We learned that the Mini Cooper can have a convertible top, a six-speed transmission, and all-wheel drive. We learned that local Israelis love to kayak, picnic, and celebrate their birthdays in Park Hayarkon. And we learned that fans of the Grateful Dead, called Deadheads, enjoy wearing tie-dyed clothing, decorated with dancing bears and skulls with roses. I pointed out that the specificity and accuracy of Renay's details proved she was on her way to becoming an authority on her topics. Of course, to fill out her narratives, she would have to do research, just as the students would have to do.

I then shared my intention to write about famous sites in New York City by imagining a day in the life of a tour guide. I explained that my choice was based on my love of Manhattan and all the amazing sites that brought tourists to our city. I also informed students that my experiences in New York as well as my research helped me decide which tourist sites to include. My Just for a Day writing follows:

> One bright summer day, you wake up early and quickly get dressed, slipping on your red blazer, the one with the Big Apple Tour logo on the pocket. You hail a taxi and ask to be dropped off at the corner of 49th and 6th Avenue. Before boarding the double-decker bus, you stop to buy a large container of coffee and a buttery croissant from the vendor on the corner. You greet the bus driver, sip your coffee, and check the microphone. Fifteen minutes later, tourists start to board the bus. You welcome all of them, take their tickets, and review your plans for today's tour. You are as eager to get started as a beaver building a dam. Finally, the driver turns the key and pulls the big bus into the lane of traffic. Your day as a New York City tour guide has begun.
>
> "First stop," you announce to the tourists, "is the Empire State Building on Fifth Avenue, between 33rd and 34th streets. Even if you have never visited this famous and popular architectural masterpiece, I am sure you have seen it as it has shown up in over 250 television shows and movies. Most of you will remember it from the movie *King Kong*. The building is named after our New York City nickname, the Empire State. There are 102 stories with observation decks on the 86th floor and the 102nd. It is an Art Deco structure that attracts over 4 million tourists every year. If you come back to see the city from one of these observation decks, be prepared for the space to be as crowded as Times Square on New Year's Eve. Okay, get your cameras ready to see one of the Seven Wonders of the Modern World.
>
> "Now we will drive East, and our next stop will be the famous Chrysler Building on the corner of Lexington and 42nd street. This is another example of Art Deco architecture. We will disembark the bus this time to visit the lobby of the building, which was completed in 1931." When you enter the lobby, you explain to the tourists that "this building used to be the home of the Chrysler car company. That's why the murals on the ceiling tell the story of the invention of transportation." You suggest the tourists touch the wall as it is covered with African marble.

You travel further East and point out the United Nations located on the East River between 42nd and 48th streets in the neighborhood known as Turtle Bay. "The United Nations," you announce, "is an international organization with 193 members. The complex was begun in 1945 at the end of World War II and completed in 1952. It is made up of 5 buildings. Four are right here in New York City—the General Assembly, the Security Council, the Economic and Social Council, and the UN Secretariat. The 39-story glass skyscraper known as the Secretariat has become a symbol of the United Nations throughout the world. The fifth part of the United Nations is the International Court of Justice, which is located at The Hague, a city in the Netherlands in Europe. The mission of the U.N. is to keep international peace, promote friendship between countries, protect human rights, and provide humanitarian aid." After tourists snap a few photos, you suggest they return to the U.N. one day to visit the gardens and the beautiful sculptures throughout the grounds.

You ask the driver to head North to Museum Mile where you point out a string of famous New York City museums. You say to the visitors, "If you have free time during your stay in our city be sure and tour the Metropolitan Museum of Art, the Solomon R. Guggenheim Museum, the Jewish Museum, the Cooper–Hewitt National Museum of Design, the Museo del Barrio, and the Museum of the City of New York." You hear the oohs and aahs of the passengers as you pass each famous cultural site.

Then you continue North, showing off the major sites in Harlem including the Apollo Theater, the Abyssinian Baptist Church, the Schomburg Center for Research in Black Culture, and the Studio Museum in Harlem.

As you travel, the tourists ask you if the city traffic is always so noisy. They have noticed that the air is filled with the honking of horns, the screeching of sirens, the vroom, vroom of delivery trucks, and the blasting of jackhammers at construction sites.

Your hungry tourists are now ready for refreshments and are thrilled that you are taking them to Sylvia's Restaurant, a highlight of Harlem and this tour. Sylvia is known as the Queen of Soul Food. You recommend the smothered chicken, the grilled catfish, or the bar-b-que ribs with Sylvia's original sassy sauce. For sides you describe the mouth-watering collard greens, candied yams, and black-eyed peas. You end your recommendations by suggesting that they share desserts as they will be very full. You tell the tourists to "Order coconut cake, sweet potato pie, or banana pudding with a few forks."

On the way downtown you pass through the Broadway theater district, the Chelsea neighborhood, and on to Greenwich Village. The tourists loved seeing Washington Square Park and the famous Arch. They also want you to talk about New York University, the Stonewall Inn, and the opening of the new downtown Whitney Museum of Art. After that, you point out the highlights in Little Italy and Chinatown, especially the unusual shops and tasty restaurants.

Before ending your full-day tour and returning to 49th St., you answer any additional questions and offer dinner recommendations to the tourists.

At the end of the day you feel exhausted, but proud of your work and proud of the city you call home. You grab a taxi back to your apartment, order a cheese pizza from the local Italian restaurant, and fall asleep reading up on the Highline, another popular tourist attraction you'll be visiting tomorrow.

To get a handle on students' ideas for their writing to come, we asked students to sign up for a topic and whose day in the life they would imagine. Most selections were attached to the students' hobbies, collections, and other personal interests. These included:

martial arts—sensei

Mount Everest—mountain climber

Germany—tourist

cats—veterinarian

butterflies—entomologist

White House—president

braces—orthodontist

tornadoes—weather forecaster

the Olympics—gold medal winner

origami—Japanese art expert

birds—ornithologist

wolves—zoologist

Several children needed assistance in deciding on the expert that would be knowledgeable about their area of interest. Some students began *not* with a topic but with a job held by someone in their family. Students who struggled to come up with a topic of interest can be prompted by looking at the cover of Lucy Cousins's (2017) picture book *Hooray for Birds!* Teachers need only ask, "What would you say hurray for?" And then, "What worker is connected to that topic?" Teachers can also show the cover of Chris Butterworth's (2018) *The Things I Love About Trees*, asking students, "How would you fill in the blank: The things I love about _____? What topic do you care so much about that you could complete that title with your own interest?" This question could be followed by "What worker knows that subject best?"

Gathering Information

Once students commit to a topic, they need to gather information. We asked students to jot down their research needs and what resources they might tap. We encouraged them to read books, visit helpful sites, and reach out to experts in the field. Of course, we helped them gather resources, posting their topics throughout the school community.

Lifting the Quality of Student Writing

Once students began gathering information, we asked them to think about a structure for delivering a typical day in the life of that person. Just as I chose making stops on a double-decker tour bus to present the information on NYC sightseeing, they would have to think about a structure/device that would allow them to present information about their worker's area of expertise. Students added an organizational structure to their topic/expert sign-up sheet. These included a cardiologist's appointments during the day, an egg farmer's series of daily chores, and an entomologist's butterfly presentations to students on a school visit.

As expected, several students needed support in choosing an organizing structure that would allow them to present specific information to their readers. We helped students find additional information about that worker, searching for what typically filled their days—appointments, scheduled visits, performances, phone calls, letter writing, chores, meetings, classes to teach, and so on.

Then it was time to give students an image of where they might be headed, so that they would remember to seek very specific bits of information as they continued their research. Weaving in accurate information would prove to their readers that they had become authorities on their chosen topic and on their chosen occupation. We talked about the kinds of information that would prove knowledge of a worker's life. These include tucking in the workers' tools, materials, or supplies as well as details that presented their work setting, the clothing they wear, any specialized vocabulary used, kinds of coworkers, and possible accomplishments in any one day.

I then stressed the importance of crafting an engaging lead. I was thrilled to find a *New York Times* article entitled "A Day in the Weather Room, Catching Storms on the Horizon," written by Alan Blinder (2019). Not only does the journalist follow a day in the life of meteorologists in Norman, Oklahoma, he offers a lead (*lede* to journalists) worth sharing with children. It reads, "The atmosphere was in turmoil before sunrise one day last week, and more than 58 million people were at risk." Who could resist continuing to read this intriguing opening?

To inspire and inform students, I shared my process of creating a lead for my NYC tourist guide narration. I informed students that I reread the opening pages of Joanne Ryder's *Just for a Day* books to remind me to use direct address.

I showed students how I had experimented with beginning at different points in time. (I reminded students that I need not physically change my body into that of a tour guide as Joanne Ryder morphs children into animals.)

I explain to students that I finally decided on the last lead as rain in the first lead would make the tour more difficult and leading a tour for the very first time might not be that successful. (See possible leads on page 112.) Students reread my entire piece and noticed my attempts to borrow several Ryder techniques. Their collaboratively created list follows:

The opening lines mention the weather and the start of the day.

The piece is written in direct address.

Several lines are rich in sensory detail.

The similes were understandable and made the meaning clear.

There was some onomatopoeia.

The piece was filled with specific and accurate bits of information.

There are several examples of the power of three.

The narration ends with the close of the day.

> ## POSSIBLE LEADS FOR
> ## A DAY IN THE LIFE OF A NYC TOUR GUIDE
>
> Your alarm clock goes off. It's 6 a.m. You awake to the sound of rain tapping on your windowpane. You realize your day is going to be very hard. You are a tour guide, and holding an umbrella and pointing out sites to enthusiastic tourists becomes extra hard on a stormy day.
>
> You have just passed the test and are now a licensed tour guide in the city of New York, and you are eager to begin your new job. You enter the office of the Big Apple Tour Company, hopefully ready to handle your first assignment. Your boss asks you to lead a walking tour of Lower Manhattan. You meet a group of 10 tourists on the corner of 14th Street and 6th Avenue. You greet the visitors and check to see if they have good walking shoes, sunscreen, and cameras. You distribute guide maps and your walk begins.
>
> One bright summer day, you wake up early and quickly get dressed, slipping on your red blazer, the one with the Big Apple Tour logo on the pocket. You hail a taxi and ask to be dropped off at the corner of 49th and 6th Avenue.

I invited students to respond to my weaknesses as well as what they saw as strengths. I encouraged them to make suggestions, note gaps, and suggest revisions. Above all, the young writers thought I could have chosen more precise verbs.

Throughout this challenge (and all the others in this book), we shared information about the tools that are in a writer's toolbox. To do so, I usually read aloud beautifully crafted texts. In addition to the Ryder titles, a few picture books that are worthy of returning to repeatedly include:

Sneed B. Collard's III's Most Fun Book Ever About Lizards by Sneed B. Collard III (2012)

Monet Paints a Day by Julie Dannenberg (2012)

Tracks of a Panda by Nick Dowson (2007)

The Everlasting Embrace by Gabrielle Emanuel (2014)

Imagine by Juan Felipe Herrera (2018)

My Island Grandma by Kathryn Lasky (1993)

The Cat Man of Aleppo by Irene Latham and Karim Shamsi-Basha (2020)

A Ruined House by Mick Manning (1994)

Butterfly Tree by Sandra Markle (2011)

Come to the Ocean's Edge: A Nature Cycle Book by Laurence Pringle (2003)

Feathers: Not Just for Flying by Melissa Stewart (2014)

Steady Hands: Poems About Work by Tracie Vaughn Zimmer (2009)

Once students had gathered enough information to describe a day in the life of *their* chosen worker, it was time for them to begin drafting their own Just for a Day narratives. We challenged them to create beginnings as inviting as Joanne Ryders's opening pages. We also reminded them to experiment with direct address.

Krystal Mitchell, then a grade two teacher at Dows Lane Elementary School, prepared a worksheet for students to experiment with leads. Eva researched a day in the life of a butterfly expert. See Figure 9.2 for her attempts.

Once students were satisfied with their leads, our minilessons and conferences focused on weaving in bits of specific and accurate information as the workers went through their days. The organizing device or structure they chose helped the young writers stick to the chronology of their workdays. Many students came to rely on transition words that showed that time was passing as they moved through the day (*after that, following this, next, soon, finally,* and so on).

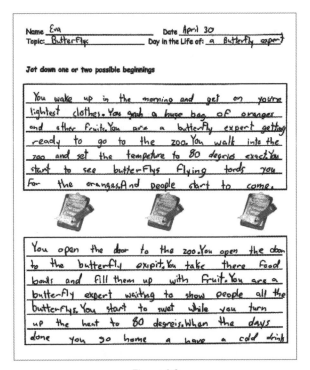

Figure 9.2

Student Writing Samples

My granddaughter Andie, then a second grader in Krystal Mitchell's class, researched what life might be like for a NASA worker on Take Your Daughter to Work Day. Her piece, "Rings in Rotation," appears in Figure 9.3.

Figure 9.3

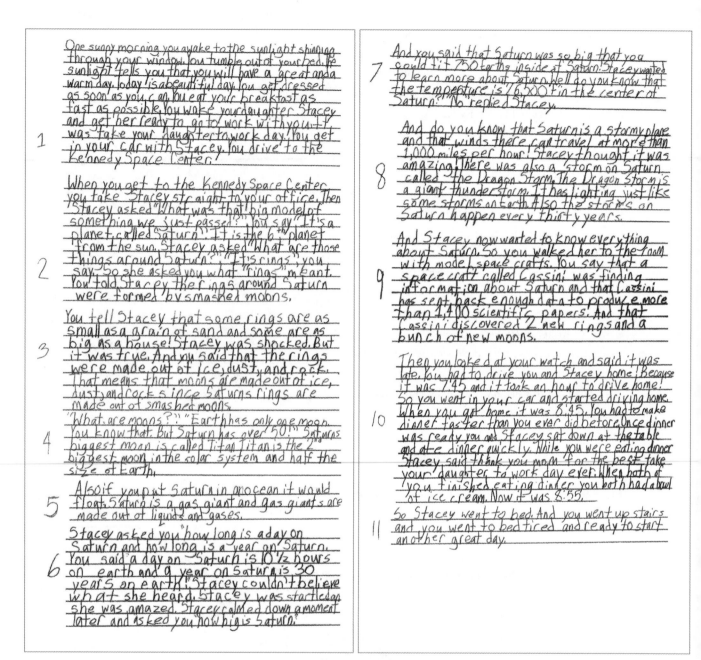

1 One sunny morning you awake to the sunlight shining through your window. You tumble out of your bed. The sunlight tells you that you will have a great and a warm day. Today is a beautiful day. You get dressed as soon as you can. You eat your breakfast as fast as possible. You woke your daughter Stacey and get her ready to go to work with you. It was take your daughter to work day. You get in your car with Stacey. You drive to the Kennedy Space Center.

2 When you get to the Kennedy Space Center you take Stacey straight to your office. Then Stacey asked "What was that big model of something we just passed?" You say "It's a planet called Saturn." It is the 6th planet from the sun. Stacey asked "What are those things around Saturn?" "It is rings," you say. So she asked you what "rings" meant. You told Stacey the rings around Saturn were formed by smashed moons.

3 You tell Stacey that some rings are as small as a grain of sand and some are as big as a house! Stacey was shocked. But it was true. And you said that the rings were made out of ice, dust, and rock. That means that moons are made out of ice, dust, and rock since Saturns rings are made out of smashed moons.

4 "What are moons?" "Earth has only one moon. You know that. But Saturn has over 50!" Saturns biggest moon is called Titan. Titan is the 2nd biggest moon in the solar system and half the size of Earth.

5 Also if you put Saturn in an ocean it would float. Saturn is a gas giant and gas giants are made out of liquids and gases.

6 Stacey asked you "how long is a day on Saturn and how long is a year on Saturn. You said a day on Saturn is 10 ½ hours on earth and a year on Saturn is 30 years on earth!" Stacey couldn't believe what she heard. Stacey was startled and she was amazed. Stacey calmed down a moment later and asked you "how big is Saturn?"

7 And you said that Saturn was so big that you could fit 750 earths inside of Saturn! Stacey wanted to learn more about Saturn. Well do you know that the temperature is 16,500°F in the center of Saturn." "No" replied Stacey.

8 And do you know that Saturn is a stormy plane and that winds there can travel at more than 1,000 miles per hour! Stacey thought it was amazing. There was also a storm on Saturn called the Dragon Storm. The Dragon Storm is a giant thunderstorm. It has lighting just like some storms on earth. Also the storms on Saturn happen every thirty years.

9 And Stacey now wanted to know everything about Saturn. So you walked her to the room with model space crafts. You say that a space craft called Cassini was finding information about Saturn and that Cassini has sent back enough data to produce more than 1,400 scientific papers. And that Cassini discovered 2 new rings and a bunch of new moons.

10 Then you looked at your watch and said it was late. You had to drive you and Stacey home. Because it was 7:45 and it took an hour to drive home! So you went in your car and started driving home. When you got home it was 8:45. You had to make dinner faster than you ever did before. Once dinner was ready you and Stacey sat down at the table and ate dinner quickly. While you were eating dinner Stacey said thank you mom for the best take your daughter to work day ever. When both of you finished eating dinner you both had a bowl of ice cream. Now it was 8:55.

11 So Stacey went to bed. And you went upstairs and you went to bed tired and ready to start another great day.

Figure 9.3, *continued*

Quin, a student in Renay's third-grade class at P.S. 87, took on the role of a zoologist studying wolves. Unfortunately, the coronavirus pandemic closed the school, and Quin didn't have an opportunity to complete his suspenseful narrative. See Figure 9.4.

Name _Quin_____   Date_____

~~░░░░░░░░░░░~~ Tracking The Trackers_____

Introduction: You hear a faint howl in the distance that wakes you up. You slide out of bed, pull on your muddy outfit, grab a stack of crackers, your pencil, and your notebook, and rush out the door of your small wooden cottage. You zip through the wood and hear a rustling sound. You peer through the bushes to see what it is with your hopes high. And it is what you're looking for. A wolf. You are a zoologist ready for a long day of tracking and recording.

Then you see more wolves slyly walking out of the bushes around the first one you saw. You write down in your notebook who you think the alpha male and female are, how many members of the pack there are and that you wonder where the den is. You look up and to answer your question you see the alpha female climbing out of a rock formation and pups following.

She is a majestic, large wolf, her ears, and tail high, like ~~three~~ skyscrapers. They see a squirrel climbing around the tree next to the bush you are hiding behind. They rush over but one of the (gaurd) wolves sees a tiny bit of your notebook. and snatches it out of your hand! After realizing it's not food, he or she (you cannot tell it's gender from your current perspective.) tosses it to the pups. You watch upset as a large percodian of your work is ripped up by the little rascles.

Then you are snapped out of your distraction by the Alpha Male. letting out an earsplitting howl to siglal to his packmates it is time to hunt. Everything after that is a flash. you remember that you're on Planet Earth but at that exact ~~motion~~ you trip over a tree root and go flying forwards. You are slammed into a tree a few feet away. Then everyth goes black.

When you come to, you look at your watch to see the time. Unfortunately, it had been broken when you fell. You suddenly had a rush of memories. You were running with the wolf pack when you fell. The wolves had taken you in and draged you back to the den!

Figure 9.4

Carving Out Time for Celebration

Students proudly shared their finished work at a classroom family celebration. If teachers can carve out additional time and have technological know-how or support, this challenge lends itself especially well to slide-show presentations. Students can use visual documentation as they take their audience through the worker's day. How powerful it would be to see photographs of origami constructions, tourist sites in Germany, or the Oval Office, Blue Room, and State Dining Room as the president escorts us through the White House.

BOOKS NOTED

Butterworth, Chris. 2018. *The Things I Love About Trees.* Somerville, MA: Candlewick.

Cousins, Lucy. 2017. *Hooray for Birds!* Somerville, MA: Candlewick.

Ryder, Joanne. 1993. *Sea Elf.* New York: HarperCollins.

————. 1994. *Winter Whale.* New York: Morrow Junior Books.

————. 1996. *Jaguar in the Rain Forest.* New York: HarperCollins.

————. 1989. *Catching the Wind.* New York: HarperCollins.

————. 1989. *White Bear, Ice Bear.* New York: Morrow Junior Books.

————. 1990. *Lizard in the Sun.* New York: Morrow Junior Books.

————. 1997. *Shark in the Sea.* New York: Morrow Junior Books.

————. 1999. *Tyrannosaurus Time.* New York: Morrow Junior Books.

Cunnane, Kelly. 2006. *For You Are a Kenyan Child.* New York: Atheneum.

————. 2013. *Deep in the Sahara.* New York: Schwartz & Wade.

TEXTS USED TO STUDY WRITING TECHNIQUES

Collard III, Sneed B. 2012. *Sneed B. Collard's 111's Most Fun Book Ever About Lizards.* Watertown, MA: Charlesbridge.

Dannenberg, Julie. 2012. *Monet Paints a Day.* Watertown, MA: Charlesbridge.

Dowson, Nick. 2007. *Tracks of a Panda.* Somerville, MA: Candlewick.

Emanuel, Gabrielle. 2014. *The Everlasting Embrace.* New York: Viking.

Herrera, Juan Felipe. 2018. *Imagine.* Somerville, MA: Candlewick.

Lasky, Kathryn. 1993. *My Island Grandma.* New York: William Morrow Co.

Latham, Irene, and Karim Shamsi-Basha. 2020. *The Cat Man of Aleppo.* New York: G.P. Putnam's Sons.

Manning, Mick. 1994. *A Ruined House.* Cambridge, MA: Candlewick.

Markle, Sandra. 2011. *Butterfly Tree.* Atlanta, GA: Peachtree.

Pringle, Laurence. 2003. *Come to the Ocean's Edge: A Nature Cycle Book:* Honesdale, PA: Boyds Mills.

Stewart, Melissa. 2014. *Feathers: Not Just for Flying.* Watertown, MA: Charlesbridge.

Zimmer, Tracie Vaughn. 2009. *Steady Hands: Poems About Work.* New York: Clarion Books/Houghton Mifflin Harcourt Publishing.

TEACHER REFERENCE MATERIAL

Blinder, Alan. 2019. "A Day in the Weather Room, Catching Storms on the Horizon." *The New York Times.* April 22.

A FEW TITLES TO ENRICH YOUR TEACHING

Alatalo, Joako. 2011. *Ilna-Marja's Day: From Dawn to Dusk in a Lapp Village.* London: Frances Lincoln Children's Books.

Brett, Anna. 2020. *World's Coolest Jobs: Discover 40 Awesome Careers.* Franklin, TN: Lonely Planet.

Campbell, Nicola I. 2017. *A Day with Yayah.* Northampton, MA: Crocodile Books.

Charles, Tami. 2021. *My Day with Panye.* Somerville, MA: Candlewick.

Cusolito, Michelle. 2018. *Flying Deep: Climb Inside Deep-Sea Submersible ALVIN.* Watertown, MA: Charlesbridge.

King, Dedie. 2019. *I See the Sun in India.* Hardwick, MA: Satya House.

————. 2020. *I See the Sun in Botswana.* Hardwick, MA: Satya House.

Kurtz, Kevin. 2007. *A Day in the Salt Marsh.* Mount Pleasant, SC: Arbordale.

————. 2010. *A Day on the Mountain.* Mount Pleasant, SC: Arbordale.

————. 2013. *A Day in the Deep.* Mount Pleasant, SC: Arbordale.

————. 2018. *A Day in the Forest Wetland.* Mount Pleasant, SC: Arbordale.

Lasky, Kathryn. 2009. *Georgia Rises: A Day in the Life of Georgia O'Keefe.* New York: Melanie Kroupa Books.

Roman, Carole P. 2017. *If You Were Me and Lived in Scotland: A Child's Introduction to Cultures Around the World.* North Charleston, SC: Create Space Independent Publisher. (series)

See additional materials in online Book List 10.

CHAPTER 10
Doing What the Animals Do
(Grades 1-3)

Adam, a student in Delia Marshall's first-grade class at P.S. 87, writes about peregrine falcons. See Figure 10.1.

Do you live with your mom and dad?

Peregrine Falcons do, too!

Peregrine Falcons take care of ther babys. The babys are born and the Peregrines sit on them. Wen they are ten days old they drop a animal so the babys will fly out of the nest to try to kach it. so they can lern to fly. They lay 2 to 4 eggs at a time. Thay are white and rlufe.

Figure 10.1

Exploring the Roots of the Writing Challenge

I had been talking to my friend and colleague Andrea Lowenkopf about a wonderful picture book I had discovered titled *Animals Do, Too! How They Behave Just Like You* written by Etta Kaner (2017). I told her that I wondered if young children would be interested in studying how animal behavior can be very similar to human behavior. A few days later, she sent me an email suggesting I listen to a podcast that addresses the question "What is unique about human beings?" One of the speakers, Princeton sociologist Dalton Conley, suggested, "The answer is absolutely nothing. One by one, the supposed attributes that we had thought were unique to humans have been shown to be present in other species. Crows use tools. Elephants can recognize themselves in a mirror. Whales form social networks of the same size and complexity as we do. Penguins mourn their dead. Gibbons are monogamous. Bonobos are polyamorous. Ducks rape. Chimpanzees deploy slaves. Velvet spiders commit suicide. Dolphins have language." Although I wouldn't share all these discoveries with young children, I was more convinced than ever that students would find this topic fascinating. This challenge taps into the notion that the activities of humans and animals overlap more than we realize.

Engaging Students in the Challenge

When I first read *Animals Do, Too! How They Behave Just Like You* by Etta Kaner (2017), I knew it would be a well-received read-aloud in any early childhood classroom. After all, the book is interactive, asking students to answer the kind of questions most children enjoy answering, beginning with "Do you like to dance?" and "Do you like to play tag?" The book is filled with surprising information about a favorite topic of most children—animals. The full-page, double-spread illustrations are appealing, as are the back pages containing additional information about honeybees, gazelles, cattle egrets, leaf-cutter ants, flamingos, marmosets, and gray tree frogs. The book promotes rich discussions about each of these intriguing animals and led us to talk about other activities carried out by animals and humans alike. Children were eager to tell stories about their own pets who liked such human activities as taking a bath, eating chicken, or listening to music.

Young writers searching for information together.

If this Kaner book is not available, the same message can be delivered by sharing her books with such intriguing titles as *Have You Ever Seen a Hippo with Sunscreen?* (2010a), *Have You Ever Seen a Duck in a Raincoat?* (2009a), *Have You Ever Seen a Stork Build a Log Cabin?* (2010b), and *Do Frogs Drink Hot Chocolate? How Animals Keep Warm* (2018). In addition, the following titles will come in handy: *Animal Dads* by Sneed Collard III (1997), *Bugs Don't Hug: Six-Legged Parents and Their Kids* by Heather L. Montgomery (2018), or *Eat Like a Bear* by April Pulley Sayre (2013). The book *If You Were a Penguin* by Wendell and Florence Minor (2009) (highlighted in the Imagine If You Were . . . challenge on page 126) ends with the thought that children and penguins have a lot in common. This book would also serve to kick off this writing challenge as it also begs the question "What do we do that animals do too?"

I then introduced the challenge that awaited the students. Just like the authors we read, we would also write about things that both humans and animals do. I asked, "Can you think of any other things that both animals and humans do?" Young children's initial responses are often rather general like, "We both eat." That's prime time to remind children to be more specific. It's an important writing lesson to ask, "What animal are you referring to? What food are you referring to?" I then suggest that "Do you like to eat shrimp? Flamingos do, too," would be more specific.

Continuing to Support Students' Efforts
Sharing Your Own Writing

Rather than share my own writing, I shared my own reading. To be more precise, I shared my own fascination and sense of awe at what I had read about animals doing what humans do. I told the first graders that I had recently read in the newspaper that dolphins have their own language, that elephants recognize themselves in a mirror, and that chimps want other chimps to be treated fairly. I explained to the students how surprised I continue to be when I learn that animals share so many human behaviors and feelings. I added that I know that I will be just as surprised when I learn from their discoveries.

Gathering Information

I heard Jane Goodall, one of the most famous animal researchers in the world, interviewed on CNN and she said, "When you're studying animals, you must have patience." I would add that when you are a young student reading about, researching, and writing about animals, you must also have patience. It took a lot of browsing for students to discover things that animals like to do that humans do as well. Many animal/human overlap discoveries were made when students were invited to flip pages, read captions under photographs, use tables of contents, confer with a classmate, and so on. Real research can't be rushed. We surrounded students with a rich library of animal resources, and they discovered that animals are able to do many activities that humans do as well. These included:

drinking cool water	*sunbathing*
taking long naps	*pretending to be asleep*
eating salad	*making funny noises*
playing in the snow	*eating corn on the cob*
fussing about food	*play-fighting*
playing with brothers and sisters	*sticking out tongues*

When asked to finalize their choices, first graders shared a wide range of opening questions and responses. They appear below.

STUDENT QUESTIONS AND RESPONSES

Do you like to sing songs? Humpback whales do, too!

Do you like to smile? Three-toed sloths do, too!

Do you like to play hide and seek? Sea horses do, too!

Do you like to eat juicy sweet corn? Chickens do, too!

Do you like to jump in puddles? Frogs do, too!

Do you like to run in the park? Dogs do, too!

Do you like to play in the snow? Polar bears do, too!

Do you like to relax in warm tropical waters? Angelfish do, too!

Do you like to move slowly? Sloths do, too!

Do you like to lie around your home? Cats do, too!

Do you like to take walks in the cool morning air? Wolves do, too!

Do you like to have a food fight? Gulls and pelicans do, too!

Do you like to pretend? Hognose snakes do, too!

Do you like to have staring contests? Dogs do, too!

At P.S. 87, Delia Marshall guided her first-grade students to study animals that were native to New York City as part of her social studies curriculum. The cover to each child's research appears in Figure 10.2.

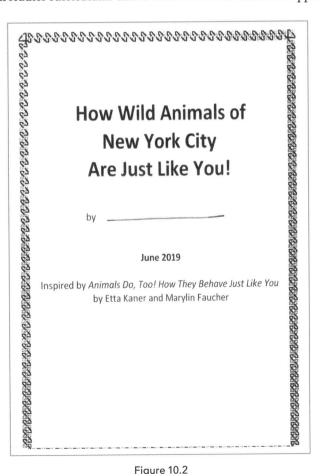

Figure 10.2

Lifting the Quality of Student Writing

First, we provided appropriate resources so that young students would have enough content material to come up with their questions and explain their answers. Then we turned toward helping them write effective and clear paragraphs. We returned to author Etta Kaner and lifted lessons from *Animals Do, Too! How They Behave Just Like You* (2017). After rereading the book aloud, we listed the following techniques that young writers might choose to borrow:

What writing lessons can we take from Etta Kaner?

1. She sticks with her pattern (refrain) throughout her book. (Do you like to _____ ? _____ do, too!)

2. She offers paragraphs that explain the animal's specific behavior.

3. She creates opening sentences for each paragraph that introduce her idea.

4. She includes information that is accurate and specific.

5. She presents additional facts in a "More About the Animals in This Book" section in the back of the book.

Each of these points became the focus of the minilessons that began our writing workshops. In addition, we reminded students of the importance of rereading their work to make sure their meaning was clear and to be sure they answer any questions their readers might have.

Student Writing Samples

The first graders in Delia's class at P.S. 87 wrote the pieces in Figures 10.3, 10.4, and 10.5. Vivien wrote about American robins (see Figure 10.3). Ares wrote about eastern red bats (see Figure 10.4). Amelie wrote about porcupines (see Figure 10.5).

Do you like to sing?

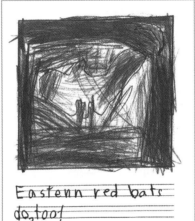

American Robins do too! Robins screech and dive at the animals

That are tring to eat then or their babies. When American Robins bill their nests they sing. They are the first to sing in the morning. They sing to make friends. That the last to sing in the nite. They sing to signbol other American Robins when predators are neart. They dont sing in the afternoon!

Figure 10.3

Do you like to stay up at night?

Eastenn red bats do,too!

Eastenned bats are awak in the night because they hunt for food. They eat kakurachis and other inses. They danit see well but they hear the Insects flying and hoping around.

Figure 10.4

Do you like to eat fruit?

Porcupines do too!

Porcupines eat fruit and uthr plants because they are herbivores. Herbivores only eat plants. Porcupines allso eat seeds flowers and mostly bark in winter. They live in forests and medos. In forests and medos they have all they nede their. They allso eat leaves and grass and buds and pine needles

Figure 10.5

Carving Out Time for Celebration

The classroom celebration for this completed challenge can be as interactive as the book that inspired it. Children can ask their original question to audience members, including classmates and family members, as well as students from other classrooms. They can wait for audience members' response, and then surprise them with the name of the animal that shares that human behavior as well as the additional information they have learned about the animal. In preparation for such a celebration, teachers can work on public speaking requirements—using appropriate volume, making eye contact, scanning the room, and using appropriate pacing. Completed and illustrated pages can be bound in an anthology and copied for all members of the class.

BOOKS NOTED

Collard III, Sneed B. 1997. *Animal Dads*. Boston, MA: Houghton Mifflin .

Kaner, Etta. 2009a. *Have You Ever Seen a Duck in a Raincoat?* Toronto, Ontario, Canada: Kids Can Press.

_____. 2009b. *Have You Ever Seen an Octopus with a Broom?* Toronto, Ontario, Canada: Kids Can Press.

_____. 2010a. *Have You Ever Seen a Hippo with Sunscreen?* Toronto, Ontario, Canada: Kids Can Press.

_____. 2010b. *Have You Ever Seen a Stork Build a Log Cabin?* Toronto, Ontario, Canada: Kids Can Press.

_____. 2017. *Animals Do, Too! How They Behave Just Like You*. Toronto, Ontario, Canada. Kids Can Press.

_____. 2018. *Do Frogs Drink Hot Chocolate? How Animals Keep Warm.* Toronto, Ontario, Canada: OwlKids Books.

Minor, Florence, and Wendell Minor. 2009. *If You Were a Penguin*. New York: Katherine Tegen Books/ HarperCollins.

Montgomery, Heather L. 2018. *Bugs Don't Hug: Six-Legged Parents and Their Kids*. Watertown, MA: Charlesbridge.

Sayre, April Pulley. 2013. *Eat Like a Bear*. New York: Henry Holt.

TEACHER REFERENCE MATERIAL

Conley, Dalton, and Stephen J. Dubner. 2018. "The Invisible Paw." *Freakonomics* podcast, episode 329. April 4. freakonomics.com/podcast/animal-economics/

A FEW TITLES TO ENRICH YOUR TEACHING

Aston, Dianna Hutts. 2016. *A Beetle Is Shy*. San Francisco, CA:

Bishop, Nic 2017. *Penguin Day: A Family Story*. New York: Scholastic Press.

Colby, Rebecca. 2020. *Crocodiles Need Kisses Too*. New York: Viking.

Ehrlich M.D., Fred. 2014. *Does a Seal Smile?* Maplewood, NJ: Blue Apple Books.

Haynes, Richard. 2021. *Orangutan Hats and Other Tools Animals Use*. Somerville, MA: Candlewick.

Henn, Sophy. 2021. *All Kinds of Animal Families*. New York: Kane Miller

Jenkins, Steve, and Robin Page. 2015. *How to Swallow a Pig*: Step-by-Step Advice from the Animal Kingdom. Boston, MA: HMH Books for Young Readers.

Markle, Sandra. 2020. *What If You Could Sniff Like a Shark: Explore the Superpowers of Ocean Animals*. New York: Scholastic.

_____. 2021. *What If You Could Spy Like a Narwahl? Explore the Superpowers of Amazing Animals.*
   New York: Scholastic.
Newson, Karl. 2019. *The Same but Different Too.* Somerville, MA: Nosy Crow.

See bibliography for Doing What the Animals Do in online Book List 11. See additional animal resources in online Book Lists 2, 4, and 12.

CHAPTER 11
Imagine If
You Were . . .

(Grades 1-3)

Jade, a second grader in Alyssa Fisher's class at Dows Lane Elementary, wrote about rabbits:

If you were a rabbit, you would come in lots of shapes and sizes. If you were a Flemish Giant Rabbit, you would be the biggest rabbit in the world. If you were a Netherland Dwarf Rabbit, you would be very small.

If you were a rabbit, you would eat very healthy foods. You would eat lettuce, grass, rabbit pellets, carrots and apples.

If you were a rabbit, you could have as many as eight babies per litter and two to three litters per year.

But you are not a bunny or a rabbit. You are a human being. But you can have a pet rabbit and you can save them and keep them safe.

Exploring the Roots of the Writing Challenge

I was touring in in Ireland and came across a children's book titled, *If I Were a Bee,* written and illustrated by an Irish writer named Dolores Keaveney (2010). The book caught my eye because I had recently clipped an article in *The New York Times* titled "Just Imagine You're a Bee," written by a science writer named Joanna Klein (2016). Both writers teach a great deal by imagining the life of a bee and sharing that life with their readers. One writer imagines herself as the bee, the other uses the direct address voice, suggesting to readers what their lives would be like if they were bees.

When I returned home, I began thinking about how the "If you were . . ." or "If I were . . ." stance always leads to rich conversations in early childhood classrooms. Children like to imagine and pretend and are probably *not* invited to do so often enough in today's overloaded curriculums. Share such poems as "If I Were in Charge of the World," by Judith Viorst (1984), "If It Were My Birthday," by Zaro Weil (1992), or "If I Were King" by A.A. Milne (1924) and listen for the children's interesting responses. They are eager to tell what they would do if they were in charge of the world, if they were king, or if it were their birthday. The same thing happens with fictional picture books such as *If I Were Your Mother* (1999b) or *If I Were Your Father* (1999a) by Margaret Park Bridges, or Fred Hiatt's (1997) *If I Were Queen of the World*. (See additional titles in bibliography in online Book List 12.)

Shortly thereafter, I was asked to help design an animal research project for second graders, and I decided to combine this wonderful imaginary stance with the more serious business of presenting animal research. Wendell and Florence Minor's picture books titled *If You Were a Penguin* (2009) and *If You Were a Panda* (2013) got all our juices flowing.

My goal in this challenge was to simplify nonfiction research and writing for second graders. Having watched young students struggle with topic choice, note taking, and turning notes into cohesive paragraphs, I was determined to make the experience joyful and to tap into students' strengths. I wanted young writers to take pleasure in reading and writing informational texts.

Young students delight in using their words and their drawing to record what they are learning.

Engaging Students in the Challenge

We began this challenge by gathering many picture books that asked students to imagine being something other than a human child. We showed the covers of the following books, asking students why they might be shelved together. Students noticed that some asked the reader to imagine being something else, and in a few the author imagined being a lion, a kangaroo, or a bee.

If You Were Born a Kitten by Marion Dane Bauer (2001)

If You Were My Baby: A Wildlife Lullabye by Fran Hodgkins (2007)

If You Were a Penguin by Florence and Wendell Minor (2009)

If You Were a Panda by Florence and Wendell Minor (2013)

If You Were the Moon by Laura Purdie Salas (2017)

If I Were a Bird by Gladys Conklin (1965)

If I Were a Bee by Dolores Keaveney (2010)

If I Were a Kangaroo: A Bedtime Tale by Mylisa Larsen (2017)

If I Were a Lion by Sarah Weeks (2004)

I then read aloud both *If You Were a Penguin* and *If You Were a Panda* and talked about what the children learned from the books. The students noticed that the authors shared brief nonfiction information on every page of their books. We reread the books, talking about any additional information they would have liked the authors to include. They appreciated the list of animal fun facts that ended each book.

We then invited students to think of an animal they were interested in. We suggested that they select one that they knew a little about but would like to know more or one that they were curious about but knew very little. For sure, some students chose animals that they already knew a great deal about.

We gave each second grader a sheet of paper with the following words typed across the front:

If You Were a _____ by _____

We asked them to imagine this sheet as the cover to a book they were to write just as the Minors did.

Then we arranged stacks of lined paper on every tabletop, asking students to write one piece, and *only* one, of information on every page, borrowing the structure used by the authors.

If you were a _____ , you would (or you'd)_____ .

Students were encouraged to write one such informative sentence on as many pages as they could fill. We didn't worry if students had inaccurate or skimpy information, knowing they would be able to confirm, delete, revise, or expand their original thinking as they researched their animals.

Continuing to Support Students' Efforts
Sharing Your Own Writing

The next day, I shared the beginnings of my book about koalas. I showed students the following statements, one per page.

If you were a koala, you would eat eucalyptus leaves.

If you were a koala, you would be called a joey when you were young.

If you were a koala, you would have to take care of yourself at a young age.

If you were a koala, you would be great climber.

If you were a koala and you were a male, you would rub your scent on trees to claim them as your own.

If you were a koala, you would have thick, oily fur that helps you keep dry.

If you were a koala, you would be found only in Australia.

If you were a koala, you would be a marsupial and would stay in your mother's pouch.

Then, I showed them the same statements after I had done some research about koalas. I had learned from several books including *The Life Cycle of a Koala* by Bobbie Kalman (2002) and *Pocket Babies and Other Amazing Marsupials* by Sneed B. Collard III (2007). I added on to each statement, combined two of them (marsupial and joey statements), and put the statements in an order that made sense (young joey information before marking trees with scent). I pointed out how my research led me to revise my original statements. The revised work follows:

If you were a koala, you would only be found in Australia. Originally your koala ancestors were stranded in Australia. They had no way to travel to other continents and they adapted well to the Australian environment, eating the leaves of the native Australian eucalyptus tree. That's why you are found in Australia today.

If you were a koala, you would be a marsupial and would stay in your mother's pouch when you were young. There are several animal species that are called marsupials. These include kangaroos, wallabies, wombats, Tasmanian Devils, possums, gliders, bandicoots and you and your relatives, the koalas. Marsupial mamas have pouches to carry their babies. You were called a joey when you were young. And when you were born you were the size of a jellybean without hair, without ears and eyes that cannot see yet.

If you were a koala, you would have to take care of yourself at a young age. You and other koalas begin to take total care of yourselves between 1 and 2 years of age, as soon as another baby joey appears in your mother's pouch. You are fully grown between 3 and 4 years of age and you search for your own forest filled with eucalyptus trees.

If you were a koala, you would be great climber. You would have strong paws with extra thumbs that help you grip onto trees. You would search for leaves to eat in the trees and places to sleep.

If you were a koala, you would eat eucalyptus leaves. You would eat about ten ounces of leaves every day (300 grams) when you were young and even more when you grew older. When you are full-grown you would eat about 500 grams of leaves every day. It's a good thing that you have very sharp teeth as you need to grind up the leaves and chew them a lot.

Believe or not, your mama fed you a form of her poop when you were just a joey. This mushy "pap" was your first solid food. That poop contains microbes which help you digest the leaves. There are 800 kinds of eucalyptus leaves so your mama koala taught you which ones are best to eat.

If you were a koala, you would have thick oily fur that helps you keep dry. During the rainy season, koalas have their own built-in raincoats. They are built in such a way, that their fur quickly releases rainwater.

If you were a koala and you were male, you would rub your scent on trees to claim them as your own. You wouldn't like to share your trees with other koalas. You use your scent to attract female partners and keep away other males. Your scent helps you communicate.

Gathering Information

Students understood that they were about to create their own If You Were . . . animal book, filling each page with separate ideas about their chosen animals, adding illustrations, and, if they desired, a fun fact page at the back, the way the Minors had done.

Our reason for asking students to place separate ideas on separate pages was to make research easier. For example, if a student were to write, "If you were a skunk, you would give off a bad smell," at the top of a page, they would then have the rest of the page to add relevant information about skunk spray. This, we sensed, would make researching, note taking, and the organization of ideas much easier for young writers. We also suggested that as they looked up information, their ideas might change. They might realize that they did not have correct information and/or they might even eliminate a page or combine pages that are related. Above all, they would gather more information and would have the space to add on.

Early on, we circulated the room making sure the students were writing separate ideas on each page. Again, we didn't worry if their recorded ideas did not seem specific or accurate, as we knew that the research to follow would add specificity, accuracy, and clarification.

For students who needed extra practice, we spent time reading aloud well-written, content-rich nonfiction picture books about animals of interest and asking students to recall what they learned from them. We then practiced formulating "If you were . . ." statements and creating a book together before students began their individual booklets.

All the while, we collected resource materials about the students' chosen animals from the school library and public libraries, and we encouraged students to bring in any information they might have at home.

Lifting the Quality of Student Writing

We began each writing workshop with minilessons to support the students' efforts. The most important lesson dealt with writing with specificity and accuracy. I shared Frank Asch's (1998) poem, "If I Were an Ant," in his collection *Cactus Poems*, to make my point crystal clear.

"IF I WERE AN ANT" BY FRANK ASCH

If I were a leaf-cutter ant,
I wouldn't be a worker who carts leaves to the nest,
one of ten million chewers, just like all the rest.
      If I were a leaf-cutter ant,
I wouldn't be a minor tending to the queen,
just another fungus farmer keeping things clean.
If I were a leaf-cutter ant,
I wouldn't be a soldier who has to guard and fight,
defending the colony all day and night.
If I were a leaf-cutter ant,
I wouldn't be a male flirting and flying around,
only to fall down and die alone upon the ground.
If I were a leaf-cutter ant,
I'd be the pampered queen, the one and only,
Supreme, royal egg-laying machine!

It seemed important to point out to students, "Look how much specific and accurate information the poet included. Look how he cleverly proves he is an authority on leaf-cutter ants."

We then taught several other minilessons that served as reminders about the power of the information gathered.

- Some information will lead to brand-new pages in booklets.

- Some information will expand ideas already noted.

- Some information will challenge ideas and result in elimination of pages.

- Some information will result in the combining of pages.

- Published information should not be copied but retold in the student's own unique way.

We addressed the following issues as well:

- The use of such nonfiction features as tables of contents and indices will help student locate needed information.

- The order of the pages should make sense (e.g., information about early life would come before adult behavior).

- Endings should sound like endings.

As we conferred, we helped students formulate "If you were . . ." statements, find relevant information, confirm or deny their original statements, and write with clarity, specificity, and accuracy. We also asked students to double-check the order of their pages and number them. When students were close to compiling and completing their own fleshed-out statements, we shared ideas about how to end their If You Were . . . booklets. We asked students to create an ending for their booklets by breaking the pattern and/or adding a surprise. The following kinds of endings were discussed.

End with a Question

Would you like to be a _____?

Would you like to see a real _____?

Would you like to learn even more about _____?

End with a "You're Not" Statement

But you're not a _____, so you can't . . .

Since you're not a _____, you can't . . .

Even though you are not a _____, you still can . . .

End with a Superlative

Most of all, if you were a _____, you would_____.

Best of all, if you were a _____, you would _____.

Most important of all, if you were a _____, you would _____.

Most surprising of all, if you were a _____, you would _____.

End with a Closing Statement

Now that you know a lot about hummingbirds, I think you could spot them in your backyard.

_____ are interesting animals, aren't they? If you want to know even more, keep reading about them.

So now you are an expert on_____. Please pass on what you have learned.

Student Writing Sample

Here are a few pages from Zoe's *If You Were a Polar Bear . . .* book written in Alyssa Fisher's second-grade class at Dows Lane.

If you were a polar bear, you would be a carnivore. Your favorite prey would be the ringed seal. You would dig into the ice or lie for hours near an ice hole, waiting to grab a seal with your sharp teeth and claws. You would also attack young walruses. If you are very hungry, you would hunt smaller prey such as sea birds or fish. Sometimes you might even eat plants or look around for trash.

If you were a polar bear, your fur would be so thick and warm that you could overheat. Sometimes you could take a swim in freezing icy water just to cool off. If you were a male polar bear, you would be much bigger than the females. If you were a male, you might have play fights. During a play fight, you would both stand up and try to push each other over.

If you were a polar bear you would be endangered. You would need people to protect you. If not, you might become extinct. If that happens, we would only be able to learn about you from books like this.

Carving Out Time for Celebration

Second graders very proudly typed up their revised and edited work, creating picture books containing one page for each interesting, researched idea. Each page was accompanied by either a drawing or a downloaded image. Family members and siblings attending the school were invited to a classroom celebration with students reading their favorite page aloud to all visitors. In some classrooms, children were encouraged to bring matching stuffed animals to accompany their presentations. (A soft and adorable lion, turtle, and even a wolf attended!)

BOOKS NOTED

Bauer, Marion Dane. 2001. *If You Were Born a Kitten*. New York: Aladdin.

Bridges, Margaret Park. 1999a. *If I Were Your Father*. New York: Morrow Junior Books.

_____. 1999b. *If I Were Your Mother*. New York: Morrow Junior Books.

Collard III, Sneed B. 2007. *Pocket Babies and Other Amazing Marsupials*. Minneapolis, MN: Millbrook.

Conklin, Gladys. 1965. *If I Were a Bird*. New York: Holiday House.

Hiatt, Fred. 1997. *If I Were Queen of the World*. New York: Margaret K. McElderry Books/Simon & Schuster Children's Publishing.

Hodgkins, Fran. 2007. *If You Were My Baby: A Wildlife Lullabye*. Nevada City, CA: Dawn.

Kalman, Bobbie. 2002. *The Life Cycle of a Koala*. St. Catharine's, Ontario, Canada: Crabtree.

Keaveney, Dolores. 2010. *If I Were a Bee*. Westmeath, Ireland: Dbee.

Larsen, Mylisa. 2017. *If I Were a Kangaroo: A Bedtime Tale*. New York: Viking/Penguin Random House.

Minor, Wendell, and Florence Minor. 2009. *If You Were a Penguin*. New York: Katherine Tegen Books/HarperCollins.

_____. 2013. *If You Were a Panda*. New York: Katherine Tegen Books/HarperCollins.

Salas, Laura Purdie. 2017. *If You Were the Moon*. Minneapolis, MN: Millbrook.

Weeks, Sarah. 2004. *If I Were a Lion*. New York: Aladdin Paperbacks/Simon & Schuster Children's Publishing.

POEMS NOTED

Asch, Frank. 1998. "If I Were an Ant." In *Cactus Poems,* San Diego, CA: A Gulliver Green Book/Harcourt Brace.

Milne, AA. 1924. "If I Were King." *When We Were Very Young*. New York: E.P. Dutton.

Viorst, Judith.1984. "If I Were in Charge of the World." In *If I Were in Charge of the World and Other Worries: Poems for Children and Their Parents*. New York: Aladdin Paperbacks.

Weil, Zaro. 1992. "If It Were My Birthday." In *Mud, Moon and Me*. Boston, MA: Houghton Mifflin.

TEACHER REFERENCE MATERIAL

Klein, Joanna. 2016. "Just Imagine You're a Bee," *The New York Times*, Science Section. December 19.

A FEW TITLES TO ENRICH YOUR TEACHING

Baptiste, Tracey. 2018. *If You Were a Kid in the Wild West*. New York: Children's Press. (series)

Gregory, Josh. 2018. *If You Were a Kid During the California Gold Rush*. New York: Children's Press. (series)

Markle, Sandra. 2017. *I Wish I Was a Lion*. New York: HarperCollins.

————. 2017. *I Wish I Was an Orca*. New York: HarperCollins

O'Connor, George. 2014. *If I Had a Raptor*. Somerville, MA: Candlewick.

Schimel, Lawrence. 2017. *If You Were a Kid Building a Pyramid*. New York: Children's Press. (series)

Stewart, David. 2021. *How Would You Survive as a Whale?* Danbury, CT: Franklin Watts. (series)

Wise, Bill. 2021. *If Animals Built Your House*. Nevada City, Ca: Dawn Publications.

Zimmerman, Andrea. 2021. *If I Were a Tree*. New York: Lee & Low.

See additional resources in bibliography online in Book List 12.

CHAPTER 12
Wearing a Mask

(Grades 2-5)

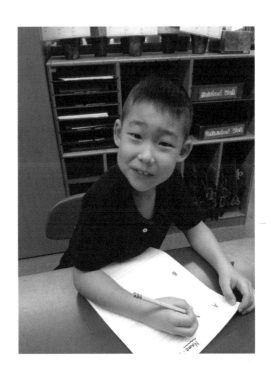

Sophia, a third grader in Liz Lynch and Teresa Edwards's class at P.S. 87, imagined being the moon:

> ## I AM THE MOON
>
> I am the moon. I shine in the sky and the stars love me. I may look like a thin sliver or maybe round like a cookie. This is because I have phases. They depend on how the sun's light hits me. I belong to the Earth. The Earth and I move together as if we are dancing. You might see me in the West. When I am in the West, I will set soon. I could be in the East. That is when I am rising and waking up. I rise in the sky at night and when you are sleeping, I watch over you. Astronauts like to come visit me. Only 12 people have walked on me. You weigh less on me and when you jump, you can go so high in the sky! During the day, I am as hot as the sun. At night, I am as cold as an ice cube. You know me. I am the moon.

Exploring the Roots of the Writing Challenge

Some writing challenges would rise to the top of a popularity contest, if one existed. I think young writers would unanimously vote for persona/mask writing, in both poetry and prose, much the way Mariano Rivera was chosen for the Cooperstown Baseball Hall of Fame. Children love to pretend, to use their imaginations, to step into a make-believe world. Mask writing allows them to do so. This challenge was inspired by poetry, reinforced by a newspaper clipping, and then, perhaps surprisingly, clinched by a tissue box.

I have several poetry anthologies brimming with persona/mask poems, and children always seem to delight in these surprising points of view. In persona/mask poems, the poets imagine what it would be like

135

to *be* the objects, places, animals, or phenomena they are thinking about. They share their thoughts from these new perspectives.

I have tried my hand at writing persona poems. One is called "Worth the Trip," and to write it, I became Staten Island, the island where I used to live. (See poem in Appendix 4.) This borough is frequently denigrated by many New Yorkers, the butt of many jokes with punchlines referring to the garbage dump, the conservative politics, and the abundance of pizza parlors, strip malls, and track housing. By filling this poem with lots of positive information, I hoped to show that Staten Island is an appealing and unique part of New York City.

The newspaper clipping that added to my belief that our students could do this kind of writing was entitled "Baby Trip Advisor" by Rosemary Counter (2018). In this clever piece of writing, the author writes from a baby's point of view. In part, she reviewed life in a Flamingo Bay hotel and wrote, "There were lots of colorful pillows for grabbing and lamps for throwing them at. Many cords were available for pulling and nobody had blocked the electric plugs, so everyone had to pay me more attention than ever before." Older students understood the humor and the insights in this article.

Now to the tissue box. I have never longed for a tissue box before, but when I saw the one in my son and daughter-in-law's apartment, I knew I needed one just like it. The box was a Trader Joe's brand, and each side of the box had clever notes written from the tissues' point of view, one on each of the four sides and a fifth on top. With old-fashioned illustrations and font, the tissues explained how helpful and essential they are, especially in challenging situations. These included picking up something disgusting, running out of toilet tissue, and being helpful on tearful occasions.

Someone in the advertising department of Trader Joe's certainly has a soft spot for persona/mask writing because I also discovered a clever persona/mask ad in a *Trader Joe's Fearless Flyer* advertising publications. The dog snack ad read:

PEANUT BUTTER FLAVOR DOG TREATS—
A First-Person (Dog?) Narrative, as Told to Trader Joe's by Keltie the Corgi Mix

Do you like peanut buttery things? I really do. They're so good and salty and tasty and—SQUIRREL!—I just love when my humans give me peanut butter-flavored snacks, especially Trader Joe's Peanut Butter Flavor Dog Treats. They're super crunchy and slightly sweet, thanks to oats and whole wheat flour—HEY, A CAT!—and molasses. Sometimes I get to go in the car to buy them—YAY CAR!—and sometimes I'm even allowed to eat them on the couch. My humans like them because they aren't as messy as real peanut butter—LOOK, A BONE!—and also because a 24-ounce box of these Treats—OHMYGOSH TREATS!—is just $3.49, which means I don't have to share with my sister.

Engaging Students in the Challenge

To get ready for this challenge, I sorted many persona/mask poems. You're bound to find many that will be of interest to your students if you browse the pages of *Dirty Laundry Pile: Poems in Different Voices* selected by Paul Janeczko (2001), *Desert Voices* by Byrd Baylor (1981), and *Cat Talk* (2013) and *I Didn't Do It* (2010) by Patricia MacLachlan and Emily MacLachlan Charest. If you are interested in persona/mask poems that are filled with more factual nonfiction information, select some from the pages of Stephen R. Swinburne's (2010) clever *Ocean Soup: Tide Pool Poems,* Joyce Sidman's (2010) brilliant *Dark Emperor & Other Poems of the Night,* or Frank Asch's (1998) content-rich poems in *Cactus Poems.* (See bibliography in online Book List 13 for a list of persona/mask poems in these collections and others.)

Students need lots of opportunities to hear fine literature read aloud.

I selected ones that contained a great deal of rich nonfiction information and ones that didn't. Shirley Mozelle's (2006) persona poems in *The Kitchen Talks* were lighthearted and cleverly told through the voice of a refrigerator, a cookie jar, a potholder, and a rolling pin without any nonfiction information. On the other hand, Stephen Swineburne's (2010) content-rich poems in *Ocean Soup: Tide Pool Poems* were told through the point of view of sea urchins, sea stars, and hermit crabs.

I also gathered stacks of picture books written in the persona/mask style. The authors of these books chose to tell their stories from an object or animal's point of view. These included *I'm a Duck* by Eve Bunting (2018) (the story of a duck who fears swimming), *I, Doko: The Tale of a Basket* by Ed Young (2004) (a fable through the eyes of a basket), and *Drawing Lessons from a Bear* by David McPhail (2000) (the life of a bear who is a talented artist).

These books were all fictional tales that did not include extensive nonfiction information. I planned to contrast these books with other persona/mask picture books that contained lots of nonfiction information. I chose these books from a wide range with very distinct formats. See the following descriptions.

PERSONA/MASK PICTURE BOOKS USING VARIOUS STRUCTURES

- Journal/diary format—These include *My Awesome Summer by P. Mantis* by Paul Meisel (2017) and Angela Royston's (2007) *See How They Grow—Puppy* and others in the DK series. Devin Scillian's (2010) lighthearted, humorous, and charming *Memoirs of a Goldfish* are written in journal format, but the author entertains more than informs. The same can be said for *Diary of a Wombat* (2002) and *Diary of a Baby Wombat* (2009) by Jackie French. In the wildly popular books by Doreen Cronin, *Diary of a Worm* (2003), *Diary of a Spider* (2005), and *Diary of a Fly* (2007), that author does weave in some factual information, but the content is limited.

- Narratives based on true stories—These include *Gretchen: The Bicycle Dog* by Anita Heyman (2003).

- Several first-person voices across a topic—These include *My First Day: What Animals Do on Day One* by Steve Jenkins (2013) and *Animal Faces* by Darlyne Murawski (2005). Thomas Locker's *Water Dance* (2002), which appears in the poetic style section, also contains many first-person voices all connected to the theme of water. These include "I am the mountain stream, I am the mist, and I am the storm." He also includes end pages filled with thorough information about the water cycle.

(continues)

> ### PERSONA/MASK PICTURE BOOKS
> ### USING VARIOUS STRUCTURES (continued)
>
> - Dialogue between humans, animals, and plants—These include *I'm a Seed* by Jean Marzollo (1996), a Hello Science Early Reader! with two seeds talking to one another about their lives, and *So What's It Like to Be a Cat?* by Karla Kuskin (2005) in which a young boy interviews a talking cat.
> - Poetic style—These include *My Light* by Molly Bang (2004), *Water Dance* by Thomas Locker (2002) and *Atlantic* by G. Brian Karas (2002). (See Vicki Vinton's [2011] insightful blog, in which she thoughtfully describes a creative nonfiction unit she designed for grade three students using as a mentor text, G. Brian Karas's [2002] *Atlantic*.)

I began my first get-together with third-grade students at P.S. 87 by sharing several persona/mask poems from the anthologies listed in the bibliography at the end of this chapter, highlighting those that were rich in content information. (See my Staten Island poem in Appendix 4.)

I then explained the new challenge to the students. They would write persona/mask materials that were filled with rich content information about topics of their own choosing. They would be writing prose, not poetry, and their prose could be shaped into formats of their own choosing (picture books, essays, articles for a class newspaper, etc.).

I then shared two picture books written in persona/mask style. I asked students to note the differing amounts of nonfiction information in *My Awesome Summer by P. Mantis* by Paul Meisel (2017) and *I'm a Duck* by Eve Bunting (2018). Students understood how much they learned about the praying mantis from reading Meisel's book.

Finally, I asked students what mask they would want to wear if they were to do what Paul Meisel did. Their first responses included writing from the point of view of such diverse things as a submarine, a pine tree, a sunflower, a cello, a globe, the moon, a hurricane, a waterfall, and Frederick Douglass. In another classroom, third graders chose Valentine's Day, a subway car, lightning, a Manx cat, the Olympics, an airport, a rainbow, Poseidon, a snowflake, Carnegie Hall, the Eiffel Tower, an aardvark, Madison Square Garden, a red panda, and the Empire State Building.

We were pleased by the wide range of student choices, falling into such categories as animals, plants, space, locations, inventions, holidays, foods, sports, history, nature, and transportation. The student who chose Frederick Douglass was the only one who chose a person from history for this study, ignoring the request to choose an inanimate object or write through an animal's perspective for this creative approach to nonfiction writing. In the second class, Poseidon, the god of the sea from Greek mythology also stood out. We encouraged these students to read Brad Meltzer biography series I Am . . . , Kay Winters's Voices from . . . series and Kate Waters's first-person historical fiction accounts. (See titles in bibliography in online Book List 13.)

Continuing to Support Student's Efforts
Sharing Your Own Writing

As has become my custom, I shared with students my process of creating my own I Am . . . prose piece of writing. I began my research by reading *Panda Kindergarten* by Joanne Ryder (2009), paying close attention to the fast facts about giant pandas in the back of the book. This list taught me that "a newborn giant panda is about the size of a stick of butter and weighs about four ounces." I also learned that they weigh over 200 pounds when fully grown and that they make many different sounds. They eat mainly bamboo, have become endangered for several reasons, and are very important in China.

Then I jotted down the additional information I wanted to know about giant pandas. My questions included:

What does a panda look like?

What do bamboo plants look like? How do they grow?

What else weighs 200 pounds?

What are the threats to giant panda habitats? Why do those threats exist?

How are pandas treated in China?

Next, I searched the library and the Internet for material that would help me answer those questions. I took notes from Gail Gibbons's book *Giant Pandas* (2004).

My finished piece appears here:

I am a Giant Panda. I've been told that when I was born, I was "as small as a stick of butter" and weighed only four ounces. * I grew to be a very cute cub, but my screeching squeals made some folks shudder. That surprised me because I am a most peaceful creature. Today, as a full-grown giant panda, my sounds seem even more frightening. I've been told that they are as chilling as the sound of thunderbolts on a stormy night. I've become an expert at barking like a dog, honking like a goose and growling like a lion, especially when I'm hungry. I can devour 40 pounds of bamboo leaves every single day. Yum, Yum. They're my favorite food, really the only thing I eat. Did you know that bamboo is the fastest-growing plant on Earth? One plant grew 36 inches in 24 hours. Bamboo plants are the express trains of the plant world.

If I'm lucky, I find all these scrumptious snacks growing in the wild. It is beautiful here, high in the mountains of our bamboo forests in the southwest of China. The wildlife that surrounds us includes dwarf blue sheep, multi-colored pheasants, crested ibis and golden monkeys.

(continues)

(continued)

Bamboo leaves make my mouth water. I love the shoots, the stems and the leaves of this beautiful flowering evergreen. Of course, I must be a clever climber to reach the highest leaves.

By the way, bamboo plants do not flower very often. Unfortunately, you might have to wait a hundred years to see a plant produce flowers and once they do flower, the plant dies. The good news is that when they flower, they produce lots of seeds which allow more bamboo plants to grow. You can think of me as a gardener as I help spread those seeds.

Do you know why I eat so much? It's because I am now a strong and sturdy adult panda weighing 200 pounds. Some of my friends weigh even more, some are three hundred pounds! But I am very impressive at just two hundred pounds. That's about the weight of a typical refrigerator, a manhole cover or two Bloodhound dogs put together! So, you see, I'm huge and heavy, but also rather attractive. I'm black and white like a zebra or a raccoon but I don't look like them at all. No way! I am much cuter than those creatures. In fact, I'm so adorable that friendly folks in China think of me as their unofficial national mascot. Mascots, you know, excite, entertain and energize people!

Being so adorable, you'll be surprised to discover that I am an endangered animal. It's true. You will only find about 1600 of us living in the bamboo forests in this part of China. You are probably wondering right now, "Why are there so few Giant Pandas living there?" Well, one reason has to do with poachers. These illegal hunters are meaner than playground bullies. They come after us, capture us and kill us. Then they sell our skins for big bucks. Imagine that, selling our skin for big bucks! Sometimes, we aren't hunted, but die accidentally because we are caught in traps and snares set out to capture other animals. I must be so careful when I roam around, sniffing and searching for bamboo.

Another reason that I am endangered is that as the population in China gets bigger and bigger, our habitats are getting smaller and smaller. People are logging our trees for lumber to build new houses. That's not surprising because I've heard that bamboo is stronger than wood, brick or concrete. Farmers are also clearing our ground to grow foods to feed the growing population of Chinese people. In addition, some folks are disturbing our habitats because they need parts of nearby plants to create Chinese medicines. Then too, every day it seems, more and more tourists are visiting our habitats. When builders create hotels for these tourists, they also disturb our lush and green forests. When all these bamboo plants are cut down, many Giant Pandas can't find enough food. Our stomachs remain empty, we grow weak and we sometimes even die of starvation.

Finally, builders are also creating roads and railways to transport all the people in the new neighborhoods. These roads break up our forests into separate sections, so Giant Pandas can't meet one another, form families and breed baby pandas. Our birthrate is dropping and dropping. It's no wonder we are endangered. How can people do all this to the Giant Panda, a true treasure in China?

Thankfully, scientists in China are working hard to protect and preserve my species. They have created 50 panda reserves to help take care of us. Three cheers for the scientists! Three cheers for the Giant Panda!

*from *Panda Kindergarten* by Joanne Ryder

After sharing the giant panda writing with students, I asked them for their response. I insisted that we talk about giant pandas before talking about the strengths and weaknesses of the writing. Some of discussion questions follow:

> *What surprised you about giant pandas?*
>
> *What concerns do you have about giant pandas?*
>
> *What are your new thoughts about giant pandas?*

Gathering Information

Students took on such varied persona that their resources needed to be as varied. We brainstormed with students all the ways they could collect information and learn about their chosen topics. These included:

> *browsing approved sites on the Internet*
>
> *visiting nonfiction shelves in the school and public library*
>
> *checking classroom resource materials*
>
> *finding experts in that field*
>
> *doing firsthand observation if possible*

In addition, we discussed the importance of making our quests for information known in the community. This included sending a letter to families listing all class topics and requesting information or leads that would help us locate experts. Class topics were also posted for faculty members to see. You never know who has expertise in a field apart from school subjects.

Lifting the Quality of Student Writing

As students approached drafting their mask writing, we began talking about how to craft an effective piece of writing. We returned to my giant panda writing and I asked students the following questions: "Are any parts unclear? Are there places where you need more information? How did I organize the writing? What tools from my writer's toolbox are evident?"

The discussions following this last question led to many worthwhile minilessons. Not surprisingly, the first thing students noticed was that the piece was persona/mask writing and that I stuck to the voice of the giant panda throughout. They also noticed that the piece was written in direct address, with the panda talking directly to its readers. We also talked about what students called a friendly, chatty tone, especially when the panda refers to herself as being so cute and adorable.

From previous studies, students were familiar with many writing tools taught at their elementary school. Other crafting issues they pointed out included:

Similes: These include "as chilling as the sound of thunderbolts on a stormy night"; "meaner than playground bullies."

Metaphors: One example is "Bamboo plants are the express trains of the plant world."

Strong verbs: Examples include shudder, devour, sniff, roam, preserve.

Sensory details: One example is "When builders create hotels for these tourists, they also disturb our lush and green forests."

Power of three: These include "stronger than wood, brick, or concrete"; "excite, entertain, and energize people!"

Specific and accurate information woven in: Examples of this include "can devour 40 pounds of bamboo leaves"; "adult pandas weighing 200 pounds"; "The wildlife . . . includes dwarf blue sheep, multicolored pheasants, crested ibis, and golden monkeys."

Alliteration: These include "clever climber"; "roads and railways"; "a true treasure"; "separate sections"; "protect and preserve"; "strong and sturdy"; "cute cub"; "big bucks."

Variety of sentence lengths: "Being so adorable, you'll be surprised to discover that I am an endangered animal. It's true."

Repetition: These include "more and more"; "bigger and bigger"; "smaller and smaller"; "dropping and dropping."

Ending sounds like an ending: "Three cheers for the scientists! Three cheers for the Giant Panda!"

We followed the same procedure when we read and reread published persona/mask materials. After discussing the content of the material, we continued asking, "What writing tools are available to us that will help us write in high-quality, engaging ways?"

I deliberately shared excerpts from published texts that represented several genres as we hadn't yet answered the question of how students would shape their persona/mask writing into finished genre. Students were aware that nonfiction information could be woven into poetry, picture books, essays, speeches, or articles for school publications. It became clear that my giant panda persona/mask writing influenced the writing done by the students. They were, however, not sophisticated enough at eight years of age to be writing lengthy essays. Instead, their persona/mask attempts sounded more like brief introductions as children pretended to be animals, objects, locations, and so on. (See samples later in this chapter.) Fourth and fifth graders were more likely to have written lengthier essays.

Had I written my giant panda persona/mask ideas as a picture book, so would the children. Had I shaped those ideas into poetic form, so would the children. For now, all the students' brief persona/mask pieces would be bound into a class anthology. At a future date, even young students could recast their persona writing into picture books, poetry, or any other genre that supports their content. The big lesson for teachers remains: we must be careful what we demonstrate as children will attempt to do what we do.

Teachers also pored over students' drafts, selecting those that would lead to minilessons with benefits for all students. With student permission to share and the use of a document camera we looked at the work of several students, making suggestions and generalizing the takeaways to make the ideas applicable to the work of other students.

Other minilessons taught included:

- keeping the persona/mask voice consistent

- combining direct address with persona/mask, talking directly to the reader, use of *you*

- chunking information into paragraphs

- introducing paragraphs with topic sentences

- making decisions about the tone of writing (Did they want their piece to sound chatty and conversational? Formal and serious? Sarcastic and humorous?)

Student Writing Samples

Kasten, a third grader in Renay Sadis's and Mayra Romero's class, imagined being a New York City subway. The border that surrounds his words lists the name or number of our subway lines. See Figure 12.1.

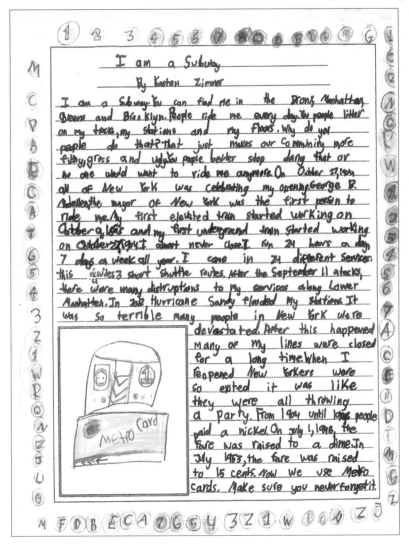

Figure 12.1

Indira, a third grader in Liz Lynch and Teresa Edwards's class at P.S. 87, imagined being India, and Jack, another student in that class, looked at the world through the eyes of a Komodo dragon.

"I AM INDIA" BY INDIRA

I am the country of India. If you are visiting me, you will hear 12 languages. Did you know my two main languages are Hindi and English? My most famous building is the Taj Mahal. It is decorated with dazzling diamonds, elaborate decorations and jewels.

Can you guess my favorite food? It's juicy, scrumptious and sweet. It's mango.

I am the 7th largest country on Earth. I know that's pretty big. In fact, I'm so big, my population is about one billion, two hundred sixty million people. Can you believe it? They probably are very entertained because I have the largest movie industry in the world. It's called Bollywood. Bollywood produces more than 800 movies a year. That is more than Hollywood.

You can think of me as a class with 29 students. Those are my states. My capital is New Delhi. If you see women wearing beautiful dresses, they are called saris. If the women have dots on their heads, those are called bindis.

Cricket is one of the most popular games played on me. Indian sports fans will spend hundreds of rupees (Indian money), just to be cheering in the humungous crowds watching a game of cricket. So, if you are a cricket player reading this, people on me might be laying around on the couch watching you on TV. I am India. India is me.

"I AM A KOMODO DRAGON" BY JACK

I am a Komodo dragon. I am the world's largest lizard. Remember if you are any animal except for a human and I am hungry, if you want to stay alive, run for your life! I will eat you. I have a large amount of bacteria (to be exact, I have 50 types of deadly bacteria), in my mouth that can poison my victim usually within twenty-four hours.

Many of my relatives can live about thirty to fifty years. When I am hunting, I rely on camouflage and patience. I'm able to hide for long amounts of time while I hunt my prey. I lie in bushes or tall grasses until a victim passes by. After that, I pounce on my prey with my powerful legs, sharp claws, and then I sink my jagged shark like teeth in my prey.

I weigh about one hundred fifty pounds. This is odd, but I smell with my tongue. I am also known as an ora. The name ora means "land crocodile." The people of Komodo Island named me that. My species has been around for millions of years. Hope you never run into me in the wild!

Carving Out Time for Celebration

In one classroom, the students' persona/mask writing was typed, illustrated, and bound into a class anthology, and every student received a copy. It made for great reading material. Another more ambitious approach would be to turn the celebration into a costume party. Could the children become the subject of their writing? With a homemade mask? With a costume? With appropriate props? Would you dress as a basketball player to share "I Am a Basketball"? Would you create a sandwich board map of India to share "I Am India"? Would you design a mask to become Poseidon, a Komodo dragon, or a rainbow?

BOOKS NOTED

PERSONA/ MASK PICTURE BOOKS THROUGH THE EYES OF MANY ANIMALS, CONTAINING NONFICTION INFORMATION:

Jenkins, Steve, and Robin Page. 2013. *My First Day: What Animals Do on Day One.* Boston: MA: Houghton Mifflin Harcourt.

Murawski, Darlyne A. 2005. *Animal Faces.* New York: Sterling.

PERSONA/MASK PICTURE BOOKS WITH POETIC LANGUAGE (NOT ANIMALS):

Bang, Molly. 2004. *My Light.* New York: Scholastic (told from the sun's point of view).

Karas, G. Brian. 2002. *Atlantic.* New York: Puffin Books/Penguin Young Readers Group (told from the Atlantic Ocean's point of view).

Locker, Thomas. 2002. *Water Dance.* San Diego, CA: Harcourt Brace (from point of view of many forms of water).

PERSONA/MASK IN SCRAPBOOK FORMAT, BASED ON A TRUE STORY:

Heyman, Anita. 2003. *Gretchen: The Bicycle Dog.* New York: Dutton Children's Books/Penguin Putnam Books for Young Readers.

PERSONA/MASK PICTURE BOOKS IN DIALOGUE FORMAT:

Kuskin, Karla. 2005. *So, What's It Like to Be a Cat?* New York: Atheneum Books for Young Readers/ Simon & Schuster Children's Publishing (cat and boy talk to each other).

Marzollo, Jean. 1996. *I'm a Seed.* New York: Scholastic. (two seeds converse with one another).

PERSONA/MASK PICTURE BOOKS IN JOURNAL OR DIARY FORMAT:

Cronin, Doreen. 2003. *Diary of a Worm.* New York: Joanna Cotler Books/HarperCollins.

_____. 2005. *Diary of a Spider.* New York: Joanna Cotler Books/HarperCollins.

_____. 2007. *Diary of a Fly.* New York: Joanna Cotler Books/HarperCollins.

French, Jackie. 2002. *Diary of a Wombat.* New York: Clarion Books/Houghton Mifflin.

_____. 2009. *Diary of a Baby Wombat.* New York: Clarion Books/Houghton Mifflin.

Meisel, Paul. 2017. *My Awesome Summer by P. Mantis.* New York: Holiday House (from praying mantis' point of view).

Royston, Angela. 2007. *See How They Grow—Puppy*. London, England: DK.

Scillian, Devin. 2010. *Memoirs of a Goldfish*. 2010. Ann Arbor, MI: Sleeping Bear Press.

PERSONA/MASK PICTURE BOOKS TO READ ALOUD (WRITTEN FROM AN ANIMAL'S POINT OF VIEW WITHOUT ABUNDANT CONTENT INFORMATION):

Bunting, Eve. 2018. *I'm a Duck*. Somerville, MA: Candlewick.

McPhail, David. 2000. *Drawing Lessons from a Bear*. New York: Little, Brown.

PERSONA/MASK PICTURE BOOK TO READ ALOUD (WRITTEN FROM AN OBJECT'S POINT OF VIEW):

Young, Ed. 2004. *I, Doko: The Tale of a Basket*. New York: Philomel.

NEWSPAPER ARTICLES (WRITTEN FROM A BABY'S POINT OF VIEW)

Counter, Rosemary. 2018. "Baby Trip Advisor." *New York Times*. May 27.

PERSONA/MASK POETRY RICH IN NONFICTION INFORMATION

Asch, Frank. 1998. *Cactus Poems*. San Diego, CA: A Gulliver Green Book/Harcourt Brace.

Sidman, Joyce. 2010. *Dark Emperor & Other Poems of the Night*. Boston, MA: Houghton Mifflin Books for Children/Houghton Mifflin Harcourt.

Swinburne, Stephen R. 2010. *Ocean Soup: Tidal Pool Poems*. Watertown, MA: Charlesbridge.

ADDITIONAL POETRY COLLECTIONS WRITTEN IN PERSONA/MASK VOICE

Baylor, Byrd. 1981. *Desert Voices*. New York: Charles Scribner's Sons.

Janeczko, Paul (selected by). 2001. *Dirty Laundry Pile: Poems in Different Voices*. New York: HarperCollins.

MacLachlan, Patricia, and Emily MacLachlan Charest. 2010. *I Didn't Do It*. New York: Katherine Tegen Books/HarperCollins (through the eyes of a dog).

———. 2013. *Cat Talk*. New York: Katherine Tegen Books/HarperCollins.

Mozelle, Shirley. 2006. *The Kitchen Talks*. New York: Henry Holt.

PANDA RESOURCES

Gibbons, Gail. *Giant Pandas*. 2004. New York: Holiday House.

Ryder, Joanne. 2009. *Panda Kindergarten*. New York: HarperCollins.

TEACHER REFERENCE MATERIAL

Trader Joe. 2018. "Peanut Butter Flavor Dog Treats—A First Person (Dog?) Narrative, as Told to Trader Joe's by Keltie the Corgi Mix." *Trader Joe's Fearless Flyer*. May. Page 14.

Vinton, Vicki. 2011a. "Beyond All About Books—Part 1." Blog: *To Make a Prairie* (blog), November 16. https://tomakeaprairie.wordpress.com/2011/11/16.

———. 2011b. "Beyond All About Books—Part 2." *To Make a Prairie* (blog), November 30. https://tomakeaprairie.wordpress.com/2011/11/30.

A FEW TITLES TO ENRICH YOUR TEACHING

Bernstein, Galia. 2018. *I Am a Cat*. New York: Harry N. Abrams.

Coppo, Marianna. 2018. *Petra*. Northhampton, MA: Tundra.

Gonzalez, Maya Christina. 2014. *Call Me Tree*. New York: Children's Book Press.

Jenkins, Steve. 2014. *Creature Features: Twenty-Five Animals Explain Why They Look the Way They Do*. Boston: HMH Books for Young Readers.

Jones, Karl. 2020. *Heart on Pluto*. New York: Penguin Random House.

Levine, Sara. 2019. *Flower Talk: How Plants Use Colors to Communicate*. Brookfield, Ct: Millbrook Press.

Lewis, J. Patrick. 2019. *I Am Polar Bear*. Mankato, MN: Creative Editions.

Meisel, Paul. 2019. *My Happy Year by E. Bluebird* (A Nature Diary Book). New York: Holiday House.

Miller, David Lee, and Steven Jay Rubin. 2019. *The Cat Who Lived with Anne Frank*. New York Philomel Books.

Miller, Kelly Leigh. 2019. *I Am a Wolf*. New York: Dial Books for Young Readers.

Morpurgo, Michael. 2016. *Coming Home*. Somerville, MA: Candlewick.

Motum, Markus. 2017. *Curiosity: The Story of a Mars Rover*. Somerville, MA: Candlewick.

Newton, Vanessa Brantley. 2020. *Just Like Me*. New York: Knopf. (poems) "I Am a Canvas," "The Day I Decided to Become Sunshine," "Warrior."

Paul, Pamela. 2021. *Rectangle*. New York: Philomel.

Schonfeld, Sara. 2019. *Birthday on Mars!* New York: Penguin Random House.

Summurtok, Nadia. 2020. *In My Anaana's Amautik*. Nunavut, Canada: Inhabit Media.

See additional resources in online Book List 13.

CHAPTER 13
Doing What They Do Best

(Grades 1-3)

Ari is a first grader in Paola Jeon's class at P.S. 87. See Figure 13.1.

Figure 13.1

Lifeguards sit on high chairs,
watch people swim,
and save people if they're drowning.

Lifeguards dive really well,
use whistles,
and warn people not to go too deep.

Lifeguards swim very fast,
give kids swimming lessons,
and wear special bathing suits.

But most of all,
lifeguards make you feel safe.

Exploring the Roots of the Writing Challenge

Early childhood students seem surprised yet comforted when I show them books from their preschool years, those familiar titles from their nursery school libraries, their own bedroom shelves, or those that are currently being read to their younger siblings at bedtime. I do so not to create a feeling of nostalgia, but rather to teach the tools the writers have in their toolboxes. Of course, I choose these "baby" books with care. (See list of these books in bibliography in online Book List 14.)

One of my most favorite preschool materials to share with young writers was written by Laura Numeroff. Her popular board book series often contains two stories for the price of one. Finish reading *What Mommies Do Best* (1998), turn it over and upside down and begin again with *What Daddies Do Best.* Do likewise with *What Grandmas Do Best/What Grandpas Do Best* (2000), *What Aunts Do Best/What Uncles Do Best* (2004), *What Sisters Do Best/What Brothers Do Best* (2009), and *What Puppies Do Best/What Kittens Do Best* (2011). In addition to listing specific everyday actions of these characters, Numeroff makes the big point that moms and dads (and all the other pairs) can do exactly the same things. After reading and discussing the author's ideas, I love pointing out Numeroff's consistent use of the power of three.

Engaging Students in the Challenge

Students love hearing the Numeroff books read aloud. They readily pick up on the similarities between all the books in this series, particularly the repetition of phrases ("Mommies can," "Daddies can," etc.), the specificity of all the details, the illustrations of animals as main characters, the use of direct address (*you*), the last lines that always deal with "lots and lots of love," and the clever manner of publishing so that two stories appear in one book. To this list, I add the power of three, with authors offering three different ideas in one long sentence.

Young students share surprising discoveries with one another.

In the books in this series, the three ideas are stretched out over three pages. The first two ideas are separated by commas, followed by the word *and* before the third idea. Once students know that this technique is called the power of three, they are ready to hear the books again, paying close attention to the sound of the power of three. I inform even our youngest writers that many writers use this tool because clusters of three words, three phrases, or even three short sentences sound rhythmic and readers find the clustered information easy to remember.

I then ask students to orally practice creating interesting sentences using the power of three. To support their efforts, I ask them to use the power of three to talk about any or all of the following prompts. (Note the prompts all required students to choose three verbs, as that is what they will be doing in the writing challenge to come.)

- What you like to do on Sundays? (For example, "On Sundays, I like to eat pancakes, play ping-pong, and visit my grandma.")

- What you do before you go to sleep? (bedtime rituals) (For example, "Before I go to sleep at night, I line up my teddy bears, turn on my nightlight, and listen to my dad read a book to me.")

- What you do during the summer vacation? (For example, "In the summer, my family visits my cousins in Pennsylvania, has barbecues, and swims in the town pool.")

- How you help at home? (chores) (For example, "I always help mom fold the laundry, set the table for dinner, and throw out the trash.")

- What you do after school? (For example, "After school, I eat a snack, do my homework, and practice the piano.")

When the young students are comfortable and successful using the power of three. I suggest that we could write our own Doing What They Do Best books. Teachers can decide if this challenge will be connected to an occasion, a hot topic in the class, or a curriculum area.

For example, students can choose people in their lives as Numeroff has done, even turning their tributes into Valentine's Day gifts. In addition to the people Numeroff has chosen, students could create such books about what friends, neighbors, babysitters, cousins, grandsons, granddaughters, or even stepbrothers or stepsisters do best. Or teachers could ask students to choose a class pet to research and write up what gerbils, hamsters, fish, parakeets, rabbits, turtles, and so on do best.

This format would also serve a school study well with students selecting such topics as what school librarians, school aides, custodians, assistant principals, guidance counselors, school crossing guards, or school security guards do best.

This book was written during an election year, and I can easily imagine focusing on political careers with third graders learning what mayors, senators, vice presidents, presidents, or representatives do best.

Similarly, third-grade teachers can tilt this project toward the study of a wide range of science and math careers with students researching the work done by actuaries, anthropologists, astronauts, botanists, chemical engineers, environmentalists, epidemiologists, forensic technicians, geographers, meteorologists, and paleontologists, among others.

As noted in the Monica Wellington study in Chapter 4 and the riddle-writing challenge presented in Chapter 20, most New York City first graders study community workers. This topic is a perfect match for this writing challenge as well. We began by asking one group of first graders at P.S. 87 to name the workers in their community. In addition to the expected firefighters, police officers, and mail carriers, students added jobs held by members of their families. One group of first graders brainstormed the following list:

WORKERS IN OUR COMMUNITY

Pediatricians	Pilots	Firefighters
Veterinarians	Secretaries	Musicians
Hair stylists	Attorneys	Party planners
School crossing guards	Accountants	Principals
Electricians	Sanitation workers	Actors
Gardeners	Mail carriers	Chefs
Mayors	Lifeguards	Cashiers

Fashion designers	Bus drivers	Flight attendants
Pharmacists	Subway operators	Travel agents
Waiters	Dog walkers	Nannies
Construction workers	Elevator operators	Jewelers
Taxi drivers	Manicurists	Tailors
Doormen (and women)	Barbers	Plumbers
Dentists	Computer programmers	Carpenters
Emergency medical technicians	Bakers	Teachers
	Pizza makers	Architects
Train engineers	Farmers	

Continuing to Support Students' Efforts
Sharing Your Own Writing

Once again, serving as a model for student writers can be very beneficial. Following is one example of my *Doing What They Do Best* writing. In this class, I shared *What Chefs Do Best* as these students were all going to write about a worker in their community.

WHAT CHEFS DO BEST

Chefs can create recipes, plan menus, and choose fresh ingredients.

Chefs can prepare dishes, teach assistants, and clean up their kitchens.

Chefs can measure ingredients, control portions, and add seasonings.

Chefs can order kitchen supplies, store leftovers, and work long hours.

Chefs can read cookbooks, study with master chefs, and open their own restaurants.

Best of all, chefs can cook delicious meals for their own families.

Note, I did *not* to use direct address in my writing as Laura Numeroff had done. She frequently talks directly to the reader, using the words *you* and *your*. I thought this requirement might detract from the main goals of learning about community workers and practicing the power-of-three writing tool. I was happy to discover that many children included the *you* voice without being directed to do so.

I began by explaining to students how I went about creating my short book. First, I thought about what a chef could do, recording statements I was sure of. Then I researched other information about the work of a chef. Sometimes, my research changed my original ideas. I tried to list fifteen things that my subject could do (five long sentences, each with three parts), saving one idea for a powerful or surprise ending.

I then grouped these ideas into sentences that made sense and then put the sentences into an order that made sense. I had to ask myself, "Should certain bits of information come before other pieces of information?" I also made sure to place a comma after each of the first two ideas, followed by the word *and* before the third idea. Finally, I had to copy the three-part sentences over three pages, illustrating each page.

Gathering Information

As evident, I created five power-of-three sentences before my ending, following the lead of Laura Numeroff. We challenged our young writers, however, to create only three power-of-three sentences. Each would be stretched out over three pages, and then an ending sentence would break the pattern of the book. This task required young writers to think of nine interesting things that their subjects could do (three actions in each of three sentences). This is when gathering additional information became essential. If students couldn't think of nine actions, they spoke to classmates, teachers, or family members. They also paid close attention on class field trips to the post office, police station, firehouse, and so on, and they took notes on class interviews of community workers and of course read appropriate books about chosen occupations. (See bibliography in online Book List 14.)

Lifting the Quality of Student Writing

Some teachers choose to collaborate on a whole-class Doing What They Do Best book before sending students off to work on their own. When students seemed ready for independent work, teachers began by asking a few volunteers to orally compose a power-of-three sentence for their worker.

> *"Dentists can teach children how to brush their teeth, clean kids' teeth, and give out little tubes of toothpaste."*
>
> *"Bakers can bake birthdays cake, decorate cupcakes, and make chocolate cookies."*
>
> *"Bus drivers can make sure you use your Metro card, beep their horn, and drive you to school."* (Note, this student naturally used the direct address voice without being asked to.)

The classroom teacher, Paola, distributed rehearsal/draft paper to serve as a template for the students' writing. The worksheet had space for the three long sentences, with stars in the left margin to remind students to include three ideas in each. She also printed the word *and* to remind students of the grammatical structure in the Numeroff books. She might have included the word *can* in her template, if she wanted students to stick even closer to the Numeroff format. Students were not yet asked to plan their endings.

Jade planned her book about dogwalkers, a very New York City profession. See Figure 13.2.\
Lydia planned her book about hairdressers. See Figure 13.3.

What _dog walkers_ do best

Dog walkers
* wach your dog when no wun is home
* take your dog for a run,
* and give your dog a treat.

■ Dog walkers
* teech **trix**,
* givr dogs watrr,
* and play with dogs,
■ Dog walkers
* walk more then one dog,
* wach the dog play,
* and cleen up aftr dogs,

Jade

Figure 13.2

Name: Lydia Kendall Do
What _hairdress_ do best
ers
* Hair dress ers
give you intfrsting haircuts,
* can braid your hair in neet ways,

* and dye your hair in cool ways,

* Hairdressers
can wash your hair,
give you diffrint Ideas of how
theyCan cut your hair,
* and brsh your hair,
* dairdressers
put clips In your hair to daiv
tha seashorg,
* but masks on you if you want
so it's a sapries when your don
* and give you hair exsusareds,

Figure 13.3

Some of the very best minilessons involved sharing carefully chosen student work. For example, when a group of teachers read Colin's *What Construction Workers Do Best* (see Figure 13.4), they selected several issues that the whole class would benefit from considering.

Figure 13.4

"WHAT CONSTRUCTION WORKERS DO BEST" BY COLIN

Construction workers make buildings with bricks, dig up big holes, and use cranes to reach high places.

Construction workers use a lot of tools like shovels, use a lot of machines like forklifts, use hard hats for falling objects.

Construction workers use gloves to carry heavy things, use wrenches to fix things, and use cement to make streets.

But most of all, construction workers make the city beautiful.

This piece could spark conversation about the following important writing issues:

- putting ideas in appropriate order (Should making holes and using cranes come before building with bricks?)

- paying attention to the precision of language, particularly verbs (Do we use a hat or wear a hat?)

- honoring an established pattern (If the author wants to stick to the pattern, does he want to add the word *and* to the second power-of-three sentence?)

- adding a powerful ending (Here, the author pays tribute to construction workers.)

In addition to analyzing student work, additional minilessons (as well as one-on-one conferences) focused on the following topics:

- reminders about using of the power of three
- stretching sentences over three pages
- looking in resource books for ideas
- gathering ideas through reading, interviewing, and observing workers
- adding specificity and accuracy to sentences
- selecting three ideas that sound right together
- reordering ideas in an order that makes sense
- creating endings that are powerful and sound like endings
- preparing illustrations to accompany words on each page

Lifting the quality of writing in early childhood classrooms involves reading aloud well-written texts. After rich conversations about the ideas in the picture books, teachers can reread those books aloud and highlight such writing techniques as using the power of three, the importance of including specific and accurate information, and the effect of closing with a strong ending. Other accessible writing techniques for young writers are highlighted in the list of books at the end of this chapter (A Few Titles to Enrich Your Teaching), as well as in Book List 14.

Student Writing Samples

Nick, a first grader in Paola's class at P.S. 87, wrote *What Firefighters Do Best*. His cover appears in Figure 13.5.

Figure 13.5

> Firefighters go down big poles, use hoses to put out fires, and climb big ladders.
>
> Firefighters ride in big trucks, break down doors and windows with axes, and wear thick clothes.
>
> Firefighters use fire sirens, have dogs, and keep us safe.
>
> But most of all, firefighters are kind, brave, and prepared.

Carving Out Time for Celebration

Family members can be invited to a publishing party with students reading their booklets aloud and visitors jotting down compliments on sticky notes. Duplicate copies of completed booklets could also be offered as gifts to other first-grade classrooms that are studying community workers. Another possibility is to divide the class into clusters of students according to the kindergarten teacher the students had the year before. Teachers can arrange classroom visits for small groups to share their writing in each kindergarten. (New students could be assigned to any group that is low in number.) No doubt, teachers would delight in seeing how much their former students have grown, and kindergarteners would learn about community workers and have an image of what it means to be a first-grade learner.

BOOKS NOTED

Numeroff, Laura. 1998. *What Mommies Do Best/What Daddies Do Best*. New York: Aladdin Paperbacks/Simon & Schuster.

———. 2000. *What Grandmas Do Best/What Grandpas Do Best*. New York: Simon & Schuster Books for Young Readers.

———. 2004. *What Aunts Do Best/What Uncles Do Best*. New York: Simon & Schuster Books for Young Readers.

———. 2009. *What Sisters Do Best/What Brothers Do Best*. San Francisco: Chronicle Books.

———. 2011. *What Puppies Do Best/ What Kittens Do Best*. San Francisco: Chronicle Books.

A FEW TITLES TO ENRICH YOUR TEACHING

Books to Teach Craft to Young Writers (Of course, they should be enjoyed as works of literature before being studied for craft).

Byers, Grace. 2020. *I Believe I Can*. New York: Balzer + Bray. (similes)

Cabrera, Cozbi A. 2020. *Me & Mama*. Denene Millner Books/Simon & Schuster. (sensory details, repetition, alliteration, onomatopoeia)

Gonzalez, Maya Christina. 2012. *I Know the River Loves Me*. New York: Lee & Low. (personification)

Ho, Joanna. 2021. *Eyes That Kiss in the Corners*. New York: HarperCollins. (similes, repetition)

Hoang, Zara Gonzalez. 2020. *A New Kind of Wild*. New York: Dial. (sensory details, alliteration, similes)

Isdahl, Nansubuga Nagadya. 2018. *Sing to the Moon*. Oxford, UK: Lantana. (sensory details)

Luyken, Corinna. 2019. *My Heart*. New York: Dial. (metaphor)

Medina, Meg. 2020. *Evelyn Del Rey Is Moving Away*. Somerville, MA: Candlewick. (sensory details, strong ending)

Meddour, Wendy. 2019. *Grandpa's Top Threes*. Somerville, MA: Candlewick. (sensory details, power of three)

Nelson, Marilyn. 2020. *Lubaya's Quiet Roar*. New York: Dial Books. (alliteration, power of three, strong ending)

Oh, Joowon. 2019. *Our Favorite Day*. Somerville, MA: Candlewick. (power of three, repetition, authentic dialogue)

Roundtree, Dovey Johnson, and Katie McCabe. 2021. *We Wait for the Sun*. New York: Roaring Brook Press. (sensory details)

Scott, Jordan. 2020. *I Talk Like a River*. New York: Neal Porter Books. (sensory details, strong verbs, repetition, simile/metaphor)

Sriram, Meera. 2020. *A Gift for Amma: Market Day in India*. Cambridge, MA: Barefoot Books. (sensory details, onomatopoeia, strong verbs)

Underwood, Deborah. 2020. *Outside In*. Boston, MA: Houghton Mifflin Harcourt. (personification)

Yang, Kao Kalia. 2019. *A Map into the World*. Minneapolis, MN: Carolrhoda Books. (sensory details, similes)

Yolen, Jane and Heidi E.Y Stemple. 2020. *I Am the Storm*. New York: Rise-Penguin Workshop. (sensory details, similes, strong verbs)

See additional resources in online Book List 14.

CHAPTER 14
Writing with Refrains

(Grades 2–5)

Siri, a second grader in Eileen Scanlon's class at Dows Lane Elementary School, created an original refrain for her publication on ruby-throated hummingbirds.

IN THE FOREST . . .

In the forest, I found a ruby-throated hummingbird. A ruby-throated hummingbird has a ruby throat, a green head, and a green body.

In the forest, I see a ruby throated hummingbird flying through the air. Ruby-throated hummingbirds make a humming sound while flying.

In the forest, I see a ruby-throated female hummingbird laying a blue egg. Female hummingbirds lay their eggs in their cup-shaped nests. After they hatch, the female gets insects for the baby. Female hummingbirds sit on their eggs for about 14-16 days. The female can lay about 2 eggs at a time.

In the forest, I see a ruby-throated hummingbird constructing a nest. Ruby-throated hummingbirds live in North America. They build nests in the shape of cups. They mostly construct their nests near forest edges, streams and meadows.

In the forest, I see a ruby-throated hummingbird soaring with its babies looking for food. Ruby-throated hummingbirds sip nectar from flowers. They mostly sip their nectar from red flowers, and they eat the insects that are in the flowers.

When you go to the forest, would you want to see a ruby-throated hummingbird?

Exploring the Roots of the Challenge

Refrains or repeated phrases are staples in early childhood reading materials. When key phrases are repeated throughout a book, the book becomes predictable and helps young children learn to read. They can add their voices to read-alouds, develop sight vocabulary from seeing words repeatedly, and learn to appreciate the rhythm and lyrical quality of books with patterns and refrains. It's no wonder that *Brown Bear, Brown Bear, What Do You See?* by Bill Martin Jr. and Eric Carle (1967) and *Where Is the Green Sheep?* by Mem Fox (2004) are as common in an early childhood classroom as tofu and lentils in the kitchen of a vegetarian.

Picture books with refrains have played a starring role in a few of the challenges presented previously. These included biographical sketches (Spinelli's [2010] *Do You Have a Cat?*), Doing What the Animals Do (Kaner's [2017] *Animals Do, Too! How They Behave Just Like You*), and Imagine If You Were . . . (the Minor and Minor's [2009] *If You Were a Penguin*). In this challenge, students are presented with an array of books with refrains, not focusing on any one book as in previous challenges. Students are invited to experiment with published refrains and then eventually to invent their own. In this challenge, students were invited to weave refrains into their nonfiction writing.

When children "borrow" refrains written by others or invent their own, these short, repeated phrases can accomplish several big goals.

- **A refrain can take good nonfiction writing and make it memorable writing.** One of the most effective nonfiction refrains I have ever come across comes from the pen of Anna Baccelliere (2017) in her stunning picture book about child labor entitled *I Like, I Don't Like*. These five words not only make up the title, but they appear on every powerfully and dramatically illustrated page. Some children like soccer balls because they get to play; some don't like soccer balls because they must work hard making them. Some children like rice because it's tasty; others don't because they must work in the fields growing rice. Some children like cars because they have toy ones to play with; other children don't like cars because they must wash windshields to earn money.

- **A refrain can be used to break nonfiction information into manageable chunks for the writer and the reader.** In *Living Fossils: Clues to the Past*, Caroline Arnold (2016) uses the words *then* and *now* to divide contrasting information about ancient plants and animals with the same plants and animals in today's world.

- **A refrain can be used to highlight and reinforce important ideas.** In *Boy, Were We Wrong About the Weather!* Kathleen V. Kudlinski (2015) uses the words in her title as a refrain throughout her book to remind the reader that people used to have major misunderstandings about the weather.

- **A refrain can help a nonfiction writer develop a stance or an angle on a topic.** David Bouchard's (1993) picture book *If You're Not from the Prairie . . .*, which repeats the words in the title throughout the text, persuades the reader that prairie life contains unique qualities that can be known only by people who have lived on the prairie.

- **A refrain can help build suspense or help the reader anticipate what will appear on the following page.** Marilyn Singer (2000) does this in *On the Same Day in March: A Tour of the World's Weather*. Ending each page with the repeated phrase "On this same day in March" motivates readers to turn to the next page.

- **A refrain can make a young writer's nonfiction ideas sound literary.** Perhaps this is the goal that is most important to students and their teachers. Young children have limited access to new information, but their nonfiction writing can sound new and of high quality, if students are shown how to present their research in new and surprising ways. Refrains can help young writers present their ideas in fresh ways.

Some third graders borrowed the title of Mary Ann Hoberman's (2002) picture book *Right Outside My Window* to share what they learned about New York City immigration at the turn of the century. Each page began with the refrain, "Right outside my window . . ." They proceeded to describe many different street scenes on the Lower East Side. (See student samples on pages 167–168.) Some second graders used the same refrain to teach others about the all the different kinds of birds they were studying. Again, they began each page with the words, "Right outside my window . . ."

Engaging Students in the Challenge

Over the next few days, we read aloud several fiction books that contained refrains and talked to students about the effect and the power these repeated phrases had on readers. There are so many titles to choose from including A. H. Benjamin's (2000) *It Could Have Been Worse*, Lucy Cousins's (2010) *I'm the Best*, Douglas Wood's (2011) *No One But You,* Yamile Saied Mendez's (2019) *Where Are You From?*, Sophy Henn's (2017) *Pass It On*, and Amy Krouse Rosenthal's (2008) *It's Not Fair!* All the titles serve as refrains in these picture books. We realized that these expressions could apply to so many life situations that we challenged students to do a quick write, selecting one and seeing how that borrowed phrase could be woven into their own experiences. We then began a study of nonfiction books with refrains, as described next.

So many books, so many refrains!

- *Looking Closely in the Rain Forest* by Frank Serafini (2010). The repeated phrases in this book read, "Look very closely. What do you see?" Other books in this series focus on gardens, ponds, forests, deserts, and shores. These repeated phrases would work well for students who are studying such science topics as oceans, clouds, stars, beaches, minerals, and jungles.

- *Boy, Were We Wrong About the Weather!* by Kathleen V. Kudlinski (2015). Other books in this series focus on the solar system, the human body, and dinosaurs. The words in the title are used throughout the book to emphasize misunderstandings, and they add a friendly, conversational tone to the book.

- *What Forest Knows* by George Ella Lyon (2014). In this poetic description of forest life, the author uses the words in the title throughout the book to present elements of life in the forest. Students can borrow this structure for many topics, repeating such lines as "What Earth knows . . ." "What architects know . . ." "What tigers know . . ."

- *Living Fossils: Clues to the Past* by Caroline Arnold (2016). The author uses the repeated words *then* and *now* to teach readers how five different animals lived in the past and how they live today. Students can adapt this structure to explain things that have changed over time.

- *If You Lived Here: Houses of the World* by Giles Laroche (2011). In this picture book, the title serves as the refrain throughout the book. Each double-page spread explains what life would have been like had you grown up in the setting of the depicted house. (See Across-the-Globe Writing challenge on page 11).

- *On the Same Day in March: A Tour of the World's Weather* by Marilyn Singer (2000). Each double-spread page of this picture books ends with the phrase "on the same day in March." Turn the page and the author presents the weather, on the very same day in the month of March, in settings across the globe. Here, students learn that refrains can end a page, not necessarily begin a page.

- *The House That George Built* by Suzanne Slade (2012). In this picture book, the author uses the refrain from the classic and cumulative British nursery rhyme "This Is the House That Jack Built." In addition to prose passages explaining George Washington's role in the design and construction of the White House, the author also provides rhyming verses that accompany the prose explanations. All the verses conclude with the repeated line, "for the President's House that George built."

- *Here Is the Tropical Rain Forest* (Dunphy 2006b), *Here Is the Arctic Winter* (Dunphy 2007), and *Here Is the African Savanna* (Dunphy 2006a). (See online Book List 15 for additional titles.) In this series, Madeleine Dunphy uses the title as the refrain throughout the books. All the books in this series also use the cumulative and repetitive structure of "This Is the House That Jack Built."

- *Fireflies, Fireflies Light My Way* by Jonathan London (1996). In this picture book, the refrain is a line from a Native American lullaby that reads, "Lead me to the place . . ." London presents woodland life filled with forest animals, using the refrain to thread the text together and add a gentle, musical quality to the words.

- *Home at Last: A Song of Migration* by April Sayre Pulley (1998). This picture book shares the travels of many migrating animals including monarch butterflies, caribou, and Arctic terns. Again, students can realize the power of using refrains to end pages. Each passage in this picture book ends with the words *home at last*.

- *Who Likes the Snow?* by Etta Kaner (2006a) (see other books in this Exploring the Elements series including *Who Likes the Rain?* [Kaner 2007a], *Who Likes the Wind?* [Kaner 2006b], and *Who Likes the Sun?* [Kaner 2007b]). In this book, the author lists lots of reasons why children like the snow and adds a childlike wondering connected to each reason. Flip the folded page open and read a thoughtful, accurate, and easy-to-understand explanation of the scientific phenomena. Throughout the book are the repeated phrases, "I like the snow because . . ." followed by "I wonder . . ."

- *Somewhere Today* by Bert Kitchen (1992) (see more on this book on page 166). This book describes rituals in the life of unusual animals. The simplicity of this design was most appealing to students. Nazar, a fourth grader in Diane Berman's class at P.S. 87, borrowed this refrain to create a picture book for his class's in-depth study of duck egg incubation. Every other page began with the phrase "Somewhere today a Lucky Duck . . ." (See Figure 14.1.)

Figure 14.1

Fictional picture books with refrains that can be adapted to nonfiction writing include the following.

FICTIONAL BOOKS WITH REFRAINS

- *Whale Trails: Before and Now* by Lesa Cline-Ransome (2015). This beautifully illustrated picture book (artwork created by G. Brian Karas) can easily be labeled as historical fiction. The author weaves in the rich history of whale watching, as she shares the story of a young girl helping her father, the captain of a whale boat. She describes how people whale watch today, following each bit of current information with the refrain, "Before now . . ." and proceeds to explain how things used to be done. Students can borrow such a compare-and-contrast structure if it supports their own writing.

- *Right Outside My Window* by Mary Anne Hoberman (2002) is a fictional picture book, but the refrain served students well when they wrote about immigrant neighborhoods in New York City, local birds, animals, or insects in their backyards and styles of architecture on their block. (This refrain could also be used for clouds, modes of transportation, and community workers). (See student sample on page 167–168).

- Rita Gray's *Have You Heard the Nesting Bird?* (2017). In this picture book, beautifully illustrated by the accomplished author/illustrator Kenard Park, readers hear the sound of a dozen different birds. The only quiet one is the robin, nesting in a tall tree. Every few pages, the reader is asked the question, "Have you heard the nesting bird?" Students could borrow the use of a repeated question in their own writing.

- Mo Willems's *That Is Not a Good Idea!* (2013). As humorous and charming as we have come to expect from this popular author, a friendly goose outwits a hungry fox. Throughout, the baby geese call out the refrain, "That is not a good idea!" Lucy, a fourth grader in Diane Berman's class at P.S. 87, created a clever "touch and feel" picture book for her duck study that also uses a strong negative declaration as a refrain. Her pages begin with "That's not my baby . . ." (The dog's body is covered with a fluffy brown pom-pom. The alligator's neck is patched with a leathery fabric.) (See Figure 14.2.)

When students were fully immersed in the use of refrains to deliver nonfiction information, we described the new writing challenge. "What would you like to teach other children? What topic interests you and you would like to learn even more about? Once you have a significant amount of information, you'll be asked to create a nonfiction picture book that contains a refrain. These repeated phrases will make your writing more memorable and more clearly organized. You will be able to borrow a refrain from a published writer, one that supports your content, or you can invent an original one."

That's not my baby. My baby isn't hairy, shaggy, and fluffy like a dog.

That's not my baby. My baby doesn't have huge, sharp, and smooth teeth like a crocodile.

Figure 14.2

Continuing to Support Students' Efforts
Sharing Your Own Writing

To help students understand the task at hand, I borrowed a refrain from *If You're Not from the Prairie . . .* by David Bouchard (1993). In this Canadian publication, the author describes several elements of life on the prairie that can't possibly be understood or appreciated if one didn't come from that part of the world. I borrowed that refrain to create the nonfiction picture books that follows. (Teachers could just as easily share the posts that frequently appear on Facebook screens with titles like "36 Things You Will Naturally Understand If You're from Colorado," "Signs You're from Florida," and "You Know You're from Long Island If . . .")

IF YOU'RE NOT FROM NEW YORK CITY . . .

If you're not from New York City, you don't know dog walkers.

You can't know dog walkers.

Dog walkers are a big business in New York City, especially in Manhattan. It's not unusual to see a person holding on to a dozen leashes making his or her way to the nearest park. The dog walkers belong to licensed and insured businesses, which walk dogs for busy New Yorkers. Most Manhattanites live in apartments and can't just open backdoors to their back yards and let their dogs take care of their own business. Visitors sometimes think some New Yorkers are lazy because they don't walk their own dogs. Truth be told, these New Yorkers usually work long hours and want to be sure that their dogs are walked at regular intervals.

If you're not from New York City, you don't know dog walkers.

You can't know dog walkers.

(continues)

IF YOU'RE NOT FROM NEW YORK CITY . . . *(continued)*

If you're not from New York City, you don't know yellow taxi cabs.

You can't know yellow taxi cabs.

In New York City souvenir shops, you can buy t-shirts adorned with yellow taxi cabs, snow globes with yellow cabs inside, and even pencil cases, coffee mugs, and keychains boasting the iconic yellow cabs of New York City. If you have enough money to take a cab, you must stand on the sidewalk with your arm up waving down an empty cab. The light-up sign atop the roof of the cab lets you know if the cab is available. If the light highlights the cab's medallion number, it is available. If it lights up the medallion number and two side lights, the cab driver is off duty. If no lights are on, the driver already has a passenger. If you are lucky enough to hail a cab, be prepared to meet an interesting driver from countries far and wide. If you can't find a cab or want a new experience, try calling for an Uber or Lyft ride. As you make your way through New York City traffic, don't be surprised to see green cabs, which pick up passengers north of 96th street.

If you're not from New York City, you don't know Nathan's hot dogs.

You can't know Nathan's hotdogs.

Nathan's Famous opened in 1916 selling 5-cent hot dogs at their stand in Coney Island, Brooklyn. It was started by Nathan Handwerker, a Polish immigrant, and his wife, Ida. She came up with the recipe for the now very famous hot dog, using her grandmother's secret spices. Today there are Nathan's Famous Hot Dog shops all over our country and the world. Every July, the Coney Island store hosts a Nathan's Hot Dog–Eating Contest. A man named Joey Chestnut has been the champion hot-dog eater several times and in 2018 boasted eating 74 hot dogs and buns in 10 minutes. That's almost hard to imagine, isn't it?

(See Appendix 5 for entire text.)

Gathering Information

To demonstrate writing with a refrain as well as researching information to surround that refrain, I worked with students to create a text about life in France. The refrain was borrowed from *You See a Circus, I See . . .* by Mike Downs (2005). We began by listing lots of iconic French things including crepes, croissants, baguettes, berets, the Louvre, Notre Dame Cathedral, the Mona Lisa, the Eiffel Tower, the fleur-de-lys, and Chanel No. 5. Teachers, student teachers, and a few students who had visited France contributed a few of the items. Then we asked students how to describe these items without naming them. We put those together using the "You see . . . I see . . ." format in the next text box. The children were sent off in pairs to gather additional information about these French classics. The students used books about France as well as appropriate Internet searches to find out more. Once they had enough information, we composed the following text.

YOU SEE THIS AND THAT, I SEE FRANCE.

You see thin, round pancakes, moon-shaped buttery breads, and long loaves of bread. I see crepes, croissants, and baguettes, typical French food.

Crepes are very thin pancakes that can be sweet or savory. Sweet ones, made from wheat flour, are often filled with Nutella, sugar, maple syrup, or jams. Savory ones, made from buckwheat flour, are often filled with cheese, eggs, ham, or mushrooms. Crepes are strongly associated with Brittany, a region of northwest France, but are served throughout France, Belgium, and Canada. Croissants are flaky crescent-shaped pastries that are served for breakfast in France and are sold in most French bakeries. Baguettes are long, thin, crispy-crusted loaves of French bread. Baguettes, which also means wand, baton, or stick, has been popular since the 18th century in France.

You see a flat, tilted hat. I see a beret, a traditional French hat.

The beret is a soft, round, and flat-crowned hat that is worn worldwide but became strongly associated with the French people, both male and female. Today it is worn by the military and police of many countries. Actors, artists, and other creative types are often seen with a beret atop their heads. If ever you are in France for the celebration of a traditional event, you will see many, many folks wearing berets.

You see a big building with a glass pyramid in front. I see the Louvre, a famous art museum in Paris, France.

The Louvre is one of the biggest museums in the world. The new entrance is called the Glass Pyramid. Tour the museum and view the *Mona Lisa*, the *Venus de Milo*, and the *Winged Victory of Samothrace*. Be prepared to wait your turn to get close to these works of art as the crowds surrounding them can be huge.

You see a big, big church. I see Notre Dame, one of the most famous cathedrals in France.

This Gothic-style cathedral represents the Middle Ages. Construction was begun in 1160 and was completed in 1260. When tourists visit, they snap photographs of the towers, the spire, the gargoyles, the organ, the stained-glass windows, and the sculptures.

You see a painting of a gently, smiling woman. I see the *Mona Lisa*, one of the most famous paintings housed in the Louvre.

The *Mona Lisa* was painted by Leonardo da Vinci and today sits at the Louvre behind a sheet of bullet-proof glass. The painting is a realistic portrait, but experts have never agreed on the identity of the woman who sat for the portrait. People from all over the world remain fascinated by her steady gaze and her unusual smile.

(continues)

YOU SEE THIS AND THAT, I SEE FRANCE. *(continued)*

You see a tall, pointy, and arched metal structure. I see the Eiffel Tower.

The Eiffel Tower is a true symbol of France and can be seen no matter where you are in Paris. It was built between 1887 and 1889 as the entrance to a World's Fair. It is made from wrought iron in a lattice design. It is 1063 feet tall, similar to an 81-story building. An average of 25,000 visitors come to eat in the many restaurants and take in the views from the observation decks.

You see a small flower design. I see the fleur-de-lys, a popular symbol of France.

The fleur-de-lys is a decorative design depicting a stylized lily. It has its roots in Catholicism, and as France historically has been a Catholic nation, the fleur-de-lys became a symbol for the country, often representing the French monarchy.

You see a small bottle of perfume. I see Chanel No. 5, a perfume made famous by French designer Coco Chanel.

Chanel No. 5 is a very popular French perfume (eau de parfum) that was developed by fashion designer Coco Chanel. The perfume is known for its wonderful aroma as well as its iconic bottle. The bottle has remained the same since 1924. The number 5 held special meaning for Coco Chanel.

You see airplanes, luggage, and a sign that reads *Bienvenue!* I see Charles de Gaulle Airport.

WELCOME TO FRANCE!

(Note, this class text was composed before the tragic Notre Dame fire of April 2019.)

Lifting the Quality of Student Writing

We reviewed the tools in our students' writer's toolboxes by rereading and dipping into the two exemplars, my New York City writing and the collaboratively created text about France.

The texts led us to discuss the following tools in our toolboxes:

- consistent use of repeated refrains
- use of direct address, the "you" voice talking directly to reader
- power of three
- long list sentences
- accurate and specific information
- consistent tone throughout

In addition, we read and reread several of the published nonfiction texts containing refrains that were previously described. For example, we studied the text and illustrations of Bert Kitchen's (1992) *Somewhere Today* in which the author beautifully presents the distinctive activities of many different birds and animals. Each page begins with the refrain "Somewhere today" followed by short, well-developed paragraphs that thoughtfully introduce each animal to readers. It is easy to spot the rich sensory details, the accurate and specific bits of information, and the use of the power of three. This picture book demonstrates how valuable illustrations are in nonfiction texts. It also illustrates how a simple design with a repeated refrain adds elegance to a nonfiction text and how the simple addition of the word *and* to begin the last page breaks the pattern ever so gently and helps readers know they have reached the last page. Above all, this book demonstrates the importance of having something original to say. The author selected interesting birds and animals and focused on surprising behaviors. Imagine a blue bird of paradise hanging upside down, a spotted skunk doing a handstand, or a speckled salamander striking a pose.

Once students made final choices about the topics for their independent studies, we taught whole-class minilessons and conferred on essential instructional goals such as:

- borrowing effective refrains and creating original ones

- deciding if a refrain belongs at the beginning, in the middle, or at the end of a page

- creating satisfying endings

Student Writing Samples

Third graders in Carmela Brutto's class at P.S. 87 borrowed Mary Ann Hoberman's (2002) *Right Outside My Window* to present what they were learning about immigration in New York City at the turn of the century. Each vignette was accompanied by a colorful and detailed illustration.

Right outside my window, I see an organ grinder with children holding hands to play a game with the hurdy-gurdy melody that the organ grinder is playing. I see the organ grinder's pet monkey with a rope on it, so it doesn't run away. It has a coat and hat and is taking coins with one hand and taking off his hat with the other. I wish that I can go outside to play with the other children, but I have to work. —Tyler (See Figure 14.3)

Figure 14.3

Right outside my window, I see Hester Street busy with peddlers selling used clothes and cigars and especially hard flat wheat bread. There also were a lot of Italian banana peddlers because they were shouting, "*Buongiorno*, bananas for sale!" Plus, I could hear their Italian accents. I can also see Jewish peddlers selling the fish they caught earlier that morning. They were shouting, "Fish for sale!" I knew they were Jewish because they didn't have perfect English, plus they had on a little hat called a yarmulke. Also, they were wearing religious scarves with the Star of David on them. I can also spot a little sign in in Yiddish, saying "Kleyder" which is Yiddish for clothes. I learned that from my Jewish friend from school. I wish I could go down there because all of my clothes are rags. —Colin

Right outside my window, on this hot day, I see the ice man with a big block of ice tied to a plank of wood. My friend Joe's job was to get a chunk of the ice for his mom. The ice man lifted it up and Joe went back to his tenement, 5 flights up. The ice man is letting the kids rub their faces on those cold silver cubes. The ice is so tempting on this hot day. I ask my mom if I can have some money to buy ice but she says, "No, you have to cook stew for dinner for our family and for our boarder.
—Dashiell (See Figure 14.4.)

Figure 14.4

Third-grader Katharine, a student in Anne Marie Reardon's class at Dows Lane Elementary School, created an original refrain, with each page of her book about Korea beginning with the words, "If you visit South Korea…"

If you visit South Korea, you will see people wearing hanboks on special occasions.

People in South Korea wear hanboks for a baby's 100th day and the baby's first birthday. They also wear their hanboks for New Year's Day. Hanboks are a long dress for women, and men have their tops and bottoms that are baggier than regular tops and bottoms in the U.S.A.

If you visit South Korea, you will see that schools are different. Korean high school students have a 14-hour day! They start at 8 a.m. and end at 10 p.m. Since they don't get home until almost midnight, they eat their dinner at school. Also, students have to bow to their new teachers when they first meet them in the beginning of the school year.

If you visit South Korea, you will see that famous things are made there. South Korea is the home of Samsung. Samsung is a South Korean company that makes electronic goods such as televisions and computers. Dae Woo and Hyundai make cars. South Korea has made modern goods to sell to other countries for the past 30 years. Now, it is in the world's top ten countries for making ships, cars, and tires.

If you visit South Korea, you would have seen the Olympic torch in 2018. The torch bearer carried the flame for 200 meters. The relay ended in Peyong Changs Olympic Stadium, the main venue for the 2018 Olympics. The final torch was lit by figure skater Yuna Kim.

If you visit South Korea, you will hear a different language. Following the traditions of teachers and philosophers, South Koreans are careful to use respectful language. A Korean uses special words to talk to someone who is older or who has an important title. In fact, there are seven different levels of speech, depending on how much respect a person wants to show and how formal or casual the conversation may be. People who are the same age and know each other use a casual form of speech. Koreans can usually tell exactly what region a person is from by the dialect or ancient use. The Seoul dialect is the one taught in schools.

If you visit South Korea, you will learn about the Chuseok holiday. Chuseok is a traditional Korean holiday of beautiful harvest. Chuseok is the Korean Thanksgiving Day, one of the biggest and most important holidays in South Korea. Family members from near and far come together and share food and stories and to give thanks to their ancestors. In 2017, Chuseok fell on October 4th.

If you visit South Korea, you will see different kinds of transportation. There is every kind of modern transportation in Korea. There are highways and other main roads called expressways. The roads are between all the main towns and cities. There are trains for passengers and freight. Trains are a good way to carry heavy things like cars. The country's main airport is in Seoul. It is called Gimpo Airport. Some flights are to and from other countries. Others are between cities in South Korea.

If you visit South Korea, you will see that Valentine's Day is different. Valentine's Day in South Korea is a bit different from Valentine's Day elsewhere in the world. In fact, Valentine's Day is one of 12 love days celebrated on the 14th of every month in South Korea. These days range from the popular to the depressing to the bizarre and everything in between. Big money is spent and made on the popular Valentine's Day, White Day, while the other love days receive little or no commercial attention.

If you visit South Korea, you will see people eating food differently. All the different foods cooked for one meal are put on the table together. They can be eaten in any order. People use spoons for soup, but usually eat everything else with chopsticks. Everyone waits until the oldest person starts to eat. Then everyone waits until the oldest person finishes. Nobody leaves the table until the oldest person is finished.

If you visit South Korea, you will discover that South Korea had a war. The Soviet (Russian) army took control of Korea when Japan lost World War II. Russia and the United States agreed to divide the country into two parts. Russians moved into North Korea, while U.S. troops entered South Korea. Neither country officially recognized the other. With Chinese and Russian help, North Korea built a huge army and invaded South Korea in 1950. North Korea hoped to make a single country controlled by a Communist government. The United States and other countries sent help to South Korea. Millions of people died, but no one won the war. A peace treaty still has not been signed. Today, North Korea and South Korea are still separate countries.

IF YOU VISIT SOUTH KOREA . . .
REMEMBER TO SAY:
AN NYEONG HA SE YO (hello!)

Carving Out Time for Celebration

The use of refrains certainly makes student writing sound more literary. How thrilling it would be to work with the school librarian to create a shelf or two in the school library to house original and high-quality work created by students throughout the grades. It would make sense then to invite family members and other classes to a launch of this special section of the library along with a publishing party for student accomplishments. Students can turn their refrain writing into illustrated picture books that they would proudly house in the school library for other members of the school community to read.

BOOKS NOTED

Arnold, Caroline. 2016. *Living Fossils: Clues to the Past.* Watertown, MA: Charlesbridge.

Baccilliere, Anna. 2017. *I Like, I Don't Like.* Grand Rapids, MI: Eerdmans Books for Young Readers.

Benjamin, A.H. 2000. *It Could Have Been Worse.* London, England: Little Tiger Press/Penguin Random House.

Bouchard, David. 1993. *If You're Not from the Prairie . . .* Vancouver, British Columbia, Canada: Raincoast Books.

Cline-Ransome, Lesa. 2015. *Whale Trails: Before and Now.* New York: Christy Ottaviano Books/Henry Holt.

Cousins, Lucy. 2010. *I'm the Best.* Somerville, MA: Candlewick.

Cuyler, Margery. 1993. *That's Good, That's Bad.* New York: Henry Holt.

Downs, Mike. 2005. *You See a Circus, I See . . .* Watertown, MA: Charlesbridge.

Dunphy, Madeleine. 2006a. *Here Is the African Savanna.* San Francisco: Web of Life Children's Books.

———. 2006b. *Here Is the Tropical Rain Forest.* San Francisco: Web of Life Children's Books.

———. 2007. *Here Is the Arctic Winter.* San Francisco: Web of Life Children's Books.

Fox, Mem. 2004. *Where Is the Green Sheep?* San Diego, CA: Harcourt Children's Books.

Gray, Rita. 2017. *Have You Heard the Nesting Bird?* Boston: HMH Books for Young Readers.

Henn, Sophie. 2017. *Pass It On.* New York: Philomel Books.

Hoberman, Mary Ann. 2002. *Right Outside My Window.* New York: Mondo.

Kaner, Etta. 2007a. *Who Likes the Rain?* Toronto, Ontario, Canada: Kids Can Press.

———. 2007b. *Who Likes the Sun?* Toronto, Ontario, Canada: Kids Can Press.

———. 2006a. *Who Likes the Snow?* Toronto, Ontario, Canada: Kids Can Press.

———. 2006b. *Who Likes the Wind?* Toronto, Ontario, Canada: Kids Can Press.

———. 2017. *Animals Do, Too! How They Behave Just Like You.* Toronto, Ontario Canada. Kids Can.

Kitchen, Bert. 1992. *Somewhere Today.* Cambridge, MA: Candlewick.

Kudlinski, Kathleen V. 2015. *Boy, Were We Wrong About the Weather!* New York: Dial Books for Young Readers/Penguin Group (USA).

Laroche, Giles. 2011. *If You Lived Here: Houses of the World.* Boston: MA: Houghton Mifflin Books for Children/Houghton Mifflin Harcourt.

London, Jonathan. 1996. *Fireflies, Fireflies Light My Way.* New York: Viking.

Lyon, George Ella. 2014. *What Forest Knows.* New York: Atheneum Books for Young Readers/Simon & Schuster Children's Publishing.

Martin Jr., Bill. 1967. *Brown Bear, Brown Bear, What Do You See?* New York: Henry Holt.

Mendez, Yamile Saied. 2019. *Where Are You From?* New York: Harper.

Minor, Florence, and Wendell Minor. 2009. *If You Were a Penguin*. New York: Katherine Tegen Books/ HarperCollins.

Rosenthal, Amy Krouse. 2008. *It's Not Fair!* New York: HarperCollins.

Sayre, April Pulley. 1998. *Home at Last: A Song of Migration*. New York: Henry Holt.

Serafini, Frank. 2010. *Looking Closely in the Rain Forest*. Toronto, Ontario, Canada: Kids Can Press Ltd.

Singer, Marilyn. 2000. *On the Same Day in March: A Tour of the World's Weather*. New York: HarperCollins Publishers.

Slade, Suzanne. 2012. *The House That George Built*. Watertown, MA: Charlesbridge.

Spinelli, Eileen. 2010. *Do You Have a Cat?* Grand Rapids, Michigan: Eerdmans Books for Young Readers.

Willems, Mo. 2013. *That Is Not a Good Idea!* New York: Balzer + Bray/HarperCollins.

Wood, Douglas. 2011. *No One but You*. Somerville, MA: Candlewick.

Woodson, Jacqueline. 2013. *This Is the Rope: A Story from the Great Migration*. New York: Nancy Paulsen Books/Penguin Group (USA).

A FEW TITLES TO ENRICH YOUR TEACHING

Clinton, Chelsea. 2020. *Don't Let Them Disappear: 12 Endangered Species Across the Globe*. New York: Philomel.

Cowley, Joy. 2019. *Song of the River*. Wellington, New Zealand: Gecko Press.

Gonzalez, Maya Christina. 2012. *I Know the River Loves Me*. New York: Lee & Low.

Gundersheimer, Ben. 2020. *Lilah Tov Good Night*. New York: Nancy Paulsen Books.

Horáček, Petr. 2020. *The Best Place in the World*. Somerville, MA: Candlewick.

Murphy, Mary. 2020. *What I Like Most*. Somerville, MA: Candlewick.

———. 2020. *Only a Tree Knows How to Be a Tree*. Somerville, MA: Candlewick.

Ramos, NoNiega. 2021. *Your Mama*. Boston MA: Houghton Mifflin Harcourt.

Recio, Sili. 2020. *If Dominican Were a Color*. New York: Denene Miller Books: Simon & Schuster.

Richards, Doyin. 2021. *Watch Me: A Story of Immigration and Inspiration*. New York: Feiwel & Friends.

Robinson, Christian. 2020. *You Matter*. New York: Atheneum.

Smith, Monique Gray. 2017. *You Hold Me Up*. Victoria, BC: Orca Book.

Sorrell, Traci. 2021. *We Are Still Here!: Native American Truths Everyone Should Know*. Waterton, MA: Charlesbridge.

Tsarfati, Einat. 2021. *It Could Be Worse*. Somerville, MA: Candlewick

Turk, Evan. 2019. *You Are Home: An Ode to the National Parks*. New York: Atheneum.

Woodson, Jacqueline. 2018. *The Day You Begin*. New York: Nancy Paulsen Books.

See additional resources in online Book List 15.

CHAPTER 15
Definitional Picture Books

(Grades 3-5)

Lulu, a third grader at P.S. 87, filled out the planning sheet in Figure 15.1 as she defined the concept of regret.

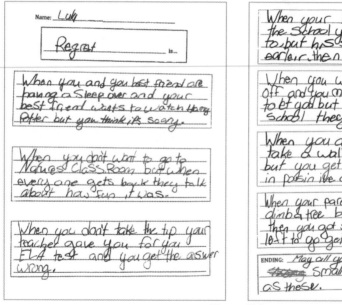

Figure 15.1

Exploring the Roots of the Writing Challenge

Teachers of a certain age might well recall Charles Schulz's (1963) *Security Is a Thumb and a Blanket* and Johnny Carson's (1967) *Misery Is a Blind Date*. In these entertaining and humorous little books, the authors chose a broad concept (security, misery) and explained the meaning of the concept by providing clever examples and illustrations on every page. In this writing challenge, students are asked to do likewise. They are invited to select a broad concept that has significant meaning in their own lives and then craft short, powerful examples on every page. Students are surrounded with excerpts from children's literature, with titles that utilize this "definitional" format.

The structure of this writing is so straightforward and accessible that many students can compose more than one book within a week of school, if they are invited to write daily. The challenge also fits with my trust in the notion that short children benefit from short genres. In other words, elementary-age students can learn a great deal from writing tasks that are of reasonable length, thus warding off the lethargy, inattentiveness, and even frustration that can arise if young writers spend too much time on one writing assignment. When working on this challenge, students can also concentrate on improving the quality of the writing because they are not bogged down with complicated issues of design and structure. Children can then choose their best work to revise, edit, illustrate, and publish.

This project is particularly useful at the beginning of the school year as teachers will learn a great deal about their new students from the topics they choose, asking themselves, "Why did this student choose to define sadness, regret, disappointment . . . ?" Of course, they will also learn about students' writing abilities from the examples they craft to explore these concepts.

Teachers have also challenged older students to create definitional picture books connected to a social studies or science unit of study. (See content-related topics on page 174.)

Engaging Students in the Challenge

All it takes is a copy of Bernard Waber's (2002) *Courage*, or Tobi Tobias's (2000) *Serendipity,* or Kevin Maillard's (2019) *Fry Bread: A Native American Family Tradition*, or Matt de la Peña's (2018) *Love*, or Bryan Collier's (2004) *Uptown*, or Angela Joy's (2020) *Black Is a Rainbow Color,* to successfully launch this writing challenge. After reading a few of these books aloud, teachers carve out time for students to respond to their content. Courage and love are familiar concepts to students and serendipity usually a new one. (We do have a well-known restaurant in New York City called Serendipity, which students often mention. It is famous for its frozen hot chocolate!) Collier's beautifully crafted and illustrated presentations of Harlem ring true for our city students. Discussing Kevin Maillard's *Fry Bread* leads to many new understandings about Native American culture. Angela Joy's celebration of Black color and culture also leads to serious and important conversations as do de la Peña's descriptions of love in ordinary and extraordinary moments. To keep our conversations going I add such questions as:

Students take turns sharing their drafts with one another.

Why do suppose the author chose this concept to define?

Does this concept connect to your own life?

What does this book make you think about?

Which examples touch you deeply?

What do these books have in common?

What example would you compose if you wanted to add an additional page to any one of these books?

Students appreciate that the authors of all these books took a concept that they were interested in and decided to explain that concept by giving an example of the concept on every page.

We then ask students to brainstorm concepts they might like to define. Each student is asked to come up with a list of concepts that they would consider exploring through very powerful one-liners that would help the reader appreciate the concept. After creating a list of possibilities, students star the one that most appeals to them. The following are topics that third, fourth, and fifth graders often list.

YOUNGER WRITERS

adventure, anger, annoyance, astonishment, beauty, boredom, bravery, calm, caring, celebration, concentration, cooperation, creativity, curiosity, danger, dedication, delight, determination, disappointment, effort, embarrassment, excitement, fairness, fancy, fear, forgiveness, friendship, fun, gentleness, happiness, helpfulness, honesty, hope, humor, joy, kindness, loneliness, love, luck, mischief, misery, nature, neatness, noise, peace, politeness, pride, quiet, respect, rudeness, sadness, shock, shy, stubbornness, strength, surprise, suspense, sweetness, teamwork, thoughtfulness, wonder

OLDER WRITERS

adversity, anxiety, awe, bittersweet, boldness, chaos, charisma, charity, charm, coincidence, comfort, compassion, compromise, conformity, confusion, dedication, determination, devotion, discipline, elegance, empathy, enthusiasm, exaggeration, exhaustion, flexibility, frustration, generosity, grace, gratitude, heroism, honor, hopelessness, horror, hospitality, humility, hysteria, impatience, impulsivity, initiative, inspiration, independence, integrity, jealousy, leadership, loneliness, loyalty, motivation, nostalgia, obsession, optimism, patience, perseverance, persistence, pessimism, regret, relaxation, reliability, resilience, resourcefulness, responsibility, revenge, rivalry, sacrifice, security, self-confidence, serenity, sibling rivalry, simplicity, sophistication, sorrow, sportsmanship, stress, stubbornness, sympathy, tragedy, trustworthiness, vanity, virtue, wisdom

Tobi Tobias, author of *Serendipity*, might inspire teachers to view this writing challenge as a means of introducing unfamiliar and surprising vocabulary to students. Imagine upper-elementary students creating books that define such million dollars words as *anguish, arrogance, calamity, camaraderie, conundrum, eccentricity, ennui, hypocrisy, irony, mayhem, procrastination, prudence, remorse, solitude, tolerance, tranquility,* or *versatility.*

If more content-related topics are requested, possibilities include: activism, child labor, communism, community, censorship, citizenship, civil rights, civil war, climate change, democracy, discrimination, diversity, equality, freedom, global warming, going green, government, homelessness, immigration, justice, liberty, patriotism, pollution, poverty, racial harmony, recycling, religion, Revolutionary War, socialism, social justice.

Then too, students can define various holidays (Gail Gibbons's [2006] *Valentine's Day Is . . .*), seasons of the year (Charlotte Zolotow's [1983] *Summer Is . . .*), or sports (Louise Borden's [2014] *Baseball Is . . .*).

One second-grade class created definitional books for their study of New York City. Their topics included NYC architecture, NYC transportation, NYC sightseeing, NYC shopping, NYC eating, NYC art, and NYC recreation. In addition, some students focused on sections of the city including Chinatown, Greenwich Village, the Broadway Theater District, Museum Mile, Little Italy, Central Park, and the Upper West Side. Others defined qualities as they related to New York City including happiness, bravery, adventure, fun, nature, noise, sportsmanship, and relaxation.

Continuing to Support Students' Efforts
Sharing Your Own Writing

Two teacher samples follow. In the first, I use personal experiences to define the concept of quiet. In the second, in addition to background knowledge and personal experience, I tuck in specific bits of content information because the text is anchored to happiness in a specific locale.

QUIET IS . . .

Dedicated to my mom who loves peace and quiet

Quiet is lying awake at night and hearing the wind whooshing right through your windowpanes.

Quiet is a fire drill when the teacher is serious about "No Talking!" and all you can hear is the shuffling of feet out the schoolhouse doors.

Quiet is an empty house after the movers have carried out all the boxes and the last bit of furniture.

Quiet is tiptoeing into your baby sister's room to listen to her breathing when she has been asleep for a very long time.

Quiet is hearing the soft crunch of your winter boots when you are the first to sink your feet into the freshly fallen snow in your front yard.

Quiet is being by yourself in the backyard at nightfall, looking up at the dark sky, and spotting the Big Dipper.

Quiet is not being able to sleep because you hear the ticking of the wall clock or the dripping of the bathroom faucet.

(continues)

QUIET IS . . . *(continued)*

Quiet is walking barefoot on the beach very early in the morning accompanied by a lone speckled sandpiper on the dunes.

Quiet is sitting at the kitchen counter softly slurping a chilled glass of apple juice as you listen to the refrigerator hum.

Quiet is the sound of a book closing when you are alone in the library. Go ahead, try closing this one quietly.

NEW YORK CITY HAPPINESS IS . . .

Dedicated to all NYC first responders and essential workers

New York City happiness is . . . arriving just in time to catch the number 2 or 3 express train when you are running late for school on the Upper West Side.

New York City happiness is . . . getting to the Central Park Zoo just as the Delacorte Musical Clock is about to chime and the seals are going to be fed.

New York City happiness is . . . standing on the Ticketmaster line in Times Square and getting front row seats to *Lion King* at a discount price.

New York City happiness is . . . being invited to a Central Park West apartment to view the Macy's Thanksgiving Day parade.

New York City happiness is . . . feeling hungry and arriving at Shake Shack when there is no line.

New York City happiness is . . . receiving a Zabar's gift certificate and buying your favorite bagels, cream cheese, and lox.

New York City happiness is . . . watching the Mets and Yankees in a Subway Series World Series and your preferred team wins. (Go Yankees!!)

New York City happiness is . . . attending a Shakespeare play in Central Park on a beautiful summer's evening.

New York City happiness is . . . hailing a taxicab quickly on Broadway during a heavy downpour.

New York City happiness is . . . visiting the dinosaur exhibit at the Museum of Natural History and being the only one there.

New York City happiness is . . . taking an out-of-town friend to the Guggenheim Museum for the very first time.

Above all, New York City happiness is visiting the memorial built in Lower Manhattan to honor those lost in the tragedy of 9/11 and knowing we will never forget.

Gathering Information

Students will need support with research techniques if the concepts they are working on are curriculum related. For example, if a student has chosen global warming as their topic, the student will need to know how to locate appropriate information, take notes, use and credit quotes, use notes to craft meaningful sentences, and so on.

If students are working on more experienced-based concepts such as jealousy, kindness, or creativity, they might need a very different approach to gathering ideas. Their preparation for writing might include recalling memories, rereading journals or writer's notebooks, and talking to friends and family members. Then, too, they will need opportunities to try out their tentative ideas looking for emotional responses. They will benefit from asking, "Did I move my audience with the images I have created?" Students should be encouraged to share their work in progress, noting if their classmates sigh, nod, laugh, tear up, laugh, cry, or show any other emotion. If there is no emotional response, students will need to revise their ideas or gather new ones. (See "Lifting the Quality of Student Writing" on how students can inspire an emotional response.)

Lifting the Quality of Student Writing

Whenever teachers share their own writing with their students, they create an enormous well from which to draw. Potential minilessons topics include the following:

- how you thought of items included

- how you wove in specific and/or sensory details to make your examples come alive

- how your dedication connects to the topic of the book

- how you created a satisfying yet surprising ending

- how you turned your draft into a page-turning book complete with illustrations

Additional minilessons include the following:

- Offer and explain preprepared drafting paper that enables students to plan and organize their ideas. Students write concepts to be defined in the rectangular box at the top of the sheet. In the additional boxes, students jot down examples they will use to define the concept and then fill out the box labeled "Ending." (See Lulu's drafting sheet for "Regret Is . . ." on page 172.)

- Remind students to write in a way that will "move" their audience. If teacher has written their own definitional material, places with an emotional tug can be highlighted as well as the writing tools used to create such an effect. Classmates can talk about how student writers can improve their writing if there is no audience response. Suggestions might include choosing more powerful examples as well as adding more sensory details, precise verbs, specific information, powerful similes, and so on.

- Review the tools in their writer's toolboxes. I don't think we can do this enough. For easy reference, tape the list of writing tools in students' writer's notebooks or writing folder or laminate on a card that sits in middle of desk or on a chart that hangs in a prominent place.

- Refer to published literature to discuss how authors move their audience.

I say something like, "Each time I read aloud a page from *Serendipity* by Tobi Tobias, I can tell that the author really touched you. After some pages you sighed. After other pages you smiled, laughed, or nodded in agreement. Sometimes I could tell that you were bursting to comment on the example the author chose. In other words, Tobi Tobias knows how to move her audience. When you choose your examples, aim high. You, too, can move your audience. Let's begin by figuring out what Tobi does that we can try to do."

Then I lifted sentences from the text so students could figure out what author has done that they could do. We ask students, "Why are these lines so powerful? "

One of Tobias's definitions reads, "Serendipity is putting a quarter in the gumball machine and having three pieces come rattling out instead of one—all red." Students were reminded to be specific when they write, recalling Nancy Hale's oft-quoted, "The more particular, the more specific you are, the more universal you are." Teachers might then lift lines from other published definitional books after enjoying, appreciating, and responding to the texts in their entirety. A few examples follow:

Note the alliteration in Judi K. Beach's (2003) *Names for Snow*: "Call snow lace when it lines the limbs of the lilacs."

Note the strong verbs in Bernard Waber's (2002) *Courage:* "Courage is being sudsed and scrubbed by strangers."

Note the rich sensory details in Angela Joy's (2020) *Black Is a Rainbow Color.* "Black are the eyes on salted peas. Black are the shadows of ooo-old magnolia trees."

Similarly, de la Peña shakes awake your senses in *Love* (2018) when he writes, "Love, too, is the smell of crashing waves, and a train whistling blindly in the distance, and each night the sky above your trailer turns the color of love."

Every page of Kevin Maillard's tribute to fry bread and Native American culture provides content for valuable minilessons. One page is filled with similes to describe the shape of the bread. He writes that it is "flat like a pancake" or "round like a ball" or "puffy like Nan's softest pillow." On another page describing the sound of fry bread cooking, he tantalizes the reader with his choice of powerful and precise verbs including "clangs," "blazes," "sizzles," and "pops."

Note all the effective writing tools in Louise Borden's (2014) *Baseball Is . . .*

Power of three: "There are floats, bands . . . and big balloons."

Repetition: "Baseball is front row seats and top row seats, bleacher seats and box seats."

Simile: the American flag is "like a familiar friend."

Long list sentences, brimming with specific and accurate information: "Baseball is the fastball, the curveball, the knuckleball, the slider, the crack of the bat, the balk, the steal, the ground out, the frozen rope, the triple, the squeeze play, the double play, the pop fly, the sacrifice fly, the warning track, the walk, the RBI, the error, the tag, and the grand slam."

- Explore the use of introductions in definitional picture books. Some published books have them, some do not. Rather than offering introductory words, some authors get right to their list of examples on the very first page. This is done in Gail Gibbons's (2004) *Thanksgiving Is . . .* Louise Borden's *Baseball Is . . .* (2014) and *America Is . . .* (2002), Charles Schulz's Happiness Is series, and Tobi Tobias's (2000) *Serendipity.* Other authors do provide introductions before beginning their list of examples. Jen Hochhauser (2004) begins her misery books with short rhymes. Judy K. Beach's (2003) *Names for Snow* begins with a question, "Mama, what is snow?" Bernard Waber (2002) begins *Courage* with a traditional topic sentence, "There are many kinds of courage."

- Remind students that the word *when* is not required, even though most students automatically include it. "Happiness is when you get to stay up late to watch a Harry Potter movie with your whole family" vs. "Happiness is getting to stay up late to watch a Harry Potter movie with your whole family."

- Place student work in progress on document camera for public conferences. Select issues that apply to many students.

- Teach ending possibilities. Teacher can share the variety of ways authors have chosen to end their definitional books. Several examples follow.

ENDINGS FOR DEFINITIONAL BOOKS

Most of all . . . (use of superlative):

"Most of all, luck is winning the lottery on your birthday!"

May your . . . . (a wish for the reader, a switch to direct address):

"May your stressful situations pass quickly!"

Pose a question related to the concept being defined:

"What do you find frustrating?"

So . . . (give advice to reader):

"So if you are feeling bored, find a little kid to read this book to."

But . . . (set up for shift in thinking or present an opposite):

"But, mischief is not scooping some extra ice cream; that's just being a growing, hungry kid!"

(continues)

ENDINGS FOR DEFINITIONAL BOOKS *(continued)*

Circle back to beginning, introductory ideas as Louise Borden (2002) does in *America Is . . .* She repeats the same lines on the first and last pages:

> "America is our country. It is the place we call home."

Make a clever comment referring to topic of book:

> "Go ahead, try closing this book quietly."

Present a big idea statement as Charles M. Schulz (1962) does in *Happiness Is a Warm Puppy:*

> "Happiness is one thing to one person and another thing to another person."

Shift to a very different genre as Jen Hochhauser (2004) does in *Misery Is a Spider in the Bathtub.* She begins and ends the book with rhyming lines while all her other examples of misery are written in prose.

End with character going to sleep, a very common and natural ending to books. Deborah Underwood (2010) does in this in *The Quiet Book.*

End with a comment on learning the meaning of the concept presented as Tobi Tobias (2000) does in *Serendipity:* "Serendipity is a word that, when you find out what it means, is as wonderful and surprising as it sounds."

Minilessons are based on needs assessed during writing conferences:

- If you notice that student examples are rather skimpy, share carefully selected ones aloud, asking students how to turn such minimal statements, such as "Happiness is going to Yankee Stadium" into more effective writing. (For example, "Happiness is going to Yankee Stadium to watch your favorite teammates in pinstripes play the Boston Red Sox, and the Yankees score a grand slam in the first inning.")

- If you notice that student examples are overlapping or repetitive, thereby losing the element of surprise with the turn of each page, share these drafts aloud. Ask students to listen for places that are not as effective as others because similar ideas are being used repeatedly. Discuss with students how to brainstorm additional, original alternatives to strengthen their writing.

- If you notice that students are struggling with how to move from "_____ is . . . " to the example that follows, point out a range of possibilities. In *Summer Is . . .* Charlotte Zolotow (1983) begins all her examples with nouns ("Summer is barefeet"; "Summer is porches"). In *Courage*, Bernard Waber (2002) includes a mix of structures, verbs ("Courage is going to bed without a nightlight"), and nouns ("Courage is a spelling bee"). Harriet Ziefert (2005) in her *Misery Is a Smell in Your Backpack* begins several examples with the word *when* ("Misery is when your . . . ").

Finally, students were asked to choose their best work for publication. After completing revisions, provide time for students to edit, illustrate, and share their definitional picture books.

Student Writing Samples

Cleo, a third grader in Renay Sadis's class at P.S. 87, defined *peaceful* in Figure 15.2.

Figure 15.2 *(continues)*

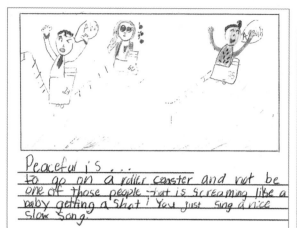

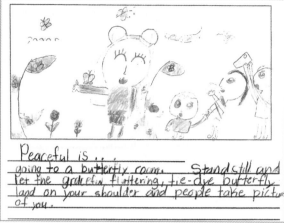

Peaceful is . . .
to go on a roller coaster and not be one of those people that is screaming like a baby getting a shot! You just sing a nice slow song.

Peaceful is . . .
going to a butterfly room. Stand still and let the graceful, flattering, tie-dye butterfly land on your shoulder and people take picture of you.

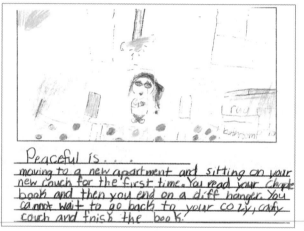

Peaceful is . . .
moving to a new apartment and sitting on your new couch for the first time. You read your Chapter book and then you end on a diff hanger. You cannot wait to go back to your cozy, comfy couch and finish the book.

Figure 15.2 (continued)

Third-grade Campbell, another one of Renay's students, writes "Luck Is . . ."

Luck is . . . going to the movies to see *The Secret Life of Pets 2* and suddenly you see your best friends and you get to sit with them.

Luck is . . . driving to the beach on a July morning, watching tropical fish glide across the rippling water, and you're the only one there.

Luck is . . . having a snow day from school and running across the fluffy snow, with your beautiful Bichon behind you, making tracks in the snow.

Luck is . . . finding your sister's hilarious toy, which you secretly want for yourself, and your sister says you can have it.

Luck is . . . right after Halloween, your sister's full-to-the top candy bag shouts, "I'm almost empty!" but yours is still full.

Luck is . . . jumping from stone to stone across the stream and you start to wobble and shake, but you reach out and balance yourself and you don't fall.

Luck is . . . the reader wanting to read this book again, over and over, over and over.

Classmate Matthew writes "Shyness Is . . ."

Shyness is . . . when you're in a school show and your mouth gets zipped up by your memory and you're the main character in the show.

Shyness is . . . going to 16 Handles, Pinkberry, or Forty Carrots frozen yogurt shops and you want to ask for a sample, but you just can't.

Shyness is . . . meeting someone new and feeling as blank as a book with no words.

Shyness is . . . not wanting to give your own order at a fancy restaurant and when you do your voice is as soft as kids at a fire drill, lockdown, or shelter-in.

Shyness is . . . someone asking you, "Are you upset, sad, or lonely?" and you really want to say "yes," but your brain won't allow you.

Shyness is. . .being new to the school, and you mutter to someone if they will be your friend, but just when you're about to say it, your brain gets pushed away by your heart.

Shyness is . . . being the only person at the best birthday party ever that doesn't know anybody except the birthday boy/girl and feeling that your heart is desperate for love, importance, and attention.

Please don't be shy to read this book again! Tip . . . sometimes you can be shy at the beginning, but you warm up in the end!

Carving Out Time for Celebration

Definitional picture books have become so popular that several classes usually take on this challenge simultaneously. This across-the-grade event can result in a larger-than-usual publishing event with several classes gathering in the school gymnasium, auditorium, or cafeteria so that students can roam the room and read one another's short picture books. Children who might have chosen the same concept to define can be grouped together to appreciate how different authors present the same concept.

Then too, a student from each class can volunteer to read their definitional book aloud to the entire group gathered. Of course, teachers can invite family members to smaller classroom celebrations in which each student reads aloud his or her favorite page from their definitional book, having been asked to choose the page that they think will best evoke an emotional response.

BOOKS NOTED

"Definitional" picture books:

Beach, Judi K. 2003. *Names for Snow.* New York: Hyperion Books for Children.

Borden, Louise. 2002. *America Is . . .* New York: Margaret K. McElderry Books/Simon & Schuster Children's Publishing.

_____. 2014. *Baseball Is . . .* New York: Margaret K. McElderry Books/Simon & Schuster Children's Publishing.

_____. 1997. *Thanksgiving Is . . .* New York: Cartwheel Books/Scholastic.

Collier, Bryan. 2004. *Uptown.* New York: Square Fish.

de la Peña, Matt. 2018. *Love.* New York: G.P. Putnam's Sons.

Gibbons, Gail. 2004. *Thanksgiving Is . . .* New York: Holiday House.

_____. 2006. *Valentine's Day Is . . .* New York: Holiday House.

Hochhauser, Jen. 2004. *Misery Is a Spider in the Bathtub.* Maplewood, NJ: Blue Apple Books.

Joy, Angela. 2020. *Black Is a Rainbow Color.* New York: Roaring Brook Press.

Maillard, Kevin. 2019. *Fry Bread: A Native American Family Tradition.* New York: Roaring Brook.

Tobias, Tobi. 2000. *Serendipity.* New York: Simon & Schuster Books for Young Readers.

Turner, Ann. 2001. *In the Heart.* New York: HarperCollins Children's Books.

Underwood, Deborah. 2010. *The Quiet Book.* Boston, MA: Houghton Mifflin Books for Children/ Houghton Mifflin Harcourt.

Waber, Bernard. 2002. *Courage.* Boston, MA: Walter Lorraine Books/Houghton Mifflin.

Ziefert, Harriet. 2005. *Misery Is a Smell in Your Backpack.* Maplewood, NJ: Blue Apple Books.

Zolotow, Charlotte. 1983. *Summer Is . . .* New York: Thomas Y. Crowell.

Definitional books intended for adults:

Carson, Johnny. 1967. *Misery Is a Blind Date.* Garden City, NY: Doubleday.

Schulz, Charles M. 1962. *Happiness Is a Warm Puppy.* Kennebunkport, ME: Cider Mill Press.

_____. 1963. *Security Is a Thumb and a Blanket.* San Francisco: Determined Productions.

_____. 972. *Happiness Is a Sad Song.* New York: Scholastic.

A FEW TITLES TO ENRICH YOUR TEACHING

Barnes, Derrick. 2020. *I Am Every Good Thing.* New York: Nancy Paulsen.

Beer, Sophie. 2019. *Kindness Makes Us Strong.* New York: Dial Books for Young Readers.

_____. 2018. *Love Makes a Family.* New York: Dial Books for Young Readers.

Franco, Betsy. 2009. *Zero Is the Leaves on the Tree.* Berkeley, CA: Tricycle Press.

Ledyard, Stephanie Parsley. 2019. *Home Is a Window.* New York: Neal Porter Books.

Paul, Baptiste and Miranda Paul. 2021. *Peace.* New York: Simon & Schuster.

Salas, Laura Purdie. 2012. *A Leaf Can Be...* Brookfield, CT: Millbrook Press.

_____. 2014. *Water Can Be . . .* Brookfield, CT: Millbrook Press.

_____. 2015. *A Rock Can Be . . .* Brookfield, CT: Millbrook Press.

Talle, Mariahadessa Ekere. 2019. *Layla's Happiness.* New York: Enchanted Lion Books.

Yeomans, Ellen. 2019. *Some Snow Is . . .* New York: G.P. Putnam's Sons.

See additional definitional publications including poetry in bibliography in online Book List 16.

PART FOUR

MORE THAN
AN AUDIENCE OF ONE

Students need to see that their words can really inform, entertain, and have an impact. They need to see that their words can change someone's behavior or attitude. The writing challenges in the pages that follow all have the potential to result in work that reaches a wide audience. The writing is not intended to wind up in a folder, on a bulletin board display, or tossed in the trash at the end of the semester. During the writing of this book, I had surgery to repair a torn rotary cuff. I was not able to use my left arm for many, many weeks. "Think of it as an ornament," suggested my physical therapist. "Do not use it." Students' writing should not be an ornament, mere decoration. It must be put to good use. Completed work should take its place in the real world, and students alongside their classmates, teachers, and family members should proudly admire and appreciate one another's efforts.

- Chapter 16: Would You Rather . . .? (Grades 2–5)
- Chapter 17: Nonfiction Calendars (Grades 2–5)
- Chapter 18: Creating Readers' Notes (Grades 3–5)
- Chapter 19: Creating Glossaries (Grades 3–5)
- Chapter 20: Research and Riddles (Grades 1–5)
- Chapter 21: Every Day of the Week (Grades 2–5)
- Chapter 22: Author Scrapbooks (Grades 3–5)

CHAPTER 16
Would You Rather . . . ?
(Grades 2-5)

Bella, a third grader in Renay Sadis and Mayra Romero's class at P.S. 87, asks her readers a literary question:

WOULD YOU RATHER WRITE AN ODE OR A SONNET?

Do you know the difference between an ode and a sonnet? First, sonnets are lyrical poems that have 14 lines, whereas odes are not very lengthy. Next, there is only one kind of sonnet, however there are three kinds of odes—Pindar ode, Horatian ode and Irregular ode. Third, the name sonnet comes from the Italian word sonnet which means little song. On the other hand, the Horatian ode comes from a guy named Horace. Did you know that odes have a technique that is lyrical in nature? The word *ode* comes from the Greek word "aedine" which means to chant or sing. Sonnets feature two contrasting characters, events, beliefs or emotions. One example of a sonnet is "Shall I compare thee to a summer's day?" That was written by William Shakespeare. Shakespeare was a famous writer from England who wrote books and poems. He was very dramatic and romantic. "Ode to the Nightingale" was written by John Keats. "Ode to My Socks" was written by Pablo Neruda. So, now that you know about odes and sonnets, which one would you rather write?

Exploring the Roots of the Writing Challenge

When my children were little and then when their children were little, I often read aloud John Birmingham's (1978) *Would You Rather . . .* , a favorite bedtime picture book. The author passed away in January of 2019, and in his obituary, a publishing executive described him as "a true original, a picture-book pioneer and an endlessly inventive creator of stories that could be by turns hilarious and comforting, shocking and playful" (Genzlinger 2019). My grandchildren probably loved this Birmingham title for all those qualities and additionally because the book delayed their bedtimes. As the title suggests, this picture book is filled with "Would you rather . . . ?" questions, questions that demand answers. Young listeners want to answer every single question and explain why their answer makes more sense than any contrary one offered by a sibling. Who could resist explaining why it would be preferable to have your house surrounded by snow than surrounded by water or a jungle? Who could resist explaining why it would be preferable to be soaked with water than covered in jam or pulled through the mud by a dog? These interesting questions continued and so did the long conversations, way past their bedtimes.

But some "Would you rather . . . ?" questions are not so easy to answer. They are not merely opinion questions based on our tastes, interests, and past experiences. No, the other kind of "Would you rather . . . ?" question fuels curiosity and demands that the reader have information before answering. In other words, there are questions that require informed decision making, and isn't *that* what we want for all our students? We want them to be armed with information before they choose which after-school program, summer camp, middle school, high school, or college to attend. We want them to grow into citizens who read the newspaper before they vote, who read consumer reviews before they make expensive purchases, who read up on side effects before choosing medical options. These kinds of questions abound in today's world.

Realizing how children delight in answering "Would you rather . . . ?" questions, I speculated on the possibility of turning this format into a nonfiction research challenge for students, beginning in grade two. To entice a room full of seven-year-olds, I worked with classroom teachers to tap into another surefire interest of young children: animals. Second graders always seem to take great delight in class pets, animal read-alouds, and field trips to zoos and aquariums. So, in this thinking-through-possibilities stage, we wondered about combining "Would you rather . . . ?" questions *and* a love of animals. To this combination, I added a third ingredient: the desire to teach others. I capitalized on the idea that children especially love to test, tempt, and teach their caregivers, proving that they know things that adults may not. The challenge solidified into creating "Would you rather . . . ?" questions about animals that would be hard for classmates as well as family members to answer if they didn't have enough information. The children would have to have a question of interest to themselves, their peers, and their family members. Then they would have to research and write up the kind of information that would help their readers make informed decisions. Luckily, most school and classroom library shelves are filled with a wide range of books about animals, many that second graders can read independently.

(For older students in grades 3–5, we did not limit topics to animals, but invited students to craft "Would you rather . . . ?" questions in a wide range of topics. (See pages 189–190 as well as Appendix 6 for an extensive listing of "Would you rather . . . ?" questions.)

Engaging Students in the Challenge

I began my work with second graders by reading aloud the John Birmingham (1978) picture book, *Would You Rather . . .* Their responses were like those of my own children and grandchildren. They had opinions and their opinions came quickly. I then suggested that some "Would you rather . . . ?" questions would be harder to answer. I said, "What if I asked you, 'Would you rather pet an ostrich or an emu?'" Several students called out, "What's an emu?" "What if I asked you if you would rather spend time with an alligator or a crocodile?" "Oh, I always mix those up," volunteered one child. "Would you rather become an expert on African elephants or Asian elephants?" I continued. "What's the difference between them?" a young student asked. The students understood my point. Sometimes you can't answer a question without additional information. (Note, that this challenge could have been introduced without the John Birmingham book. Teachers simply need to share some of the "Would you rather . . . ?" questions for children that are easy to find online or read aloud any of the picture books listed at the end of this chapter and in online Book List 17.)

Students are working side by side, creating "Would you rather . . . ?" questions.

I then announced our new writing challenge: to gather many pairs of animals that people either mix up with one another or include an animal that is so unfamiliar that people can't readily answer a "Would you rather . . . ?" question. We spent a long time generating a list of these kinds of questions. The only constraint was that the animals had to be frequently confused by young and old alike. We brainstormed many possibilities in class, and then students as well as their teachers contributed additional ones. Collecting the names of animals that are frequently confused or ones that many people are unfamiliar with can become contagious. Try asking a colleague or family member, "Can you name two animals that you have mixed up with one another?" You can even google "animals that are often confused." Our list kept growing and growing.

We also spent time brainstorming the use of different verbs, realizing that the verb used would help direct and narrow the research. If you were being asked to choose between two animals you might take care of, you would need different information than if you were being asked to choose between two animals that might attack you. Some of the questions generated included: Would you rather *train* a dolphin or a porpoise? Would you rather *swim* with sea lions or seals? Would you rather *be chased by* a great white shark or a bull shark? Would you rather *spot* a hedgehog or a woodchuck in your yard? Would you rather *feed* an alpaca or a llama? Would you rather visit Australia to *observe* a dingo or a bilby? Would you rather *sketch* a chinstrap penguin or a macaroni penguin? Would you rather *pet* a porcupine or an echidna? (See Appendix 6 for additional "Would you rather . . . ?" animal questions.)

Continuing to Support Students' Efforts

Students composed an original question or chose a question from the class list. (Students who composed original questions were asked to check in with teachers to be sure that readers would need background information to answer.) A sampling of students' questions follows:

Would you rather . . .

> *have a guinea pig or a gerbil for a pet?*
>
> *take care of a frog or a toad?*
>
> *ride a camel or a dromedary?*
>
> *feed an alpaca or a llama?*
>
> *race a cheetah or a jaguar?*
>
> *watch a walrus or a manatee?*

study the habits of a rhinoceros or a hippopotamus?

ride a mule or a donkey?

catch a salamander or a lizard?

snorkel near a narwhal or a walrus?

take photographs of a gorilla or a chimpanzee?

spot an elk or a moose on your travels?

Sharing Your Own Writing with Young Students

I decided to write about woodchucks and hedgehogs (although currently the real visitors to my garden are opossums and raccoons). I gathered background information about each animal and then focused on possible backyard behaviors. I told the children that as I read about each animal, I asked myself, "Would there be any benefits to having these animals in your backyard? Would there be any problems with having these animals in your yard?" As I researched, I jotted down any answers to these questions. I also downloaded images of each animal to accompany my writing. I showed children my notes and then my drafts. Finally, I read aloud my finished work to the second graders and gave them copies to reread and discuss.

After learning about woodchucks and hedgehogs, students engaged in a lively discussion and were ready to make their opinions known. (Most students preferred woodchucks, as they didn't want to leave the United States, and they worried about the possibility of skin infections from hedgehogs.)

Would you rather see a woodchuck or a hedgehog in your backyard?

WOODCHUCKS

There is a lot to understand about woodchucks. These animals are also called groundhogs, so we hear a lot about them on February 2nd when we celebrate Groundhog's Day.

One thing you might want to know about woodchucks, especially if you see them in your yard, is that they are great diggers. They have short, powerful limbs and curved, thick claws so they can dig very well. Be prepared to see several holes in the lawn. The woodchuck creates a big den, one with two entrances and many rooms. They use their underground homes to get away from bad weather and predators, to sleep, to take care of their babies, to poop, and, of course, to hibernate in the winter. Can you believe that they often create a separate room in their burrow for pooping?

Woodchucks also like to eat plants that might grow in your garden, especially grasses, dandelions, clover, and berries. They seem to be especially fond of raspberries, so beware if you grow these in your yard. Although they are mainly plant eaters, groundhogs have been known to eat insects and even baby birds.

Another issue that you will have to deal with if a woodchuck lives in your neighborhood is noise. Woodchucks make several different sounds. For example, they make a high-pitched whistle to warn other woodchucks that danger is near. They also squeal if they get into a fight with a predator. Woodchucks also produce a low bark and a noise from grinding their teeth. So, would you want to see one in your yard?

HEDGEHOGS

Hedgehogs are fascinating animals. Of course, if you live in America, you probably won't see this interesting animal in your backyard. You might have to move to Europe, Asia, Africa, or New Zealand to spot one. Even if you live in places that hedgehogs call home, you will have to stay up late to see one as they are usually only seen in the dark of night. (That's why they are called nocturnal animals.)

If you spy one in your yard, you might be amazed to see some unusual behaviors. For example, the hedgehog can roll itself into a tight ball to defend itself. The hollow hairs, also called quills, do not cover the hedgehog's face, feet, or belly, so when it rolls itself into that tight ball, it is protecting the other parts of its body. You might also see a hedgehog licking and biting anything in your yard that is giving off a new scent. The hedgehog gathers that scent and mixes it with its own saliva. The hedgehog spreads that mixture on its body. Some scientists think that the hedgehogs are camouflaging themselves with a new aroma to keep predators away.

Besides being killed by predators, hedgehogs have been known to starve to death because they get their heads stuck in containers or cups and can't remove them. So, if you have a hedgehog in your yard, be sure not to leave any empty food containers around!

Hedgehogs eat plants, especially berries and even watermelon and animals including birds' eggs, snakes, snails, and frogs. Some countries think of hedgehogs as pests because they have destroyed so many shore birds, insects, snails, and lizards. They can also be considered annoying because of the sounds they make which include grunting, snuffling, and squealing.

A final warning—do not touch a hedgehog! They have been known to spread a skin infection to the people that handle them. Well, what do you think? Would it be worth moving to different continent in order to see a hedgehog in your yard?

Gathering Information

Students needed to think about the kind of information readers would need to make informed decisions about their individual "Would you rather . . . ?" questions. Before beginning their own research, we worked collaboratively with the whole class to think through the following research challenges.

We asked the question, "Would you rather take care of a ferret or a guinea pig?" We then asked, "What information would help you make an informed decision?" We brainstormed the following list of questions that would have to be asked about ferrets and then repeated for guinea pigs.

- What are ferrets' eating habits and costs?
- What kind of home do you need to provide for ferrets, and how do you keep it clean?
- How often do ferrets need to see a veterinarian?
- What are ferrets' sleeping habits?
- How noisy are ferrets?
- How playful are ferrets?

We followed with another question, "Would you rather ride a camel or a dromedary?" Again, we asked, "What information would help you make an informed decision?" We brainstormed the following list of questions that would need to be asked about dromedaries as well.

- How fast do these animals move?
- How tall are camels?
- How comfortable are camels to sit on?
- How do camels behave with children riders?
- Are there news stories about people having accidents while riding camels?

Finally, we asked students to record what information would be needed for their own individual research question. We reviewed students' individual research plans, and then students copied each of their questions on a separate sheet of paper or index card. We helped students gather relevant research material encouraging them to search the shelves in their classroom as well as the school library. We also asked students to visit the public libraries in their neighborhoods for appropriate books on their chosen animals. (See online Book Lists 2 and 4 for bibliographies of animal reference materials.) Students read reference materials and took notes to answer each question. We demonstrated taking notes without copying directly from resource materials, making sure that students recorded facts and phrases in their own words. We also taught students how to use direct quotations, and we suggested looking for useful, yet surprising bits of information, the kind that makes them say, "Hey, I never knew that!"

Lifting the Quality of Student Writing with Young Students

Once students had abundant information on both animals, they began to draft their passages. They revised as needed, making sure their information was clear, complete, accurate, and specific. Throughout, we reminded students that their goal was to help readers make an informed choice. A few minilessons follow:

- We talked to students about possible topic or opening sentences. A few possibilities appear below:

  » Do you need more information about _____?

  » Would you like to know more about _____?

  » There is so much to understand about _____.

  » _____ are interesting animals.

  » Welcome to the world of _____!

- We shared chapters from Joan Axelrod Contrada's (2012) *This or That Animal Debate: A Rip-Roaring Game of Either/Or Questions,* highlighting how the author provided the kind of information that would help readers answer her "This or that?" questions. For example, when the author posed a question about preferring to swim with a great white shark or with a box jellyfish, she was sure to include information about the number of people killed in a year by each, the percent of people who die from being attacked, and the quality of the venom. Teachers also pointed out her use of bulleted information alongside her prose paragraphs and the way she separated information about each animal into two distinct pages.

- We shared a few sections of *What's the Difference? 40 Pairs of the Seemingly Similar* by Emma Strack (2018). The author offers bulleted lists of descriptors about the paired similar items, including camels and dromedaries, grasshoppers and crickets, and penguins and auks. We pretended these lists were research notes and asked students to practice turning each list into a meaningful paragraph complete with an opening sentence and a sensible concluding one.

- We talked about the benefits of providing accompanying illustrations to help the reader make informed choices. Illustrations were drawn or downloaded from Internet sites.

- We stressed the importance of clarity, accuracy, and specificity.

- We talked about the importance of rereading drafts, becoming critical readers of one's own writing.

- We encouraged volunteers to place their drafts under the document camera so that we could publicly confer, making helpful suggestions.

- We asked students to make sure they were including the kind of information that addressed their question. In other words, if your question was about getting chased by an animal, be sure to include the size, speed, and predatory habits of the animal. If your question was about having the animal as a pet, be sure to include the eating, cleaning, and sleeping habits of the animal. Such young writers, in their urgency to share information, often forgot to address the question they posed.

Working with Older Writers

The "Would you rather . . . ?" challenge can become even more enticing with older students. Third, fourth, and fifth graders can branch out and ask questions in a wide range of categories. In other words, it no longer felt necessary to create a classroom theme to provide abundant research materials. We no longer worried about the availability of readable materials, knowing there are appropriate and accessible Internet sites for upper-grade students. We appreciated the older students' abilities to independently find additional information online and on the shelves of school and public libraries. We looked forward to the contagious energy that would fill the room when students were choosing and learning about so many different and surprising topics simultaneously.

(Note, I can easily imagine third-, fourth-, and fifth-grade teachers successfully designing a "Would you rather . . . ?" course of study within a content area. Teachers and students could create a long list of questions related to Colonial America, the Olympics, or nutrition. Students would research a wide range of topics under each of these broad umbrellas.)

In one third-grade class, I introduced the challenge similarly to our work in grade two. Once again, I began by sharing John Birmingham's book *Would You Rather . . .* and then suggested how easy it was to answer the questions posed. I then introduced the idea of questions that would be more difficult to answer because we lacked necessary background information. It was easy to prove my point by asking a few questions, not limiting them to any one area of study. These included "Would you rather eat vegemite or marmite for breakfast?" "Would you rather visit Iceland or Greenland?" "Would you rather get caught in a cyclone or a tornado?" "Would you rather suffer from claustrophobia or acrophobia?" "Would you rather have been a cooper or a chandler in Colonial times?" "Would you rather become an archeologist or an anthropologist?" Students understood that before they answered these questions, they would need information.

Another way to launch an upper-grade study would be to share *What's the Difference? 40 Pairs of the Seemingly Similar*, written by Emma Strack (2018). The author includes interesting matches in a variety of categories. These include stalactites and stalagmites, clementines and mandarin oranges, Antarctica and the Arctic, The Netherlands and Holland, Great Britain and England, the iris and the pupil, the tibia and the fibula, a cathedral and a basilica, white chocolate and dark chocolate, and a terrace and a balcony.

We placed a wide range of categories on the board and asked children to choose their main area of interest. We listed sample questions in each category and invited students and observing teachers to add additional ones. Questions referred to topics that people often confused or ones that might be unfamiliar.

Categories included geography ("Would you rather take a vacation in Slovakia or Slovenia?"), food ("Would you rather eat Gorgonzola or Roquefort cheese?"), sports ("Would you rather become an expert at spelunking or zorbing?"), famous people ("Would you rather have worked for Milton Bradley or Milton Hershey?"), science ("Would you rather have deciduous or evergreen trees in your backyard?"), history/social studies ("Would you rather be asked to filibuster or gerrymander?"), occupations ("Would you rather become an astronomer or an astrologer?"), transportation ("Would you rather ride on a funicular or a monorail?"), construction/architecture ("Would you rather design buildings like Frank Lloyd Wright or Antoni Gaudí?"), the arts ("Would you rather star in a performance of Rapunzel or Rumpelstiltskin?"), clothing/fashion ("Would you rather wear a fez or a fedora?"), mathematics ("Would you rather study algebra or trigonometry?"), and even a category labeled "miscellaneous" ("Would you rather win a Nobel Prize or a Pulitzer Prize?"). Of course, older students are still interested in animals, so that category was listed on the board as well, but now their questions could be more sophisticated ("Would you rather have as a pet a Siberian husky or a Belgian Malinois?"). (See Appendix 6 for additional categories and questions and online Book List 17 for resource materials.)

Then students went off into small groups based on their selected categories. We handed out lists of questions for the categories chosen to spark conversation and encourage students to select those that interested them and/or to create original ones. After half an hour we gathered to share their preferences. In the days ahead, before students made a final choice, they were encouraged to talk to family members as well, adding even more interesting questions.

Mayra and Renay, third-grade teachers at P.S. 87, created a chart to keep tabs on their students' choices and progress. It appears in Figure 16.1 and illustrates the wide range of fascinating topics that filled the classroom. Students chose topics that piqued their interests and ones they would be proud to share with classmates and family members.

Name	Would You Rather... question	Research completed?	Final draft done?	Work edited?
Asher	be ambidextrous or have achromatopsia?			
Ava	win a Pulitzer Prize or a Nobel Prize?			
Bella	write an ode or a sonnet?			
Carson	Alpine ski or Nordic ski?			
Eduardo	order a taco or a burrito?			
Ellie	prepare a timeline of Alexander Graham Bell or Alexander Hamilton?			
Ginny	wear a fez or a fedora?			
Iris	ride in funicular or on a monorail?			
Jack	learn about the 1st amendment or 2nd Amendment?			
Jacob	pilot a blimp or a zeppelin?			
Juliet	use a microscope or a magnifying glass?			
Kasten	live in a forest or a rain forest?			
Leah	build a suspension bridge or an arch bridge?			
Liam	get caught in a cyclone or a tornado?			
Matthew P.	own the Hope Diamond or a Moon Rock ?			
Matthew T.	ride in a kayak or a canoe?			
Max	become an expert at spelunking or zorbing?			
Maxton	eat jam or jelly?			
Robert	view lightning or thunder?			
Sadie	read a myth or a legend?			
Sebastian	get lost in a labyrinth or a maze?			
Sophia	design like Frank Lloyd Wright or Antoni Gaudi?			
Sydney	swim in the Red Sea or the Dead Sea?			
Theodora	explore the North Pole or the South Pole?			
Valentino	be an archeologist or an anthropologist?			
Veranica (Nica)	visit Iceland or Greenland?			

Figure 16.1

At our next class meeting, just as we did in grade two, we talked about the information students would have to gather to help their readers make informed choices. Again, we worked collaboratively at a whole-class gathering to answer the question "Would you rather visit Sweden or Switzerland?" We began by asking students what information they would need to make an informed decision. Students suggested the following questions for each country.

What are the travel costs? What languages are spoken? What are the most popular tourist sites? What is the food like and how much do the restaurants cost? What is the quality of the hotels and what is their average cost? What are the best cities to visit and how to travel between them?

For homework, we asked students to think through the information that would be needed if their questions were the following:

Would you rather climb Mt. Everest or Mt. Kilimanjaro?

Would you rather become a member of the Senate or the House of Representatives?

Would you rather learn judo or karate?

Finally, students were asked to think about their own individual topic and list the information that would need to be provided (or the questions that would need to be answered).

We helped older elementary students understand that information could be presented separately, as I did in the woodchuck vs. hedgehog in your backyard question that appears on pages 190–191. We also introduced the idea that sometimes you might choose to combine the two choices, preparing a compare-and-contrast piece of writing. Students would have to choose the structure that made the most sense for their content. For example, if the question dealt with subjects that are often confused, such as mangos and papayas, it might make sense to compare and contrast these two fruits. If the question contained very unfamiliar items, such as "Would you rather become an expert at zorbing or spelunking?" it might be easier to present information in totally separate pieces of writing.

Sharing Your Own Writing with Older Students

Below is a passage I wrote about the similarities and differences between mangos and papayas, fruits that people sometimes confuse. Here, I chose to combine information in a compare-and-contrast format, and I provided accompanying images.

WOULD YOU RATHER EAT A MANGO OR A PAPAYA?

Have you ever mixed up a mango and a papaya? Both these fruits are tropical, and they come in various sizes, shapes, and colors. Also, they both taste sweet, have wonderful aromas, and are usually very fleshy. However, there are several differences between these fruits. First, the papaya is a tropical American evergreen tree, whereas a mango is a tropical Asian fruit tree. Another difference is that mangoes have only a single seed (a pit), while papayas have lots of them. Then too, ripe mangoes usually feel firm, but ripe papayas are quite soft. And even though both these fruits taste sweet, they do have different flavors. The mango seems to be a mixture of sweet and sour, kind of like a peach, pineapple, and apricot put together. On the other hand, the papaya tastes a bit like apricots mixed with ginger. Both fruits are nutritious; however, a papaya is a better source of vitamin A, vitamin C, and potassium. Now that you know more about these fruits, which would you rather have as a snack? Maybe, you still need to taste them to help you decide.

Lifting the Quality of Student Writing with Older Students

Both examples of teacher writing can be mined for minilessons. Depending on class needs, these might include:

- providing a broad opening/topic sentence that introduce the ideas to come

- giving targeted information that would help readers answer the specific question being asked (the taste of the two fruits, the likely activities of the two animals in a backyard)

- using transition words to help readers better understand the information including such words and phrases as *besides, another issue, also, then too,* and *a final warning.*

- using direct address, with references to *you* and *your*

- using a conversational tone ("Can you believe they often create a separate room in their burrow for pooping?" and "Maybe, you still need to taste them.")

- including sensory details to make meaning clear

- closing passages with satisfying endings

Additional minilessons include the following:

- After sharing my mango/papaya writing, we challenged students to think about other ways of beginning a compare-and-contrast piece. A few of the gathered suggestions follow:

   » People often confuse _____ and _____ .

   » Do you know the difference between _____ and _____ ?

   » It's hard to answer the question, "Would you rather_____?" if you do not have enough information about these _____.

   » Have you ever confused a _____ and a _____ ?

   » Would you like to understand the difference between _____ and _____ ?

- We reviewed ways to make transitions between different chunks of information.

   » Another difference is . . .
   » First . . .. Second . . .
   » In addition to . . .
   » Then, too, . . .
   » Also . . .
   » A final thought . . .

- We brainstormed words often used in compare-and-contrast writing. These include:

   » similarly
   » in comparison

- » on the other hand
- » as opposed to
- » in contrast
- » however
- » but
- » yet
- » meanwhile

- We reminded students that the writer's tools they have been studying apply to all genres, including nonfiction.

- We continued to share well-written nonfiction writing. One of the end pages in Doug Wechsler's (2017) picture book *The Hidden Life of a Toad* is titled "What's the difference between a frog and a toad?" The half-page explanation serves as a powerful model for students attempting compare-and-contrast writing.

- Teachers are well advised to save student work from year to year. Sometimes, students are satisfied with work that we know can be improved, but we know students no longer have energy to keep on revising their work. At some point, the pieces must be placed in the finished bin. These pieces or excerpts of them, however, can be shared anonymously with next year's students to help students learn from the work of their peers.

Student Writing Samples

Grade two writers in Kari Carlson and Kyle MacDowell's class at Dows Lane Elementary School sorted out the difference between often confused animals.

Layla asked, "Would you rather live near turtles or tortoises?" She provided the following information, first with each animal described in a separate paragraph, then combining the two in a final paragraph.

> **Do You Know the Difference Between Tortoises and Turtles?**
>
> Turtles eat fruits, plants, insects, other animals, and sometimes poisonous jellyfish. Turtles have flat shells and small bodies. Turtles are usually green or green and brown. They live in North America, Central America, Africa, Asia, Australia, and all oceans except the Arctic Ocean. They mostly live in water. Turtles have webbed or flipper-like feet.
>
> Tortoises eat all kinds of fruits and plants. Tortoises have large bodies and round shells. Tortoises are green or greenish brown. Tortoises live in dry areas like deserts.
>
> Tortoises are herbivores, but turtles are omnivores. Tortoises are usually bigger than turtles. Tortoises live in dry areas, but turtles live in wet areas. Turtles live up to 80 years. Tortoises live up to 150 years.

Michael asked, "Would you rather study salamanders or lizards?" He shared the following information with his second-grade classmates, using the same structure as his classmate Layla.

Salamanders are amphibians. They eat small animals such as insects and worms. Salamanders have smooth skin. They come in many colors. Most are only a few inches long. They live in dark damp places. There are a hundred kinds of salamanders.

Lizards are reptiles. Some lizards only eat plants. Some eat animals and some eat both. They have scaly, rough skin. Their skin is dry. Lizards come in many colors. They live in warm dry places. There are 5,000 kinds of lizards on Earth.

The biggest difference between a salamander and a lizard is that a salamander is an amphibian and a lizard is a reptile.

Third-grade writers in Renay Sadis and Mayra Romero's class at P.S. 87 asked a broad range of "Would you rather . . . ?" questions. Max, a third grader asked, "Would you rather go zorbing or spelunking?" He provided the following information to his readers.

Zorbing is adventurous. It will be a memorable moment. Get out of bed and welcome to the world of zorbing! Imagine a soccer ball rolling down a hill. What if you're in that soccer ball? Zorbing balls are designed to minimize damage done to the rider. There are different kinds of zorbing such as aqua zorbing and harness zorbing, etc. This is just the beginning of zorbing. Zorbing can be done anywhere as long as it has a hill and grass. It can't be too bumpy unless you want to get hurt and terrified. You just need a zorbing ball to go zorbing. You don't need anyone to teach you how to zorb, just keep on rolling and steering and you'll get better.

Are you ready for fun? For danger, adventure, a once-in-a-lifetime trip? Spelunking is going in a cave and exploring around it. It may include finding water and animals like bats or fish. Looking for a thrill? Well, you're in luck. Bring a bathing suit and go swimming or exploring the rocks. Today in bed, tomorrow spelunking. You better get prepared; spelunking is done in a cave. (Not in New York City.) You usually need a person to teach you how to spelunk. After you get the hang of it, it is easy. Get a tour guide and you should probably buy yourself a trip to a journey of wonder. You better get prepared, ready when you are!

So, would you rather go zorbing or spelunking? Both are very good sports, unusual, but fun.

Liam asks, "Would you rather get caught in a cyclone or a tornado?" He helped his readers decide by providing the following information.

A cyclone is a fascinating kind of storm. It is a rough storm. The calmest part of a cyclone is the eye. The eye is the very center of the storm. Did you know a cyclone is tall and often exceeds 30,000 feet in height? Cyclones form over warm ocean waters and draw their energy from the evaporation and condensation of the water. Cyclones are also associated with strong thunderstorms, high winds, and flooding. Zap, crash, whoosh! Did you know as the storms move across land; the air pressure may fall rapidly to below 980 millibars? Cyclones are rapid rainstorms. This is a storm not to mess with. Run!

There is so much to understand about tornadoes. A tornado is a violent spinning tube of air. Did you know about sixty people are killed by tornadoes each year? A tornado can have wind speeds over 300 miles per hour. Whoosh! Most tornadoes are calmer and have wind speeds of less than 110 miles per hour. Tornadoes are about 250 feet. Did you know a tornado does not have to be visible? However, the low pressure made by the high winds and fast rotation can cause water vapor in the air to condense into a visible condensation funnel. A single storm may produce multiple tornadoes and mesocyclones. Tornadoes are wild whirlwinds. These twisters will destroy anything! Watch out! Boom!

Now that you know the difference between a cyclone and a tornado, do you know which storm you would rather get caught in? I would choose neither.

Jacob asks, "Would you rather ride in a blimp or a zeppelin?" His helpful information appears in Figure 16.2, just as it did in his illustrated class anthology.

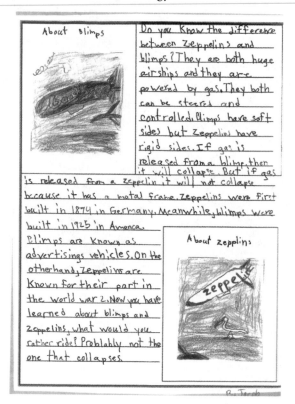

Figure 16.2

Carving Out Time for Celebration

We invited students across the grades to think through how their research might be put to real-world use, not merely tucked in a folder or hung on a bulletin board. Most classes decided to create an anthology, with each child's question and research included. But first, family members would be invited to a celebration and be asked the "Would you rather . . . ?" questions. Students would show family members that they would have an easier time answering those questions if they were filled with information. Students would then share their research and ask their questions again. Family members could be called upon to share their choices and explain their reasons for those choices.

BOOKS NOTED

Birmingham, John. 1978. *Would You Rather . . .* New York: Thomas Y. Crowell.

Contrada, Joan Axelrod. 2012. *This or That Animal Debate: A Rip-Roaring Game of Either/Or Questions.* Mankato, MN: Capstone.

Strack, Emma. 2018. *What's the Difference? 40 Pairs of the Seemingly Similar.* San Francisco: Chronicle Books.

Wechsler, Doug. 2017. "What's the Difference Between a Frog and a Toad?" *The Hidden Life of a Toad.* Watertown, MA: Charlesbridge.

TEACHER REFERENCE MATERIAL

Genzlinger, Neil. 2019. "John Birmingham, Author Who Piqued Young Imaginations, Dies at 82." *The New York Times.* January 16.

This challenge also requires that students have access to abundant nonfiction reference materials as well as appropriate Internet sites to research a wide range of topics.

A FEW TITLES TO ENRICH YOUR TEACHING

Goodhart, Pippa. 2019. *This or That? What Will You Choose at the British Museum?* Somerville, MA: Noisy Crow/Candlewick.

Castaldo, Nancy, and JR Mortimer. 2015. *This or That 3.* Washington D.C. National Geographic Kids.

Chang, Kirsten. 2019. *Rabbit or Hare?* Minnetonka, MN: Bellwether Media.

———. 2019. *Wolf or Coyote?* Minnetonka, MN: Bellwether Media.

Daly, Lindsey. 2020. *Would You Rather? Made You Think Edition.* New York: Zeitgeist.

Hall, Katharine. 2014. *Polar Bears and Penguins.* Mount Pleasant, SC: Arbordale.

———. 2014. *Clouds: A Compare and Contrast Book.* Mount Pleasant, SC: Arbordale.

———. 2014. *Trees: A Compare and Contrast Book.* Mount Pleasant, SC: Arbordale.

———. 2015. *Amphibians and Reptiles.* Mount Pleasant, SC: Arbordale.

Herrington, Lisa M. 2015a. *What's the Difference? Turtles and Tortoises.* New York: Children's Press.

———. 2015b. *What's the Difference? Crocodiles and Alligators.* New York: Children's Press.

———. 2015c. *What's the Difference? Monkeys and Apes.* New York: Children's Press.

———. 2015d. *What's the Difference? Frogs and Toads.* New York: Children's Press.

———. 2015e. *What's the Difference? Butterflies and Moths.* New York: Children's Press.

Kurtz, Kevin. 2016. *Sharks and Dolphins.* Mount Pleasant, SC: Arbordale.

See additional resources in online Book List 17.

CHAPTER 17
Nonfiction Calendars
(Grades 2–5)

Leah, a third grader in Laura Leibman's class, created an informative calendar based on Colonial Williamsburg. One page appears in Figure 17.1.

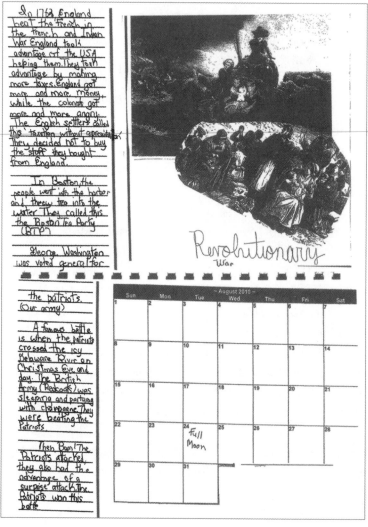

Figure 17.1

Exploring the Roots of the Writing Challenge

Twenty years ago, I wrote about inviting students to create nonfiction calendars. In *Writing Through Childhood*, I shared the work of Joanne Hindley Salch's third-grade class at the Manhattan New School. In that book, I explained that students selected topics they really cared about, created twelve subcategories for that topic, researched, and then wrote twelve prose passages to accompany illustrations for each month of the year. Joanne downloaded calendar pages for the upcoming year 2000 (one set for each student), attached original student work, and bound the pages, and students proudly took their original calendars home. My guess and my hope are that those calendars are still tucked away between original Valentine's Day poems, kid-made potholders, and kindergarten self-portraits in a carton labeled "handmade treasures." In other words, the calendars became family heirlooms.

I still believe in inviting students to create calendars, ones that will be content rich, highly valued, and hung in their homes for the full year ahead. But here I want to focus on the value of attaching those calendars to grade-level, whole-class content studies. Teachers are under such time pressures nowadays that curriculum-connected calendars allow them to accomplish two goals at once—not "killing" two birds with one stone, but effectively attending to two objectives at the same time. Teachers can nourish the teaching of writing as well as an in-depth topic in social studies, science, music, art, and so on. Students get to choose individual topics within a broad whole-class umbrella topic. They are invited to create their own content-area subcategories. They are expected to craft twelve high-quality passages, using the tools in their writer's toolboxes.

Earlier in this book, I listed the many elements that guide the work I do and help me stay true to my beliefs about the teaching of writing. (See pages 5–6.) The following elements stand out for the writing of nonfiction calendars: calendars appeal to students and become joyful gifts when brought home to families. They can be done at any grade level, and the work can be scaffolded with the use of a template. Students have opportunities to write one prose passage and then another, and another, all the way up to a dozen if they are working independently. No matter the grade level, there is an expectation for high-quality work.

Engaging Students in the Challenge

It is helpful to show children a stack of calendars that not only appeal to them topic-wise but also come close to the image you have in mind for the kind of writing you expect your students to do. In Manhattan, the calendar I frequently show students in grades three through five is the one published each year by the Central Park Conservancy. Students like calling out the names of familiar park structures (Belvedere Castle and the statue of Balto), appreciate learning the names of spots they recognize but never knew what to call them (Bethesda Fountain and the Ramble), and enjoy seeing totally unfamiliar places inside their wonderful park (Literary Walk and Bow Bridge). Then, too, the paragraphs that accompany the lush photographs are just the length you would hope older elementary students will be able to write, and each is filled with specific, clear, and accurate information. Other foundations

Students are swapping ideas for writing to come.

that publish calendars that are useful as models include The National Park Foundation, the World Wildlife Fund, the National Audubon Society, and the Colonial Williamsburg Foundation.

It is also helpful to show students calendars that do not contain much more than a label under each photograph. The conversation can easily move to "What else would you like to know? What lingering questions do you have? What more could have been added to each page?" One year, the wildlife calendar published by the Ocean Conservancy contained breathtaking photographs of the banded butterflyfish, the tufted puffin, and the sandy lightfoot crab, but the reader was not told anything beyond the name of the creature. Students were hungry for more information, and that feeling headed them in the right direction when they were invited to create their own calendars.

In recent years, I have supported teachers and students as they created calendars connected to many ongoing classroom studies. These included birds, foreign countries, architecture, outer space, community workers, and ocean creatures. In some classrooms, creating a calendar is one option among many, as students research topics connected to a broad umbrella theme. Although some students may choose to create a calendar, others may be creating alphabet books, counting books, true-or-false books, among others. (See Simple Scaffolds on page 59.) No matter if this is a small-group challenge or a whole-class study, students select subtopics that fit under the broad class topic.

Continuing to Support Students' Efforts
Sharing Your Own Writing

The only calendar I ever created was based on my interest in poetry. I showed students my plans to create a poetry calendar with subcategories that explore twelve different forms of poetry.

BROAD TOPIC FOR CALENDAR: POETRY

Twelve subtopics: (one per calendar page)

1. January: list poems

2. February: mask/persona poems

3. March: poems of direct address

4. April: haiku poems

5. May: narrative poems

6. June: found poems

7. July: riddle poems

8. August: concrete poems

9. September: sonnets

10. October: odes

11. November: limericks

12. December: how-to poems

I explained my intention to research and then write up any rules attached to each form and to find one wonderful example of each to include on my calendar page. I showed students the resource materials I used when I needed a few more forms to complete the dozen required for a calendar as well as the information I needed to explain the forms accurately. I showed students Paul Janeczko's *A Kick in the Head: An Everyday Guide to Poetic Forms* (2005) and his *Poetry from A to Z: A Guide for Young Writers* (1994).

Gathering Information

In one classroom, students were asked to create nonfiction calendars connected to their third-grade global studies. Each child was asked to create a calendar about a country of their choice. Additionally, they were asked to use the planning sheet that appears in Appendix 7 to plan their subtopics, just as I did for my poetry calendar. Students were told that they might change their subtopics based on what they were learning from their research. Reviewing students' planning sheets helped teachers get a handle on student intentions and on the kind of reference material and resources the students would need. Teachers were able to guide students whose subtopics were too similar, too broad, or too narrow.

One student intent on learning about Ireland planned the following:

BROAD TOPIC FOR CALENDAR: IRELAND

Twelve subtopics: (one per calendar page)

1. January: biggest cities in Ireland

2. February: major moments in history

3. March: the Gaelic language

4. April: relationship between Ireland and Northern Ireland

5. May: traditional Irish food

6. June: Irish holidays

7. July: religion in Ireland

8. August: geography of Ireland

9. September: famous Irish writers

10. October: traditional Irish music and dance

11. November: Irish sports teams

12. December: most popular tourist sites

After students decided on their subcategories, teachers supported their intentions by helping them locate relevant sources of information. Having an overarching theme, like the study of a foreign country, made it easier for teachers to gather stacks of nonfiction books about the chosen countries and to recommend appropriate websites. Teachers were also able to arrange classroom interviews with community members who had extensive knowledge about the chosen countries. Throughout, teachers reviewed note-taking strategies including those work habits that would allow students to file notes under appropriate headings or subcategories.

Lifting the Quality of Student Writing

Teachers planned a wide range of minilessons based on students' needs. Their focus included:

- reminders about topic sentences for calendar paragraphs
- teaching the use of transitions if text of calendar page required more than one paragraph
- public conferring to highlight the need for clarity, specificity, and accuracy
- reviewing of all techniques presented in students' writer's toolbox
- noting illustration possibilities (sketches, photographs, downloaded Internet images, and so on)

Student Writing Samples

Third graders in Carmela Brutto's class at P.S. 87 collaborated on pages for a calendar on China. The twelve subtopics in their 2018 calendar included geography, government, terra-cotta warriors, language, Chinese New Year, food, sports, education, medicine, good luck symbols, and Chinese weddings, holidays, and festivals, as seen in Figures 17. 2 and 17.3.

Carving Out Time for Celebration

The most meaningful celebration of completed calendars would be to see students and families appreciating and using the calendars in their homes or offices. Perhaps students can be asked to bring in photos of their calendars hung in various settings in their homes. Captions can be added to the photos and displayed at school.

Chinese Weddings

By Christy Demaliaj and Kate Moore

Imagine you were sitting in a Chinese wedding. Your brain would probably be racing with curiosity. There are a lot of traditions in Chinese weddings.

One of these traditions is the tea ceremony. In Chinese "cha" means tea. They have the tea ceremony to welcome the bride into the groom's family.

Another custom is people give gifts. These gifts represent some kind of luck. For example, the bride's family gives the groom a wallet to represent wealth in their future. Children also go to the wedding to bring good luck. This is because it gives the couple a better chance of having a kid.

Some other tradition is that the oldest uncle writes the bride and groom's names on a red cloth. Then he gives them advice. This advice should help the couple in their marriage.

Besides the traditions, there are different ways to pick up the bride. 200 years ago the groom would carry the bride on his back. 100 years ago his friends would carry the bride on the chair. Today, he picks her up in a car. The bride also has to change her dress often. 100 years ago she would change her dress 100 times to show her wealth. 200 years ago the bride would change so many times that she wouldn't be able to eat her cake or food. When she is getting married, the bride wears a red dress because red represents good luck. The groom does not have to change outfits.

There is also a ceremony where the bride and groom exchange rings. This is important just like in America. Another custom that is just like American weddings is when the bride throws the bouquet at the end.

In conclusion, there are many different ceremonies and traditions in Chinese weddings which makes them so different, special, and extraordinary compared to any other wedding.

June 2018

Sunday	Monday	Tuesday	Wednesday	Thursday	Friday	Saturday
					1	2
3	4	5	6	7	8	9
10	11	12	13	14	15	16
17 Father's Day	18	19	20	21	22	23
24	25	26	27	28	29	30

Figure 17.2

Chinese Medicine

Bv Michael

Different cultures have different ways to get people to feel healthy. Chinese people mostly use herbs, plants and tools.

Most people don't just go to the hospital or doctors, they first try traditional Chinese medicine and herbal treatments. Ginseng is the most popular herb used. Ginseng has been used for over 2,000 years. You can buy Ginseng at the market. It can be made into pills or creams and put in tea or soup. Qigong is a way to help you feel better or to heal. It is a kind of meditating martial art. Qigong gets rid of sickness and bad energy. Another way to get rid of bad energy is to do Tai-chi. It makes you peaceful and gives you positive healing.

Acupuncture is when a doctor uses tiny needles and the needles get rid of pain and bad energy. It cures illness. Also, it doesn't hurt. Besides a lot of Americans use it. In addition, it has been used for over 2,000 years. Then too, you can get it in a hospital or you can get pressure point needles from a clinic.

Another tool is cupping. Bamboo cups are immersed in hot water to apply to the body at acupuncture points. Cups are put on your skin and there is hot air inside the cup to create suction. Your skin swells into a cup. Cupping is believed to relieve congestion of asthma and accompanying aches and pains.

Now you've learned about China's most popular medicine. We hope you stay healthy.

November 2018

Sunday	Monday	Tuesday	Wednesday	Thursday	Friday	Saturday
				1	2	3
4	5	6	7	8	9	10
11 Veterans Day	12	13	14	15	16	17
18	19	20	21	22 Thanksgiving Day	23	24
25	26	27	28	29	30	

Figure 17.3

BOOKS NOTED

Janeczko, Paul. 1994. *Poetry from A to Z: A Guide for Young Writers*. New York: Simon & Schuster Books for Young Readers.

_____. 2005. *A Kick in the Head: An Everyday Guide to Poetic Forms*. Somerville, MA: Candlewick Press.

TEACHER REFERENCE MATERIAL

Harwayne, Shelley. 2001. *Writing Through Childhood*. Portsmouth, NH: Heinemann.

Resources for this challenge depend on the umbrella topic chosen for study. In addition to picture books, students are encouraged to browse appropriate Internet sites. Teachers are also encouraged to save commercial calendars that come their way, those with well-written passages and those that contain meager, skimpy labels. Both can be used to instruct students.

A FEW TITLES TO ENRICH YOUR TEACHING

For teachers who decide to invite students to create calendars on topics of their own choosing rather than as part of a whole-class study, the following nonfiction titles may serve as inspiration. If the entire class is working on calendars devoted to one broad curriculum topic, well-crafted content texts will be an important support. In other words, if every student is asked to create a calendar as part of a class study of global warming, social justice, or immigration, they will need a classroom shelf filled with high-quality resource materials.

Barton, Bethany. 2020. *I'm Trying to Love Rocks*. New York: Viking. (calendar of things kids collect)

Bryant, Jen. 2020. *Above the Rim: How Elgin Baylor Changed Basketball*. New York: Harry N. Abrams. (sports heroes calendar)

Eggers, Dave. 2017. *Her Right Foot*. San Francisco, CA: Chronicle Books. (a calendar of 12 iconic statues around the world)

Gillingham, Sara, 2018. *Seeing Stars: A Complete Guide to the 88 Constellations*. New York: Phaidon. (a dozen constellations calendar)

Green, Sara. 2021. *The Taj Mahal*. Minnetonka, MN: Bellwether Media. (calendar of 12 famous buildings)

Ignotofsky, Rachel. 2021. *What's Inside a Flower? (And Other Questions About Science & Nature)*. New York: Random House. (a calendar with information about a dozen flowers)

Larkin, Shabazz. 2019. *The Thing About Bees: A Love Letter*. Bellevue, WA: Readers to Eaters. (a dozen insects calendar)

Markel, Michelle. 2019. *Out of This World: The Surreal Art of Leonora Carrington*. New York: Balzer + Bray. (calendar of a dozen artists)

Patent, Dorothy Hinshaw. 2019. *At Home with the Beaver: The Story of a Keystone Species*. Berkeley, CA: Web of Life Children's Books. (a dozen animals calendar)

Peterson, Cris. 2019. *Popcorn Country: The Story of America's Favorite Snack*. Honesdale, PA: Boyds Mills Press. (a dozen snack foods calendar)

Roth, Susan L. 2019. *Birds of a Feather: Bowerbirds and Me*. New York: Neal Porter Books. (a dozen bird species calendar)

Siber, Kate. 2018. *National Parks of the USA*. London: Wide-Eyed. (a dozen national parks calendar)

Stone, Tanya Lee. 2018. *Pass Go and Collect $200: The Real Story of How Monopoly Was Invented*. New York: Henry Holt. (a calendar presenting the history of 12 toys and games)

Therme, Jennifer. 2019. *Manhattan: Mapping the Story of an Island*. New York: Harry N. Abrams. (12 famous cities of the world calendar)

Winter, Jonah. 2019. *Thurgood*. New York: Schwartz & Wade. (a dozen social justice heroes calendar)

See nonfiction planning sheet in Appendix 7.

CHAPTER 18
Creating Reader's Notes

(Grades 3-5)

Sasha, my granddaughter, then a fifth grader in Loren Holand and Lindsay Donlon's fifth-grade class at Main Street School, read Junot Diaz's (2018) *Islandborn* and wrote the Dear Readers letter that appears in Figure 18.1.

A "Tru" Monster

Dear Readers,

In the book Islandborn by Junot Diaz, a young girl asks many different people to share their memories of the Dominican Republic. Their memories include the music, the food and the beaches. When I interviewed Fatima Contreras, an immigrant from the Dominican Republic, about her memories, she said "The best memory was when I was a child. I remember the freedom to play outside with my friends without fear of anyone doing anything bad to us. Another fun time was when we made our own toys to play. We made balls from old socks, cars with palm trees and used tomato paste cans. When it rained, we took a shower in the rain. Also, I had a bike and I could ride far away from my house for hours. As I grew up I started going to the beach." Fatima had very good childhood memories, but one person in Islandborn remembered a monster.

When you read this book, you'll probably wonder who the monster is. The monster is Rafael Trujillo. He was the president of the Dominican Republic from 1930 to 1952. He was called a monster because he tortured people and even assassinated people who criticized him. He killed more than 50,000 people and 30,000 were Haitians. He also tried to kill the Venezuela president and hid money that wasn't his. Finally, he didn't let people leave the country without his permission and forbid anyone to talk openly.

When I interviewed Fatima she also remembered the following about Trujillo. " If someone was a thief he would cut off their hands so that they couldn't steal anymore and so that other people would not attempt to do that," she said.

In the book, the author says that there were smart women who protested against Rafael Trujillo. They were the Mirabal sisters. Their names were Patria, Minerva, and Maria Teresa and later on their other sister Dede joined their underground movement to get rid of Trujillo. But, unfortunately in 1960, Trujillo had Patria, Minerva, and Maria Teresa killed (Dede lived). Then in 1961 the people in the Dominican Republic got so mad at Trujillo for assassinating the three sisters that they killed Rafael Trujillo.

You might be wondering, *what was the Dominican Republic like after Trujillo's death*? Many people left the Dominican Republic because Rafael Trujillo was such a disgusting, dangerous, and despicable dictator. 44,000 Dominican people immigrated to Puerto Rico and 300,000 immigrated to New York in the US. 50 years later Rafael Trujillo died the Dominican Republic improved a lot in getting more freedom in religion, expression, and movement but it still isn't great like there are issues in education, poverty, and health care. There was also a Civil War in 1965 and then 50 years after Rafael Trujillo died there were no more political exiles, prisoners or firing squads. Another thing is that after Rafael Trujillo died Joaquin tried to liberalize the government. There was the first democratically elected president then, too. I hope that you learned a lot about Rafael Trujillo!!

PATRIA   MINERVA   MARIA TERESA

Sincerely,

Sasha

Figure 18.1

Exploring the Roots of the Writing Challenge

As an avid reader of novels, I've often had the feeling of needing more information to make the most of the book in my hands. I would have gotten more out of Hilary Mantel's (2009) *Wolf Hall* had I brought with me a fuller understanding of England in the 1500s. I know this to be true, as I so appreciated Lisa Halliday's (2018) *Asymmetry* because I know a lot about Philip Roth. I made the most of Rachel Kushner's (2009) *Telex from Cuba* because I have long been an aficionado of all things Cuban. (That's no surprise as my father came to this country from Cuba, and I have wonderful Cuban first cousins in Miami.)

The writing challenge in this chapter takes a hard look at author's notes, those additional nonfiction passages that often appear in picture books dealing with content-rich topics. These picture books can be fiction, nonfiction, poetry, or historical fiction. No matter the genre, adults who read to children appreciate these extra pages of information as they often help the grown-ups answer children's inevitable questions. In other words, author's notes can make grown-up readers seem very clever in their children's eyes.

Sometimes these notes explain the writer's process of creating the book or their inspiration for the writing. Occasionally, the writer explains the literary heritage of their tale, or the author includes a call to action—how the reader can take part in solving a problem posed by the picture book. More often, the writer offers additional information that provides background for the slice of the story being told, or the writer anticipates any lingering questions the reader might have. No matter their purpose, author's notes have become a common feature of many recently published picture books, especially in biographical narratives and historical fiction.

Engaging Students in the Challenge

One way to launch this challenge is to fill the room with a wide range of interesting picture books, ones with valuable and varied author's notes. Teachers might begin their search by reading Elizabeth Dillow's (2016) column for the Nerdy Book Club titled "Top Ten Picture Books with Fascinating Author's Notes for All Ages." In several fifth-grade classes at Main Street School in Irvington, New York, I rolled in a suitcase chock-full of books with intriguing author's notes, inviting students to read ones they found interesting. If books are chosen carefully, fifth graders are pleased to have a welcome change from the chapter books they usually read. We gave students time to read several picture books and time to share their responses to these books. We stressed the importance of paying attention to the author's notes, a feature that students often view as optional. We made sure to ask students to share their thoughts about the contents of the book, the illustrations as

A fourth grader is busy crafting notes to share with her classmates

well as the author's notes. (A list of books appropriate for students in grades three through five that contain various forms of author's notes appears at the end of this chapter and online in Book List 18. If the topic of the book is not obvious from the title, I have added the subject in parentheses.)

We explained to students that they would be writing a note to readers to be slipped into a picture book that did not have one but would be enriched if it did. We reminded students that they couldn't write an author's note, as they were not the authors of these books. They couldn't talk about their inspiration or their process of writing, but there were several goals they could accomplish by creating a note to readers. These varying goals included:

- provide background for adults sharing the book with children

- place the story in a historical context

- suggest ways for readers to learn more about the topic

- anticipate readers' questions and provide additional information to answer those questions

- present a call to action for a problem noted in the book

- entertain with surprising additional facts or events

After several days of browsing, reading, and responding to these carefully chosen picture books, we began using the books as resources for minilessons for the writing challenge to come.

MINILESSONS

- We discussed the placement of the author's notes. Should they be in the front of the book or the back?

- We shared collections of books written by the same author, ones who create extensive and helpful notes like Carole Boston Weatherford, Mara Rockliff, Lesa Cline-Ransome, Jane Yolen, Sandra Markle, Barb Rosenstock, Phil Bildner, Kelly Starling Lyons, April Pulley Sayre, Claire Saxby, Deborah Hopkinson, and Louise Borden.

- We talked about authors who often include authors notes but sometimes don't. We asked, "Why did Lesa Cline-Ransome include author's notes in *Whale Trails: Before and Now* (2015b) and in the back of *Words Set Me Free: The Story of Young Frederick Douglass* (2012), but none in *Freedom's School* (2015a)?"

- We talked about why author's notes that provided information about the setting, time, and place in which the events occurred were particularly helpful in understanding historical picture books. (Carole Boston Weatherford includes timelines in the back of *Box: Henry Brown Mails Himself to Freedom* [2020] and in *Voice of Freedom: Fannie Lou Hamer: Spirit of the Civil Rights Movement* [2015]. Debbie Levy includes notes on Supreme Court cases in the back of her book *I Dissent: Ruth Bader Ginsburg Makes Her Mark* [2016].)

- We talked about picture books that combined several genres of writing in their back matter. (In the back of *Out of Wonder: Poems Celebrating Poets* [2017], Kwame Alexander with Chris Colderley and Marjory Wentworth include biographical sketches, relevant lists, and information about the authors. Doug Kuntz and Amy Shrodes include an author's note, a map, and photographs in *Lost and Found Cat: The True Story of Kunkush's Incredible Journey* [2017].)

- We shared several narrative nonfiction picture books, especially those starring animals. They often had very straightforward and brief author's notes with such basic titles as "About Otters," "About Hippos," "Information About Red Kangaroos," "More About Geckos," "About Orcas," "Information About Dingoes."

(continues)

MINILESSONS *(continued)*

- We discussed author's notes that were surprising and full of voice.
- We pointed out author's notes written as letters to readers.
- We discussed picture books that included author's notes but did not satisfy the reader's thirst for more information.
- We noted features and formats of author's notes. These included:

» bulleted lists	» recipes	» advertisements
» time lines	» glossary	» scrapbook
» quotations	» poems	» call to action
» questions and answers	» reader's guide	» two columns: what we know/what we don't know
» photographs/ and other primary source documentation	» songs	» table of statistics
	» a note on sources	
	» sources of learning more	» pronunciation guide
» illustrations/ sketches	» explanation of literary features	» did you know? section
» fun facts	» acknowledgments	» suggestions for writing a biography
» diary entries	» map	» song lyrics

(See bibliography in online Book List 19 for additional information on these minilessons as well as titles containing the various formats listed here.)

Several days later, I rolled in a second book-filled suitcase. This one was also packed with a wide range of picture books for upper-elementary students, but these did not have author's notes, notes for readers, or any other sections devoted to additional background information. They did, however, have intriguing enough topics that background information for readers would be beneficial. (See list of titles in online Book List 20.)

Students were given time to browse, read, and respond to this second set of picture books. We asked students to commit to one picture book, one with a topic that really sparked their interest. We suggested that some of the books that they had read earlier, those *with* accompanying author's notes, could still be considered. We announced, "Don't discount books that already have author's notes, especially if those author's notes left you wanting more information."

An effective way to demonstrate how helpful reader's notes can be and what they might contain is to read aloud very simple picture books such as Charlotte Zolotow's *The Moon Was the Best* (1993). This book is filled with beautiful descriptions of Paris scenes, each accompanied by photographs taken by Tana Hoban. Students can be asked to think about what kind of back matter would make sense for this book. Their responses will probably include more information about the River Seine, French bookstalls on the banks of the river, outdoor cafes, baguettes, and the fountain sculptures throughout the city. Similarly, in Gaia Cornwall's *Jabari Tries* (2020), the young main character attempts to build a flying machine and he seeks inspiration from Lewis Howard Latimer, Dr. Flossie Wong-Staal, Roy Allela, and Dr. Shirley Ann

Jackson. No doubt, students will suggest that adding back matter information about these successful inventors, engineers, and scientists would be beneficial to readers. Then too, after listening to Bryan Collier's *Uptown* (2004), students will want more information about photographer James Van Der Zee, Rucker Park, and The Boys Choir of Harlem.

Continuing to Support Students' Efforts
Sharing Your Own Writing

To give students an image of where we were headed in this writing challenge, I shared my own experience with needing background information. I came across a delightful early childhood picture book entitled *The Thing About Yetis* written by Vin Vogel (2015). I couldn't quite recall anything about yetis, wondering where I had heard the term before. I saw the odd creature in the illustrations but knew that I would not be able to answer any questions about yetis if my grandchildren asked. For me, I would have been quite pleased to find some yeti information at the back of the book in a note to readers, but unfortunately there was none. I decided to research yetis before sharing the book. In other words, I created my own back matter. The information I gathered follows:

> Yetis are sometimes called Abominable Snowmen. They are mythical creatures that some people think live in the Himalayan Mountains across Nepal, Bhutan, and Tibet. They are usually described as being large, hairy, and ape-like. There have been "sightings" of yeti, just as there have been sightings of Big Foot and the Loch Ness Monster. Adventurous explorers and photographers have, over the years, claimed to have seen a yeti, taken their photos, and found their bones. In a recent article in *The New York Times* (May 1, 2019), the author Sandra E. Garcia quotes a yeti expert, Daniel C. Taylor. He wrote a book titled, *Yeti: The Ecology of a Mystery*, in which he suggests that there are three kinds of yeti. First, is the kind that is a legend, much like the tooth fairy, leprechauns, or Santa Claus. Second is the kind that lives inside of human beings, inspiring them to be more interested in nature. The third is the kind that leaves footprints, and Mr. Taylor concludes that these can be explained by the presence of other real creatures. In a latest supposed sighting, Mr. Taylor suggests that the unusual footprint was made by a mother bear being followed by her cub. In other words, the thing about yetis is that you are as likely to find one in the mountains as you are to spot a real unicorn at the mall.

I shared Vin Vogel's book with students and the background information I prepared to tuck into the book so I would be more prepared when my grandchildren asked me about yetis. I showed the students my sources of information, and we had an interesting discussion about the possible existence of such a creature.

Gathering Information

We helped students who selected a picture book but were struggling to come up with a specific research topic. We also asked students to decide on their purposes in creating a note to readers. We distributed a planning sheet to support students as they made decisions about the research to come. The sheet also helped teachers stay on top of their student's needs and interests.

Name: _____

Title of text that inspired nonfiction research: _____

Research topic for note to readers: _____

Questions or subcategories to guide research: _____

Possible sources of information: _____

(Include Internet sites to browse, people to interview, books to read, places to conduct firsthand observation, videos to view, and so on.)

Following is a sample planning sheet that I filled out about yetis. (Of course, I could not do any firsthand observation or talk to any yeti experts in the community.)

Name: *Shelley*

Title of text that inspired nonfiction research:

The Thing About Yetis by Vin Vogel

Research topic for note to readers:

An explanation of yetis

Questions or subcategories to guide research:

What is a yeti?

Where are they found?

Who has studied them?

Are they real creatures or myths?

Possible sources of information:

"Those Big Yeti Footprints? Just a Mama Bear and Cub" (*New York Times,* May 2019)

"The Yeti (Abominable Snowman)" online article from factfictionandconjecture

Daniel C. Taylor's *Yeti: The Ecology of a Mystery* (2017)

Name: *Renay*

Title of text that inspired nonfiction research:

Immigrant Girl: Becky of Eldridge Street by Brett Harvey

Research topic for note to readers:

Immigration to the Lower East Side of Manhattan from Eastern Europe at the turn of the twentieth century

Questions or subcategories to guide research:

Why did so many immigrants come at that time?

What were the problems immigrants faced when they settled in NYC?

Why was education so important to the immigrants?

Possible sources of information: (Include internet sites to browse, people to interview, books to read, places to conduct first-hand observation, videos to view, etc.)

Read *My Name Is Not Gussie* by Mikki Machlin (1999)

Read *Immigrant Kids* by Russell Freedman (1995)

Interview elderly immigrant neighbor

Visit Tenement Museum in Manhattan

After each student thought through their research plans, our next task was to help the young researchers find accessible and appropriate information. We reached out to the school community as well as to family members for resources needed.

Teachers can post research topics in the staff room and send a letter of request to families. One such letter follows:

Dear families,

Our class is beginning a new reading and writing challenge. After spending time reading many picture books intended for older students, each fifth grader has chosen one book that appeals to them, and they will now conduct research connected to the subject of that book. All students will create a Reader's Note to accompany their chosen picture book. To that end, we are asking for your support.

We want students to appreciate that research is not only done in in front of a computer screen, although credible and appropriate sites will of course be used. Students will also learn that nonfiction writers spend time in the field talking to experts and doing firsthand observations.

Attached you will find a list of our students' chosen areas of interest. We are now on the hunt for additional and appropriate resource materials (books, magazine articles, videos, etc.) and connections to experts to be interviewed, in person or via email. Then too, please send in any suggestions you may have for places to be visited or organizations to be contacted for any of the students' chosen topics. Please include yourselves or other family members as potential experts. And please know that any material you send to class will be handled with extreme care and returned at the end of our study.

Thanks in advance for your support, and we look forward to sharing our finished work with you at the end of our study.

Lifting the Quality of Student Writing

During writing workshop time, students took notes for their research topic and organized the notes they took when they were away from school. Eventually, they began drafting their reader's notes. Our minilessons included the following topics:

- We selected authors who consistently provide rich and varied author's notes and back matter. After sharing stacks of the author's books, we looked closely at what they tended to do in their notes to their readers.

- We selected several published author's notes as exemplars, knowing that the kind of writing contained was within reach of most students. We were careful to choose ones that did not highlight the author's process or source of inspiration. Instead, we selected ones that accomplished other goals including providing background information, offering additional related facts, presenting the current status of the book's topic, and including a call to action. Appropriate models include the notes found in the following books:

» *At the Mountain's Base* by Traci Sorell (2019). In two prose passages, the author presents helpful background information on the role Native women play in the military. She offers biographical information on one of these women, Ola Mildred "Millie" Rexroat, an Oglala Lakota pilot who served in the Air Force.

» *The Cart That Carried Martin* by Eve Bunting (2013). In four easy-to-read paragraphs, the author adds additional background information about the life and death of Martin Luther King Jr.

» *Galápagos Girl/Galapagueña* by Marsha Diane Arnold (2018). In the back-of-the-book note titled "About the Galapagos Islands," Arnold describes the islands as well as the native plants and animals and the current problems facing the Galapagos Islands.

We chose additional titles as needs arose. For example, different author's notes were perfect for demonstrating the use of paragraphs and topic sentences or presenting information in chronological order. We encouraged students to keep reading author's and reader's notes for inspiration, as well as information about writing well. Our stacks of picture books remained in the classroom throughout the study.

We compiled a list of ways that authors labeled their additional notes. Students added some original ones as well. The class chart looked as follows:

POSSIBLE TITLES FOR NOTES

Historical Notes	For a More Complete Understanding
Scientific Notes	Filling in the Gaps
Author's Notes	Extra, Extra, Read All About It!
Reader's Notes	Background Information
About	Some Facts Pertaining to . . .
Companion Note	What May Be Floating Around in Your Head
Dear Reader,	
What You May Be Wondering	A Note to Readers
Answers to Your Questions	Message for Readers
The Rest of the Story	Questions You May Have
Did You Know . . . ?	Afterword
A Feast of Facts	Information About:
More on This Topic	Extra Tidbits

See additional minilessons about author's notes in online Book List 19.

Student Writing Samples

Isabelle and Kale, fifth graders in Julie Cangelosi's classroom at Main Street School, created the notes to readers in Figures 18.2 and 18.3.

Kale

Companion Note

A companion note for the book:
At The Edge of the Forest, by Jonathan London

When you think of a farm dog, you think of a dog that sits on a farm and looks adorable, right?. What you don't know is that a farm dog has a really hard life. It does multiple things to make a farm successful. This piece will teach you a little bit about farm dogs.

Farm dogs have multiple jobs on the farm. These jobs are very complex. Some dogs need to be big, while some need to be small. Certain dogs are right for each job. These jobs are guarding livestock, herding livestock and controlling pests. I will give you some information about each job. Without these dogs, the farm would not be successful.

There are multiple farm dog breeds. They are all great at certain jobs. Here are some of the best farm dogs breeds: the Australian cattle dog, Belgian Shepherd, Border Collie, German Shepherd, Old English Sheepdog, Rottweiler and Welsh Corgi.

As you know there are three jobs for farm dogs on the farm. The first one is herding livestock. These dogs herd the animals to go into the pen and out of the pen. They should herd them out of the pen in early morning and return them to the pen at night. They herd the livestock by barking very loudly and making eye contact with the animals. They also will run around the livestock to form them in a group. The animals they herd can be big or small. They will herd sheep, cattle, chicken, ducks, llamas and pigs. These dogs do not need command to do their job.

The next job farm dogs do is pest control. They can also be called ratters. This job is very important. These dogs stop pests from destroying crops and stored food. Pests can also eat eggs and farms need that source. These animals will track rats and mice most often. But these are not the only animals they will encounter. They will track badgers, ferrets, possums, raccoons and stoats. The dogs that do this job need to be very athletic, fast and have tons of energy. These are the skills these dogs need to catch fast and tiny rats and mice. These dogs were bred in the 18th and 19th century in the U.K (United Kingdom).

These last job is guarding livestock. These dogs are in charge of keeping the livestock safe from predators. These type of animals they protect are birds, pigs, sheep, cows, goats and chickens. These dogs have a very tough job. They have to be alert day and night. They can rest but always have to be alert. Predators can come at any moment. It helps when these dogs are big so they look strong and scary to the predator. If they can bark loud they can also scare the intruder with the sound.

Now that you know what a farm dog does, you now know how active their day is. Without these dogs, a farm would not be as successful. They do things that the farmer can't do during his day because they are working. Farm dogs are very hardworking dogs!

Figure 18.2

Isabelle

What may be floating around in your head......

A companion note to Soccer Fence by Phil Bildner

In this wonderful book, <u>The Soccer Fence</u>, it mentions the name Nelson Mandela and about him being president and getting released from jail and creating a soccer team, but doesn't really talk much about him. So I thought I might talk a little bit about him.

Who was Nelson Mandela?

Nelson Mandela was the very first black president of South Africa. He thought that black people should have the same rights as those whose skin is light. He was against apartheid* and he was also a philanthropist**. He loved soccer and changed many things about South Africa.

What changed once he became president?

Nelson Mandela changed the way South Africans lived. He gave out money to improve sewers and houses in disadvantaged area. He also let people take back the land that was stolen from them and he increased welfare payments.

Is Nelson Mandela still alive to day? (Written as of 2017)

Nelson Mandela passed away on December 5, 2013. He passed away from a respiratory tract infection. Even though he is not with us today his changes to South Africa have changed the world for the better.

Why did Nelson Mandela make South Africa a Soccer Team?

In his eyes, Nelson Mandela thought of sports as a way to connect with his people. He thought since he loved soccer

South Africa's soccer team

or *futbol,* and so did his people, He thought that he should make South Africa a futbol team.

What did he do that put him behind bars?

Nelson Mandela stood up against a government that was committing egregious*** human rights abuses against black South Africans. He was trying to get the government to give black people better rights and convince them that we are all equal. He organized boycotts, strikes, marches, and made many speeches that inspired many people to join him in the fight.

*a person who seeks to promote the welfare of others, especially by the generous donation of money to good causes.
**(in South Africa) a policy or system of segregation or discrimination on grounds of race.
***outstandingly bad; shocking.: "egregious abuses of copyright"
****showing a great deal of variety; very different.
*****lack of fairness or justice.

Figure 18.3

Carving Out Time for Celebration

When completed, students edited and then published their work. Finished work could then be placed in a plastic sleeve (or laminated) and slipped inside the picture books. Students explained their work to classmates and family members who were invited to a classroom celebration.

PICTURE BOOKS NOTED

Alexander, Kwame with Chris Colderley and Marjory Wentworth. 2017. *Out Of Wonder: Poems Celebrating Poets*. Somerville, MA: Candlewick.

Arnold, Marsha Diane. 2018. *Galápagos Girl/Galapagueña*. New York: Lee & Low Books.

Bunting, Eve. 2013. *The Cart That Carried Martin*. Watertown, MA: Charlesbridge.

Cline-Ransome, Lesa. 2012. *Words Set Me Free: The Story of Young Frederick Douglass*. New York: Paula Wiseman.

———. 2015a. *Whale Trails: Before and Now*. New York: Christy Ottaviano Books.

———. 2015b. *Freedom's School*. New York: Disney—Jump at the Sun.

Collier, Bryan. 2004. *Uptown*. New York: Square Fish.

Cornwall Gaia. 2020. *Jabari Tries*. Somerville, MA: Candlewick.

Diaz, Junot. 2018. *Islandborn*. New York: Dial Books for Young Readers.

Freedman, Russell. 1999. *Immigrant Kids*. Glenview, IL: Scott Foresman.

Harvey, Brett. 1987. *Immigrant Girl: Becky of Eldridge Street*. New York: Holiday House.

Kuntz, Doug, and Amy Shrodes. 2017. *Lost and Found Cat: The True Story of Kunkush's Incredible Journey*. New York: Crown Books.

Levy, Debbie. 2016. *I Dissent: Ruth Bader Ginsburg Makes Her Mark*. New York: Simon & Schuster.

London, Jonathan. 1998. *At the Edge of the Forest*. Cambridge, MA: Candlewick.

Machlin, Mikki. 1999. *My Name Is Not Gussie*. Boston, MA: Walter Lorraine Books/Houghton Mifflin Books.

Sorell, Traci. 2019. *At the Mountain's Base*. New York: Kokila.

Vogel, Vin. 2015. *The Thing About Yetis*. New York: Dial Books.

Weatherford, Carole Boston. 2015. *Voice of Freedom: Fannie Lou Hamer: Spirit of the Civil Rights Movement*. Somerville, MA: Candlewick.

———. 2020. *Box: Henry Brown Mails Himself to Freedom*. Somerville, MA: Candlewick.

Zolotow, Charlotte 1993. *The Moon Was the Best*. New York: Greenwillow Books.

TEACHER REFERENCE MATERIALS

Dillow, Elizabeth. 2016. "Top Ten Picture Books with Fascinating Author's Notes for all Ages." https://nerdybookclub.wordpress.com/?s=Elizabeth+Dillow&x=0&y=0. December 24.

Garcia, Sandra E. 2019. "Those Big Yeti Footprints? Just a Mama Bear and Cub." *The New York Times*. May 1.

Halliday, Lisa. 2018. *Asymmetry*. New York: Simon & Schuster.

Kushner, Rachel. 2009. *Telex from Cuba*. New York: Scribner.

Mantel, Hilary. 2009. *Wolf Hall*. New York: Henry Holt and Company, LLC

Radford, Benjamin. 2007. "The Truth About the Abominable Snowman." https://www.livescience.com/2061-truth-abominable-snowman-html. December 3.

Taylor, Daniel. 2017. *Yeti: The Ecology of a Mystery*. Oxford, England: Oxford University Press.

A FEW TITLES TO ENRICH YOUR TEACHING
PICTURE BOOKS WITH AUTHORS' NOTES AND/OR BACK MATTER

Allman, John Robert. 2020. *American Ballet Theatre Presents Boys Dance!* New York: Doubleday.

Bildner, Phil. 2014. *The Soccer Fence: A Story of Friendship, Hope and Apartheid in South Africa.* New York: G.P. Putnam's Sons/Penguin Group.

Grimes, Nikki. 2017. *One Last Word: Wisdom from the Harlem Renaissance.* New York: Bloomsbury USA.

Hillery, Tony. 2020. *Harlem Grown.* New York: Simon& Schuster.

Isdahl, Nansubuga Nagadya. 2018. *Sing to the Moon.* Oxford, UK: Lantana Publishing.

Khorram, Adib. 2021. *Seven Special Somethings: A Nowraz Story.* New York: Penguin.

King, Shani Mahiri. 2021. *Have I Ever Told You Black Lives Matter.* Thomason, ME: Tilbury House Publishers.

Langley, Sharon: 2020. *A Ride to Remember: A Civil Rights Story.* New York: Abrams.

Lindstrom, Carole. 2020. *We Are Water Protectors.* New York: Roaring Brook Press.

Morales, Yuyi. 2018. *Dreamers.* New York: Neal Porter Books.

O'Meara. Kitty. 2020. *And the People Stayed Home.* Miami, FL: Tra Publishing.

Singer, Marilyn. 2019. *Who Named Their Pony Macaroni? Poems About White House Pets.* New York; Hyperion.

Sotomayor, Sonia. 2019. *Just Ask! Be Different, Be Brave, Be You.* New York: Philomel.

Vilela, Fernando. 2019. *Along the Tapajós.* 2019. Seattle, WA: Amazon Crossing Kids.

See additional resources in online Book List 18, Book List 19 (minilessons), and Book List 20.

CHAPTER 19
Creating Glossaries

(Grades 3-5)

Lincoln, a third grader in Renay Sadis's class at P.S. 87, chose Japanese words as well as unfamiliar English words when he prepared a glossary for *Yoshi's Feast* by Kimiko Kajikawa (2000). See Figure 19.1.

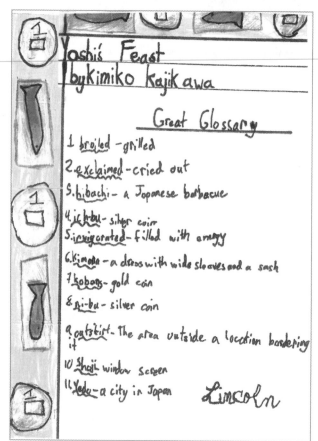

Figure 19.1

Exploring the Roots of the Writing Challenge

Teachers frequently call students' attention to nonfiction text features when the class reads weekly news magazines, nonfiction picture books, or textbook chapters. Elementary teachers often highlight side bars, subheadings, indices, tables of contents, captions, labeled diagrams, charts, graphs, footnotes, bibliographies, and glossaries. One way to help students appreciate such text features is to ask students to create their own. When a student attempts to write a sidebar, for example, the student looks at sidebars differently, with more scrutiny and deliberation. In this challenge, students will study picture books with glossaries and then search for picture books that would be enriched by a glossary. They will scour the text, lifting words they think should be defined in a mini-dictionary, and then they will define those words.

This is a seemingly simple challenge, but it carries many benefits. First, students will pay heightened attention to unfamiliar words and phrases. Teachers will be able to observe if students use illustrations, context clues, or familiar word parts to figure out the meaning of new words. Teachers will have an opportunity to teach students how to use dictionaries in ways that have real-world payoff. The finished glossary could be added to the class library. In this case, the glossary could be published as a laminated bookmark that will be slipped into the book and used when readers are unsuccessful using other strategies to figure out the meaning of unfamiliar words. Then too, students will have many opportunities to improve their vocabulary by working on their own glossary and responding to ones written by classmates. They will also have many opportunities to read upper-grade picture books, ones rich in content. In fact, books that have glossaries or need glossaries are usually rich in history or science. Not only will students learn new words and concepts, but so will the teachers and family members who read these books and the accompanying glossaries. As an important side benefit, picture books that have glossaries or need glossaries are frequently multicultural, filled with words in other languages and customs from other countries. In addition to their important global citizen content, these books also remind students that they too can weave words in other languages into their own writing, especially when they choose to write about their home countries, their family vacations, or immigrants in their neighborhood.

Some students will complete this challenge in a short amount of time. Perfect. They can do it again. They can read additional books and create additional glossaries. I always half-joke that short kids need short genres, and this is one of them. Elementary-aged students belong in the Little League of writing, not in Yankee Stadium. Short and sweet challenges like this one are often a breath of fresh air when children sometimes spend weeks on other writing assignments. And to top it off, this writing has real-world value. The finished work is not stuffed in a folder or filed in a portfolio or hung on a bulletin board. Glossaries belong in books, and that is where the students' glossaries will be placed.

Engaging Students in the Challenge

I began this challenge by sharing a favorite cookbook of mine that has a glossary. I explained how grateful I was that the editors of Williams-Sonoma's Kitchen Library collection, *Hors d'Oeuvres & Appetizers* (Williams 1992), included definitions for *Emmenthaler, garam masala*, and *tarama* in the glossary at the back of their book. Glossaries really do help readers. Then I asked students to share their own experiences using glossaries. Most referred to nonfiction books.

Next, I shared a collection of picture books that have glossaries. My choice of titles always depends on the grade level and interests of the students. In one fourth-grade class, I began with fictional picture books that had glossaries because the author interspersed words in other languages or made references to other cultures or had rich content information to share. Some titles include *Auntie Yang's Great Soybean Picnic* by Ginnie Lo (2012) (glossary of Chinese words), *Mama's Saris* by Pooja Makhijani (2007) (glossary of Hindi words), Aunty Joy Murphy and Andrew Kelly's *Birrarung Wilam: A Story from Aboriginal Australia* (2019) (glossary of words in Woiwurrung, a language of the Aboriginal culture), and *Goodbye, Havana! Hola, New York* by Edie Colon (2011) (glossary of Spanish words). (See additional titles at the end of this chapter and in online bibliography in Book List 21.)

Third grader has his supplies ready for writing to come.

I then shared the more traditional use of glossaries in such nonfiction texts as *Behold the Beautiful Dung Beetle* by Cheryl Bardoe (2014) (glossary of scientific terms), *Flying Deep: Climb Inside Deep-Sea Submersible ALVIN* by Michelle Cusolito (2018) (glossary of scientific terms), *A President from Hawai'i* by Terry Carolan and Joanna Carolan (2012)(glossary of Hawaiian words), and *Cows, Cats, and Kids: A Veterinarian's Family at Work* Jean L.S. Patrick (2003) (glossary of medical terms). (See additional titles at the end of this chapter and in online bibliography in Book List 21.)

In addition, I shared biographical picture books that contained glossaries including: *No Small Potatoes: Junius G. Groves and His Kingdom in Kansas by* Tonya Bolden (2018) (glossary of farming terms) and *Fab Four Friends: The Boys Who Became the Beatles* by Susanna Reich (2015) (glossary of music terms and British-English terms).

I also shared poetry anthologies that are so content rich that the poets added glossaries to support their readers' understanding of the material. These included *Dark Emperor & Other Poems of the Night* by Joyce Sidman (2010) (scientific glossary), *Ocean Soup: Tidal Pool Poems* by Stephen Swinburne (2010) (tide-pool creatures glossary), and *The Day the Universe Exploded My Head: Poems to Take You into Space and Back Again* by Allan Wolf (2019) (space terms glossary) (See additional titles at the end of the chapter and in online bibliography in Book List 21.)

We followed the usual protocol when sharing picture books. After reading aloud, we carved out time to talk about the content of the books, the illustrations, and any author's notes or additional information that was included. We encouraged honest questions, opinions, and insights. Eventually, we talked about the usefulness of the glossaries.

Continuing to Support Students' Efforts

We then filled the classroom with carefully selected books that lent themselves to the creation and addition of glossaries. Readers benefit from the inclusion of a glossary when the world of the picture book might be unfamiliar to many students and/or contain highly specialized vocabulary such as *Cowboy Up! Ride the Navajo Rodeo* by Nancy Bo Flood (2013), *The Secret Kingdom: Nek Chand, A Changing India, and a Hidden World of Art* by Barb Rosenstock (2018), and *An Amish Year* by Richard Ammon (2000). (See additional titles at the end of this chapter and in bibliography in Appendix 8.)

Students were given time to browse, read, and respond to these picture books and then decide if a glossary was in order. They were invited to contribute other picture books for consideration.

Sharing Your Own Writing

Rather than complete a glossary on my own for this writing challenge, I decided to work collaboratively with students. We chose one book, *Mazes Around the World* by Mary D. Lankford (2008), and wrote a glossary together. We reread the book aloud, selecting words that were unfamiliar to most students. Working in pairs, student partners were given a word to define and then contribute to the class glossary. Some definitions could be inferred from surrounding sentences in the book, and some needed to be looked up in a dictionary. We also had to revise student contributions if they chose an incorrect meaning or defined a related word that was a different part of speech. When we were unsure of the accuracy of the definition, students were asked to read aloud the entire sentence that contained the word in *Mazes Around the World*. We also had to make sure that students understood how to place words in alphabetical order. Our collaborative glossary appears below.

grotto: an artificial structure that is made to look like a real cave

hibiscus: a flowering hedge shrub

House of litoi: a Pima Native American labyrinth basket design that represents the twists and turns of life

maize mazes: temporary planted cornstalk mazes that can be quite complicated

Minotaur: a monster in Greek mythology that had the head of bull and the body of a man

multicursal: many paths

pilgrimage: a journey to a sacred place

puzzle mazes: also called hedge mazes; are found in many European countries and have dead ends and wrong turns

sepulchers: tombs or burial vaults

Soekershof: Afrikaans for "seeker's court"

succulent: a kind of fleshy plant like the cactus that conserves moisture

Tapu'a: Hopi design meaning mother and child

tecomaria: a flowering hedge shrub

turf mazes: often found in England; these mazes are made by digging out soil, creating a raised path

Trojborgs: also called Troy Towns; were stone mazes built by Scandinavian fisherman to ward off trolls

unicursal: one-path

veld: the grassland in South Africa scattered with shrubs

water mazes: fountains of water added to a maze and if you step on the wrong stone, you get sprayed

Woven mazes: labyrinth patterns used by Native American basket weavers

After working collaboratively, students chose picture books that would be enriched by glossaries and began working independently. The classroom was alive with conversations about such disparate topics as ballerinas, rodeos, China, India, Pilgrims, the Amish, and the printing press. (See Appendix 8 for words chosen for various titles.) Students reread their chosen books, selecting words that would be appropriate, and then began to create definitions.

Gathering Information

The main source of information for this challenge was the dictionary, an essential resource throughout the grades. Teachers might need to instruct students on how to use a traditional dictionary, rather than simply asking Siri for a definition. Many students were surprised to find themselves using these heavy tomes because outside of school they had gotten used to digitally checking out the meaning of unfamiliar words. Teachers had to introduce and/or review the use of alphabetical order, the use of guide words at the top of dictionary pages, sorting through multiple meanings, using pronunciation guides, understanding word origins, and using initials to indicate parts of speech. Teachers also had to demonstrate how to use dual-language dictionaries as so many of the words selected were in a language other than English. Occasionally, bilingual students were able to provide translations for their classmates. We hoped students would find the browsing of dictionary pages to be satisfying. (Of course, we also encouraged students to infer the meaning of words from context.)

Lifting the Quality of Student Writing

Our minilessons began with a conversation about how authors might go about choosing words for a glossary. We then focused on the specifics of writing definitions within glossaries. We came up with the following list of elements to consider:

- Different fonts are used for the word and for the definition.
- Colons or dashes are before the definitions.
- Labeled sketches are used, as in Michelle Cusolito's (2018) *Flying Deep*.
- Photographs are used, as in Todd Wechsler's (2017) *The Hidden Life of a Toad*.
- Phrases vs. full sentences are used in definitions.
- Brevity of definitions occurs in a glossary.
- Final punctuation or no punctuation is used at the end of definitions
- Parentheses are used to give examples, as in Stephen Swinburne's (2010) *Ocean Soup: Tidal Pool Poems*: "echinoderm: A spiny-skinned animal (starfish and sea urchin)."
- Plural is introduced, as in Cheryl Bardoe's (2014) *Behold the Beautiful Dung Beetle*: "larva (Pl. larvae): A young insect that has recently hatched from its egg."
- Singular is introduced, as in Joyce Sidman's (2010) *Dark Emperor & Other Poems of the Night*: "Fungi (singular, fungus) A group of spore-making organisms that feed on decaying organic matter."
- Pronunciation guides are used, as in Susan Middleton Elya's (2018) *Our Celebracion*: "(la) calle (KAY-yeh): street."
- Other alphabets are used to teach words—Korean characters appear in glossary of Frances Park and Ginger Park's (2008) *The Have a Good Day Café*.

In Renay's third-grade classroom at P.S. 87, students created glossaries for a collection of picture books connected to their study of Asian heritage. In addition to words that belonged to Chinese, Korean, and

Japanese culture, students chose English words that were unfamiliar. We were surprised by how honest students were and were equally surprised which words were new to students. Observing students at work also revealed their use of context clues to figure out word meanings.

The work taught us many lessons about how to support students as they created glossaries. First, we discovered that students needed to pay very close attention to the context of the words they chose. Since many English words have several meanings, students could err and provide a definition that did not fit the material at hand.

We also realized that students would need to reread the passages containing the selected words before they provided definitions. Therefore, students needed to record page numbers if they existed or mark pages with sticky notes so that they could easily return to the needed pages. Another possibility is to ask students to copy the sentences down for easy access. Having the sentence as a reference enables students to see if their definition makes sense. This requirement was therefore added to Renay's planning sheet. (See Appendix 9.)

Then too, students' definitions often did not match the part of speech of the chosen word. They might substitute, for example, an adjective for a noun, such as the student who wrote "violent, savage, and brutal," when creating a definition for *barbarian*. Teachers will need to help students revise their words to match the correct part of speech. The student's revised definition read "people who are violent, savage, and brutal."

Finally, some students might need instruction in how to use dictionaries if they are unfamiliar with their design. Many dictionaries offer so much information that young writers can feel overwhelmed with their contents.

Student Writing Samples

Third graders in Renay's class at P.S. 87 prepared the glossaries that appear in Figures 19.2–19.5.

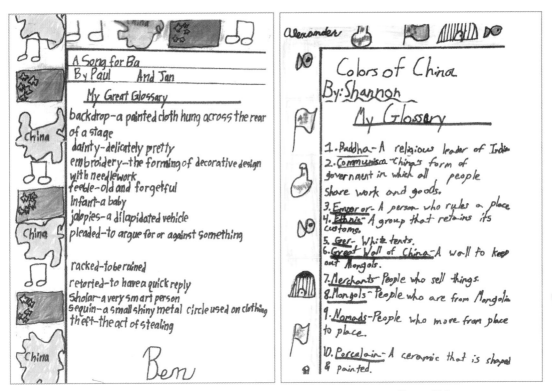

Figure 19.2   Figure 19.3

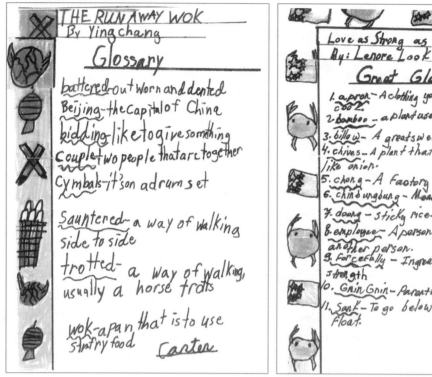

Figure 19.4   Figure 19.5

Carving Out Time for Celebration

When complete, revised and edited glossaries can be turned into laminated bookmarks. These can be slipped inside the books, much as reader's notes were. (See page 219.) They can remain in the class and school library. Copies can be made in case glossaries are misplaced with use.

BOOKS NOTED

Ammon, Richard. 2000. *An Amish Year.* New York: Atheneum Books for Young Readers/Simon & Schuster Children's Publishing.

Bardoe, Cheryl. 2014. *Behold the Beautiful Dung Beetle.* Watertown, MA: Charlesbridge.

Bolden, Tonya. 2018. *No Small Potatoes: Junius G. Groves and His Kingdom in Kansas.* New York: Knopf Books for Young Readers.

Carolan, Dr. Terry, and Joanna Carolan. 2012. *A President from Hawai'i.* Somerville, MA: Candlewick.

Colon, Edie. 2011. *Goodbye, Havana! Hola, New York.* New York: A Paula Wiseman Book/Simon & Schuster Books for Young Readers.

Compestine, Ying Chang. 2011. *The Runaway Wok: A Chinese New Year Tale.* New York: Dutton Books for Young Readers.

Cusolito, Michelle. 2018. *Flying Deep: Climb Inside Deep-Sea Submersible ALVIN.* Watertown, MA: Charlesbridge.

Elya, Susan Middleton. 2018. *Our Celebración.* New York: Lee & Low Books.

Flood, Nancy Bo. 2013. *Cowboy Up! Ride the Navajo Rodeo.* Honesdale, PA: Wordsong/Highlights.

Kajikawa, Kimiko. 2000. *Yoshi's Feast.* London, England: DK.

Lankford, Mary D. 2008. *Mazes Around the World.* New York: Collins/HarperCollins.

Lo, Ginnie. 2012. *Auntie Yang's Great Soybean Picnic.* New York: Lee & Low Books.

Look, Lenore. 1999. *Love as Strong as Ginger.* New York: Atheneum Books for Young Readers/Simon & Schuster.

Makhijani, Pooja. 2007. *Mama's Saris.* New York: Little, Brown/Hatchette Book Group USA.

Murphy, Aunty Joy, and Andrew Kelly. 2019. *Birrarung Wilam: A Story from Aboriginal Australia.* Somerville: MA: Candlewick.

Park, Frances, and Ginger Park. 2008. *The Have a Good Day Café.* New York: Lee & Low Books.

Patrick, Jean L.S. 2003. *Cows, Cats, and Kids: A Veterinarian's Family at Work.* Honesdale, PA: Boyds Mills.

Reich, Susanna. 2015. *Fab Four Friends: The Boys Who Became the Beatles.* New York: Christy Ottaviano Books/Henry Holt.

Rosenstock, Barb. 2018. *The Secret Kingdom: Nek Chand, A Changing India, and a Hidden World of Art.* Somerville, MA: Candlewick.

Sidman, Joyce. 2010. *Dark Emperor & Other Poems of the Night.* Boston, MA: Houghton Mifflin Books for Children/Houghton Mifflin Harcourt.

Swinburne, Stephen. 2010. *Ocean Soup: Tidal Pool Poems.* Watertown, MA: Charlesbridge.

Wechsler, Todd. (2017). *The Hidden Life of a Toad.* Watertown, MA: Charlesbridge.

Wolf, Allan. 2019. *The Day the Universe Exploded My Head: Poems to Take You into Space and Back Again.* Somerville, MA: Candlewick.

Yee, Paul. 2004. *A Song for Ba.* Toronto, Canada: Douglas & McIntyre/A Groundwood Book.

Zemlicka, Shannon. 2001. *Colors of China.* Minneapolis, MN: First Avenue Editions.

TEACHER REFERENCE MATERIAL

Williams, Chuck, ed. 1992. *Hors d'Oeuvres & Appetizers.* Williams-Sonoma Kitchen Library. San Francisco: Weldon Owen.

A FEW TITLES TO ENRICH YOUR TEACHING
PICTURE BOOKS WITH GLOSSARIES

Averbeck, Jim. 2015. *One Word from Sophia.* New York: Atheneum Books for Young Readers.

———. 2018. *Two Problems for Sophia.* New York: Margaret K. McElderry Books.

Brown, Monica. 2011. *Waiting for the Biblioburro/Esperando el Biblioburro.* New York: Tricycle Press.

Button, Joshua and Robyn Wells. 2019. *Steve Goes to Carnival.* Somerville, MA: Candlewick.

Cunnane, Kelly. 2013. *Deep in the Sahara.* New York: Simon & Schuster.

Guidroz, Rukhsanna. 2019. *Leila in Saffron.* New York: Salaam Reads/ Simon & Schuster.

Khalil, Aya. 2020. *The Arabic Quilt: An Immigrant Story.* Thomaston, ME: Tilbury House Publishers.

Lindstrom, Carole. 2020. *We Are Water Protectors*. New York: Roaring Brook Press.

Martinez, Claudia Guadalupe. 2019. *Not a Bean*. Waterton, MA: Charlesbridge

Rodrigues, Andre, Larissa Ribeiro, Paula Desgualdo, and Pedro Markun. 2020. *The President of the Jungle*. New York: Nancy Paulsen Books.

Robertson, Joanne. 2017. *The Water Walker/Nibi Emosaawdang*. Toronto: Second Story Press.

Thompkins-Bigelow, Jamilah. 2020. *Your Name Is a Song*. Seattle, Washington: The Innovation Press.

Walker, Tricia Elam. 2020. *Nana Akua Goes to School*. New York: Schwartz & Wade.

Wills, Cheryl. 2015. *The Emancipation of Grandpa Sandy Wills*. New York: Lightswitch Learning.

See online Book List 21 for additional titles of picture books with glossaries as well as titles of books that would be enriched by the addition of a glossary. See Appendix 8 for picture books with proposed lists of words for creating glossaries. See Appendix 9 for a Glossary Planning Sheet.

CHAPTER 20
Research and Riddles

(Grades 1-5)

The students in Max's second-grade class at P.S. 87 wrote riddles about famous sights in New York City. His appears in the text box below.

When you hear crowds cheering

and smell steaming hot dogs and

sweet cracker jacks filling the air.

Where bats crack with a swing,

and dirt flies from a slide to home.

When music roars as the noise meter screams,

my bleachers go wild with a ball out of the park.

I stand proud as a symbol of New York.

Who am I?

I am Yankee Stadium

Home of World Champions

Exploring the Roots of the Writing Challenge

When two of my grandsons were little, I often entertained them with baseball riddles, especially ones about their beloved Yankees. Which Yankee likes fireplaces the most? Mickey Mantle. Which Yankee likes honey the most? Yogi Bear-a. Which Yankee likes to be so clean? C.C. Sa BATH ia. These are very simple play-with-language riddles, just right for very young children. As soon as they "get it," they like to retell it to anyone who will listen. Just share the popular question "Why is 6 afraid of 7?" and the clever answer "Because 7, 8, 9," and be prepared to hear the riddle told endless times throughout the day and the school. As children get older, we can entertain them with more complex riddles like the classic Sphinx riddle that appears in Sophocles's *Oedipus the King*: What creature walks on four legs in the morning, two legs at noon, and three legs in the evening? The answer is, of course, a human being who crawls on all fours when a baby, walks on two legs when an adult, and uses a cane when elderly. Riddles like these require out-of-the-box thinking, an understanding of metaphors, and an ability to infer. A wide range of riddles can be found in the works of such literary luminaries as Shakespeare, Jane Austen, and Edgar Allen Poe. Riddles can be traced back many centuries, to many cultures, written in many languages. It's possible to study Sanskrit riddles, ones written in clay tablets from Ancient Babylon, and riddles from the Bible.

Occasionally, students throughout the grades choose riddle and joke collections during independent reading time if that type of material is available. Teachers seem to be okay with the reading of short humorous texts if they do not dominate a student's reading life. Informed teachers see the benefits of riddle-reading including the importance of laughter in the classroom, logical thinking, puzzle solving, and the social interactions created by the sharing of riddles.

Many of the old riddles are riddle poems. Today, riddle poetry remains alive and well and the content has moved beyond Humpty Dumpty. Young students enjoy *Riddle-icious* (1996) and *Riddle-lightful* (1998) by J. Patrick Lewis and *When Riddles Come Rumbling: Poems to Ponder* by Rebecca Kai Dotlich (2013). Older elementary students enjoy *Guess Again! Riddle Poems* by Lillian Morrison (2006), *Riddle-Me Rhymes* selected by Myra Cohn Livingston (1994), and Joyce Sidman's (2006) *Butterfly Eyes and Other Secrets of the Meadow*.

Riddle poems are not to be confused with the persona/mask poems described earlier. (See page 135.) Although poets become their subjects when they write persona poems, their intention is *not* to make the reader guess their identity. They are *not* leaving clues to help the reader solve a puzzle. Instead, they are announcing the mask they have donned and create images to support that persona.

Riddle-writing challenges can be as varied as the grades in an elementary school. In this riddle-writing challenge, we are inviting early childhood students to produce simple prose riddles, providing clues for their readers to guess at selected subjects. We are asking students to have enough information about their subjects that they can write clear and clever clues so readers can guess their subjects. When teaching upper-elementary grades, older students can be asked to craft riddle poems, using various forms of poetry as models and basing their clues on acquired information about their subjects.

Engaging Early Childhood Students in the Challenge

Riddles are naturally engaging for students. The most obvious way to begin is to simply share some intriguing riddles and begin a discussion of what makes a riddle a riddle. Children often note that a riddle is a guessing game. They realize that some are very short, just one question followed by a clever answer.

What animal can jump higher than a house?
Any animal because a house can't jump.

Other riddles offer several clues as Robin Page and Steven Jenkins (2017) do in *Who Am I? An Animal Guessing Game* and John Canty (2017) does in his book *Heads and Tails*. Both these picture books present early childhood animal riddles with several factual clues for each animal.

In *Who Am I? An Animal Guessing Game,* the authors include a list of carefully crafted clues in a description of the mystery animal. They write, "a sticky, flicky tongue, bumpy green skin, two bulging eyeballs, ten webbed toes, a floating lily pad, and a fly for lunch!" Note the specificity, sensory details, and surprise ending.

In *Heads and Tails* the author offers three clues to help young readers guess the name of the animal. The clues are accompanied by an illustration of the animal's rear end. Turn the page and get the answer along with an illustration of the front end of the animal. Hence the title, *Heads and Tails*. The structure of this riddle book is an easy one for young writers to borrow. In several classrooms that I visited, teachers extended the format to their social studies curriculum, namely community workers.

Many riddles were shared with students before they began crafting their own.

Continuing to Support Students' Efforts
Sharing Your Own Writing

Inspired by *Heads and Tails* we invited first graders in Leigh Brown and Rachel Heimler's class at P.S. 151, the Yorkville Community School, to choose a community worker, provide clues, and a create a partial illustration on one page. The name of the community worker appeared on the next page along with the other half of the illustration, just as Canty had done with his animals. After sharing Canty's book with children, I shared my attempts with children. See Figures 20.1 and 20.2.

Figure 20.1

Figure 20.2

Students noticed the features I borrowed. They noted that

I became the person, writing in the I voice.

I used three clues.

I wrote "I AM A"... in capital letters.

I used an ellipsis (usually referred to by first graders as three dots) to show that sentence was unfinished.

I used all capital letters for my answers.

I showed half the illustration at a time. (I demonstrated to students how I drew a full picture and then folded it in half to borrow John Canty's illustration technique.)

After children chose their community worker, we brainstormed kinds of clues they might include. We created the following chart.

CREATING CLUES FOR COMMUNITY WORKER RIDDLES

- clothes they wear (uniforms or not)
- tools they use (equipment, machines, and other supplies
- tasks they do in an average day (routines, jobs, etc.)
- the biggest challenges they face (hardest parts of their job)
- their favorite moments at work
- vehicles they travel in (if any)
- words they frequently say
- training needed for this kind of job/what they need to learn
- people they help
- problems they solve
- description/location of their place of work
- whether they work alone, in partners, or on a team

Gathering Information

Teachers provided varied resources for students so they would have information for their riddle clues. They read aloud related picture books about community workers, organized pertinent field trips, showed worthwhile videos, and interviewed community workers. Teachers also carved out time for rich class discussions about the work of members of the community.

We then rehearsed by asking a few children to orally compose riddles in front of the class. Then the six-year-olds went off to write. In one first-grade classroom, children stuck close to the Canty text, probably because I had done so. They offered three clues, split their illustrations in half, capitalized the "I AM A…", and used an ellipsis. And perhaps not surprisingly, they chose very New York City occupations. A few samples follow.

Student samples from Leigh and Rachel's first-grade classroom appear in Figures 20.3, 20.4, and 20.5.

Figure 20.3

Figure 20.4

I clen evry day.

I use soap.

I ride in a bucit

I AM A...

window washer

Figure 20.5

In all the first-grade classrooms that I worked in, conferring primarily focused on helping children avoid being too obvious, by using give-away words, like saying, "I put out fires," for a firefighter riddle. Occasionally, students needed help coming up with their third clue, and we encouraged them to reread the easy-to-read community worker material that filled their classroom shelves. We also encouraged students to chat with friends who might be able to remind them of additional ideas about their chosen worker.

Riddle-Writing in Grade 2

In a grade two classroom where students were studying birds, I filled a scrapbook with beautiful bird photographs taken from old Audubon calendars. Students were invited to write clues to help readers guess the name of the bird in the illustration. Turn the page and you would find the answer to the riddle.

Student samples from Kari Carlson and Kyle MacDowell's second grade class follow.

Alice wrote:

They call me a gem of a beauty.

I am the only bird that can fly backward.

When I fly forward, I beat my wings 75 times per second, and I make a bee-like sound.

I am also the smartest bird in the world.

Who am I?

I am a ruby-throated hummingbird.

Layla wrote:

> I am chunky, brown and grey with a large head and brown eyes.
>
> My eggs are only colored white.
>
> Female and male feed our young.
>
> We do not migrate.
>
> We eat mammals and small birds.
>
> I have a brown chest.
>
> Who am I?
>
> I am a barred owl.

In another second-grade classroom, I shared *Water Voices* by Toby Speed (1998), an oldie but a goodie. Many years ago, in *Writing Through Childhood: Rethinking Process and Product,* I wrote about this collection of poetic water-related riddles. More recently, I shared these poetic tributes to different forms of water to challenge young writers to learn from this writing, creating poetic tributes to different aspects of life in New York City, their social studies unit. Although we did not consider this primarily a poetry-writing unit, we did trust that students would borrow many of the poetic qualities of Toby Speed's collection. These included rich sensory details, personification, precise and surprising verbs, onomatopoeia, repetition, and similes. Children also borrowed Speed's use of direct address, long-list sentences, taglines after answers are given, and the word *When* appearing at the beginning each riddle.

I tried my hand at borrowing Toby Speed's distinctive features in *Water Voices* and shared the following riddle with students:

> When you huddle in the glass shelter
>
> and your mom keeps checking her watch
>
> and the number of people keeps growing and growing,
>
> I rumble down the avenue
>
> bringing smiles to waiting faces.
>
> Then you board, sliding your card up and down
>
> or jingling just the right amount of coins in my box.
>
> *(continues)*

(continued)

You squeeze your way through all those fellow passengers

toting packages, umbrellas, and even suitcases.

You finally nestle into an empty spot,

staring out my window, spotting Fairway,

H and H Bagels, and your mom's favorite shop, Zabar's.

Who am I?

I am the M 104, the Uptown Broadway bus.

Come board me. I'll take you home.

We then brainstormed subjects for the students' riddles. They came up with many New York City people and places including the United Nations, dog walkers, the Empire State Building, fashion designers, Central Park, elevator operators, Yankee Stadium, taxi drivers, Macy's, window washers, subway conductors, The Metropolitan Museum of Art, street vendors, and skyscrapers.

Max's poetic riddle about Yankee Stadium appears in the opening of this chapter. Similarly, second-grader Leila created another New York City riddle. (See Figure 20.6.)

When you walk you see skyscrapers tower over.
You feel excitement rolling in your stomach,
like gummy bears dancing on your skeleton.
Your mom is urging you to hurry up
but you're looking up like everyone else.
It's so hard to move through the crowds,
you just want to stay still and
look up at my advertisements.
Looking up and stalling the traffic
staring at my bright lights.   Who am I?

By Leila Brenner

I am Broadway
Come see a show

Figure 20.6

Engaging Upper-Grade Students in the Challenge

In Melissa Martinez and Guia Mirasol-Tabuelin's fifth-grade class, we decided to use many forms of riddle poetry to challenge students. We made the task even more ambitious, by asking students to create riddle poems based on people, places, and events in the news. At the time, our newspapers were filled with articles about Cory Booker, Kobe Bryant, Hillary Clinton, Andrew Cuomo, Kamala Harris, Lin-Manuel Miranda, Greta Thunberg, Andrew Yang, and Alexandria Ocasio-Cortez as well as stories about Congress, the Oval office, and the California wildfires. (Asking students to keep up with current events is always a top priority as we move up in the grades.)

We read aloud several poems from Myra Cohn Livingstone's (1994) selection of riddles in *Riddle-Me Rhymes*. These included a poem made up of a series of questions ("Who" translated by Sylvia Cassedy), and two Lillian Morrison poems composed of a list of similes (one a riddle about a walnut and another about a magpie). We also shared one of Eve Merriam's poems from the same collection ("It Isn't"), in which the poet repeats the phrase, "It isn't…" followed by the phrase, "but it…" Lillian Morrison (2006) uses a similar grammatical structure in the following riddle poems. Students recognized how important the word *but* is in each.

> They have tongues
>
> but they can't talk to you.
>
> They have no legs
>
> but they can walk with you. (Sneakers)
>
> (Morrison 2006)

> It's in the river
>
> but not in the lake.
>
> It's in the raindrop
>
> but not the snowflake. (The letter R)
>
> (Morrison 2006)

Lillian Morrison uses another distinctive form when she offers clues by listing several actions taken by the subject as she does in the following two poems. They are filled with a list of precise verbs, ending with a surprising statement.

> At times it sings or softly speaks
>
> At times it bangs and shouts or shrieks,
>
> yet it can take you to wondrous places
>
> as it sits against a wall making faces. (The TV)
>
> (Morrison 2006)
>
>
> You turn it and punch it,
>
> you smoothe it and scrunch it.
>
> At times you might heave it
>
> at friends in a fight.
>
> Yet it's there for your comfort
>
> every night. (A pillow)
>
> (Morrison 2006)

We also shared haiku riddles with students. Most students remembered this traditional form from their reading in earlier grades. They were eager to count the syllables in the three lines to see if the poem conformed to their memory of lines of five, seven, five syllables, totaling seventeen in all. They needed to be reminded that haiku, this ancient Japanese form of poetry, is intended to be about nature and natural events and is written in the present tense.

We shared poems from Deanna Caswell's (2016) *Guess Who, Haiku* including the following mouse riddle.

> a chunk of Swiss cheese
>
> chewing sounds heard from a hole
>
> in the kitchen wall

To help students to write original riddles, I shared a few of my own, borrowing the structures used by each of these poets. I lifted subjects from the daily newspaper, intending to be true to the students' assignment. I showed them the riddle poems that inspired and informed me.

This following riddle poem is a list of questions like the Indian riddle about the wind.

Who is represented by an elephant?

Who was Abraham Lincoln proud of?

Who has the same initials as George Otto Powell?

Who wants to run both chambers?

Who did the Bush family party with?

Who appreciates polls, politicians, and platforms? (The Republican Party)

The following two riddles rely on a series of similes.

As brilliant as a top scholar, as determined as a pioneer.

As wise as an owl, as famous as a president.

And a long black robe covered me all.

Who was I? (Ruth Bader Ginsberg)

As well-spoken as an actor and isn't an actor.

As smart as a valedictorian and isn't a valedictorian.

As important as a president and is no longer the president.

And stands tall alongside the country's famous and favorite first lady.

Who am I? (Barack Obama)

Please see Appendix 10 for more original riddle poems.

Gathering Information

As we shared different forms of riddle poems, we also collaboratively compiled a list of newsworthy people, places, or events. To make sure that students were playing on a level playing field in their ability to create riddle clues and their ability to guess answers to current event riddles, Melissa and Guia helped students stay on top of the news. Students watched appropriate videos at morning meetings, shared news clippings, and had rich classroom conversations about local, national, and international happenings.

Lifting the Quality of Student Writing

Alongside giving children information about riddle poetry formats and current events happenings, teachers also carved out time for students to write riddle poems collaboratively. Each time we introduced a new format, the class worked together to create a riddle poem based on an item on their class list. The first poem is made up of a series of questions.

> What is mighty and majestic?
>
> What was meant to reach the sky?
>
> What might be in the background when you are munching a pain au chocolat?
>
> What was built beautifully but not loved by all?
>
> What needs 60 tons of paint every 7 years?
>
> What has 100 hundred ways to access the world?
>
> What is a sister to Liberty?
>
> What glistens in the city of light?
>
> What am I? (Eiffel Tower)

The next poem is filled with similes.

> As interesting as a museum, as historical as antique books.
>
> As yellow as the sun, almost as old as the Declaration of Independence.
>
> As ancient as my great-grandma, a world within its walls.
>
> As far away from New York City in 1799 as a country house is today.
>
> What am I? Gracie Mansion (the NYC mayor's home)

The following poem is based on Eve Merriam's and Lillian Morrison's use of a contrasting structure.

It Is, but Isn't

It is the heart of New York City,

but it doesn't beat.

It holds beautiful scenes,

but is not a museum.

It is very green,

but turns white in winter.

It has strawberry fields,

but there aren't any strawberries.

It is a great place for recreation and relaxation,

but please don't litter, don't loiter and don't get lost.

What is it? (Central Park)

The following original riddle poem reveals Lillian Morrison's use of a string of precise verbs.

It screams, shouts, shrieks up above

where everyone could see

its clapper swinging

from side to side, like a monkey,

vibrating, announcing liberty.

People rejoicing, laughing, jumping for joy

"We are free! We are free!"

What am I? (The Liberty Bell)

This collaboratively created poem is a haiku.

> I destroy the world
>
> Dark, smoky skyline
>
> You struggle to breathe
>
> What am I? (air pollution)

Each time a poem was created, we asked a student from another class to visit. The student read the riddle poem and tried to guess the answer. If the student could not guess the answer, we rethought our clues, refining them to give better hints. For example, the first draft of the haiku poem had read:

> I destroy the world
> Eating up all Earthly life
> You struggle to breathe.

The first student we invited into the classroom to solve the riddle could not figure it out. Students realized that the first two lines essentially shared the same information, and the reader needed another clue. They therefore changed the second line, although a bit reluctantly, as they loved the poetic sound of "Eating up all Earthly life." After changing the second line to include a "Dark, smoky skyline," the second invited guest reader was able to solve the riddle.

We always asked visiting students which clue was the most helpful and we analyzed those. Most importantly, we analyzed the process that we went through to create each poem, compiling a few suggestions for writing riddle clues independently.

Suggestions for writing riddle poems

- Start with your answer and work backward.
- Consider becoming the subject to offer clues.
- Don't make clues too obvious or too easy.
- Don't make clues too generic so that clues apply to many subjects.
- Consider using words with double meanings as well as puns.
- Limit the number of clues; otherwise the riddle can become overwhelming.
- Think about the order of your clues, and rearrange them in a sensible order.
- Listen to the sound of your lines, remembering your desire to be poetic.
- Don't hesitate to use techniques from your writer's toolbox, including similes, metaphors, precise verbs, power of three, specific sensory details, alliteration.
- Include the question "Who am I?" or "What am I?"
- Feel free to borrow structures used by other riddle-poetry creators.

We sent students off with copies of the published riddle poems, teacher-composed riddle poems, and the collaboratively created ones. After selecting a subject, children jotted down anything they already knew about their subject. Many realized that they needed to do additional research to create meaningful clues. Over the next few days, they took notes on the subjects they had chosen.

Our minilessons, conferences, and share meetings focused on finding appropriate information and strengthening the clues offered. Students volunteered to share the drafts of their riddles, and classmates were encouraged to give honest, yet tactful feedback.

Student Writing Samples

The following fifth graders in Melissa and Guia's class wrote content-rich riddle poems.

Hannah relied heavily on similes when she created the following three riddle poems.

> As jointed as an octopus, as slow as a slug.
>
> As mysterious as a Sherlock Holmes and Watson book.
>
> As metallic as a knight's armor,
>
> As well thought out as a robber's escape plan.
>
> As intelligent as Albert Einstein.
>
> What am I? (The Mars Curiosity Rover)
>
>
> As elegant as a swan, as tragic as the Great Depression.
>
> As terrifying as a horror movie, as famous as the Mona Lisa.
>
> As mysterious as the board game, Clue.
>
> As ruined as the Mayan temples.
>
> I am submerged under water.
>
> What am I? (the *Titanic*)
>
>
> Like an alarm clock, it vibrates and rings to get your attention.
>
> Like a pendulum, it swings from side to side.
>
> Like a quote, it brings inspiration.
>
> Like a captain, it announces things for everyone to hear.
>
> Like the Bill of Rights, it stands for freedom.
>
> What Am I? (the Liberty Bell)

Amani wrote a riddle poem filled with a series of questions:

> What is hated by all and loved by none?
>
> What cannot be seen by anyone?
>
> What is the outcome of carelessness, greed, and ignorance?
>
> What gives people lung disease?
>
> What cannot be stopped by one, but by all?
>
> What am I? (air pollution)

Clarissa shows her political leanings with the following riddle poem also created with a series of questions:

> Who represents and speaks for two boroughs?
>
> Who is very ethnic and not ashamed of it?
>
> Who used to be a waitress?
>
> Who is very smart?
>
> Who is the youngest woman to ever be elected to Congress?
>
> Who am I? (Alexandria Ocasio-Cortez)

Alex contributed this riddle poem created as well with a series of questions.

> What has been preserved through the ages?
>
> What witnessed Napoleon become king?
>
> What holds treasured artworks?
>
> What has burned but sustained?
>
> What is prayed in till it falls?
>
> What still lives in the city of light?
>
> What am I? (Notre Dame Cathedral)

Carving Out Time for Celebration

In the early childhood grades, classes visited one another and shared their riddles aloud. Their riddles about community workers, birds, and New York City were copied and distributed to all members of the class.

In one fifth grade, teachers compiled students' completed riddle poems into an anthology. Titles for such collections include *Are You Stumped Yet?*; *Newsworthy Poetry Riddles: How Up to Date Are You?*; *What's Happening?*; *Are You as Smart as a Fifth Grader?*; *Clues in the News: An Anthology of Riddle Poems*; and *Poetic Riddles That Make You Read, Research, and Remember*. All students hoped to stump their friends and family members.

BOOKS NOTED

Canty, John. 2017. *Heads and Tails*. Somerville, MA: Candlewick.

Caswell, Deanna. 2016. *Guess Who, Haiku*. New York: Abrams Appleseed.

Dotlich, Rebecca Kai. 2013. *When Riddles Come Rumbling: Poems to Ponder*. Honesdale, PA: Wordsong/Boyds Mills.

Lewis, J. Patrick. 1996. *Riddle-icious*. New York: Knopf Books for Young Readers.

———. 1998. *Riddle-lightful: Oodles of Little Riddle Poems*. New York: Knopf Books for Young Readers.

Livingston, Myra Cohn (selected by). 1994. *Riddle-Me Rhymes*. New York: Margaret McElderry Books.

Morrison, Lillian. 2006. *Guess Again! Riddle Poems*. Little Rock, AR: August House.

Page, Robin, and Steve Jenkins. 2017. *Who Am I? An Animal Guessing Game*. Boston, MA: HMH Books for Young Readers.

Sidman, Joyce. 2006. *Butterfly Eyes and Other Secrets of the Meadow*. Boston, MA: Houghton Mifflin.

Speed, Toby. 1998. *Water Voices*. New York: G.P. Putnam's Sons/Putnam & Grosset Group.

TEACHER REFERENCE MATERIAL

Harwayne, Shelley. 2001. *Writing Through Childhood: Rethinking Process and Product,* Portsmouth, NH: Heinemann.

A FEW TITLES TO ENRICH YOUR TEACHING

Alemagna, Beatrice. 2019. *The Big Little Thing*. Mustang, OK: Tate Publishing.

Canty, John. 2020. *Heads and Tails: Insects*. Somerville, MA: Candlewick.

———. 2021. *Heads and Tails: Underwater*. Somerville, MA: Candlewick.

Gillingham, Sara. 2020. *Animals in the Sky*. New York: Phaidon Press.

Lewis, J. Patrick. 2009. *Spot the Plot: A Riddle Book of Book Riddles*. San Francisco, CA: Chronicle.

———. 2015. *National Geographic Kids Just Joking Animal Riddles: Hilarious Riddle Jokes and More—All About Animals!*: Washington, DC: National Geographic Kids.

Lupton, Hugh. 2016. *The Barefoot Book of Riddles from Around the World*. Somerville, MA: Barefoot Books.

Paul, Miranda. 2016. *Whose Hands Are These?: A Community Helper Guessing Book*. Minneapolis, MN: Millbrook Press.

Porter, Antoinette. 2020. *A New Green Day*. New York: Neal Porter Books.

Salas, Lara Purdie. 2019. *Lion of the Sky: Haiku for All Seasons*. Brookfield, CT: Millbrook Press.

Ziefert, Harriet. 2014. *What Ship Is Not a Ship?* Maplewood, NJ: Blue Apple Books.

See additional resources in online Book List 22.

CHAPTER 21
Every Day
of the Week
(Grades 2-5)

Fourth graders in Diane Berman's class wrote short texts for younger students learning to read. Using the seven days of the week as a predictable structure, Ruby wrote the following:

No More Sports

On Monday, Nina quit basketball.

On Tuesday, Nina gave up soccer.

On Wednesday, Nina left baseball.

On Thursday, Nina stormed out of hockey.

On Friday, Nina walked out on volleyball.

On Saturday, Nina turned her back on tennis.

On Sunday, Nina said, "I think I want piano lessons."

What do you think her parents said?

Exploring the Roots of the Writing Challenge

In this challenge, I invite students throughout the elementary grades to tap into the very accessible list structure, creating reading material for their younger book buddies and other early childhood classrooms in their school. To make the challenge more interesting and at the same time more manageable for young writers, I suggested that we study emergent reader books that were structured around the seven days of the week. I believed this shape would help students keep the plot predictable, the phrasing repetitive, and the length appropriate.

This challenge has several benefits for the writers, including the following:

- The writing would serve as a manageable introduction to fiction for the writers.
- The writing would demonstrate the importance of putting student work to real-world use.
- The elegance of the design facilitates a literary sound.
- There exists a wide range of literature to inspire and inform.
- The writing would remind writers of the importance of a satisfying ending.
- The writing has a built-in audience for sharing rough drafts and for final celebrations.
- The writing demands that illustrations be taken seriously as they to enhance the meaning and support comprehension of young readers.
- The writers can work with a specific audience in mind, influencing their topic choice, vocabulary, length, and so on.
- The writers can apply the techniques in their writer's toolbox to create high-quality text.
- The writers can produce more than one seven-day-a-week book as length of text is so short.

Of course, there are also benefits for the members of the young audience as their classroom library fills with original, readable booklets.

Eric Carle's (1974) classic tale *The Very Hungry Caterpillar* is always included on lists of recommended books for our youngest children. And that comes as no surprise. It has very rich content, incredible illustrations, and a predictable structure. The structure, that of the passing of the days of the week, is one frequently used by writers of material for our youngest readers. Early childhood students usually have little or no control over how their time is used, and I think, therefore, they become particularly engaged in reading and rereading stories that offer a handle on how time passes.

Engaging Students in the Writing Challenge

In addition to *The Very Hungry Caterpillar*, there are many published picture books that are built upon the seven days of the week. (See bibliography at the end of this chapter and in online Book List 23.) The ones I choose to share with fourth graders for this challenge, however, belong to a subset of this collection. Not all the books mentioned can be read by beginning or emergent readers. Although all are worth reading aloud to young children, many cannot be read independently by beginning readers. Some have long introductions, richly detailed scenes for each day of the week, lengthy dialogue, and so on. Fourth-grade writers need to see the ones that can be described as early childhood list books. They are more bare bones, with repeated words, predictable patterns, illustrations that support the beginning reader, and endings that seem to make these simple stories add up to a meaningful whole.

Young readers delight in memorizing the text in *Cookie's Week* by Cindy Ward (1997), *Baby Penguins Love Their Mama!* by Melissa Guion (2015), and,

Young children love reading picture books structured around the seven days of the week and enjoy writing them as well.

of course, the pages in Eric Carle's (1974) *The Very Hungry Caterpillar*. After they hear the books read aloud several times, they can often recite the words along with their teachers or even on their own. These are the kind of texts that fourth-grade writers can emulate when they create their own gifts for their younger book buddies.

Perhaps the most helpful models are the ones created by teachers, especially by teachers who have worked with emergent readers and understand the kind of material that is most supportive of beginning readers. I created the following simple stories structured around the seven days of the week. I pointed out to the students that I chose the topics with young people's interests in mind. I relied on repetition of key words. I tried to honor the pattern with no distractions. I attempted to write satisfying and surprising endings. In addition, I gave thought to the feasibility of illustrating these texts, knowing how much illustrations support the emergent reader. Throughout, I had to remember that it is easy for a teacher to impress a fourth grader. Our models do not have to be publishable for real. (See additional teacher-made examples in Appendix 11.)

Continuing to Support Students' Efforts
Sharing Your Own Writing

The following are my own emergent reader texts based on the seven days of the week.

Big Adventures

On Sunday, Will flew to the moon.

On Monday, Will joined the circus.

On Tuesday, Will visited the Queen.

On Wednesday, Will climbed the highest mountain.

On Thursday, Will became the President.

On Friday, Will became a zookeeper.

On Saturday, Will had an even better dream.

Cleaning Up

On Sunday, Andie cleaned her bookcase.

On Monday, Andie cleaned her desk.

On Tuesday, Andie cleaned her closet.

On Wednesday, Andie cleaned her bed.

On Thursday, Andie cleaned her drawers.

On Friday, Andie cleaned her floor.

On Saturday, everyone asked,

"Whose room is this?"

(continues)

(continued)

Tiny Boo-Boos

On Sunday, Ben cut his toe. Oops! Ouch!

On Monday, Ben cut his finger. Oops! Ouch!

On Tuesday, Ben cut his elbow. Oops! Ouch!

On Wednesday, Ben cut his knee. Oops! Ouch!

On Thursday, Ben cut his forehead. Oops! Ouch!

On Friday, Ben cut his leg. Oops! Ouch!

On Saturday, Ben got a haircut and it didn't hurt at all.

Weather Forecasts

On Sunday, the weather forecaster predicted sun.

Instead, it rained.

On Monday, the weather forecaster predicted clouds.

Instead, it was sunny.

On Tuesday, the weather forecaster predicted heavy rain.

Instead, it drizzled.

On Wednesday, the weather forecaster predicted snow.

Instead, it hailed.

On Thursday, the weather forecaster predicted strong winds.

Instead, it was calm.

On Friday, the weather forecaster predicted thunder and lightning.

Instead, it was partly cloudy.

On Saturday, I didn't bother listening to the weather forecast.

Getting Ready

On Friday, Sasha prepared cranberry sauce.

On Saturday, Sasha steamed asparagus.

On Sunday, Sasha baked pumpkin pie.

On Monday, Sasha cooked vegetable soup.

On Tuesday, Sasha made mashed potatoes.

On Wednesday, Sasha roasted a turkey.

On Thursday, Sasha said "Happy Thanksgiving Everyone!"

Gathering Information

This task requires manageable amounts of research including asking students to read and reread published emergent reader material, particularly texts that are based on the seven days of the week. (Teachers might want to extend the design to include the four seasons of the year and/or the twelve months of the year. See bibliography in online Book List 23.) Additionally, as part of their research process, students benefit from talking to early childhood teachers and other literacy experts about what they look for when choosing emergent reading materials. Students will learn a lot when they ask such questions as "What makes a book so engaging that young readers will want to read it again and again?" "What supports should be present in emergent reader materials to facilitate learning to read?" "What topics are most appealing to young students?" "What kind of illustrations are most supportive?"

Lifting the Quality of Student Writing

We asked upper-grade students to borrow the seven days a week as a predictable structure to create their own meaningful list books. First, we brainstormed appropriate topics for five- and six-year-old readers. Students came up with such topics as birthday parties, playing in the snow, playgrounds, pets, sleepovers, playdates, cupcakes, learning to ride a bike, trampoline fun, playing baseball, buying new shoes, loose teeth, stuffed animals, day camp, pizza, swimming, fun at recess, helping at home, baby sisters or brothers, and getting a haircut.

Then we reviewed some of the essential ingredients in early reading material. These included:

- The main character must appeal to young children.
- Key words and phrases must be repeated.
- Illustrations must support the text.
- Vocabulary must be age appropriate.
- Sentences must be simply constructed.
- Humor, if any, must be age appropriate.
- The ending must be satisfying (could add surprise or twist).

We also prepared blank seven-page booklets, with space for illustrations as well as words so students could transfer their revised and edited ideas into reading material for younger children. Cover pages were added later.

Students' first attempts provided much grist for the minilesson mill. For example, several students wrote wild fantasy experiences and on Sunday awoke from their dreams, modeling their work on my own emergent reader material *Big Adventures*. We talked about being original and trusting your own imaginations.

We also had to remind students to think about whether what they wrote was appropriate for younger audience in terms of topic choice, vocabulary, and even humor. For example, Quinn wrote a clever book about current Broadway musicals, but had to think about her audience. Would our youngest readers know all those Broadway shows and be able to read their titles? Perhaps this book was best read by Quinn's fourth-grade classmates.

Several student pieces were used to highlight the use of consistency, repetition, and patterns. Avery repeated each verb two times, creating a satisfying pattern in her book, *A Really Bad Week*. In *Vacations*, Ruby achieved a satisfying sense of consistency by changing all her destinations to cities instead of including some countries and some continents. Similarly, she added consistency by including specific amounts for each candy in *Too Much Candy*.

Student Writing Samples

The following are students' revised books, published here without illustrations.

A Really Bad Week by Avery

On Monday, I fell off my bike.

On Tuesday, I fell off my scooter.

On Wednesday, I tripped over a rock.

On Thursday, I tripped over my laces.

On Friday, I got a splinter.

On Saturday, I got a scrape.

On Sunday, my mom said, "What's going to happen to you tomorrow?"

Trip Around the World by Ruby

On Monday, Olivia went to Cape Town.

On Tuesday, Olivia visited Dublin.

On Wednesday, Olivia toured Mexico City.

On Thursday, Olivia traveled all the way to Beijing.

On Friday, Olivia flew to London.

On Saturday, Olivia journeyed to Paris.

On Sunday, Olivia's mom said, "That was a great play. I love your creativity!"

Too Much Candy by Ruby

On Monday, Alex ate 15 gummy bears.

On Tuesday, Alex chomped on 11 Hershey kisses.

On Wednesday, Alex stuffed 20 marshmallows in her mouth.

On Thursday, Alex chewed 5 whole chocolate bars.

On Friday, Alex munched 50 Nerds.

On Saturday, Alex sucked 10 pieces of caramel.

On Sunday, Alex had a toothache and planned to visit the dentist.

Carving Out Time for Celebration

The most meaningful celebration of this challenge would be for students to share their work in early childhood classrooms. The work can be illustrated and bound into page-turning booklets. When completed, the young authors might give their work as gifts to early childhood teachers, share them aloud as guest readers in kindergarten or first-grade classrooms, or use as reading material with their younger book buddies. Book buddy time is always prime time for teachers to observe and assess their students. Teachers can observe and take notes on engagement, attention span, response to text, and reading fluency.

Then, too, students who have younger siblings, cousins, or friends could make copies of their emergent reader materials and share these outside of school.

BOOKS NOTED

Carle, Eric. 1974. *The Very Hungry Caterpillar.* New York: Puffin Books/Penguin Group.
Guion, Melissa. 2015. *Baby Penguins Love Their Mama!* New York: Philomel Books.
Ward, Cindy. 1997. *Cookie's Week.* New York: Puffin Books.

See additional resources in online Book List 23 and additional teacher made materials in Appendix 11.

A FEW TITLES TO ENRICH YOUR TEACHING

Alarcon, Francisco. 2017. *Family Poems for Every Day of the Week: Poemas familiares para cada dia de la semana.* New York: Children's Book Press.
Archer, Micha. 2016. *Daniel Finds a Poem.* New York: Nancy Paulsen Books.
Flett, Julie. 2019. *Birdsong.* Vancouver: Greystone Kids.
Isadora, Rachel. 2020. *Do I Have to Wear a Coat? A Journey Through the Seasons.* New York: Nancy Paulsen Books.
Janezcko, Paul, ed. 2014. *Firefly July: A Year of Very Short Poems.* Somerville, MA: Candlewick.

Lê, Minh. 2020. *Lift*. New York: Little, Brown.

Levine, Arthur A. 2015. *Monday Is One Day*. New York: Scholastic.

Ludwig, Trudy. 2018. *Quiet Please, Owen McPhee*! New York: Alfred A. Knopf.

Murrow, Ethan, and Vita Murrow. 2020. *Zero Local: Next Stop: Kindness*. Somerville, MA: Candlewick.

Muth, Jon J. 2014. *Hi, Koo! A Year of Seasons*. New York: Scholastic.

Ransome, James. 2019. *The Bell Rang*. New York: Atheneum.

Singer, Marilyn. 2018. *Every Month Is a New Year*. Lee & Low Books.

Sorell, Traci. 2018. *We Are Grateful: Otsaliheliga*. Watertown, MA: Charlesbridge.

Weatherford, Carole Boston. 2017. *Freedom in Congo Square*. New York: little bee books.

Wheeler, Eliza. 2019. *Home in the Woods*. New York: Nancy Paulsen Books.

CHAPTER 22
Author Scrapbooks

(Grades 3-5)

Arianna, a third grader at P.S. 87, focused on Judith Viorst and shared what she learned about elements of the author's craft.

This is a line I lifted from the book *Alexander and the Terrible, Horrible, No Good, Very Bad Day* by Judith Viorst. She used a long list sentence when she wrote, "I went to sleep with gum in my mouth and now there's gum in my hair and when I got out of bed this morning I tripped on the skateboard and by mistake I dropped my sweater in the sink while the water was running and I could tell it was going to be a terrible, horrible, no good, very bad day." Now this is an example of me trying out a long sentence. "I was on my way to school and it started to snow and I was wearing my new shoes so my shoes got messed up and my backpack was open on the train ride to school and when I got to school my friends pulled a prank on me so every time I tried to talk to them they would ignore me and pretend I'm not there."

Exploring the Roots of the Challenge

In the Learning from One Writer challenge (see page 48), all students in the class study the work of one author. In this challenge, each student in the class becomes an expert on a different author, preparing a scrapbook devoted to the life story of that popular and prolific author. Their scrapbooks include a short biography of the writer, the titles of their writer's published works, responses to a few of the writer's publications, and detailed commentaries on the authors' crafting techniques. I designed this challenge after asking students to name their favorite writers. Often, they responded with the title of a book they enjoyed, but rarely spoke about the authors of those books. I was determined that students become familiar not only with the best of children's literature but also with the writers who created these literary treasures.

I began by creating a list of writers that I thought were so wonderful that I wouldn't want children to graduate elementary school never having gotten to know their work. I jotted down authors that readily came off the top of my head, scanned my library shelves, and did Internet searches. Students and teachers were asked to add additional ones. (See list on pages 259–260.) In addition to being fine writers, I wanted to include authors who wrote across several genres and ones whose publications were readily available in public and school libraries. I made sure that the authors were diverse in ethnic background and gender. I included authors who were primarily known as fiction writers and some who were considered nonfiction writers and poets. One day, I hope to repeat this challenge exclusively with nonfiction writers and then again with poets, as students frequently cannot name a nonfiction writer or a poet when asked for their favorites.

When meeting with a team of third-grade teachers, we developed the following description of the author scrapbook project.

AUTHOR SCRAPBOOK PROJECT

1. Choose an author from the long list provided. Find several age-appropriate materials written by this author. Read, read, read works written by this author. Write short responses to your favorite books by this author. (Be sure to include what the book is about and what it makes you think about.)

2. Prepare a comprehensive list of published works by this author.

3. Create a short biographical sketch of the author, introducing the writer to your classmates. (Information will be gathered by browsing book jackets, reading biographies and autobiographies, talking to librarians or teachers, and researching on the Internet, especially the author's website.)

4. Copy down well-written lines (excerpts) from the author's works. Choose lines or passages that stood out for you as you read. Find the kind of lines that you would like to be able to write yourself.

5. Use these lines as mentor sentences. Name the technique (tool or craft element) that the author used. Attempt to write like that author, borrowing the same writing tools from your writer's toolbox to create your own high-quality sentences.

6. Be prepared to share what you learned about this author's life as well as any big ideas you gathered from reading this author's work. Share the writing lessons you learned from studying the works of this author.

Engaging Students in the Challenge

We began our study by talking about having favorite writers. "Who are the writers you would be first in line to buy or borrow a new book they just published? After all, when you have a favorite writer, you want to read all the publications of that writer." As an adult reader, I can't imagine not reading the latest book by Isabel Allende, Margaret Atwood, Louise Erdrich, Oscar Hijuelos, Alice Hoffman, Kazuo Ishiguro, Ian McEwan, or James McBride. Having favorite writers is one of life's pleasures, and I hope we are raising students who will also be delighted to hear that one of their favorite writers has a new book coming out.

A student gathers stacks of books written by a favorite author.

We distributed a list of over 100 accomplished and prolific authors that were appropriate for a wide range of third-grade tastes and abilities. We sent students off to browse the list, asking them to circle familiar names and star ones that they might like to study in depth.

AUTHORS FOR STUDY—GRADE 3

Karen Ackerman	Sneed B. Collard III	Karen Hesse
Alma Flor Ada	Floyd Cooper	Amy Hest
Aliki	Roald Dahl	Lee Bennett Hopkins
Jim Arnosky	Nicola Davies	Deborah Hopkinson
Derrick Barnes	Carmen Agra Deedy	Chen Jiang Hong
Mac Barnett	Lulu Delacre	Elizabeth Fitzgerald Howard
Chris Barton	Kate DiCamillo	Steve Jenkins
Marion Dane Bauer	Dyanne DiSalvo	Tony Johnston
Byrd Baylor	Alice Faye Duncan	Maira Kalman
Phil Bildner	David Elliott	Kathleen Krull
Maribeth Boelts	Zetta Elliott	Kathryn Lasky
Louise Borden	Margarita Engle	Irene Latham
Tom Brenner	Paul Fleischman	Ted Lewin
Monica Brown	Candace Fleming	Grace Lin
Joseph Bruchac	Ralph Fletcher	Kelly Starling Lyons
Ashley Bryan	Helen Frost	Patricia MacLachlan
Eve Bunting	Michael Garland	Patricia McKissack
Chris Butterworth	Kristine O'Connell George	Tony Medina
Nicola I. Campbell	Mordicai Gerstein	Pat Mora
Andrea Chang	Nikki Giovanni	Yuyi Morales
Jason Chin	Eloise Greenfield	Walter Dean Myers
Andrew Clements	Nikki Grimes	Kadir Nelson
Lesa Cline-Ransome	Virginia Hamilton	S.D. Nelson
Joseph Coehlo	Juan Felipe Herrera	W. Nikola-Lisa

(continues)

AUTHORS FOR STUDY—GRADE 3 *(continued)*

Jonathan London	Joanne Ryder	Carmen Tafolla
Lenore Look	Cynthia Rylant	Matt Taveres
Sandra Markle	Laura Purdie Salas	Joyce Carol Thomas
Meg Medina	Allen Say	Duncan Tonatiuh
Kate Messner	April Pulley Sayre	Eric Velasquez
Marilyn Nelson	John Scieszka	Sally M. Walker
Vaunda Micheaux Nelson	Joyce Sidman	Karen Wallace
Jerdine Nolen	Seymour Simon	Carole Boston Weatherford
Frances and Ginger Park	Marilyn Singer	Jonah Winter
Linda Sue Park	Peter Sis	Janet S. Wong
Andrea Davis Pinkney	Suzanne Slade	Douglas Wood
Brian Pinkney	Traci Sorell	Jacqueline Woodson
Patricia Polacco	Gary Soto	Sharon Dennis Wyeth
Laurence Pringle	Eileen Spinelli	Laurence Yep
Doreen Rappoport	William Steig	Jane Yolen
Mara Rockliff	James Stevenson	Ed Young
Barb Rosenstock	Melissa Stewart	Harriet Ziefert
Pam Muñoz Ryan	Stephen R. Swinburne	

When we met to share responses, we were surprised at how many writers seemed unfamiliar to students. Mentioning some of the authors' popular titles jogged students' memories. We were determined that students become aware of the authors of their favorite books. We trusted that students in a lively and interactive classroom environment would become familiar with over two dozen authors and their work.

Before asking students to make a final decision about the author they wanted to study, teachers gave students time to browse the classroom and school library. They also took a walk to the local public library. The teachers' task was to help match students with appropriate choices. Some students not only needed help with a choice of author, they also needed help with choosing appropriate books written by that author, especially for writers like Kate DiCamillo, Kadir Nelson, Jacqueline Woodson, Cynthia Rylant, Janet S. Wong, Nicola Davies, Andrea Davis Pinckney, and Walter Dean Myers who write for a wide range of age groups and many in a wide range of genres.

Continuing to Support Students' Efforts
Sharing Your Own Writing

Once students had decided on an author, I brought in a stack of picture books written by Jonathan London and presented my scrapbook devoted to the author as a model. My scrapbook contained four parts. The first was a biographical sketch of the author—see page 263. Younger writers were able to write their biographical sketches based on their author's website, published interviews with the author, and other promotional materials. If older students are asked to do more in-depth study of their author, a list of biographies and autobiographies as well as picture book biographical narratives appear in online Book Lists 3 and 24.

PART 1—BIOGRAPHICAL SKETCH

Meet Jonathan London

Jonathan London has long been one of my favorite writers because I always learn something new from his books. I learn about wildlife, outdoor activities, and how young children solve problems. I also learn about good writing because he writes so well. When reading about his life, I was surprised to learn that we have a few things in common. He was born in Brooklyn. So was I. He was born in 1947. So was I. He has two children. So do I.

After reading some biographical information about Jonathan London, I have even more reasons to appreciate his talents. I never knew that he wrote poetry. In fact, he has published over 200 poems. (I plan to read some of them.) I also never knew that he was a professional dancer when he was younger. I also discovered that he likes to collaborate with his own children. Isn't that wonderful? His son Sean illustrated his picture book *Pup the Sea Otter*, and he illustrated the three novels his dad wrote for elementary school children in the Aaron's Wilderness series (*Desolation Camp, Grizzly Peak*, and *Bella Bella*). I didn't even know he wrote chapter books. Then too, he wrote the picture book *White Water* with his son Aaron, the story of a real-life rafting trip they took together. I also learned that most of his Froggy books are based on experiences he had with his two sons. His ideas took shape when the boys asked him to tell them a story. Isn't it amazing to learn that Jonathan London didn't publish any children's books until he was 45 years old? Above all, I was surprised to learn that Jonathan London has written an autobiography titled, *Tell Me a Story*. I definitely want to read that book.

It is not surprising that Jonathan London has won many awards and received many honors, especially for his Froggy series. Those books are as popular as chicken nuggets, pizza, and hot dogs in a school cafeteria. Aren't we lucky that Jonathan London loves to write? So far, we can choose from 120 of his published books.

Part 2—List of Author's Publications

In this section, I listed all the author's published works. (It was a very long list!)

Part 3—Reader Responses to a Sampling of Author's Publications

Next were my reading responses to several of my favorite Jonathan London picture books. I briefly told what the book was about and what the book made me think about. In other words, after a quick summary, I referred to the popular notion that a good piece of literature is like a window and a mirror. It leads you to look at the world and to look at yourself. Following are three of the five responses I shared with students.

AT THE EDGE OF THE FOREST
BY JONATHAN LONDON (1998B)

In this suspenseful narrative, a young boy and his father must protect their sheep from predator coyotes. Just as the dad is about to shoot two coyotes, four young coyote pups appear eager to eat the food brought by their parents. Through the voice of the young boy, we realize that his dad is relieved that he did not kill the parents of these young animals. Instead, he plans to solve their problem by getting a big shepherd dog to protect his sheep. This poetically written story, tenderly illustrated by Barbara Firth, reminds us to care for animals and to remember that they have loving families, just as human beings do. It also reminds me that there is more than one way to solve a problem and that violent solutions should not be a first thought, but a last resort.

PUDDLES BY JONATHAN LONDON (1997)

This book is a poetic tribute to the childhood joy of jumping in puddles. The main characters explore the outdoors the morning after a big rainstorm. They splash in puddles, jump in mud, watch worms, observe frogs in a pond, march through wet grass, and get soaking wet. This book reminds me of how little time most city kids get to spend exploring nature with no set agenda. It also reminds me that nowadays city children are rarely allowed to leave their homes alone without adult supervision. In today's world, most children are too busy with their electronic devices to even think about simply taking a walk to explore their surroundings. In today's world, most children are told to use hand sanitizer frequently to not pick up germs. They would not be found playing in the mud. This book makes me wonder what we have lost by being so obsessed with being clean (except during a pandemic, of course!).

HURRICANE!
BY JONATHAN LONDON (1998C)

The author did experience a hurricane when he was a "Navy brat" child living in Puerto Rico. London taps into his vivid memories to create this realistic first-person account of a family's response to a hurricane in Puerto Rico. The family packed quickly, protected their home, and took shelter in an old Navy barracks. With rich sensory details, the author makes us feel the storm, his life in a shelter, and the cleanup after the storm. The book is a comforting one, quite different from today's newspaper accounts of brutal hurricanes, earthquakes, wildfires, and tsunamis. Not every family is as fortunate as the one in *Hurricane!* And that is why governments and private citizens need to provide emergency assistance to victims of natural disasters.

Part 4—Learning from Jonathan London's Writing Techniques

In this section, I shared lines I admired from several of London's picture books. I grouped the lines by the writing technique that they demonstrate. I then tried to take lessons from London's craft, writing original sentences using these same writer's tools.

Following are three of the techniques I shared with students. I chose those writer's tools that would most benefit students at the time. I also selected and prepared sentences to illustrate additional writer's tools as

Jonathan London can provide much grist for the minilesson mill. These techniques include the use of precise verbs, alliteration, repetition, sensory details, long-list sentences, onomatopoeia, and specific bits of information. See these additional examples in Appendix 12.

Personification

From *Puddles* (1997): "Birds flap from the trees and we think **the trees are applauding***!*"

From *Dream Weaver* (1998a): "A sudden wind, and **the trees hum**, the branches creak, and yellow spider's web shimmers like wind across a pond."

From *Giving Thanks* (2003a): "He says, 'Thank You' to the **trees that wave their arms** and spin their leaves in the breeze."

From *Like Butter on Pancakes* (1995): "Papa's kettle whistles. Mama's bacon sizzles. **Slippers whisper** across the kitchen floor."

From *At the Edge of the Forest* (1998b): "**The wind bit my face** as I came upon a meadow."

I used personification:

"The **sun welcomed** me as I walked out the door."

"The **playground was calling my name** so I raced there as fast as I could."

"My empty **backpack slept** in the corner of my bedroom all summer long."

Similes

From *Phantom of the Prairie: Year of the Black-Footed Ferret* (1998d): "**Quiet as the moonlight**, Phantom creeps toward a flower, crouches, stares . . . and pounces!"

From *Hurricane!* (1998c): "Schools of tropical **fish flashed by like flocks of birds turning in a wind**, while langostas—tasty Puerto Rican lobsters—hid in dark cracks in the huge reef."

From *Hippos Are Huge!* (2015): "Then they **swing their tails like baseball bats** and swat balls of dung at each other—SPLAT! SPLOP!"

From *Otters Love to Play* (2016): "Within days, the otter pups **gracefully spin and flip and swish like underwater acrobats.**"

From *Dream Weaver* (1998a): "A sudden wind, and the trees hum, the branches creak, and yellow **spider's web shimmers, like wind across a pond.**"

From *White Water* (London and London 2001): "All of a sudden the water was **white, as if thousands of white rabbits were jumping around us.** I clenched my teeth and fists as we whipped and bounced on the waves."

From *Let the Lynx Come In* (1996): "The lynx steps in, shakes first one paw then the other. **Stands still as a stone, quiet as an owl**, in the middle of the room. Firelight glows in its yellow eyes."

From *At the Edge of the Forest* (1998b): "The wind bit my face as I came upon a meadow. And there below was Coyote . . . When he saw me, he froze again, then **took off like a streak of furred lightning . . . Sheep scattered like huge balls of cotton.**"

I used similes:

"The reading room in the public library was **as quiet as fresh-fallen snow.**"

"She loved to read, going through books **like hungry people devouring a big bag of potato chips.**"

"The cover of the antique book was **as fragile as an eggshell.**"

Power of Three

From *Dream Weaver* (1998a): "A sudden wind, and **the trees hum, the branches creak, and yellow spider's web shimmers**, like wind across a pond."

From *Otters Love to Play* (2016): "Within days, the otter pups gracefully **spin and flip and swish** like underwater acrobats."

From *When the Fireflies Come* (2003b): "The screen doors slam. Slam-bang. Slam-bang. Outside, the smell of summer. **The smell of fresh-picked corn, barbecued hot dogs and burgers in the air.** The tinkle of ice in tall iced-tea glasses."

From *Froggy Rides a Bike* (2006): "**His bike zigged and zagged and wobbled.**"

From *Like Butter on Pancakes* (1995): "**Papa's kettle whistles. Mama's bacon sizzles. Slippers whisper across the kitchen floor.**"

From *Into This Night We Are Rising* (1993): "Into this night we are rising, **leaving our shoes, our toys, and our night-lights.**"

I used the power of three:

"Every day when lunch time is over, we find **water bottles, lunch boxes, and sweatshirts** left in the cafeteria."

"The cafeteria is very noisy because **children are chattering, the teachers are shushing, and the aides are trying to make announcements.**"

"**The mac and cheese is gooey. The pizza is spicy. The peanut butter and jelly sandwich is delicious.**"

Gathering Information

Students' first job was to gather a substantial stack of books by their chosen author. This involved tapping resources in the school, class, and neighborhood libraries. In addition to gathering books to read, we suggested students read book jackets, about the author pages, and any available book reviews. Students searched for even more information as they were asked to write a biographical sketch of their chosen author. To gather information on their author's life story, we suggested students ask themselves the following questions:

- Has your author written an autobiography?
- Has a biography been written about your author?
- Does your author have a website?
- Does your author's publisher have promotional material or videos online?
- Has an interview with your author ever been published? Are we able to find and read it?
- Has your author won any awards and/or given published speeches? Are we able to find and read them?

Lifting the Quality of Student Writing

Recently, I heard a cable news host compliment a guest commentator on his choice of words to describe a politician. The speaker said that the congressmember was "flummoxed and vexed." The host noted, "Those are very impressive words on a late Friday afternoon!"

Similarly, my husband shared a comment made by a Watergate prosecutor who said, "No matter how thin the pancake, it has two sides." He thought it was a great metaphor for analyzing news stories.

Then, too, my daughter-in-law Alison sent me the following email:

I loved the Thomas Friedman lines I heard on CNN last night. "The core problem is that we have a president without shame who is backed by a party without spine that is supported by a Network called Fox News without integrity. Fasten your seatbelt."

Whether you agree or disagree with Friedman, you must admit, he knows how to choose powerful words and arrange them effectively. The question for those of us who teach writing is, What makes his sentences so memorable?

The heart of this challenge is to do what the TV host, my husband, and my daughter-in-law did. They paid attention to powerful language. Students are asked to carefully read and reread their author's work. They are asked to save and savor lines they love. Then they are asked to name the writing techniques used and eventually borrow them to share their own ideas.

To support students as they began their search for lines they loved, I taught the following minilessons and small-group instruction:

- I reviewed the tools in our writer's toolbox. (See pages 18–19, 31–34, 63–65, 87–88, 141–142, 166–167, 178–179, and 263–265.) Students needed to become very familiar with these terms.

- I shared pages from Part 4—Learning from Jonathan London's Writing Techniques, handing out pages containing his use of personification, similes, and the power of three. I wanted to help students imagine what they would be doing with their chosen author. I shared my attempts at borrowing London's techniques, then asked students to do likewise.

- I read aloud picture books written by authors that students had chosen for their in-depth studies. The first was April Pulley Sayre's (2008) picture book *Trout Are Made of Trees*. I purposefully selected this text as it is short, making it easy to share in a minilesson. Then, too, I wanted students to know that they could take writing lessons from fine nonfiction writers. We began by discussing the content of the book so that we honor published material as works of literature. We postponed zooming in on the author's craft until we had responded to the meaning of the whole text. I always imagine the author making a surprise visit to our classroom, and I want the author to be pleased with our discussion. I would never want an author to think I only appreciate their work because I can point out similes, powerful sensory details, or strong verbs. I would never want to be accused of trivializing books that a writer worked so hard to create. Instead, after students read, we want them to develop new insights, rethink their opinions, and solve or identify problems.

In our discussion, we answered the question, "Why does the author state that trout are made of trees?" We also explored why the author ends the book by stating that bears and people are also made of trees. Eventually, I distributed a typed text of Sayre's book, numbering the pages for easy referral. Students were given time to mark up their typed texts, naming the tools in this writer's toolbox. We encouraged students to ask themselves, "What can I do that this author does?"

Among the many tools they listed were alliteration, onomatopoeia, the power of three, repetition, long-list sentences, precise verbs, and using a variety of sentence lengths. To that, I added what the late Don Murray described as writing with authority. He writes, "Effective writing is built from specific, accurate pieces of information" (1984). Sayre fills her writing with this kind of information." We also talked about her engaging lead. Why would the author select as a title and begin with the words "Trout are made of trees"? Students understood the power of a surprising, engaging, irresistible beginning. A reader can't resist turning the page. Additionally, we talked about several nonfiction features that children could borrow when they write their own nonfiction. These included the extra information that ends the book, about the trout life cycle, which provides rich background information for readers. At the back of the book, Sayre also includes a bulleted list of ways for readers to take care of streams and a list of resources for further study.

Once the list of writing tools was complete, we sent off the student who was becoming an April Pulley Sayre expert, to read other Sayre books. She needed to figure out if the author relied on these same tools to make her other books come alive. Among her choices were *The Hungry Hummingbird* (2001b), *Crocodile Listens* (2001a), *Eat Like a Bear* (2013a), *Best in Snow* (2016), *Home at Last: A Song of Migration* (1998), *Vulture View* (2007), *Meet the Howlers!* (2010), *Here Come the Humpbacks!* (2013b), and *Stars Beneath Your Bed: The Surprising Story of Dust* (2005).

In a fourth grade classroom, I led small-group instruction for students who needed extra support in lifting lines, naming tools, and borrowing techniques. Each time, I chose a work by an author being studied by one of the students in the group. The following authors and their selected picture books can be viewed as a well to draw on. Of course, books need to be read aloud and their important meanings discussed before attention turns to issues of craft.

Lesa Cline-Ransome's biographical picture book *Helen Keller: The World in Her Heart* (2008) (Students are inspired to add rich sensory details to their own writing.)

Andrew Clements's picture book *Workshop* (1999) (Students can borrow his use of the power of three, his varying use of short and long sentences, and the precision of his verbs.)

Kelly Starling Lyon's picture book *Sing a Song: How "Lift Every Voice and Sing" Inspired Generations* (2019) (Students can lift lines with repetition, the power of three, and precise verbs.)

Monica Brown's bilingual biographical picture book *Tito Puente: Mambo King/ Rey Del Mambo* (2013) (Students can try their hand at onomatopoeia.)

Jane Yolen and Heidi E.Y. Stemple's *I Am the Storm* (2020) (Students can learn to craft similes by studying the pages in this book.)

Nicola Davies's *The Promise* (2013) (Students can aspire to fill the original writing in their author's scrapbooks with similes, personification, repetition, and alliteration.)

Choosing a book written by an author that a struggling student is researching is an effective means of giving the student a leg up in this challenge.

Once students had gathered abundant information about their author's life, they began to draft their biographical sketches. (See also Quirky Questions and Biographic Sketches on page 23.) We reread my sketch on Jonathan London to remind students that they need not sound as bland as a Wikipedia entry. Students were given copies of my "About Jonathan London" piece and were asked to mark up techniques that stood out. A few they noticed included the power of three, variety of sentence lengths, direct address, a conversational tone, and specific bits of accurate information woven throughout.

Student Writing Samples

Auggie, a student in Liz Lynch and Teresa Edward's third-grade class at P.S. 87, studied the works of Aliki and lifted lines from his favorite texts. In part, he wrote:

My author Aliki Brandenburg (1998) used similes and sensory details in *Marianthe's Story* when she wrote:

"In summer, our house was as dusty and dry as a beetle."

I used simile and sensory detail when I wrote,

"Rosetta was as graceful and beautiful as all the flowers combined."

Campbell and Maggie, third graders in Renay's class at P.S. 87, took lessons from Tom Brenner, the author of *And Then Comes Halloween* (2009), *And Then Comes Christmas* (2014), and *And Then Comes Summer* (2017). They highlighted his long sentences that follow the structure of "When . . . , then . . . ," and are filled with rich sensory details clustered in groups of three. Their attempts follow.

Maggie wrote:

When doorbells ring over and over, boxes pile at the door, and parents keep sneaky secrets in their room, then Christmas is coming.

When malls open, we gather school supplies, and more and more nerves build up inside me, then a new school year is coming.

When we buy a costume, get face paint, and leave candy at the door, then Halloween is here.

Campbell wrote:

When you put on your bathing suit, fill up your water bottle, and hop in the cold pool, then it's time for the swim team.

When ornaments hang on the tree, pine needles spread around the house, and elves hide in the cupboard, then it's time for Christmas.

When jellybeans arrive in your bag, eggs hide themselves in the house, and chocolate bunnies hop around, then it's Easter time.

Carving Out Time for Celebration

Once students had completed their scrapbooks, it was time to plan a celebration. This time, family members were not invited. Rather, teachers and students decided that the most appropriate audience members were other grade three students and their teachers. After all, the goal was to teach other readers about new authors. Students wore badges that read, "Ask me about _____," filling in their author's name. They prepared their scrapbooks and kept a stack of picture books at their sides as visitors made their way around their classroom.

BOOKS NOTED

Aliki. 1998. *Marianthe's Story: Painted Words and Spoken Memories.* New York: Greenwillow Books.

Brown, Monica. 2013. *Tito Puente: Mambo King/Rey del Mambo.* New York: HarperCollins.

Brenner, Tom. 2009. *And Then Comes Halloween.* Somerville, Massachusetts: Candlewick Press.

_____. 2014. *And Then Comes Christmas.* Somerville, Massachusetts: Candlewick Press.

_____. 2017. *And Then Comes Summer.* Somerville, Massachusetts: Candlewick Press.

Clements, Andrew. 1999. *Workshop.* New York: Clarion Books.

Cline-Ransome, Lesa. 2008. *Helen Keller: The World in Her Heart.* New York: Collins.

Davies, Nicole. 2013. *The Promise.* Somerville, MA: Candlewick.

London, Jonathan. 1993. *Into This Night We Are Rising.* New York: Viking.

_____. 1995. *Like Butter on Pancakes.* New York: Viking/Penguin Group.

_____. 1996. *Let the Lynx Come In.* Cambridge, MA: Candlewick.

_____. 1997. *Puddles.* New York: Viking/Penguin Group.

_____. 1998a. *Dream Weaver.* Orlando, FL: Silver Whistle/Harcourt Brace.

_____. 1998b. *At the Edge of the Forest.* Cambridge, MA: Candlewick.

_____. 1998c. *Hurricane!* Lothrop, Lee & Shephard Books/William Morrow.

_____. 1998d. *Phantom of the Prairie: Year of the Black-Footed Ferret.* San Francisco: Sierra Club Books for Children.

_____. 2003a. *Giving Thanks.* Somerville, MA: Candlewick.

_____. 2003b. *When the Fireflies Come.* New York: Dutton Children's Books.

_____. 2006. *Froggy Rides a Bike.* New York: Viking/Penguin Young Readers Group.

_____. 2015. *Hippos Are Huge!* Somerville, MA: Candlewick.

_____. 2016. *Otters Love to Play.* Somerville, MA: Candlewick.

London, Jonathan, and Aaron London. 2001. *White Water* New York: Viking/Penguin Group.

Lyons, Kelly Starling. 2019. *Sing a Song: How "Lift Every Voice and Sing" Inspired Generations.* New York: Nancy Paulsen.

Sayre, April Pulley. 1998. *Home at Last: A Song of Migration.* New York: Henry Holt.

_____. 2001a. *Crocodile Listens.* New York: Greenwillow/HarperCollins.

_____. 2001b. *The Hungry Hummingbird.* Brookfield, Connecticut: Millbrook.

_____. 2005. *Stars Beneath Your Bed: The Surprising Story of Dust.* New York: Greenwillow Books/HarperCollins.

_____. 2007. *Vulture View.* New York: Henry Holt.

_____. 2008. *Trout Are Made of Trees.* Watertown, MA: Charlesbridge.

_____. 2010. *Meet the Howlers!* Watertown, MA: Charlesbridge.

———. 2013a. *Eat Like a Bear.* New York: Henry Holt.

———. 2013b. *Here Come the Humpbacks!* Watertown, MA: Charlesbridge.

———. 2016. *Best in Snow.* San Diego, CA: Beach Lane Books.

Yolen, Jane, and Heidi E. Y. Semple. 2020. *I Am the Storm.* New York: Rise.

TEACHER REFERENCE MATERIAL

Murray, Donald. 1984. *Write to Learn.* New York: Holt, Rinehart and Winston.

In addition to a stack of books written by every author chosen, biographies, autobiographies, and memoirs of these same authors will come in handy for upper-grade readers.

A FEW TITLES TO ENRICH YOUR TEACHING

Alznauer, Amy. 2020. *The Strange Birds of Flannery O'Conner: A Life.* Brooklyn, New York: Enchanted Lions.

Barnett, Mac. 2019. *The Important Thing About Margaret Wise Brown.* New York: Balzer + Bray.

Bryant, Jen. 2019. *Feed Your Mind: A Story of August Wilson.* New York: Harry N. Abrams.

Duncan, Alice Faye. 2019. *A Song for Gwendolyn Brooks.* New York: Sterling Publishing.

Engle, Margarita. 2016. *Enchanted: Two Cultures, Two Wings: A Memoir.* Atheneum Books for Young Readers.

Hegedus, Bethany. 2019. *Rise! From Caged Bird to Poet of the People, Maya Angelou.* New York: Lee & Low.

Maslo, Lina. 2020. *Through the Wardrobe: How C. S. Lewis Created Narnia.* New York: Balzer + Bray.

McDonough, Yona Zeldis. 2016. *Little Author in the Big Woods: A Biography of Laura Ingalls Wilder.* New York: Square Fish.

Paterson, Katherine. 2015. *Stories of My Life.* New York: Puffins Books.

Paulsen, Gary. 2021. *Gone to the Woods: Surviving a Lost Childhood.* New York: Farrar, Straus and Giroux.

Pinkney, Andrea Davis. 2016. *A Poem for Peter: The Story of Ezra Jack Keats and the Creation of the Snowy Day.* New York: Viking.

Rogers, Lisa. 2019. *16 Words: William Carlos Williams & "The Red Wheelbarrow."* New York: Schwartz & Wade Books.

Shulevitz, Uri. 2020. *Chance: Escape from the Holocaust: Memories of a Refugee Childhood.* New York: Farrar, Straus and Giroux.

Slade, Suzanne. 2020. *Exquisite: The Poetry and Life of Gwendolyn Brooks.* New York: Harry N. Abrams.

Williams, Alicia D. 2021. *Jump at the Sun: The True Life Tale of Unstoppable Storycatcher Zora Neale Hurston.* New York: Caitlin Dlouhy/Atheneum.

Woodson, Jacqueline. 2014. *Brown Girl Dreaming.* New York: Nancy Paulsen Books.

See online Book List 24 for additional resources.

PART FIVE

MOVING
ABOVE AND BEYOND

. . . .

In this final section of the book, I look at the big picture, moving above and beyond student writing alone. I share the big lessons teachers learn when they take on individual writing challenges, and I advocate for teachers to design their own courses of study, highlighting the joy of experimentation in the classroom.

- Chapter 23: Professional Development Opportunities
- Chapter 24: Concluding Thoughts: On Inventing, Innovating, and Inspiring One Another

CHAPTER 23
Professional Development Opportunities

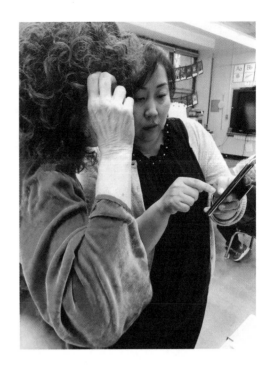

Not all writing challenges are created equal in terms of teacher content knowledge, instructional expertise, or even a teacher's relationships within the school community. For example, some writing courses of study require extensive familiarity with children's literature. Others demand a wide range of computer research skills, a solid working relationship with colleagues, or detailed information about specific genres. Of course, all rely on a teacher having effective classroom management skills, an ability to design assessment-driven minilessons, and conferring know-how.

When choosing writing challenges for their students, I hope that teachers do not avoid those that put new demands on their professional lives. We become better teachers when we are willing to step out of our comfort zones. In fact, probably the best way to get better at some aspect of teaching is to dive right in, living through the "practice makes perfect" cliché. We do get better through practice. Teachers who worry that their own writing is not good enough to qualify them to be mentors for their students must keep on writing, deliberately making efforts to strengthen their work. Similarly, teachers who hesitate to take on a challenge that requires abundant family involvement, extensive differentiation of instruction, or a deep knowledge of the tools in a writer's toolbox need to take risks and do as their students do and "have a go." Of course, it helps to have a critical friend, a caring colleague, or a knowledgeable coach at your side.

Many professional demands cut across the challenges in this book. These demands can also be thought of as professional benefits, as working through these challenges will provide opportunities for teacher growth and development in varied instructional arenas. Teachers might even consider selecting a writing challenge for their students because they understand their own professional needs. In other words, teachers might deliberately choose a challenge because it provides an opportunity to grow in any one of the baker's dozen arenas that follow. (Challenges that especially promote this professional benefit appear at the end of each section.)

Teachers need only ask themselves . . .

- Do I need to become a more effective writer?

Why should our students have all the fun? When we invent writing challenges that are joyful, accessible, and meaningful, we should want to take part in them ourselves. Not only is the work pleasurable, but if we take the work seriously, it should come in quite handy. First, students are usually impressed with our efforts and appreciate having an image in mind of where they might be heading. Then, too, we can deliberately highlight aspects of the work that we know our students would benefit from studying closely. If their writing lacks specificity, we make sure ours doesn't. If their writing lacks a satisfying design, we make sure ours doesn't. If their writing is voiceless, we make sure that ours isn't. When we write in the same format as our students, we also come to understand what kind of reading, writing, and research is needed. When we write alongside our students, we become powerful mentors for them. (All challenges suggest teachers do as their students are asked to do.)

- Do I need to reach out to the community, tapping new resources?

In the "Background on Writing Challenges" section on pages 4–6, I stress the importance of students stepping outside their own classrooms, tapping resources throughout the school and community. When we ask family members and members of the school and neighboring community to sign up for interviews about their home countries, their jobs, or their immigration stories, we help students gather important grist for their writing mill. Teachers, too, benefit from this outreach and in different ways. Relationships between staff members strengthen, and we build camaraderie when we learn more about our colleagues' personal histories, areas of expertise, and even their classroom library collections. Similarly, when we work closely with family members, relationships also change, building more trust, respect, and communication. (See especially Across the Globe, Playing Favorites, Curiosity at the Core.)

- Do I need to carve out more time for my own reading?

It is easy in our busy lives to not carve out enough time for our own reading. Being retired makes it much easier to switch that old saying of "So many books, so little time" to "So many books, almost enough time." My reading life right now is full, and many of the challenges in this book were sparked by my own reading, especially newspaper reading. I can understand when overworked teachers do not have enough time to keep up with the best-seller list, but I would argue that reading the daily newspaper is a nonnegotiable. Students deserve well-informed and knowledgeable teachers, and a major way to keep up with the world is through newspaper reading. A clipped article led to And the Award Goes to . . . and Could It Really Happen? challenges. Newspaper articles fed Across-the-Globe Writing and the current events–based work in Research and Riddles. Curiosity at the Core was sparked by a nonfiction text, and reading literature blogs supported my efforts to provide high-quality models for the writing of reader's notes. Teachers need to remember that just as their own writing informs their teaching, so, too, does their own reading. (See the importance of a teacher's own reading in "Concluding Thoughts: On Inventing, Innovating, and Inspiring One Another.")

- Do I need to enrich my content-area studies?

In the prologue of this book, I talk about getting away from the traditional school report. An effective way to do that is to adapt one of the challenges to a topic in social studies, math, science, or the arts. I can easily imagine extending Across-the-Globe Writing to a class study of birds or other animals. Rather than focus on only one bird in their science study, students can be asked to become experts on the feathers, beaks, or the nests of many birds. (The picture book *Feathers: Not Just for Flying* by Melissa Stewart [2014] can serve as an effective mentor text. See online Book List 2 for a bibliography of other picture books that span several animals.) Then too, extending writing challenges to other content areas easily applies to Research and Riddles, with students creating riddles to reinforce concepts in other disciplines. Students can be asked to prepare clues as a means of studying mathematical terms (*rhombus, trapezoid, parallelogram,* etc.) or scientific concepts (evaporation, condensation, precipitation, etc.). Or focus the creation of reader's notes to a content-related collection of picture books. Students could prepare reader's notes for picture books dealing with the civil rights movement, ecosystems, or nutrition. (See especially Across-the-Globe Writing, Research and Riddles, Imagine If You Were . . . , Definitional Picture Books, Creating Reader's Notes, Just for a Day Writing.)

- Do I need to move away from the same old genres and assignments, trying new and shorter ones?

I have long been a fan of writing assignments at the elementary level that match students' interests and sustain their attention. That belief has usually led me to shorter publications. (My mantra was short children, short genres.) Short genres are not just good for young writers, they are good for teachers. For example, just like in a poetry course, students can often attempt several pieces. The calendar challenge goes so far as to require students to create twelve nonfiction passages. We can then assess students' growth from one piece to the next, rather than evaluating only one attempt. We can ask, "What have students learned from their first attempt that they have brought to their second attempt?" The short formats in this collection also have rather accessible structures. This too, has benefits for students and teachers alike. Both can concentrate on lifting the quality of the writing. We can nudge students to work hard on creating powerful passages as the organization of most of the challenges is rather straightforward. Shorter pieces with a simplicity in their design also makes conferring easier for us and we can focus on lifting the quality of the writing. Shorter pieces are also easier to edit, duplicate, and publish. (See especially Nonfiction Calendars, Quirky Questions and Biographical Sketches, And the Award Goes to . . . , Research and Riddles, Definitional Picture Books, Every Day of the Week.)

- Do I need to become more expert in children's literature, refreshing my classroom collections?

This book is filled with recommended titles, particularly nonfiction ones on a wide range of topics and intended for a wide range of readers. This book is also filled with books that are so well written that teachers can mine them for craft lessons. I hope that these chapters and the accompanying online bibliographic lists inspire teachers to keep up with children's literature—to read related blogs, to browse bookstores and libraries, and of course to read professional texts.

Above all, I have found that one of the most effective ways for teachers to grow in their understanding of writing techniques is to read book reviews of children's literature. When I read a particularly well-written and jam-packed review, I clip the article and slip it into my copy of the book. That way, I grow in my ability to point out elements of craft. Then too, whenever I spot a well-crafted newspaper article, I clip and place it on the document camera, calling students' attention to something that the journalist did that they could do. I want to demonstrate that the writing techniques we talk about in school are the same ones that professional writers depend upon in their published work.

It is rare that teachers have all the books they would love to have, so they must choose wisely. We don't need all the titles we read about; we don't need new copies or hardcover ones. We don't need to own them, as borrowing will do. We just need the ones that will make a difference. And year by year, we need to work toward more abundant and well-organized classroom libraries. Hopefully, these libraries will include books written by a wide range of diverse writers, making sure that all students see themselves in the books on their classroom shelves. Then, too, we need to promote literature discussions at our staff meetings. Wouldn't it be helpful if teachers knew which books were sitting on shelves in the classroom across the hall? Wouldn't it be wise to create a writing resource bookroom, like the reading bookrooms stocked with leveled books for guided reading? Wouldn't it be worthwhile to leave time at all staff meetings for teachers to announce their literature needs? (The demand/benefit of knowing children's literature applies to all challenges in this collection.)

- Do I need to collaborate more with my colleagues?

In my role as an elementary school principal, and even when I served as a school superintendent, it was important to prevent teacher and principal isolation. I did not want anyone to work in silo fashion. There were too many benefits to putting our heads together, learning from one another, solving problems together, and providing emotional support for one another. The same holds true for me today, whether I am volunteering with third-grade teachers or meeting with building administrators. Creating teacher collaboration opportunities is especially important when we are inventing and discovering new ways of teaching writing. It comes as no surprise then that so many of the writing challenges in this book lend themselves to whole staff discussions, especially when teachers are grappling with a teaching idea that extends throughout the grades.

For example, teachers throughout the grades could map out what the teaching of interviewing looks like as we move up through the grades. How does interviewing grow more sophisticated? How would the techniques as well as the topics change? Working together, teachers could research this topic and prepare their own school guide. Teachers might also work together to establish best practice for the research process at each grade level. How do techniques change as we move through the grades? Are there different ways for different-aged students to locate appropriate sources, judge the reliability of sources, take notes, organize information, and weave in quoted material? Another area that would be important to look at across the grades concerns the tools in the writer's toolbox. Which crafting techniques do we teach at grade one, grade two, grade three, and so on? Does the notion of adding details mean the same thing to a first grader and to a fifth grader? Do our content and instructional techniques change with different-aged students?

I am particularly interested in writing challenges that span grade levels. Imagine how powerful the staff conversation would be if teachers at different grade levels were simultaneously working on the same writing challenge.

(Projects that span a wide range of grade levels and would lead to rich staff room talk include Nonfiction Calendars, Curiosity at the Core, Research and Riddles, and Learning from One Writer.)

- Do I need to offer my students more real-world reasons to write well?

When teachers provide authentic ways to publish student work, important benefits appear. Students are more likely to work hard and for longer blocks of time when they know their writing will be put to real use in their classrooms, school, homes, or community. Nonfiction Calendars are hung in homes. Every Day of the Week emergent reading materials are given to early childhood classes. Student-created glossaries and reader's notes are slipped into books in the school and class library. Could It Really Happen? explorations are shared with book buddies. Wearing a Mask persona pieces are performed at schoolwide celebrations. Curiosity at the Core letters are published in the school newsletter. Published student writing has a shelf of honor in classrooms and school libraries. The interviews published in Playing Favorites are displayed on a prominent school bulletin board, stopping traffic because everyone is curious about the choices made by the staff members interviewed. Then too, nothing tops sending student work out into the real world when teachers want administrators, school board members, and family members to appreciate, value, and support the teaching of writing. Teachers who have high standards for student work are wise to save copies of students' best work. They can build a file of powerful writing to share with future students. These pieces of writing can be used as exemplars to inspire and inform other young writers. (This demand/benefit is especially apparent in Creating Glossaries, Creating Reader's Notes, Every Day of the Week, and Nonfiction Calendars.)

- Do I need to learn more about the tools in a writer's toolbox?

The best way for teachers to feel comfortable teaching crafting techniques is for teachers to rely on those tools in their own writing. The more we experiment with similes, precise verbs, and the power of three, for example, the easier it becomes to teach students about their use. The more teachers try their hand at all the genres assigned to students, the easier it is to explain to students that the qualities of good writing cut across all genres. We can find many of the same craft techniques in poetry, informational writing, narratives, journalism, and so on. Teachers come to appreciate that all writing is creative and that one's imagination plays an essential role in informational writing. Informative texts can and should be filled with voice. There is no need for students to sound like Wikipedia entries. Teachers who study and experiment with the tools in a writer's toolbox find it easier to select high-quality texts and to point out effective lines and passages to their students. There is no doubt that teachers who write alongside their students and have grown familiar with a wide range of writing techniques will strengthen their own writing. (This demand/benefit applies to all writing challenges.)

- Do I need to encourage more student talk, becoming a better listener?

Teachers necessarily have different tolerances for noise in their classrooms. Some like hushed tones; others don't even notice if voices occasionally rise to the sound of recess in the playground. No matter your preference, there must be talk in a writing workshop—student talk. We can insist that there be no interruptions, no outbursts, no loud voices, but we must honor student conversation. Students learn a great deal from one another during writing workshops, and teachers learn from listening in as well. There are several different reasons why student talk produces great rewards in the writing workshop. When talk is not just permitted but encouraged, students eagerly throw out ideas to the classmates at their table who might have run out of steam. Not only does the writing improve, but students learn to defend and debate their choices. Students who regularly chat with another about their work in progress also begin to help one another conduct research.

An essential component of student talk is the student's awareness that their questions will be honored. We must continually remind students that asking questions in an essential element in the learning process. And we must make sure that our classrooms are safe places to publicly admit that you have questions. When students sense that their teachers are proud of the questions they ask, not just of the questions they answer, the room sparkles with candid curiosity. Teachers might consider brainstorming all the ways they can privilege curiosity and the asking of questions in their classrooms. (Student talk is particularly relevant in Simple Scaffolds, Could It Really Happen?, Would You Rather . . . ?, and the Award Goes to . . .).

- Do I need to promote multigenre teaching and learning?

Bread bakers know that you need a bit of sourdough starter to prepare your next loaf of sourdough bread. So too, teachers can design writing assignments by lifting bits and pieces of current challenges to create surprising new courses of study, in different genres. For example, the upper-grade research done by students in Creating Reader's Notes led to persuasive writing on related topics. Jane Yolen's (2015) *The Stranded Whale* led to persuasive writing about the human pollution of ocean water and the need to save whales. Eve Bunting's (1991) *Fly Away Home* led to persuasive writing about improving the care of homeless people. Edwidge Danticat's (2015) *Mama's Nightingale: A Story of Immigration and Separation* led to persuasive writing about improving the treatment of immigrants. Similarly, the research done for Wearing a Mask prose pieces could lead to poetry on these same topics. The short vignettes created for Definitional Picture Books could be seedbeds for personal narrative writing. Students could also write definitional poetry. (See online Book List 16.) Then too, students could prepare biographical picture books about the people they chose for Quirky Questions and Biographical Sketches. Reader's notes can also be added to genres other than picture books. These include newspaper articles and poetry. (See booklist of poetry anthologies that have informative back matter in bibliography in online Book List 16.) Similarly, there are many content-rich poetry anthologies in the fields of history and science that would be enriched by the addition of reader's notes. One need only turn to J. Patrick Lewis and ask students to read *Heroes and She-Roes: Poems of Amazing and Everyday Heroes* (2005), *A Burst of Firsts: Doers, Shakers, and Record Breakers* (2001), or *A World of Wonders: Geographic Travels in Verse and Rhyme* (2002). (See other animal poetry anthologies that would be enriched by student created back matter or reader's notes in online Book List 20.)

Then too, the addition of refrains can be used to enrich personal narratives. (See suggestion on pages 282–283 in Chapter 24: Concluding Thoughts.) Poetry, of course, becomes the handiest of resources when teachers are highlighting writing techniques. In other words, teachers can enrich the teaching of prose writing with carefully selected poetry. (Challenges that are particularly generative include Creating Reader's Notes, Wearing a Mask, and Writing with Refrains.)

- Do I need to differentiate instruction more frequently?

One way teachers differentiate instruction is to offer research and publishing options. In Doing What the Animals Do, for example, students can contribute ideas about one animal or many animals, provide simple explanations or more complex ones, read easy-to-read texts or more complicated ones, but all students can become full participants in the challenge. Similarly, Doing What They Do Best is accessible to a wide range of first graders, those that are just beginning to learn to read and those that are more accomplished readers at their young age. Some students were asked to write additional pages and write more than one book. So, too, in Playing Favorites and Imagine If You Were . . . , a wide range of student work can be celebrated.

Teachers can create opportunities for student collaboration to guarantee that all students would contribute finished work. This was done in such challenges as Across-the-Globe Writing, Nonfiction Calendars, and Simple Scaffolds.

Another way for teachers to differentiate instruction is to provide templates for students as they work their way through a challenge. Sometimes, the task is so new that all students are offered scaffolded materials. Other times, teachers don't require all students to use think sheets, planning/rehearsal worksheets, or preprepared outlines, but have them handy for those students who need organizational support.

When challenges are assigned to different-aged students, the tasks can be made more sophisticated as we move up in the grades. For example, with Author Scrapbooks in upper grades, older students could be asked to think through connections between their author's life and the author's body of work or they can be asked to search for recurring themes in their author's body of work. (Differentiation in the form of templates is highlighted in Definitional Picture Books, Creating Glossaries, Just for a Day, and Nonfiction Calendars.)

- Do I need to strengthen my students' reading/writing connections?

One major way that teachers can address students' reading as they teach writing is to involve students in the search for needed resources and examples of powerful writing. Why should we have all the fun of discovery? Students can be asked to browse bookshelves looking for content-rich, upper-grade picture books, those with author's notes and those without, those with glossaries and those that would benefit from having glossaries, and those that inspire us to ask, "Could it really happen?" Students can also be asked to search their local public libraries as well as the school library for picture books with satisfying refrains, those needed for author scrapbooks, and those that fit into the just for a day category. Then too, students can be encouraged to note places in their reading where they spot the tools in the writer's toolbox that they have been studying. This includes mining for writing treasures in preschool texts as described in Doing What They Do Best. Students can be asked to share their discoveries with their classmates.

Teachers can ensure that students' reading matches and supports their writing by encouraging students to read related material during their independent reading time. This would include students reading the newspaper when they are asked to create riddles based on current happenings, reading nonfiction resources when they are conducting research, and reading biographies and autobiographies when they are writing biographical sketches. In addition, throughout all the challenges, students should have access to the kind of mentor texts that inspire and inform their own writing.

The benefits for teachers when they connect reading to student writing are clear. Teachers become familiar with new children's literature. They share the responsibilities of teaching with their students. They learn new ways to solidify the reading-writing connection in their classrooms. In addition, when they hold reading conferences with students, they can assess students' abilities to read critically, handle unfamiliar vocabulary, and evaluate the credibility of sources. (The reading/writing connection is so crucial it applies to all challenges.)

BOOKS NOTED

Bunting, Eve. 1991. *Fly Away Home*. New York: Clarion Books/Houghton Mifflin.

Danticat, Edwidge. 2015. *Mama's Nightingale: A Story of Immigration and Separation*. New York: Dial Books for Young Readers/Penguin Group.

Lewis, J. Patrick. 2001. *A Burst of Firsts: Doers, Shakers, and Record Breakers*. New York: Dial Books for Young Readers.

———. 2002. *A World of Wonders: Geographic Travels in Verse and Rhyme*. New York: Dial Books for Young Readers.

———. 2005. *Heroes and She-Roes: Poems of Amazing and Everyday Heroes*. New York: Dial Books for Young Readers.

Stewart, Melissa. 2014. *Feathers: Not Just for Flying*. Watertown, MA: Charlesbridge.

Yolen, Jane. 2015. *The Stranded Whale*. Somerville, MA: Candlewick Press.

A FEW TITLES TO ENRICH YOUR OWN READING LIFE

One of the questions I suggest teachers ask themselves is, "Do I need to carve out more time for my own reading?" I appreciate how difficult it is for busy educators to pick up a book for their own pleasure, but if you can place reading on your to-do list, I have shared below a few titles that have enriched my life. (Thanks to the members of my book club for having made the following recommendations.)

Akhtar, Avad. 2020. *Homeland Elegies*. New York: Little, Brown.

Allende, Isabel. 2020. *A Long Petal of the Sea*. New York: Ballantine Books.

Bennett, Brit. 2020. *The Vanishing Half*. New York: Riverhead Books.

Gyasi, Yaa. 2020. *Transcendent Kingdom*. New York: Alfred A. Knopf.

Llosa, Mario Vargas. 2006. *The Bad Girl*. New York: Farrar, Straus and Giroux.

McBride, James. 2020. *Deacon King Kong*. New York: Riverhead Books.

Millet, Lydia. 2020. *A Children's Bible*. New York: W. W. Norton & Company.

Obama, Barack. 2020. *A Promised Land*. New York: Crown.

O'Farrell, Maggie. 2020. *Hamnet*. New York: Alfred A. Knopf.

Rooney, Sally. 2018. *Normal People*. London, UK: Hogarth.

Wagamese, Richard. 2012. *Indian Horse*. Minneapolis, MN: Milkweed.

Wilkerson, Isabel. 2020. *Caste*. New York: Random House.

CHAPTER 24
Concluding Thoughts: On Inventing, Innovating, and Inspiring One Another

Elementary schools are filled with living, breathing "Curiosity Rovers," hundreds of them. They carry heavy backpacks, collect stickers, and play catch at recess. If we do things right, these students reveal the same spirit of curiosity as the actual exploration robot investigating Mars, the red planet. Young children are eager to figure out how and why things work. They are eager to observe, wonder, take notes, photograph, explore, talk to experts, and share what they are learning with others.

In the classrooms I know best, children are encouraged to be inquisitive, outspoken, and independent. They are given time to pursue their passions, collaborate with others, and read, research, and write throughout the day and throughout the curriculum. In the schoolhouses I know best, the same holds true for teachers. They too are encouraged to be inquisitive, outspoken, and independent. They make time to read, research, and write.

I am always thrilled when I see teachers inventing original writing challenges for their students. Each year, whether she is teaching first grade or fourth, Diane Berman's students turn their personal narratives into breathtaking pop-up books. Liz Winnegar's third graders deliver their own version of TED Talks. Corinne Daniels reads Amy Krouse Rosenthal's picture book *I Wish You More* (2015) to her first graders and asks them to create their own pages. They write such gems as "I wish you more marshmallows than Lucky Charms." "I wish you more strikes than gutter balls." "I wish you more play-dough than slime." Her colleague, Laurel Warager, asks her first graders to write their own version of Richard Torrey's (2009) picture book *Almost*, listing such lovely thoughts as, "I can almost jump rope," and "I am almost ready for second grade."

Not only am *I* thrilled to see all these wonderful writing ideas play out in the classroom, but so are the students, and so are their teachers. In this day of overscheduled, overmandated lives, both in and out of the classroom, teachers find it energizing to design and try something brand new, and the joy that that emanates from that experimentation shows on the faces of the students and on the drafts that fill their writing folders.

Every August, in preparation for the new school year ahead, I rummage through a folder I fill all year long. It is labeled "Why not?" and brims with articles, scraps of writing in response to my reading, and titles of newly discovered picture books. (Most of my ideas are rooted in my reading life.) Each represents a potential teaching idea. Before I slip something into the file, I think to myself, "I wonder if my students can do that? I wonder if my students would enjoy doing that? I wonder what my students would learn from doing that?" In other words, I become my own Curiosity Rover. A few possibilities follow.

WRITING CHALLENGES FOR THE NEW SCHOOL YEAR

- Create a companion volume to Paul Janeczko's (2019) anthology, *The Proper Way to Meet a Hedgehog and Other How-To Poems.* His beautiful collection contains thirty-three how-to poems. Could teachers and students match that and find thirty-three additional how-to poems? I already have two dozen of them tucked into my ongoing collection. Can students find or write more? Would teachers and students be as interested in this challenge as I am? (See poetry titles in online Book List 25.)

- Share Pagan Kennedy's "Who Made That?" column from the *New York Times Sunday Magazine.* (Read her book *Inventology: How We Dream Up Things That Change the World* [2016].) Invite students to select their own invention to research and gather reference material. (My grandson Ben and I are currently researching and writing a picture book on the invention of snow globes. It's chock full of interesting science concepts.) (See bibliography in online Book List 25.)

- Conduct an in-depth study of libraries, inviting students to write in response to what they're learning through wide-open genre choices. Students could craft poetry, book reviews, interviews, school newspaper articles, persuasive letters, how-to writing, list writing, true-or-false statements, fun facts pages, cartoons, diary entries, skits, Spanish/English phrase books, or any of the formats described in this collection. Teachers would create a study stack of picture books about libraries and librarians. (See bibliography of library-related titles in online Book List 25.)

- Explain to students *The New York Times's* new feature titled "Overlooked," in which the newspaper admits neglecting many remarkable people in their obituary column. Most of their obituaries were for white men, and the newspaper is determined to make up for this privileging. In fact, the newspaper has posted, "Have an idea for an Overlooked obit? We want your suggestions." Have fifth graders write persuasive, information-filled letters to the *New York Times* in support of people who were overlooked.

- Add freshness to the personal narrative that is so frequently assigned at the beginning of the school year by suggesting alternative structures. A few possibilities follow:

WRITING CHALLENGES FOR THE NEW SCHOOL YEAR

- o   Introduce refrains to enrich students' personal narratives.
- o   Choose "time and again" events that take place on a regular basis, rather than a one-time event.
- o   Write about an event from multiple points of view.
- o   Weave chunks of informational text into narratives.
- o   Write about how an event or experience changed over time.
- o   Write about an experience that is anchored to a treasured object.

(See bibliography in online Book List 25 for titles that contain alternative personal narrative structures.)

Some women's fitting rooms in large department stores have hooks labeled "definitely," "possibly," and "never." They're there to hold the hangers, helping customers sort the clothes they have been trying on. Perhaps surprisingly, these categories also apply to new writing challenges. Some will be marked "definitely," worthy of sharing with colleagues and offering again to next year's students. A few might be labeled "possibly," knowing that they might improve with some thoughtful tweaking. Yet others will be tossed into the "never" or "never-again" pile.

Through my half a century of teaching adventures, I have learned that there's much value in all these attempts, even the ones that turn out to be a bit bland and boring. I opened this book with a quote from Tom Newkirk (2009). He writes, "When we stop experimenting, we stop living as teachers." Even the "never-again" experiments involve thinking, planning, gathering resources, talking to colleagues, revising, and assessing. Duds also demonstrate that sometimes our students can be less critical, more patient, and more ambitious risk-takers than we are.

Throughout this book, I have shared the process that led me to design each new writing challenge. Including that information was deliberate and purposeful. I hope to inspire teachers to create their own worthwhile writing challenges, to trust in their ability to invent those new challenges.

Following is a supportive guide for teachers who take pride in thinking out of the box, experimenting alongside their students, and sharing new ideas with colleagues.

ELEMENTS TO THINK ABOUT AS YOU DESIGN YOUR OWN WRITING CHALLENGES

1. Are there elements of choice for students?

2. Does the challenge tap into your students' interests?

3. Do you have abundant high-quality literature to serve as models?

4. Are you willing to take on the challenge yourself?

5. Can the challenge be adapted by your colleagues who work with different-age students?

6. Are the demands of the challenge appropriate for your students?

7. Do you have high expectations for the finished work?

8. Does the completed challenge require a reasonable amount of time?

9. Will students have opportunities to produce more than one piece of writing?

10. Will helpful templates be available if needed?

11. Are publishing demands reasonable?

12. Will the workshop be filled with a feeling of joy?

Finally, as this book draws to a close, I want to tuck in a pitch for occasionally having no units, no studies, no challenges at all. Wouldn't it be eye-opening to simply follow our students' leads, to have blocks of time with no set agenda, simply inviting students to do the kind of writing that they themselves choose? This, of course, would require that administrators trust their teachers and that teachers trust their students.

Thomas Friedman wrote an op-ed article for the *New York Times* in July 2018. It was titled "Where American Politics Can Still Work: From the Bottom Up," and in it he quotes business philosopher Dov Seidman's belief that "trust is the only legal performance-enhancing drug." As teachers, whether we have a specific writing task in mind or we are inviting students to invent their own, trust plays a significant role. We place our trust in our content knowledge, our instructional abilities, the literature on our shelves, the camaraderie of our colleagues, and most of all in the students in our care. Then and only then, do we keep the groundbreaking spirit alive and provide ways for student performance as well as our own to move above and beyond and become our personal best.

BOOKS NOTED

Janeczko, Paul (selected by). 2019. *The Proper Way to Meet a Hedgehog and Other How-To Poems.* Somerville, MA: Candlewick.

Rosenthal, Amy Krouse. 2015. *I Wish You More.* San Francisco: Chronicle Books.

Torrey, Richard. 2009. *Almost.* New York: HarperCollins.

TEACHER REFERENCE MATERIALS

Friedman, Thomas. 2018. "Where American Politics Can Still Work: From the Bottom Up." *The New York Times.* July 3.

Kennedy, Pagan. 2016. *Inventology: How We Dream Up Things That Change the World.* New York: Mariner Books.

_____. "Who Made That?" columns in *The New York Times Sunday Magazine.* Overlooked Column in *The New York Times.*

Newkirk, Tom. 2009. *Holding On to Good Ideas in a Time of Bad Ones.* Portsmouth, NH: Heinemann.

Padnani, Amisha, and Jessica Bennett. 2018. "Overlooked No More." *The New York Times,* Special Section. March 11.

Padnani, Amy. 2018. "How an Obits Project on Overlooked Women Was Born." *The New York Times.* March 18.

A FEW TITLES TO ENRICH YOUR TEACHING
PICTURE BOOK NARRATIVES ANCHORED IN A TREASURED OBJECT

Avingaa, Susan and Maren Vsetula. 2016. *Fishing with Grandma.* Toronto: Inhabit Media.

Berry, James. 2020. *A Story About Afiya.* Oxford, UK: Lantana.

Coelho, Joseph. 2019. *Grandpa's Stories: A Book of Remembering.* New York: Harry N. Abrams.

Garbutt, Loretta. 2020. *A Stopwatch from Grampa.* Toronto: Kids Can Press.

Laínez, René Colato. 2019. *My Shoes and I: Crossing Three Borders.* Houston, TX: Pinata Press/Arte Público.

Meddour, Wendy. 2019. *Lubna and Pebble.* New York: Dial.

Muhammad, Ibtihaj. 2019. *The Proudest Blue.* New York: Little, Brown.

Musleh, Helal. 2019. *Secret Recipe Box.* Toronto: Ruqaya's Bookshelf.

Oliveros, Jessie. 2018. *The Remember Balloons.* New York: Simon & Schuster.

Raven, Margot Theis. 2007. *Circle Unbroken: The Story of a Basket and Its People.* New York: Farrar, Straus and Giroux.

Smith, Cynthia Leitich. 2020. *Jingle Dancer.* New York: Heartdrum/ HarperCollins.

Stubbs, Rachel. 2020. *My Red Hat.* Somerville, MA: Candlewick.

Tafolla, Carmen. 2008. *What Can You Do with a Rebozo?* Berkeley, CA: Tricycle Press.

Thompkins-Bigelow, Jamilah. 2020. *Mommy's Khimar.* Holland, Ohio: Dreamscape Media.

Wolfer, Dianne. 2017. *Nana's Button Tin.* Somerville, MA: Candlewick.

Yousafzai, Malala. 2017. *Malala's Magic Pencil.* New York: Little, Brown.

See additional resources to support the other suggested writing challenges in online Book List 25.

ACKNOWLEDGMENTS

During the last dozen years, I have been volunteering in the two main school districts in which my grand-children live and study. Both are in New York State, but one is urban and the other suburban. I am incredibly grateful to the elementary teachers at P.S. 87 on the Upper West Side of Manhattan and those at Dows Lane and Main Street School in Irvington, New York. I also spent limited time at the Yorkville Community School (P.S. 151) on the Upper East Side of Manhattan. These schools are fertile ground for having what Eleanor Duckworth (2006) called "wonderful ideas." They meet all the Duckworth criteria described in the prologue to this book—selecting problems that are of interest to the students, providing students with the tools to solve those problems, and creating settings in which it is safe to take risks.

These schools are staffed by teachers who are interested in pushing the envelope in the teaching of writing. These teachers aren't interested in leading students through the same old same old. They had questions on their minds. Their main concerns included how to tap into their students' passion for nonfiction reading and writing, how to lift the quality of student writing without taking away ownership, and how to make time for abundant writing workshops with ever-growing curriculum demands. Fortunately, these are also schools in which teachers and administrators clearly meet Duckworth's requirement of having content knowledge to solve their problems. Most of the teachers have been teaching reading and writing for many years, and they value professional development as a lifeline. Staff members at each school have the intellectual tools necessary to address their real concerns. Most of all, it is safe to take risks at these schools. Trying new things is encouraged and appreciated. The school administrators at these schools (Dr. Andrea Kantor at Dows Lane Elementary School; Joyce Chapnick at Main Street School; Monica Berry, Kazue Takenaga, and Barbara Kissane at P.S. 87; and Samantha Kaplan and Stacie Lorraine at P.S. 151) think it is more than okay to address curriculum demands in fresh and surprising ways. They appreciate how important it is for teachers to have professional company, working hard to provide teachers with time to meet, talk, plan, reflect, and otherwise bounce ideas off one another. In other words, they understand and appreciate what teachers need to stay alive professionally. I hope this book serves as a tribute to those administrators as well as all the teachers who have invited me into their classrooms, sharing their students and their areas of expertise with me and enthusiastically puzzling over new ideas alongside one another.

An extra special thank-you to the teachers at P.S. 87 who formed a writing group: Cara Beseda, Diane Berman, Eungi Gioia, Laura Liebman, and Robyn Ulzeimer. It is always reassuring to have thoughtful listeners who are willing to provide honest feedback and advice. I so look forward to seeing their work published one day. My gratitude also extends to the early childhood teachers who gather daily for lunch in Emily Davis's kindergarten classroom. Their collegiality, conversations, and tasty treats always enriched my visits. Special thanks also go to the third-grade team that has worked with me for more than a decade and always with great enthusiasm, camaraderie, and expertise. They are always ready to take on a new challenge with gusto. These accomplished educators include Laura Liebman, Andrea Garvey, Liz Lynch, Teresa Edwards, Adriana Pena, Lisa Uhr, Carmela Brutto, Mayra Romero, Laura O'Donnell, and Michelle Owens. I am thrilled that Renay Sadis, my old friend and brilliant colleague from the Manhattan New School, joined this third-grade team a few years ago. Working in her classroom felt like a family reunion, filled with warm memories, humor, and shared interests and know-how.

My grandsons were privileged to be taught at P.S. 87 by members of my writing group including Cara, Diane, Laura, and Eungi. Hats off as well to their other teachers including Eva McKeon, Hillary Kusinitz, Sarah Mankes, Laurie Posner, Theresa Furman, and Nancy Goldstein.

This book is filled with student writing; therefore, collecting parent release forms became a major task. Since I do not have an opportunity to meet family members, I depended on many others to secure these signed forms. A special shout-out of gratitude goes to Kazue Takenaga, the assistant principal of P.S. 87 as well as my grandson Ben's sublime fifth-grade teacher. Compared with all the ways that Kazue has supported me throughout my years of volunteering at P.S. 87, sending out release forms is really a minor one. Kazue has always seen more in my teaching than I do myself. Her own expertise in the teaching of literacy, her delight in thinking out of the box, her unwavering support for the teachers in her care, as well as her logistical know-how in scheduling and covering teachers to allow for professional development meetings, are but a few of the ways that Kazue makes P.S. 87 a haven for teaching and learning. (Teachers would probably add that the big jugs filled with chocolates, mints, and Smarties on her office shelf are yet another plus.) Then too, Monica Berry, the principal of P.S. 87, has welcomed me with open arms for more than a decade, making sure to wrap staff members in the kind of support that allows them to teach with kindness, confidence, and camaraderie.

At P.S. 87, I am grateful to all the hard-working teachers that invited me into their classrooms and to Marsha Student, retired literacy expert, who for many years made my weekly visits joyous, organized, and productive. A special note of gratitude goes out to Diane Berman and Melissa Martinez, in whose stellar classrooms I probably learned more than I taught. Their classrooms are filled with joy, kindness, and always ambitious teaching and learning.

Recently, I owe another debt of gratitude to those teachers that encouraged family members to sign student release forms. This gracious group includes Diane Berman, Delia Marshall, Melissa Martinez, Robyn Ulzheimer, Adriana Pena, Paola Jeon, and Renay Sadis. Not only did these educators contact families for me, but Melissa, Renay, and Diane allowed me to spend time with their students filling in any gaps in my manuscript. As I was unable to locate several families that had left the school and/or the country, these teachers carved out time for me to invite additional students to take on these challenges. Just as I was about to collect the last few pieces of student work, the coronavirus pandemic shuttered the doors of our school buildings. I stayed out of Manhattan during this long period of social distancing, but Kazue, Renay, Diane, and Paola came to my rescue, scanning student work after they had spent hours planning the long-distance learning that awaited their students. The pandemic also made it impossible to take new photos for this book, but again Renay and Diane came to my rescue. They spent hours looking through their collections, sending appropriate photos my way. Teachers go above and beyond not only for their students and their families but also for their colleagues. Family members who attempted home schooling during those treacherous times quickly came to appreciate just how challenging, demanding, and, yes, exhausting the life of a teacher can become.

In the Irvington schools, Dr. Raina Kor, Assistant Superintendent for Curriculum and Human Resources, made it possible for me to volunteer and then spearheaded my collection of signed permission slips. Raina recently retired, but her footprints are in the snow that surrounds this Westchester school district. Joyce Chapnick, principal of Main Street, also helped in my search for families, especially of those students who had already graduated. But Joyce needs to be credited with so much more. Main Street is a close-knit fourth- and fifth-grade schoolhouse filled to the brim with a spirit of professionalism. Joyce always welcomes me with open arms, and her expert and experienced teachers are always ready to explore new ways of thinking about literacy, with priority given to meeting the needs of a wide range of students and with bookcases stacked with the finest of children's literature. And they carry out their top-notch instruction with an interest and respect for global citizenry, multiculturalism, and gender equality. Joyce lives up to the image of principal as instructional leader as she is always front and center at staff meetings, asking important questions, taking notes, and clarifying points for colleagues. Joyce's enthusiasm for literacy teaching and learning is contagious.

At Dows Lane Elementary School, a kindergarten through grade three schoolhouse, I had the privilege of working with all teachers throughout the grades for more than a decade. Staff members were always so welcoming and supportive that it would be hard to acknowledge them all in this limited space. I do want to especially thank Corinne Daniels, Eileen Scanlon, Ann Marie Reardon, Krystal Mitchell, Alyssa Fisher, and Kari Carlson for their support in securing student writing and parent permissions to publish. Then, too, thank you to Izabela Swiecka for contributing a photograph, for caring for three of my grandchildren in her kindergarten classroom, and for her kind correspondence in my time away from the school. My grand-children would be disappointed if I didn't show my appreciation for their other teachers at Dows Lane. So, *mil gracias* to Amy Blackwell, Mary Lynn Child, Kate Falcon, Alyssa Fisher, Julie Giacomantonio, Krys-tal Mitchell, Crystal Raymond, and Krista Shortino. Danielle Lee and Georgia Tasigiannis-James, now at Dows Lane, also taught my granddaughter in their fourth-grade classroom at Main Street School. Other Main Street teachers that not only invited me into their classrooms but took great care of my grandchildren include Mary Ellen Fortini, Michelle Griffin, Loren Holand, Lindsay Donlon, and Ali Meiseles.

I spent a short time at P.S. 151, the Yorkville Community School, because my grandnephew Cooper attends this warm and welcoming school. I am grateful to Samantha Kaplan, principal, and the members of her first-grade team for opening their classroom doors. I look forward to the day when Cooper's sister Millie will also call this gem of a school her home away from home.

As have so many writers before me, I stretch my arms wide to offer a heartfelt hug to Stenhouse acqui-sitions and development editor Maureen Barbieri. I can't thank my dear friend Maureen enough for her encouragement, enthusiasm, and expertise. There's no more heartwarming and inspirational professional experience than to have Maureen shadow you as you move from one classroom to another. She is an astute observer and knows just the right thing to say to keep the teaching and learning alive and enlightened. She is also an accomplished photographer, having captured several of the images that appear in this book. It is also a privilege to walk the streets of Manhattan with Maureen, as she is such a sublime visitor and, in my estimation, has become an honorary New Yorker. A sincere thank-you also goes to the Stenhouse production staff. It was a joy and a relief to have the support of Shannon St. Peter, Editorial and Production Associate. She knew just who to contact to make the permission process as painless as possible. She also kept efficient tabs on all the required student permissions. Shannon is truly a permissions maven. Then too, I extend my gratitude to Lynne Costa, Senior Production Editor, who graciously turned my unwieldy files and photos into a presentable page-turner, doing so with passion, professionalism, and lots of patience.

And finally, I raise a glass of wine to toast the members of my family. Stories of my grandchildren—Andie, Ben, Will, Zach, and Sasha—are woven throughout this book. I have always counted on them for inspiration, humor, and occasional writing samples, but now as they have all entered their teenage years, I have begun to count on them for so much more. So, thanks, dear ones, for all those music performances, the baseball and basketball games, the incredible works of art, the graduation ceremonies, the help with cooking, the carrying of heavy loads, and the computer expertise—especially the computer expertise! Of course, I toast my daughter J.J., my son Michael, and my daughter-in-law Alison, who are always there to cheer me on, to calm me down over political, pandemic, and professional issues, to get me out of my office, and then to inspire me to return. I hope their lives continue to be as fulfilling as mine, with beloved family and friends always by their side. And, finally, to my husband of fifty-three—make that fifty-four now—years (yes, I was a child bride), thank you for making my teaching and reading/writing life possible. I couldn't have accomplished much without you by my side. And, yes, I will now have more time to pick the wild raspberries in our garden, wander antique shops, and watch an occasional movie without falling asleep.

BOOKS NOTED

Duckworth, Eleanor. 2006. *"The Having of Wonderful Ideas" and Other Essays on Teaching and Learning.* New York: Teachers College Press.

APPENDICES

The pages that follow contain additional minilessons, writing samples, and a few planning sheets. In addition to these appendices, readers will find extensive bibliographies in the online book lists.

APPENDIX 1

Additional Across-the-Globe Student Writing Samples

Third graders in Laura Liebman and Andrea Garvey's class wrote the following pieces.

"AMAZING WAYS TO GO FISHING" BY MAX AND MILES

If you like waking up at 2:00 am, you would be a good fisherman. Also, if you are patient, you would be a good fisherman. It takes practice to catch lots of fish. Some kinds of fishing don't even require using a hook. There are many different ways to go fishing around the world.

Dive!
Grab a wet suit, a mask, and a sharp tool to dive under water. Haenyeo, or sea women of Korea, catch mollusks, abalone, octopus, conch, and other creatures for a living. They practice holding their breath and they swim a lot. They dive underwater and hold their breath about a minute searching for sea creatures and bringing them back up.

Cold
In Canada, when it is cold, go to a frozen lake. Fishermen use a machine that goes through ice and makes a hole. When the ice is really strong sometimes, they drive cars on the ice. They set fishing rods with bait in the holes. They sometimes sleep overnight and see if they catch anything in the morning. Popular fish you could catch are pike, bass, walleye, and whitefish.

Music
In Russia, some fishermen catch fish by making them sleepy or less watchful. They do this by playing music. In the wintertime, they dig big holes in the ice about three feet deep and fix a net called a trammel inside. Then a wooden stake from a fir tree is placed into the hole and beaten for one hour and thirty minutes in a strong rhythm. The rhythm of the "music" attracts nearby fish.

Stickrod
In Brazil, go somewhere that has sticks. Find a long stick, a piece of string and a wire. Put the string on the stick. Twist the wire into a hook shape and put the wire on the string. Put a piece of bait on the wire and go to a nearby lake. Go Fishing!

(continues)

"AMAZING WAYS TO GO FISHING" BY MAX AND MILES
(continued)

Pearls

After school in Egypt, some kids tie a string to a jar and throw it into the water. They count how many fish they catch. If they find one they like, they will open it with something sharp and see if there is a pearl inside. They will give it to his or her mom or dad for a present and they feel proud.

Dizzy and Dazed

Some South American Indian tribes use poisonous plants to fish. When the plant juice mixes together with oxygen in the water, the fish are not able to breathe correctly. The fish become dizzy and dazed, and they can be caught by hand.

Do you want to go fishing a different way? If you do, gather up the materials. You can fish with a stick, with music, with wood, with a jar, with poison, or you can dive right in.

"TRANSPORTATION AROUND THE WORLD"
BY JACOB AND PHILIPP

How do you get around town? Do you use a car, a train, a bus? In other countries, transportation is very different from transportation here. You will be amazed by how people get around all over the world.

Chicken Bus
What bus do chickens ride? A chicken bus is in Guatemala and Panama. It gets its nickname by chickens boarding and traveling to market. They get on board for no money. Lucky chickens!

Skidoo and Skiing
What if it is a snowy day in chilly Canada? Grab a skidoo. A skidoo has 2 skis in front and a caterpillar tread at the back. If you don't take a skidoo to work, some people in Canada ice-skate along the river to get to work.

Hovercraft
Do you want a boat that can drive in all directions and go on land for short periods of time? A hovercraft can go backward, forward, and sideways! It can even stay in place and turn 360 degrees. People use hovercrafts as ferries in the United Kingdom. Sometimes they're used to transport cargo.

Trolleys
Trolleys are a popular type of transport in Russia, The trolleys are economic, spacious, and clean. They can hold 20 people inside and run on tracks that are built into the road.

Shinkansen
The shikansen, or bullet train, is a superfast train in Japan. It can reach speeds of up to 2000 miles per hour! The Hokkaido Express is a rather weird one. Its rear train cars have one level while its front cars are double decker. If you don't know what Hokkaido is, it's a Japanese island off the coast of Honshu.

Three-Wheeled Motorcycle
Have you seen a three-wheeled motorcycle? It goes faster than a regular motorcycle. It is super tiny. Try to keep up! It is like a motorcycle with a side car. It is rare to see one here but not in Hungary where they are all over the streets.

These are only some of the ways people get around in other countries, Did you even know these vehicles existed? Transportation is amazing. Imagine if we had transportation like this in the United States. It would be FUN!

APPENDIX 2

Learning from Eileen Spinelli—Student Writing Samples

· ·

Third graders in Laura Liebman and Andrea Garvey's class at P.S. 87 were read aloud a stack of carefully selected picture books by Eileen Spinelli, and they were invited to take lessons from this popular author.

Lea was inspired by Spinelli's *Someday* and created her own picture book, *Dream About Someday* that appears in Figure A2.1.

Figure A2.1

In the mean time...
I'm dancing in front of my
stuffed animals.
I get to pick out the groovy music.
I will dance in the air
leaping and jumping high.
Then I start to act.
The broom is the prince
I am the princess.
Then we get our happy ending.

Someday
I am going to be a creative artist.
I will have a big art studio with
very detailed sculptures and
big, bright, bold paintings.
I will sign my name perfectly at the bottom.
I will wear a black smock.
(Just in case if paint drips on me)
Someday...

In the mean time...
I am painting, drawing, and playing
with play-dough on my small, white, shiny
desk.
I do not wear a smock.
SPLAT!
Oh no! Paint just spilled on my shirt!

Someday
I will go to the perfect tea party.
I will wear a big white dress.
With little designs on it.
And long white shiny gloves.
I will have my hair in a bun.
I will sip my tea.
When I want more tea
I will pick up the tea-pot
and ask the others if they want
more.
Just to be polite.
Someday...

Figure A2.1, *continued*

In the mean time...
I am playing tea party with my
unicorn plushy and Mr Bob the
penguin.
I'm just wearing my plain old clothes.
Mr Bob is not polite he does not ask anyone
if they want more tea.
He just takes the tea pot and pours it in his cup.

Someday
I will swim the deepest darkest sea.
I will wear a thick blue scuba suit
There will be rain bow colored fish,
big whales, and camouflaged creatures
big and small.
I will dive into the water.
   Someday...

In the meantime...
I am swimming in the pool.
I wear a colorful bathing suit.
Under water is not exciting at all.
1. The pool does not have any fish.
2. It is nothing like the deepest part
of the sea.

Now it is dawn.
A brand new day is waiting for me.
I look out my shiny window.
The sun is awakening.
It is pink, yellow, and green.
It's the prettiest thing I ever saw.
House lights turn on as it gets brighten
I guess there are things in life
you can enjoy.
Like right now.

Figure A2.1, continued

Audrey was inspired by Spinelli's *When You Are Happy* and created her own picture book, *When You are Awesome*, that appears in Figure A.2.

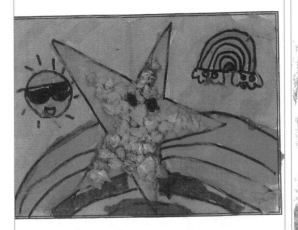

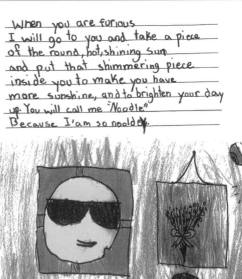

When you are furious
I will go to you and take a piece
of the round, hot, shining sun
and put that shimmering piece
inside you to make you have
more sunshine, and to brighten your day
up. You will call me "Noodle"
Because I'am so nooldey.

Figure A2.2

(continues)

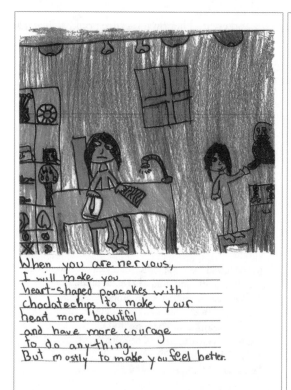

When you are nervous,
I will make you
heart-shaped pancakes with
choclatechips to make your
heart more beautiful
and have more courage
to do anything.
But mostly to make you feel better.

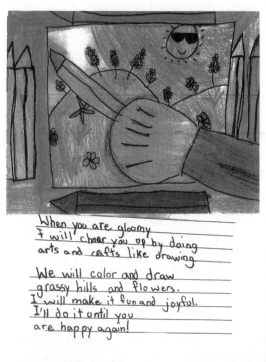

When you are gloomy,
I will cheer you up by doing
arts and crafts like drawing

We will color and draw
grassy hills and flowers.
I will make it fun and joyful.
I'll do it until you
are happy again!

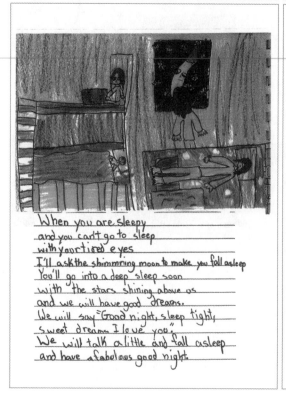

When you are sleepy
and you can't go to sleep
with your tired eyes
I'll ask the shimmring moon to make you fall asleep
You'll go into a deep sleep soon
with the stars shining above us
and we will have good dreams.
We will say "Good night, sleep tight,
sweet dreams I love you".
We will talk a little and fall asleep
and have a fabulous good night.

When you're cold I
will wrap you in
warm, loving hugs
and get your fuzzy blanket
to wrap you in. We will
hug until you are
hot and warm.

Figure A2.2, *continued*

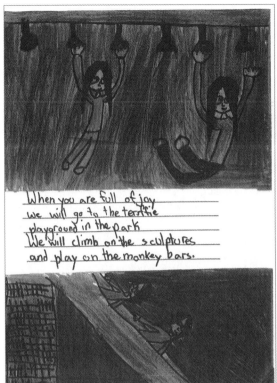

When you are full of joy
we will go to the terrific
playground in the park
We will climb on the sculptures
and play on the monkey bars.

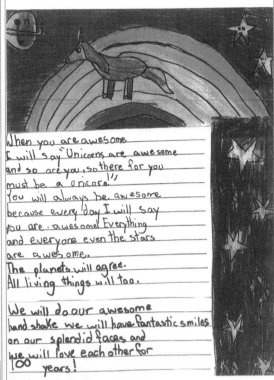

When you are awesome
I will say "Unicorns are awesome
and so are you, so there for you
must be a Unicorn."
You will always be awesome
because every day I will say
you are awesome! Everything
and everyone even the stars
are awesome.
The planets will agree.
All living things will too.

We will do our awesome
hand shake we will have fantastic smiles
on our splendid faces and
we will love each other for
100 years!

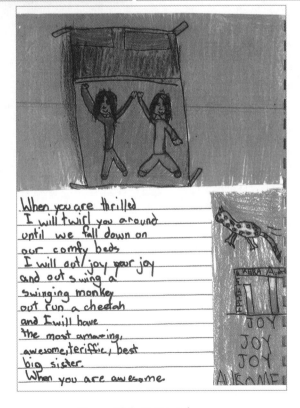

When you are thrilled
I will twirl you around
until we fall down on
our comfy beds
I will out/joy your joy
and out swing a
swinging monkey
out run a cheetah
and I will have
the most amazing,
awesome, teriffic, best
big sister.
When you are awesome

Figure A2.2, *continued*

My New York City Counting Book

COUNTING ON NEW YORK CITY

It is very difficult to write a counting book about New York City, especially if you are only counting from 1 to 10. New York City is just too big a city, with too many people, too many passions, and too many sights to see. Our skyscrapers have too many stories; our streets are filled with too many coffee shops, too many pharmacies, and too many banks. No matter your interest, you can probably count to way over 10. How many museums do we have? How many Chinese restaurants? How many subway lines? I have had to rack my brain to find things that are limited to 10 and under. The following pages, made with love and labor, demonstrate how I have learned to count on my hometown, New York City.

One is for the Statue of Liberty. This gift from France has become a symbol of freedom and democracy. This huge copper statue that sits in the New York Harbor on Liberty Island was designed by the French sculptor Bartholdi. The statue is based on the Roman Goddess of Liberty, and she holds a torch in her right hand and a tablet in her left. On the tablet is the date, July 4th, 1776 written in Roman numerals. This is the date of the signing of our Declaration of Independence from England. There are 354 steps to Lady Liberty's Crown, the top of the statue. Would you be willing to climb?

Two is for the tunnels that connect Manhattan to other boroughs. So many people who live in the outer boroughs travel to and from Manhattan, the most famous of all the five boroughs. They come for work, for shopping, for entertainment, for restaurants, for Broadway shows, and so much more. The Brooklyn Battery connects Manhattan to Brooklyn, and the Queens Midtown tunnel connects Manhattan to Queens. (There is also the Lincoln Tunnel, but that one brings folks to and from New Jersey to Manhattan.)

Three is for the airports people use to travel to and from New York City. Imagine how many visitors from around the world come to New York City every day of the year. Add to that, the number of residents of New York City that travel by airplane for work or pleasure. The airports all these people use are La Guardia and JFK in Queens and Newark Airport in New Jersey. It's no wonder these three airports are always busy!

Four is for the kinds of public mass transportation used by New Yorkers. Sure, some people ride bikes, some drive private cars, and others walk to their destinations in New York City. But many, many folks choose to use mass transportation. They travel by subway (in all boroughs except Staten Island which has its own train system, not a subway) and bus (in all five boroughs including express buses that travel directly into Manhattan), ferryboat (to all boroughs from piers on the East River), as well as the famous Staten Island ferry. You can also travel by tram (to and from Roosevelt Island).

Five is for the boroughs that make up New York City. The boroughs are Brooklyn, Queens, Staten Island, Manhattan, and the Bronx. Have you ever wondered why we always say "the" before we mention the Bronx, but we don't use the article before the other boroughs? It's because the borough was named after **the Bronx** family. Some visitors to New York City never leave Manhattan. That's too bad as there is plenty to see and do in the outer boroughs.

Six is for famous theaters. These include the Belasco theater, the Helen Hayes theater, the Al Hirschfield theater, the Lyceum theater, the Palace theater, and the Music Box theater. There are many more theaters in New York City, both on Broadway and off and throughout the outer boroughs. It's no surprise that you can often spot a famous actor or musical performer in the streets of New York. Would you ask them for an autograph?

Seven is for the daily newspapers. Every morning you can browse *The New York Times*, *The Daily News*, *The New York Post*, *The Wall Street Journal*, *The New York Amsterdam News*, *El Diario La Prensa*, or *Newsday*. Many people no longer buy a hard copy of their favorite newspaper. Instead, they read the news on their computer screens. No matter where you do your reading, it's important that all citizens stay informed.

Eight is for the islands of New York City. Two islands top this list because they are two of our boroughs, Manhattan and Staten Island. Two are famous tourist attractions, Coney Island (formerly an island and now considered a peninsula that is a great summer stop for the beach, the boardwalk, and restaurants) and Ellis Island to appreciate the Statue of Liberty and the immigrant experience. The Statue of Liberty is actually located on Liberty Island, another small island in the New York Harbor. To those four, we can add Governor's Island (a former Coast Guard base now used for recreation and cultural events), Roosevelt Island and City Island (both residential neighborhoods), and Randall's Island (co-joined with Wards Island and used for sports and other cultural events).

Nine is for the tasty foods sold by street vendors in New York City. Have you ever shopped at a cart that sold hot dogs, falafel, roasted nuts, big salty pretzels, coffee with muffins, donuts, or bagels, a full range of fruit, roasted chestnuts, and shwarma? Or have you celebrated the arrival of summer with a stop at a Mr. Softee truck? All these foods are considered NYC classics. Which one is your favorite?

Ten is for our professional sports teams. You can root, scream, and cheer for the Yankees (baseball), the Mets (baseball), the Jets (football), the Giants (football), the Rangers (hockey), the Islanders (hockey), the Knicks (basketball), the Brooklyn Nets (basketball), the New York MetroStars (soccer), New York Liberty (women's basketball), and the New York Dazzles (women's football). No matter the season, New York can satisfy sports fans.

It's clear that there are endless things to count in New York City. I know that I could write a sequel that includes the big parks, the bridges, the parades, the famous skyscrapers, the stadiums, the universities, and the zoos. Then too, perhaps one day, I will write yet another sequel, not counting to ten, but counting by tens—all the way up to 100.

(Some of you may be wondering about the New York Sharks, another women's football team. Sorry to say, I had to omit them because then I would have eleven! But thankfully, with this sidebar, they are now included.)

APPENDIX 4

Persona/Mask Poem, "Worth the Trip"

• • • • • • • • • • • • • • • • • •

Here is my persona/mask poem "Worth the Trip," in which I imagine myself as Staten Island, probably the least known borough of New York City.

Worth the Trip

I am Staten Island
and
I am worth the trip,
an island of surprises
in the borough
given short shrift.

Reach me
by ferry boat
in twenty minutes time.
View her majesty,
Miss Liberty,
and it needn't cost a dime.

Reach me by bridge,
choose any one of four:
glide across the Goethals
enter through Bayonne
cross the Outerbridge
or pay the Verrazano toll.

I am Staten Island
and
I am worth the trip,
an island of surprises
in the borough
given short shrift.

First stop—Sailors Snug Harbor,
a unique cultural sight.
Onto to Alice Austen's house,
a photographer's delight.
Next, watch the Staten Island Yankees,
the very best farm team.
Then onto my Chinese Scholar's Garden
to pause, reflect and dream.

Next, the Staten Island Zoo where
Groundhog Chuck is found.
Then learn of free black oyster fishermen
at historic Sandy Ground.
Onto the Jacques Marchais Museum,
filled with Tibetan art,
And you can't miss colonial Richmondtown
to understand our country's start.
Walk the trails of a natural preserve,
at Clay Pit Pond and then
stop at the old stone

Conference House
and learn how the Revolutionary War
really came to an end.

Now it's time to take a break
and
enjoy my island treats
Ralphs's creamy ices,
Sedutto's ice cream
and
really great pizza on all my island streets.

I am Staten Island
and
I am worth the trip
an island of surprises
in the borough
no longer given short shrift!

304

APPENDIX 5

Additional Writing with Refrains Samples

· ·

Below is the entire text of my writing, "If You're Not from New York City"

IF YOU'RE NOT FROM NEW YORK CITY . . .

If you're not from New York City, you don't know dog walkers.

You can't know dog walkers.

Dog walkers are a big business in New York City, especially in Manhattan. It's not unusual to see a person holding on to a dozen leashes making his or her way to the nearest park. The dog walkers belong to licensed and insured businesses, which walk dogs for busy New Yorkers. Most Manhattanites live in apartments and can't just open backdoors to their back yards and let their dogs take care of their own business. Visitors sometimes think some New Yorkers are lazy because they don't walk their own dogs. Truth be told, these New Yorkers usually work long hours and want to be sure that their dogs are walked at regular intervals.

If you're not from New York City, you don't know yellow taxi cabs.

You can't know yellow taxi cabs.

In New York City souvenir shops, you can buy t-shirts adorned with yellow taxi cabs, snow globes with yellow cabs inside, and even pencil cases, coffee mugs, and keychains boasting the iconic yellow cabs of New York City. If you have enough money to take a cab, you must stand on the sidewalk with your arm up waving down an empty cab. The light-up sign atop the roof of the cab lets you know if the cab is available. If the light highlights the cab's medallion number, it is available. If it lights up the medallion number and two side lights, the cab driver is off duty. If no lights are on, the driver already has a passenger. If you are lucky enough to hail a cab, be prepared to meet an interesting driver from countries far and wide. If you can't find a cab or want a new experience, try calling for an Uber or Lyft ride. As you make your way through New York City traffic, don't be surprised to see green cabs, which pick up passengers north of 96th Street.

(continues)

(continued)

If you're not from New York City, you don't know Nathan's hot dogs.

You can't know Nathan's hot dogs.

Nathan's Famous opened in 1916 selling 5-cent hot dogs at their stand in Coney Island, Brooklyn. It was started by Nathan Handwerker, a Polish immigrant, and his wife, Ida. She came up with the recipe for the now very famous hot dog, using her grandmother's secret spices. Today there are Nathan's Famous Hot Dog shops all over our country and the world. Every July, the Coney Island store hosts a Nathan's Hot Dog Eating Contest. A man named Joey Chestnut has been the champion hot-dog eater several times and in 2018 boasted eating 74 hot dogs and buns in 10 minutes. That's almost hard to imagine, isn't it?

If you're not from New York City, you don't know our skyscrapers.

You can't know our skyscrapers.

If you were asked to name the top-ten skyscrapers in New York City, could you do it? You probably could only name that many if you were a native New Yorker or a transplant that has become a devoted citizen of the city. The following buildings would probably be on your list: the Empire State Building, the Chrysler Building, the Flatiron Building, One World Trade Center (the Freedom Tower), the Woolworth Building, 30 Rock–Rockefeller Plaza, Metropolitan Life Insurance Building (Met Life Tower), the United Nations Secretariat, Citicorp Center, and the Bank of America Tower. There are many more skyscrapers in the Big Apple and more it seems are being built every day.

If you're not from New York City, you don't know the subway shuttle train.

You can't know the subway shuttle train.

This subway shuttle is also known as the Grand Central/Times Square shuttle. It only makes those two stops, shuttling people all day, every day from the East Side of Manhattan to the West Side. It has been in operation for over 100 years, having opened in 1918. The ride only takes 90 seconds and the subway car is always covered in interesting and artistic advertisements. If you want to walk around the Broadway theater district on the West Side, and then take a Metro North train to the suburbs at Grand Central Station on the East Side, you will be very grateful for the Shuttle train.

If you're not from New York City, you don't know water towers.

You can't know water towers.

The New York City skyline is dotted with water tanks that sit atop high-rise buildings. These tanks are more than 100 years old and were originated by only 3 families. Today there are more than 17,000 water tanks scattered around the 5 boroughs of New York City. Clean water is pumped into the tanks, and each hold between 5000 and 10,000 gallons of water. The upper layer of water, delivered to apartments through gravity, are for everyday use, and the lower levels are reserved for emergencies. Without water tanks, tenants living on upper floors would not be able to have good water pressure. No doubt, those residents would complain when flushing their toilets, taking a shower, or doing their laundry.

If you're not from New York City, you don't know the Broadway Theater District.

You can't know the Broadway Theater District.

The Broadway Theater District runs from West 40th St. to West 54th St, from 6th Avenue on the East to 8th Ave. on the West. The district is filled with theaters for musicals and dramatic plays, restaurant, hotels, recording studios, and movie theaters. The flashing billboards light up the Great White Way, which is a nickname for the blocks of Broadway that run through the theater district. The district is always crowded with theatergoers, tourists, and folks dressed in superhero and cartoon character costumes. If you care to look, you might even spot the guitar-playing naked cowboy. Take a walk in the theater district, you're bound to spot a celebrity or two.

If you're not from New York City, you don't know Fashion Week.

You can't know Fashion Week.

Twice a year, in September and in February, beautiful international models walk down runways, showing off the latest designer fashions to newspaper reporters, buyers, and the general public. Fashion weeks are also held in London, Milan, and Paris. In New York, the event is held in different locations throughout the city. Unfortunately, the price tags on most of these fancy fashions make it impossible for the average New Yorker to purchase any of these garments. But real New Yorkers know where to shop to get fashion bargains, discounts, and items on sale.

If you're not from New York City, you don't know MetroCards.

You can't know MetroCards.

Way back in 1904, when the New York City subways first opened, it only cost a nickel to ride the subway (as well as a bus). The fare increased to a dime in 1948. Then in 1953 the fare went up to 15 cents and since there wasn't one coin to match that cost, the subway token was invented. This small round brass disc with the letter Y carved in the middle lasted until 1993 when a plastic card was born. This MetroCard is still with us today but is expected to be replaced by a mobile scanning device in the year 2020. MetroCards can be bought at a discount for senior citizens and students. Otherwise, the one-way fare costs 2.75 cents, a far cry from the original 5 cents. MetroCards can be bought for different number of rides at different amounts. You can spend 5.50, 10.48, 20.95, 26.19, 39.29, or 61.90. You can also buy a 7-day unlimited MetroCard for 32 dollars or a 30-day unlimited MetroCard for 121 dollars. By the time you read this, the price will probably have increased once again.

(continues)

(continued)

If you're not from New York City, you don't know Fairway.

You can't know Fairway.

Fairway is one of the most popular supermarket chains in New York City. The flagship store, located in the area of Broadway and 74th Street, opened in 1933. Today, there are 15 stores. The shop is always crowded, filled with local shoppers, workers, and even firefighters. The store is huge, carrying traditional as well as exotic foods, ordinary brands as well as gourmet, raw ingredients as well as cooked foods, and specialty items such as gluten-free and kosher. You can always come in and dip a small slice of bread in an array of olive oils, for free. Fairway has always donated food to the less fortunate and has always treated firefighters especially well. Good for them, don't you agree?

If you're not from New York City, you probably don't believe that the Big Apple is the center of the Universe!!

APPENDIX 6

"Would You Rather . . . ?" Questions

· ·

The following collections of "Would you rather . . . ?" questions increase in difficulty and sophistication as you move from A to B to C. They were created and gathered by teachers over time and shared with students for inspiration as well as for possible study. They were sorted into categories suggested by students. The A lists were generally used by grade two students.

WOULD YOU RATHER . . . ?

Animal Questions

List A

Have a guinea pig or a gerbil for a pet?

Take care of a frog or a toad?

Train a dolphin or a porpoise?

Have a hedgehog or a woodchuck in your yard?

Meet up with an alligator or a crocodile?

See an emu or an ostrich?

Ride a camel or a dromedary?

Swim with sea lions or seals?

Feed an alpaca or a llama?

Race a cheetah or a jaguar?

Study amphibians or reptiles?

Watch a walrus or a manatee?

Study a Tyrannosaurus rex or a Stegosaurus?

Become an expert on wolves or coyotes?

Draw a squid or an octopus?

Take photographs of a gorilla or a chimpanzee?

See a blue jay or a bluebird?

Find a wolf or a fox in your garden?

Spot an elk or a moose on your travels?

See a porcupine or an echidna?

Be attacked by a squirrel or a chipmunk?

Get bit by a mosquito or a gnat?

Study the habits of a rhinoceros or a hippopotamus?

Snorkel near a narwhal or a walrus?

Be chased by a great white shark or a bull shark?

Be frightened by a black widow spider or a tarantula?

Own a pit bull or a bulldog?

Get stung by a hornet or a yellow jacket?

Listen to a cricket or a grasshopper?

Ride a mule or a donkey?

Own a poodle or a Labradoodle?

Discover a newt or a gecko?

Feed a ferret or a weasel?

Find a rattlesnake or a python in your yard?

See a mouse or a rat on the subway tracks?

Photograph a panda or a polar bear?

Visit Australia to see a koala or a bilby?

Sketch a chinstrap penguin or a macaroni penguin?

Have a chinchilla or a mouse for a pet?

Come face-to-face with a wombat or a dingo?

Find a possum or an opossum in your backyard?

Catch a salamander or a lizard?

Have a pet rat or a pet mouse?

Teach classmates about penguins or auks?

. . . .

List B

Care for a turtle or a tortoise? (or a terrapin?)

Care for canines or felines?

Spot a reindeer or a caribou on your travels?

See an aardvark or an anteater?

Build a hutch for a rabbit or a hare?

Describe a cheetah or a leopard?

Get stung by a wasp or a bee?

Sketch a moth or a butterfly?

See an African elephant or an Asian elephant?

Photograph puffins or penguins?

Have as a pet a Lhasa apso or a shih tzu?

Have as a pet a whippet or an Italian greyhound?

Have as a pet a Boston terrier or a French bulldog?

Have as a pet a Siberian husky or an Alaskan malamute?

Have as a pet a German shepherd or a Belgian Malinois?

Hear a fisher-cat or a weasel?

Spot a hairy woodpecker or a downy woodpecker in your garden?

Notice a soaring Cooper's hawk or a sharp-shinned hawk in the sky?

Catch a lobster or a crab?

See a bison or an ox?

. . . .

List C

Study bovine or lupine animals?

Study porcine or piscine animals?

Study equine or vulpine animals?

Spend time with a mammoth or a mastodon?

See a liger or a tigon?

. . . .

Food Questions

List A

Grow onions or scallions?

Eat a papaya or a mango?

Eat a banana or a plantain?

Eat a yam or a sweet potato?

Eat tortellini or ravioli?

Eat jam or jelly? (or preserves?)

. . . .

List B

Eat crickets or snails?

Order Manhattan clam chowder or New England clam chowder?

Taste loganberries or gooseberries?

Eat Korean barbecue or American barbecue?

Eat a persimmon or a pomegranate?

Eat escarole or kale?

Order a taco or a burrito?

. . . .

List C

Eat poutine or haggis?

Eat kimchi or adobo?

Eat truffles or mushrooms?

Be a vegan or a vegetarian?

Eat Creole or Cajun food?

Eat Gorgonzola or Roquefort cheese?

Eat grits or polenta?

Order shawarma or a gyro?

Catch sea scallops or bay scallops?

Order pastrami or corned beef?

Use confectioner's sugar or powdered sugar?

Prepare stuffing or dressing for your Thanksgiving turkey?

Taste cardamom or turmeric spice?

Order hummus or baba ganoush?

Eat a dosa or a crepe?

Drink a latte or a cappuccino?

Eat jasmine rice or sticky rice? (or arborio, or basmati?)

Add baking powder or baking soda to your cookie recipe?

Spice up your food with coriander or cilantro?

Geography Questions

List A

Visit Sweden or Switzerland?

Live in a forest or a rain forest?

Vacation in Barbados or in the Bahamas?

Have a pen pal from Puerto Rico or Costa Rica?

Grow up in the Bronx or Brooklyn?

Tour Austria or Australia?

List B

Live in the Arctic or the Antarctic?

Visit Greenland or Iceland?

Visit Washington, D.C., or Washington State?

Live on a prairie or a savanna?

Swim in the Red Sea or the Dead Sea?

Tour Prague or The Hague?

Explore the South Pole or the North Pole?

Move to Granada or Grenada?

Take a vacation in Slovakia or Slovenia?

Fly to Auckland or Oakland?

Have a pen pal in Uruguay or Paraguay?

Visit St. Petersburg, Russia, or St. Petersburg, Florida?

List C

Explain the equator or the prime meridian?

Climb Mt. Everest or Mt. Kilimanjaro?

Measure longitude or latitude?

Hike through a dale or a valley?

Live on a peninsula or an isthmus?

Visit Petra, Jordan, or the pyramids in Egypt?

Tour Great Britain or the United Kingdom?

Tour Taiwan or Hong Kong?

Visit the Galapagos or Machu Picchu?

Spend the summer in San Jose, California, or San Jose, Costa Rica?

Read about Dakar or Dhaka?

Follow the news in Chechnya or the Czech Republic?

Visit El Salvador or San Salvador?

. . . .

Sports/Games/Hobby Questions

List A

Take skiing or snowboarding lessons?

Be a wrestler or a boxer?

Scuba dive or snorkel?

Play rugby or lacrosse?

Play pool or billiards?

Practice judo or karate?

Do a somersault or a cartwheel?

Be an expert at crossword puzzles or jigsaw puzzles?

Be a champion at checkers or chess?

Learn to knit or crochet?

. . . .

List B

Be a speed skater or a figure skater?

Play for the Red Sox or White Sox?

Ride a surfboard or paddleboard?

Be great at doing tangrams or anagrams?

Be great at magic squares or sudoku?

Participate in a marathon or a triathlon?

Watch ice dancing or figure skating?

Play lacrosse or rugby?

Practice judo or karate?

List C

Be accomplished at parkouring or jogging?

Participate in the snowboard big air or the long jump in the Olympics?

Kayak on the Nile River or the Amazon River?

Skydive or bungee jump?

Become an expert at spelunking or zorbing?

Watch Olympians in the luge or skeleton sled racing event?

. . . .

Science Questions

List A

Use a telescope or binoculars?

Use a microscope or a magnifying glass?

Be an astronaut or a cosmonaut?

View a tornado or a dust devil?

Grow daffodils or dandelions?

View lightning or hear thunder?

Mix concrete or cement?

Buy a statue made of copper or bronze?

See a gibbous moon or a crescent moon?

Get caught in a hurricane or a typhoon?

Be an omnivore or a carnivore? (or herbivore?)

Explore the moon or Mars?

Control the Mars Rover Curiosity or the SpaceX Falcon Heavy?

Get caught in a cyclone or a tornado?

Grow annuals or perennials in your garden?

See clouds that are cirrus or cumulus? (or stratus?)

Walk near stalactites or stalagmites?

See a meteor or a comet in the sky? (or asteroid?)

Have deciduous trees or evergreens in your backyard?

Read a barometer or an anemometer?

Explore a cavern or a canyon?

Visit a bog or a swamp?

Visit a marsh or a fen?

See a geyser or a fumarole erupt?

. . . .

List B

Live through an earthquake or a tsunami?

See the constellation Taurus the Bull or Pegasus the Winged Horse?

Get stuck in a snow squall or a blizzard?

Walk outside during a snow shower or snow flurry?

Need an antibiotic or an antiseptic?

Watch a lunar eclipse or a super moon?

Explain rotation or revolution of our planet Earth?

Write an essay on global warming or climate change?

Have a sundial or a weathervane in your garden?

Live in a marsh or a swamp?

View a waxing gibbous moon or a waning crescent moon?

. . . .

History/Social Studies Questions

List A

Be a duke or a count in England?

Be a duchess or a princess in England?

Be a migrant or an immigrant?

. . . .

List B

Become a senator or a congressman/congresswoman?

Be asked to gerrymander or filibuster?

Read a relief map or a contour map?

Read a physical map or a political map?

Read a topographic map or a climatic map?

Learn about the First Amendment or the Second Amendment?

Become an expert on the Civil War or the Revolutionary War?

Be a Redcoat or a Patriot during the American Revolution?

Study confederate soldiers or union soldiers during the Civil War?

Be a conservative or a liberal?

Teach people about democracy or communism?

Work for the executive or legislative branch of our government?

Construction/Structures/Architecture Questions

List A

Use a wrench or pliers?

Dig with a shovel or a spade?

Ride a Ferris wheel or a carousel?

Drive a bulldozer or a backhoe?

Ride on an elevator or an escalator?

Visit the Tower of London or the Eiffel Tower?

Visit the Empire State Building or the Chrysler Building?

. . . .

List B

Design like Frank Lloyd Wright or Antoni Gaudí?

Build a suspension bridge or an arch bridge?

Live in a yurt or an igloo?

. . . .

List C

Build a pyramid or a ziggurat?

Decorate your home with a gargoyle or a grotesque?

. . . .

Music/Art/Dance/Literature Questions

List A

Dance the tango or the cha-cha?

Play the recorder or the flute?

Take banjo lessons or ukulele lessons?

Star in a performance of Rumpelstiltskin or Rapunzel?

Paint like Picasso or van Gogh?

. . . .

List B

Play the harp or the harpsichord?

Listen to hip-hop or rap music?

Play a viola or a violin?

Write a biography or an autobiography?

Write a limerick or a haiku?

Create something out of papier-mâché or clay?

Play the bass or the bass guitar?

Create similes or metaphors?

Use onomatopoeia or alliteration?

. . . .

List C

Be a lyricist or a composer?

Paint in an impressionist style or a pointillist style?

Know how to create a needlepoint or a tapestry?

Paint a mural or a fresco?

Write an ode or a sonnet?

Memorize a soliloquy or a monologue?

Dance the samba or the salsa?

Attend a show on Broadway or off-Broadway?

Tour the Museum of Modern Art or the Metropolitan Museum of Art? (or the Cooper Hewitt Smithsonian Design Museum, or The Frick Collection, or the Whitney Museum of American Art?)

Read a story containing sarcasm or irony?

Make a list of homonyms or homophones?

Know spoonerisms or idioms?

Collect palindromes or puns?

Figure out a rebus or a crossword puzzle?

Use assonance or consonance in your poetry?

Study myths or legends?

. . . .

Jobs/Occupation Questions

List A

Work as a pediatrician or a podiatrist?

Work as a botanist or a biologist?

Be an astronomer or an astrologer?

Become a knight or a gladiator?

Work on a gondola or a rickshaw?

Become an optometrist or an ophthalmologist?

. . . .

List B

Become a psychiatrist or a psychologist?

Be an ornithologist or an entomologist?

Be a philatelist or a numismatist?

Be a cooper or a chandler if you lived in Colonial times?

Be a milliner or a cobbler if you lived in Colonial times?

Be a haberdasher or a confectioner if you lived in Colonial times?

Be a lawyer that prosecutes or a lawyer that defends?

Work as a ranger in a national park or a national preserve?

Become an anthropologist or an archeologist?

Be a curator or an archivist at a museum? (or a docent?)

Become an environmentalist or a conservationist?

· ·

Transportation Questions

Sit near the caboose or the locomotive of a train?

Drive a train or a trolley?

Travel on a sailboat or a speedboat?

Drive on a parkway or a highway?

Ride in a funicular or on a monorail?

Ride in a kayak or a canoe?

· ·

Clothing/ Fashion Questions

Wear velvet or flannel?

Wear a fez or a fedora?

Wear moccasins or penny loafers?

Wear a cummerbund or an ascot?

Wear a hijab or a burka?

Wear topaz or emerald jewelry?

Wear a poncho or a serape?

· ·

Famous People Questions

Have worked for Teddy Roosevelt or Franklin Delano Roosevelt?

Prepare a time line of the life of Alexander Graham Bell or Alexander Hamilton?

Play the role of Thomas Jefferson or Thomas Edison in a play?

Write poetry like Nikki Giovanni or Nikki Grimes?

Celebrate the work of George Washington Carver or Booker T. Washington?

See a movie about Bill Gates or Bill Clinton?

Be more like Shirley Temple or Shirley Chisolm?

Become an expert on John Lennon or Vladimir Lenin?

Read a long biography of the life of Pablo Picasso or Pablo Casals?

Share character traits with Elizabeth Barrett Browning or Elizabeth Cady Stanton?

Learn from Phil Rizzuto or Phil Mickelson?

Persuade people that Magic Johnson or Lyndon Johnson would be a good role model?

Root for Serena Williams or Venus Williams?

Spend a day with Marie Antoinette or Marie Curie?

Write a long biography of Julius Caesar or Cesar Chavez?

Have worked for Milton Bradley or Milton Hershey?

Play the role of Harriet Beecher Stowe or Harriet Tubman?

Have interviewed Richard Nixon or Richard Branson?

Take lessons from the life of Gandhi or Galileo?

Have a career like Isaac Newton or Isaac Asimov?

Make a speech about Benjamin Franklin or Benjamin Banneker?

Become an expert on Sacagawea or Pocahontas?

Have character traits like Albert Einstein or Albert Schweitzer?

Have spent a day with Daniel Boone or Davey Crockett?

Play Helen of Troy or Helen Keller in a school play?

Spend an afternoon with Rachel Carson or Rachel Robinson?

Have a career like Spock in *Star Trek* or Dr. Benjamin Spock?

Spend time with Nathan Hale or Nathan Lane?

Read about Achilles or Zeus?

Mathematics Questions

Study decimals or fractions?

Study algebra or trigonometry?

Measure speed or velocity?

Use a protractor or a compass in math class?

Miscellaneous Questions

List A

Tell time using an analog clock or a digital clock?

Communicate through text or tweet?

. . . .

List B

Wear perfume or cologne?

Be a champion at playing backgammon or mancala?

Pilot a blimp or a zeppelin?

Play with a Frisbee or a boomerang?

Have trouble with your incisors or your molars?

. . . .

List C

Speak Cantonese or Mandarin?

Attend a college or a university?

Study Latin or Ladino?

Be nearsighted or farsighted?

Be a reporter covering the sinking of the *Titanic* or the crash of the *Hindenburg*?

Own the Hope Diamond or a moon rock?

Get lost in a labyrinth or a maze?

Celebrate Mardi Gras or Tanabata?

Have a pseudonym or become an eponym?

Win a Pulitzer Prize or a Nobel Prize?

Win an Emmy or an Oscar?

Be a bibliophile or a francophile?

Celebrate the Chinese New Year or the Lunar New Year?

See the Loch Ness Monster or Bigfoot?

Break your femur or your clavicle?

Be ambidextrous or have achromatopsia?

Have claustrophobia or acrophobia?

Express sympathy or empathy?

Planning Sheet for Nonfiction Calendars

. . . .

Name _____ Date_____

Broad Topic for Calendar: _____

Twelve Subtopics: (one per each calendar page)

    1. January _____

    2. February _____

    3. March _____

    4. April _____

    5. May _____

    6. June _____

    7. July _____

    8. August _____

    9. September _____

    10. October_____

    11. November_____

    12. December _____

APPENDIX 8

Sample Word Lists for Creating Glossaries

• • • • • • • • • • • • • • • • •

The following list of books and accompanying selected vocabulary illustrates the wide range of books that teachers can use to model glossary writing. Teachers can also offer these books to students, inviting them to read and then select their own words to create a useful glossary.

Quintero, Isabel. 2019. *My Papi Has a Motorcycle*. New York: Kokila/Penguin Random House LLC.

accelerator	conchas	panaderia
agarrate	con cuidado	por favor
air compressors	drywallers	raspados
albondigas	estrella	revs
asphalt	fresa	rutas naturales
carburetor	Labradoodle	tortilleria
carino	lista	trabando duro
celestial	mañana	
chicle	nopales	

Lauber, Patricia. 2006. *What You Never Know About Beds, Bedrooms, & Pajamas*. New York: Simon & Schuster Books for Young Readers.

apprentice	courtiers	renaissance
bedstaff	manor	tapestries
bedstead	Middle Ages	toga
coil-spring mattress	nightcaps	

Lauber, Patricia 2002. *What You Never Knew About Fingers, Forks, & Chopsticks*. New York: Aladdin Paperbacks.

civilization	flint	Renaissance
Crusades	medieval	Stone Age
empire	Middle Ages	tankard
etiquette	prongs	trencher

Ammon, Richard. 2000. *An Amish Year*. New York: Atheneum.

alfalfa	Eck	Pennsylvania Deitsch
Baler	Gladiolas	Shoofly pie
Belgian draft horses	Grossdawdy	Snitz pie
Chow chow	Grossmammy	"Gut marriye. Wie bischt du?"
cockscomb	Holstein cows	"Gott ist die liebe."
Datt	Joists	"Kum Lizzie. Hole Rachel und Danny. Es ist Tziet fer geb."
Doch waggle	Mamm	

Arbogast, Joan Marie. 2004. *Buildings in Disguise: Architecture That Looks Like Animals, Food, and Other Things*. Honesdale, PA: Boyds Mills.

fonda	pachyderm	stucco
howdah	pagodas	Trojan horse
innards	patent	zoomorphic
lath	petrified wood	
mimetic	sombrero	

Flood, Nancy Bo. 2013. *Cowboy Up! Ride the Navajo Rodeo*. Honesdale, PA: Wordsong/Highlights.

bareback riding	bronco	fry bread
barrel racing	calf-roper	lariat
Brahma bulls	chaps	lasso
branding	cowpokes	Navajo Nation

reins	steer wrestling	team roping
rodeo circuit	stirrups	wooly rider
saddleback riding	stockman	wrangler hat
spurs		

Friedman, Lucy, and Mary Dowdle 2012. *Becoming A Ballerina; A Nutcracker Story Starring the Dancers of the Boston Ballet.* New York: Viking Books for Young Readers.

Amane (Japanese for good fortune around)	échappé	on pointe
arabesque	épaulement	overture
arabesque sauté	épaulement effacé	Pig Latin
ballet mistress	ganbatte (Japanese for good luck)	pirouettes
barre	improvisation	plié
bunhead	kanji	polichinelles
callback slip	Kotone (Japanese for harp music)	port de bras
cavalry	Mako (Japanese for true, genuine child)	prologue
chasse		soubresaut
choreographer		stagehands
double tour	matinee	tendus

Kheiriyeh, Rasin. 2018. *Saffron Ice Cream.* New York: Arthur A. Levine Books.

Caspian Sea	kebab	Islamic
halim	Persian	saffron
Iran		

Kim, Aram. 2017. *No Kimchi for Me!* New York: Holiday House.

Anchovies	Condiment	Kkaennip kimchi
Baechu kimchi	Dongchimi	Muchae
Buchu Kimchi	Fermented	Mustard greens
Chonggak kimchi	Gat kimchi	Oisobagi
Chonggak mu (Ponytail radish)	Kimchi	Perilla leaves
		Yeolmu kimchi

Krensky, Stephen. 1996. *Breaking into Print: Before and After the Invention of the Printing Press*. New York: Little, Brown & Co.

alloy	lampblack	papyrus
antimony	Linotype	parchment
Charlemagne	linseed oil	platen
codex	manuscript	pup
cuneiform symbols	Mesoamerican	quill
Diamond Sutra	Middle Ages	typeface
Domesday Book	minotype	vellum
guilds	monastery	William the Conqueror
hieroglyphic	monk	

Krishnaswami, Uma. 2016. *Chachaji's Cup*. New York: Lee & Low Books.

beta	masala chai	refugees
gulab jamun	Partition	samosa
Hanuman		

Kyuchukov, Hristo. 2004. *My Name Was Hussein*. Honesdale, PA: Boyds Mills Press.

Arabic	identity cards	Ramadan
Bulgaria	Iftar	Roma
Gypsies	mosque	Romani
henna	Muslims	

Lynch, P.J. 2015. *The Boy Who Fell Off the Mayflower or John Howland's Good Fortune*. Somerville, MA: Candlewick.

endeavor	longshoreman	Patuxet
gables	Massasoit	plague
heathen	mast	pottage
indenture	Militiamen	rudder
keel	muskets	sachem
loathsome	nettles	Separatists

shallop	Squanto	unfurling the sails
shinning up the rigging	stockade	Wampanoag
squall	tiller	

Matula, Christina. 2018. *The Shadow in the Moon: A Tale of the Mid-Autumn Festival*. Watertown, MA: Charlesbridge.

| Ah-ma | eternal | lotus |
| archer | immortal | lunar calendar |

McDonnell, Christine. 2011. *Goyangi Means Cat*. New York: Viking/Penguin Group.

(Korean words are explained within the narrative but can be listed in a glossary for easy reference)

An-yah (no)	Chim-dae (bed)	Mok-da (eat)
AH-po (hurt)	Gom (teddy bear)	Omah (mom)
Apah (dad)	Goyangi (cat)	Po-po (kiss)
Bahp (rice)	Jip (house)	

Polacco, Patricia. 1994. *Mrs. Katz and Tush*. New York: Random House Children's Books.

borscht	kaddish	runt
bubee	kattileh	seder
bubeleh	kugel	shalom
Catskills	matzoh	tush
chuppa	mazel tov	Yiddish
Hannukah	Passover	

Rosenstock, Barb. 2018. *The Secret Kingdom: Nek Chand, A Changing India, and a Hidden World of Art*. Somerville, MA: Candlewick.

bougainvillea	kanak	oleander
burlap	kurtas	pipal trees
chapatis	Lohri	porcelain
Diwali	minstrels	Punjab
Himalayas	monsoon	rajai
Hindu	niched	

Rusch, Elizabeth. 2013. *Electrical Wizard: How Nikola Tesla Lit Up the World*. Somerville, PA: Candlewick.

alabaster	electrocute	generators
alternating current	fuses	turbines

Slade, Suzanne. 2015. *The Inventor's Secret: What Thomas Edison Told Henry Ford*. Watertown, MA: Charlesbridge.

four-cycle engine	incandescent light bulb	shocks
four-stroke cylinder	patents	Tin Lizzie
gas gauge	quadricycle	

Tahe, Rose Ann, and Nancy Bo Flood. 2018. *First Laugh Welcome, Baby!* Watertown, MA: Charlesbridge.

blue cornmeal mush	Navaho Nation	Pendleton blanket
cheii (grandfather)	nhizh'e' (father)	piñon
clan	nima (mother)	salt cedar ash
corn pollen prayer	nima-sani (grandmother in Navajo language)	tree-of-life rug
Dine awe hinaai (big brother)		

Trollinger, Patsi. 2011. *Perfect Timing: How Isaac Murphy Became One of the World's Greatest Jockeys*. New York: Viking/Penguin Group.

American Derby	jockey	procession
colt	paddock	stallion
filly	pneumonia	thoroughbred

Yang, Belle. 2018. *Angel in Beijing.* Somerville, MA: Candlewick.

Baozi	Forbidden City	Liulichang Street
Beihai Park	ginkgo tree	mung bean
cypress trees	haw fruits	Tiananmen Square
Dragon Boat festival	huamei birds	Tiantan, the Temple of Heaven
erhus	Hutong	
feather duster	Jingshan	

Young, Amy. 2005. *Belinda in Paris.* New York: Viking/Penguin Group.

baguettes	fromage	parfumerie
boucherie	la danse	pointe shoes
boulangerie	mademoiselle	patisserie
croissant	magnifique	quiche
éclair	marchand de vins	voilà
épicerie	monsieur	

Zalben, Jane Breskin. 2018. *Moon for Moe and Mo.* Watertown, MA: Charlesbridge.

(Has a brief explanation of a few terms, [rugelach, Rosh Hashanah, date cookies, Ramadan], but many more could be defined)

Arabic	iftar	sawn
brisket	Koran	shalom
challah	L'shanah tovah	star anise
crescent moon	Mecca	turmeric
Day of Atonement	pita	tzedakah
Eid Mubarak	pomegranate	Zakat al-fitr
falafel	salaam	

APPENDIX 9

PLANNING SHEET FOR GLOSSARY STUDY

. . . .

Name _____ Date _____

Book Title: _____ Author: _____

Read through your book and use sticky notes to mark sentences with your chosen words. Put list of words in ABC (alphabetical) order. Copy down the sentences from the picture book. Use a dictionary to discover parts of speech (adjective, noun, verb, etc.) and help define the word.

Word	Part of Speech	Definition	Sentence from Book

APPENDIX 10

Additional Research and Riddle Writing Samples

· · · · · · · · · · · · · · · · · · ·

In the following riddle, I borrowed the grammatical structures used by Eve Merriam and Lillian Morrison.

> I live in a mansion, but I am not a millionaire.
>
> I care for a big apple, but I am not a farmer.
>
> I tower above, but I am not a skyscraper.
>
> I run the boroughs, but I am not in the marathon.
>
> Who am I? (Mayor DeBlasio of New York City)

The following riddle is a series of carefully selected verbs forming one long sentence as Lillian Morrison has done:

> I'm protected and visited and photographed
>
> and inhabited by famous families
>
> and then my wings are redesigned
>
> because after four years, new folks might be in charge.
>
> What am I? (the White House)

The next two are haiku riddles on topics that are newsworthy.

> a cold desert world
>
> rusty iron on the ground
>
> Curiosity
>
> What am I? (the planet Mars)

> New Orleans destroyed
>
> way back in August 05
>
> such severe flooding
>
> What am I? (Hurricane Katrina)

APPENDIX 11

Additional Every-Day-of-the-Week Writing Samples

· · · · · · · · · · · · · · · · · · · ·

LOOKING AT THE MAP
On Sunday, Ellie found North America on the map.
On Monday, Ellie found South America on the map.
On Tuesday, Ellie found Africa on the map.
On Wednesday, Ellie found Australia on the map.
On Thursday, Ellie found Antarctica on the map.
On Friday, Ellie found Asia on the map.
On Saturday, Ellie found Europe on the map and she asked her family,
"Where should we go on vacation?"

COLD WEATHER FUN
On Sunday, Millie made a really big snowball.
On Monday, Millie put a smaller snowball on top.
On Tuesday, Millie put an even smaller snowball on top.
On Wednesday, Millie added a carrot.
On Thursday, Millie added rocks.
On Friday, Millie added a scarf and a hat.
On Saturday, Millie called out,
"Everyone, come look at my snowman!"

BREAKFAST FOODS
On Sunday, Cooper ate eggs for breakfast.
On Monday, Cooper ate cereal for breakfast.
On Tuesday, Cooper ate pancakes for breakfast.
On Wednesday, Cooper ate waffles for breakfast.
On Thursday, Cooper ate toast for breakfast.
On Friday, Cooper ate muffins for breakfast
On Saturday, Cooper didn't eat breakfast.

He slept late and then ate a big brunch.
He ate eggs, cereal, pancakes,
waffles, toast <u>and</u> muffins.

CIRCUS SURPRISE

On Sunday, Will broke his little sister's red ball in half.

On Monday, Will borrowed his big sister's red lipstick.

On Tuesday, Will asked for his dad's purple polka-dot bow tie.

On Wednesday, Will slipped on his big cousin's sneakers.

On Thursday, Will tried on his tall uncle's baggy pants.

On Friday, Will borrowed his mom's curly wig.

On Saturday, Will dressed up as a clown and made the whole family laugh.

YUMMY FOODS

On Sunday, Zach ate oranges.

On Monday, Zach ate grapes.

On Tuesday, Zach ate corn on the cob.

On Wednesday, Zach ate cucumbers.

On Thursday, Zach ate apples.

On Friday, Zach ate broccoli.

On Saturday, Zach's mom asked,

"Are you a vegetarian?

PLAYTIME

On Sunday, Sasha played bingo with her brother.

On Monday, Sasha played Candyland with her cousin.

On Tuesday, Sasha played on the see-saw with her sister.

On Wednesday, Sasha played on the monkey bars with her mother.

On Thursday, Sasha played the flute with her father.

On Friday, Sasha played the grand piano with her grandmother.

On Saturday, Sasha played solitaire all by herself.

APPENDIX 12
Additional Sentences Demonstrating
Jonathan London's Writing Techniques

. . . .

Following are additional sentences demonstrating Jonathan London's writing techniques. Following each set of sentences are my attempts to use these same techniques. This material was used in minilessons as the need arose.

Strong, Precise Verbs

From *Phantom of the Prairie: Year of the Black-Footed Ferret:* "Quiet as the moonlight, Phantom **creeps** toward a flower, **crouches**, **stares**... and **pounces**!"

From *Hurricane!* "Schools of tropical fish **flashed** by like flocks of birds turning in a wind, while langostas—tasty Puerto Rican lobsters—hid in dark cracks in the huge reef."

From *Puddles:* "Birds **flap** from the trees and we think the trees are applauding!"

From *Hippos Are Huge!* "Then they **swing** their tails like baseball bats and swat balls of dung at each other—SPLAT! SPLOP!"

From *Otters Love to Play:* "Within days, the otter pups gracefully **spin** and **flip** and **swish** like underwater acrobats."

From *Little Fox in the Snow:* "Two shadows **bound** across sun-sparkle snow. A snowshoe hare is no match for a fleet-footed fox."

From *Froggy Rides a Bike*: "His bike **zigged** and **zagged** and **wobbled**.*"

From *Dream Weaver:* "A sudden wind, and the tre*es* **hum**, the branches **creak**, and yellow spider's web **shimmers**, like wind across a pond."

From *Like Butter on Pancakes:* "Papa's kettle **whistles**. Mama's bacon **sizzles**. Slippers **whisper** across the kitchen floor."

From *White Water:* "All of a sudden the water was white, as if thousands of white rabbits were jumping around us. I **clenched** my teeth and fists as we **whipped** and **bounced** on the waves."

I used strong precise verbs:

Our mom **tiptoed** into our bedroom when she thought we were asleep."

"My brother and I **whispered** our plans to surprise our parents on Sunday morning."

"We were going to **yank** *weeds*, **rake** *leaves, and* **trim** *the ivy that was* **cascading** *over the fence.*

333

Alliteration

From *Hurricane!* "Schools of tropical **fish flashed** by like **flocks** of birds turning in a wind, while langostas—tasty Puerto Rican lobsters—hid in dark cracks in the huge reef."

From *Hippos Are Huge!* "Then they **swing** their tails like **baseball bats** and **swat** balls of dung at each other—**SPLAT! SPLOP!**"

From *Little Fox in the Snow*: "Two shadows bound across **sun-sparkle snow**. A snowshoe hare is no match for a **fleet-footed fox**."

From *When the Fireflies Come:* "The **tinkle** of ice in **tall** iced-**tea** glasses."

From *Froggy Rides a Bike:* "His bike **zigged** and **zagged** and wobbled."

From *Let the Lynx Come In:* "The lynx steps in, shakes first one paw then the other. **Stands still** as a **stone**, quiet as an owl, in the middle of the room. Firelight glows in its yellow eyes."

I used alliteration:

"Have you ever eaten **roasted rhubarb** or **poached pears**?"

"Do you want to **bake, broil, or bread** the chicken cutlets?"

"At **six** o'clock, please **set** the table for **seven**. Please put out **silverware**, **serving dishes,** and cups and **saucers**."

Sensory Details

From *Hurricane!* "Schools of tropical fish flashed by like flocks of birds turning in a wind, while langostas—tasty Puerto Rican lobsters—hid in dark cracks in the huge reef."

From *Little Fox in the Snow:* "Two shadows bound across sun-sparkle snow. A snowshoe hare is no match for a fleet-footed fox."

From *Candy Store Man:*

With a bip-bop-shadip

he can scoop you a dip

of ice cream, man,

in a cone or a dish,

or if you wish

he could make you a shake

that'll shake you awake

or magic you a penny candy

with a flash of his hands:

fireballs and lollipops,

jawbreakers and licorice whips,

wax lips and peppermint sticks-

you take your pick.

From *When the Fireflies Come:* "The screen doors slam. Slam-bang. Slam-bang. Outside, the smell of summer. The smell of fresh-picked corn, barbecued hot dogs and burgers in the air. The tinkle of ice in tall iced-tea glasses."

From *Dream Weaver:* "A sudden wind, and the trees hum, the branches creak, and yellow spider's web shimmers, like wind across a pond."

From *Like Butter on Pancakes:* "Papa's kettle whistles. Mama's bacon sizzles. Slippers whisper across the kitchen floor."

From *White Water:* "All of a sudden the water was white, as if thousands of white rabbits were jumping around us. I clenched my teeth and fists as we whipped and bounced on the waves."

From *Let the Lynx Come In:* "The lynx steps in, shakes first one paw then the other. Stands still as a stone, quiet as an owl, in the middle of the room. Firelight glows in its yellow eyes."

I used sensory details:

"The subway car was so crowded that I could sniff coffee, tuna fish, and oranges, from the breath of the passengers that surrounded me."

"I could feel the moisture from their dripping umbrellas and soaked raincoats."

"It was so mobbed that I couldn't even think of unfolding my newspaper, checking my cell phone, or grabbing a tissue from my pocket."

Repetition

From *When the Fireflies Come:* "The screen doors **slam. Slam-bang. Slam-bang**. Outside, **the smell of** summer. **The smell of** fresh-picked corn barbecued hot dogs and burgers in the air. The tinkle of ice in tall iced-tea glasses."

I used repetition:

"I am **thrilled, thrilled, thrilled** to watch the Thanksgiving Day parade."

"Little children love to sit **high, high** up on their parents' shoulders to watch the parade pass by."

"Everyone is cheering and chanting, **"Look at that! Look at that! Look at that!"**

Long-List Sentences

From *Candy Store Man:*

With a bip-bop-shadip

  he can scoop you a dip

of ice cream, man,

  in a cone or a dish,

or if you wish

  he could make you a shake

that'll shake you awake

  or magic you a penny candy

with a flash of his hands:

  fireballs and lollipops,

  jawbreakers and licorice whips,

   wax lips and peppermint sticks-

you take your pick.

I wrote a long-list sentence:

"If I had free time in Manhattan, I would tour an art museum, enjoy a Broadway show, shop at Macy's, dine in a fine restaurant, stroll the High-line, roam Central Park, and most of all, people-watch in Greenwich Village, Little Italy, and Chinatown."

Onomatopoeia

From *When the Fireflies Come:* "The screen doors slam. **Slam-bang**. **Slam-bang**. Outside, the smell of summer. The smell of fresh-picked corn, barbecued hot dogs and burgers in the air. The tinkle of ice in tall iced-tea glasses."

From *Hippos Are Huge!* "Then they swing their tails like baseball bats and swat balls of dung at each other—**SPLAT! SPLOP!**"

From *Like Butter on Pancakes:* "Papa's kettle whistles. Mama's bacon **sizzles**. Slippers whisper across the kitchen floor."

I used onomatopoeia:

"Outdoors, the cold and heavy rain was **split, splat, splashing** on our roof and windowsills. Luckily indoors, the logs in the fireplace were **crackling**, the potato pancakes were **sizzling** on the stove, and the **ding-dong** of the front doorbell told us that our guests had made it through the storm."

Information That Is Specific and Accurate, Proving You Are an Authority on Your Topic

From *Hurricane!* "Schools of tropical fish flashed by like flocks of birds turning in a wind, while langostas—tasty Puerto Rican lobsters—hid in dark cracks in the huge reef."

I used information that is specific and accurate, proving that I am an authority on my topic:

"If you want to visit the **American Museum of Natural History, take the number 2 or 3 train to 72nd Street in Manhattan or the number 1 to 79th Street and then walk to Central Park West and 79th Street**."

"Make sure to tour **the 94-foot blue whale, the T. rex skeleton, and the Hayden Planetarium**."

"When my mom orders a **Greek salad, she always asks for feta cheese, Kalamata olives, and stuffed grape leaves**."

"When Spanish-speaking people visit your home, it's polite to say, '**Bienvenidos.**' What do you think that means?"

INDEX